OXFORD
UNIVERSITY PRESS

sity Press, Inc., publishes works that further Oxford University's
ive of excellence in research, scholarship, and education.

OXFORD NEW YORK

CAPE TOWN   DAR ES SALAAM   HONG KONG   KARACHI
PUR   MADRID   MELBOURNE   MEXICO CITY   NAIROBI
NEW DELHI   SHANGHAI   TAIPEI   TORONTO

With offices in
STRIA   BRAZIL   CHILE   CZECH REPUBLIC   FRANCE   GREECE
HUNGARY   ITALY   JAPAN   POLAND   PORTUGAL   SINGAPORE
SWITZERLAND   THAILAND   TURKEY   UKRAINE   VIETNAM

Copyright © 2009 by Oxford University Press

Published by Oxford University Press, Inc.
198 Madison Avenue, New York, NY 10016
www.oup.com

The Library of Congress Cataloging-in-Publication Data

d by Jesse Sheidlower. -- 3rd ed.

-539311-8
nglish word) 2.   English language--Semantics.
guage--Etymology. 4.   English language--Obscene words.
esse.
2 2009

2009018730

5 7 9 8 6

Printed in the United States of America
on acid-free paper

T

EDITE

OX
UNIVE

2

Oxford Univer
object

AUCKLAND
KUALA LUM

ARGENTINA   AU
GUATEMALA
SOUTH KOREA

The F-word / edite
p.   cm.
ISBN 978-0-19
1.   Fuck (The F
3.   English lan
I. Sheidlower,
PE1599.F83
422--dc22

'Tis needful that the most immodest word
Be looked upon and learned
—Shakespeare, *Henry IV, Part II*

CONTENTS

Foreword

Fuck

It is an honor and a privilege to be asked by the esteemed Oxford University Press to write the introduction to this wondrous book about the most important and powerful word in the English language. This is like a dream come true. A scholarly publisher of worldwide prestige has blessed this most sacred, most descriptive, most moving of all words.

"*Fuck* is a sacred word?" you ask.

Fucking A right it is. It is a word that one should not utter because it is such a terrible word of epic proportions, a word whose mere utterance is a sin. A fucking sin, can you imagine? That's how fucking important *fuck* is.

And because it's a sin, using it is so enticing to the young that when they hear it for the first time they are spellbound. And when they *use* it for the first time, that F and the U bang so deliciously against the hard K, ripping through the lips, it's as if a caged animal has been unleashed. They feel that they have taken that first mighty step toward adulthood. Some of them may even repeat it over and over, testing to see if God will strike them down for saying it. It's a word you don't use in polite conversation or in front of your parents, which makes it even more glorious when chewed on and spit out in the schoolyard or in the bowels of the basement.

I can't remember the first time I actually used the word myself, but I remember the feeling I had. I am convinced it is akin to a newly converted Christian when he cries out his first hallelujah. What bliss! What joy! What freedom!

Fuck, I believe, is one of the few words in the English language with true medicinal qualities. It clears our heads of the cobwebs that our bosses, our politicians, and our pundits seem to spin with their tired words and useless clichés. I am certainly no doctor, but I believe that judicious use of the word in times of extreme stress or irritation can work wonders for your colon, blood pressure, and central nervous system. It even works as an antidepressant. The word is so efficient, it's like a miracle drug. One quick guttural expulsion is all you need (or sometimes two or three if things are really bad).

If this power isn't enough to make *fuck* the language's best word ever, remember there is no other word that is so spectacularly utilitarian. *Fuck* can work as a noun, a verb, an adverb, an adjective. And for many of us—and you New Yorkers know who you are—*fuck* isn't even a word, it's a comma. It can be placed at the end of a sentence to add emphasis to an idea. It can go at the end of a word to give it more punch. It even can be put in the middle of an existing word, giving it extra authority and impact. It's an unbe-fucking-lievable word. Its gifts are too numerous to mention.

Now I must leave you as you enter the world that is *Fuck*.

You are fucking lucky to be here.

It's almost utopian.

Lewis Black, New York, March 12, 2009

Introduction: About the F-Word

Etymology: Where It's From

The word *fuck* definitely did not originate as an acronym, as many people think. Acronyms are extremely rare before the 1930s, and etymologies of this sort—especially for older words—are almost always false. (The word *posh* does not come from "Port Outward, Starboard Home," *cop* is not from "Constable On Patrol," and *tip* is not from "To Insure Promptness.") To this editor's knowledge, the earliest suggestion of an acronymic etymology for *fuck* appears to be in the New York underground newspaper *The East Village Other*, on February 15, 1967: "It's not commonly known that the word 'fuck' originated as a medical diagnostic notation on the documents of soldiers in the British Imperial Army. When a soldier reported sick and was found to have V.D., the abbreviation F.U.C.K. was stamped on his documents. It was short for 'Found Under Carnal Knowledge.'" The more usual variant along these lines is "For Unlawful Carnal Knowledge," abbreviated to *fuck* and allegedly worn on a badge by convicted adulterers, rapists, or prostitutes in some mythical Olden Tymes; other variants include "Found in Unlawful Carnal Knowledge" (specifically for adulterers) and "Forced Unsolicited Carnal Knowledge" (for rapists).

The other common acronym is "Fornication Under Consent of the King," said to have been some form of license granted by a monarch, often specifically to repopulate the country after a plague.

This variant is first found in 1970, in the May issue of *Playboy*: "My friend claims that the word fuck originated in the 15th Century, when a married couple needed permission from the king to procreate. Hence, *F*ornication *U*nder *C*onsent of the *K*ing. I maintain that it's an acronym of a law term used in the 1500s that referred to rape as *F*orced *U*nnatural *C*arnal *K*nowledge."

In reality, *fuck* is a word of Germanic origin. It is related to words in several other Germanic languages, such as Dutch, German, and Swedish, that have sexual meanings as well as meanings such as 'to strike' or 'to move back and forth'. Ultimately these words represent a family of loosely related verbs having the structural form *f* + a short vowel + a stop (a consonant such as *k*, *d*, *g*, or *t*, in which the flow of air from the mouth is briefly interrupted), often with an *l* or *r* somewhere in between. These words have the basic meaning 'to move back and forth', and often the figurative sense 'to cheat'. English examples of this family—all found later than *fuck*—are *fiddle*, *fidget*, *flit*, *flip*, *flicker*, and *frig*.

The English word was probably borrowed in the fifteenth century from Low German, Flemish, or Dutch, though the word is found earlier in English than its equivalents in these languages. There is no way to know for sure which language is the ultimate source. *Fuck* is not an Anglo-Saxon word—the term "Anglo-Saxon" refers to the earliest period of English (now usually called Old English), before around *AD* 1100—and *fuck* is simply not found this early.

There are various claims that certain words in Old or Middle English represent early examples of *fuck*, but these are usually unprovable. For example, Carl Darling Buck, in his 1949 *Dictionary of Selected Synonyms in the Principal Indo-European Languages*, cited a 1278 example of the name "John le Fucker." However, he did not cite the source of this name, and no one has found a reference to it. More important, even if the source is authentic, there are many other possibilities for the name (the word *fulcher* 'soldier' being the most likely) other than an early example of *fuck*. However, if the bird name WINDFUCKER *noun* (or FUCKWIND *noun*) is ultimately related, it is interesting to note an occurrence of the surname *Ric Wyndfuk* and *Ric Wyndfuck de Wodehous,* found from 1287 in documents related to Sherwood Forest, which may show another form of the bird name. Use in the sense of "to strike" could perhaps also be reflected by the surname *Fuckebegger* (also 1287); perhaps compare the Anglo-Norman surname *Butevilein* (literally 'strike the churl or wretch'), found in the twelfth and thirteenth centuries.

The relevance of superficially similar words in other languages—Latin *futuere*, for example—is small. Though the Latin word is vulgar and means 'to copulate', is it almost certainly not related to *fuck*, owing to complicated linguistic reasons that are beyond the scope of this introduction. Theories attempting to tie the word to words in other languages, sometimes via a proposed Indo-European root meaning 'to strike', are also uncertain.

Despite the importance of the F-word, scholars have yet to discover an example of *fuck* (or any of its Germanic relatives) before the late fifteenth century. The lateness of this evidence for the word may have more than one explanation. One possibility is simply that the word isn't much older than that, that it was a new development at that time. The usual Middle English word for sexual intercourse was *swive*—a word that itself was considered vulgar—and *fuck* could have arisen to take its place as it became more rare. Another possibility for *fuck* is that the word carried a taboo so strong that it was never written down in the Middle Ages. The fact that its earliest known appearance in English, around 1475, is in a cipher lends surprising, though limited, support to this interpretation.

Since many of the earliest examples of the F-word come from Scottish sources, some scholars have suggested that it is a Norse borrowing, Norse having a much greater influence on the northern and Scottish varieties of English than on southern dialects. But the 1528 example at FUCKING *adj.* sense 1—found in that common source of bawdy jokes, a marginal note to a manuscript—and the pre-1500 ciphered example are both from England, proving that *fuck* was not restricted to Scotland in its earliest days. The explanation for the profusion of Scottish examples might be simply that the taboo against the word was less strong in Scotland.

Taboos against particular words or types of speech are not new. There is no shortage of evidence from the earliest times in England that certain forms of speech were restricted. As far back as the seventh century, there are records of a law from Kent reading, "If anyone in another's house...shamefully accosts him with insulting words, he is to pay a shilling to him who owns the house."

Curiously, the proposed etymology as an acronym does at least have a touch of realism about it. When purported acronymic origins are suggested, the original phrase usually sounds artificial, not like some real phrase in the language that would be common enough to be abbreviated. And so it is with "for unlawful carnal knowledge"—it has the ring of something that is made to sound like a stilted legal expression. But in fact, "unlawful carnal knowledge" is found in legal sources going back quite some time. The full phrase is first found in the *South African Law Journal*, volume 46, in 1929: "One of the latest instances occurred in the case of Alfred Ayles, sentenced at the Central Criminal Court in 1928 to seven years' penal servitude for unlawful carnal knowledge of a child." And the phrase "unlawful carnal knowledge" as used in definitions of rape under English Common Law can be found in Britain's Criminal Law Amendment Act of 1885, and is still present in Northern Ireland's current statute on sex offenders, the Statutory Instrument 1994 No. 2795 (N.I. 15) and the Criminal Justice (Northern Ireland) Order 1994: "procuring unlawful carnal knowledge of woman by threats or false pretences or representations or administering drugs...unlawful carnal knowledge of a girl under 17 years of age" and others. Even earlier, this formula was found in criminal statutes throughout the southern United States, where rape was defined as "the unlawful carnal knowledge of a female, forcibly and against her will." Such language is attested from the 1870s and 1880s from Arkansas, Tennessee, Florida, Georgia, and Texas. All this evidence for the phrase still does not mean that the word *fuck* derives from this or any other acronym; it does not. However, it is notable that the story is at least not completely absurd.

In the category of folk etymology, a recent development has been the popularity of the "pluck yew" story, which conflates the origin of *fuck* with an earlier piece of folklore about the origin of the offensive backhand two-finger gesture (the British form of what is usually an extended middle finger in America). According to the original form of the tale, before the battle of Agincourt in 1415 (immortalized in Shakespeare's *Henry V*) the French taunted the English longbowmen by waving two fingers at them, saying that those fingers—used to pull back the bowstring—could never defeat the mighty French. After the English longbowmen rather convincingly demonstrated their superiority (10,000 French dead to a mere 29 Brits, in Shakespeare's exaggerated count), the English responded by waving their two fingers back at the French in the now familiar gesture. The recent twist has been to use the fact that longbows were traditionally made of yew to claim that the act of drawing back the bowstring was called "plucking yew," and thereby to assert that the victorious English not only waved their fingers at the French but shouted "We can still pluck yew! Pluck yew!" at them. A convenient sound change and a respelling brings us to the familiar phrase "fuck you." This story, totally ludicrous in any version, was popularized on the NPR show *Car Talk*, where it was meant as a joke; it spread on the Internet in the 1990s as a serious explanation.

The Taboo Status of *Fuck*

The demand for bawdy humor meant that in the past, as now, writers found ways to use certain words even if such words were prohibited by social conventions. In Shakespeare, for instance, one can find two clear references to *cunt*. In *Twelfth Night* (Act II, scene v), Olivia's butler Malvolio receives a letter written by Maria but in Olivia's handwriting. Analyzing the script, Malvolio says, "By my life this is my lady's hand. These be her very C's, her U's and her T's and thus makes she her great P's." With the *and* sounding like "N," Shakespeare not only spells out *cunt*, but gets a pun on *pee* in there as well. And more famously, in *Hamlet* (Act III, scene ii) the prince uses the phrase "country matters" in a manner clearly alluding to *cunt* (Hamlet's next crack is about what "lie[s] between maids' legs").

Though Shakespeare never actually uses *fuck* itself, his plays contain several examples of probable puns or references to the word. A Latin grammar lesson in *The Merry Wives of Windsor* (Act IV, scene i) gives us the *focative case* (punning on the *vocative case*, used for direct address), followed up immediately with a raft of lewd wordplay, including sexual puns on Latin words and references to various English words for the sexual organs. In *Henry V* (Act IV, scene iv) the notoriously bawdy Pistol threatens to "firk" an enemy soldier; though *firk* does have a legitimate sense 'to strike', which is appropriate here, it was used elsewhere in the Elizabethan era as a euphemism for *fuck*, and it is quite likely that Shakespeare had this in mind as well. In several places Shakespeare refers to the French word *foutre*, which is the literal (and also vulgar) equivalent of *fuck*; the most notable is this passage in *Henry V* (Act III, scene iv), in which Princess Katherine is having an English lesson:

KATHERINE. Comment appellez-vous les pieds et la robe? [What do you call *le pied* and *la robe*?]

ALICE. *De foot*, madame; et *de cown* [a French pronunciation of *gown*; these English words sound like the French words *foutre* 'fuck' and *con* 'cunt'].

KATHERINE. *De foot* et *de cown*? O Seigneur Dieu! Ils sont les mots de son mauvais, corruptible, gros, et impudique! [Dear Lord! Those are bad-sounding words, wicked, vulgar, and indecent!]

Shakespeare elsewhere (*2 Henry IV* Act V, scene iii) has Pistol say, "A foutra for the world and worldlings base!" and in at least one place (*Merry Wives of Windsor* Act II, scene i) he uses *foot* as a probable pun on *foutre*. As the *Henry V* passage shows, Shakespeare was well aware that this word was vulgar—at least in French—and there is a good possibility that these examples are intended to represent the taboo English word *fuck*.

Though the evidence clearly shows that *fuck* was considered vulgar in Shakespeare's time, it's hard to tell just how bad it was. But we have a remarkably informative example from the late seventeenth century of the word's status from a source unexpected in this early era: pornography. Though the amount of truly explicit English erotica before the Victorian era is small, there are exceptions, one of which is the 1680 *The School of Venus*, a translation of an earlier French work. This graphically illustrated book—surviving in only a single copy, in the Bayerischer Staatsbibliothek in Munich—is presented in the style of a dialogue between a sexually experienced older woman and her young niece, a format (common especially in the eighteenth century) allowing highly explicit discussions to appear in the guise of instruction. The author of this work appears to have been unusually interested in language: at one point the characters discuss the precise differences in meaning among *occupy, fuck, swive, incunt*, and other verbs, and elsewhere the older woman explains why men use offensive words like *cunt* during intercourse. And the reader is also treated to a clear statement of how offensive the word *fuck* was:

> There are other words which sound better, and are often used before Company, instead of Swiving and Fucking, which is too gross and downright Bawdy, fit only to be used among dissolute Persons; to avoid scandal, men modestly say, I kissed her, made much of her, received a favor from her, or the like.

Certainly the word was considered literally unprintable except in obscure, secret, or privately printed publications throughout the nineteenth century. Important early authors known to have used the word include Lord Rochester in the seventeenth century and Robert Burns in the late eighteenth century; Burns was probably the latest important author known to use the word before the twentieth century, and he uses it only in *Merry Muses of Caledonia*, a bawdy manuscript intended for private circulation only. Even Captain Francis Grose—a friend of Burns—in his *Classical Dictionary of the Vulgar Tongue* (1785 and later editions; the word was expunged from the 1811 edition by a different compiler) felt compelled to spell it *f–k*.

In a striking example of the unfamiliarity of some Victorians with bawdy vocabulary, we see that the poet Robert Browning egregiously misunderstood one common word. He encountered the couplet "'They talked of his having a Cardinal's hat,/They'd send him as soon an old nun's twat,'"in a seventeenth-century poem. Erroneously believing from this passage that the word referred to a part of a nun's habit, Browning wrote of "Cowls and twats" in his 1848 poem *Pippa Passes*.

This does not imply that *fuck* was unused, of course. John Farmer and W. E. Henley's monumental *Slang and Its Analogues* (privately printed; the volume with *fuck* appeared in 1893) included the use of *fucking* as both an adjective and an adverb, described respectively as "A qualification of extreme contumely" and "a more violent form of *bloody*." These are labeled "common," despite the fact that this editor has been able to discover hardly any earlier examples of this sense outside Farmer and Henley's dictionary. No doubt this and various other senses were common but unprinted for some time previously. While there seem to be a large number of new senses that are first found around World War I, it seems likely that these were in use earlier, and their appearance in the 1910s is more a re sult of weakening taboos than of an actual increase in the number of words coined in that era.

For although *fuck* may have been strictly taboo in mainstream usage in the nineteenth century, it was extremely common in the flourishing world of Victorian pornography. Many explicit F-words are found in such sources from the 1860s onward, often in ways that are scarcely different from the hard-core pornography of the present day. And research in the past ten years has shown that various forms or senses that were thought to have come later were indeed in use in the nineteenth century.

In two remarkable incidents, *fuck* even found its way into the very proper London *Times* in that prudish era. Reporting a speech delivered by Attorney General Sir William Harcourt, the *Times* printed on January 13, 1882:

> I saw in a Tory journal the other day a note of alarm, in which they said, "Why, if a tenant-farmer is elected for the North Riding of Yorkshire the farmers will be a political power who will have to be reckoned with." The speaker then said he felt inclined for a bit of fucking. I think that is very likely.

It took the stunned editors four days to run an apology for what must have been a bit of mischief at the typesetter:

> No pains have been spared by the management of this journal to discover the author of a gross outrage committed by the interpolation of a line in the speech of Sir William Harcourt reported in our issue of Monday last. This malicious fabrication was surreptitiously introduced before the paper went to press. The matter is now under legal investigation, and it is hoped that the perpetrator of the outrage will be brought to punishment.

And later that year, on June 12, 1882, the following advertisement appeared: "Every-day Life in our Public Schools. Sketched by Head Scholars. With a Glossary of Some Words used by Henry Irving in his disquisition upon fucking, which is in Common Use in those Schools."

Changing Standards

Different kinds of language have been considered incendiary at different times. Several hundred years ago, for example, religious profanity was the most unforgivable type of expression. In more recent times, words for body parts and explicitly sexual vocabulary have been the most shocking: in nineteenth-century America even the word *leg* was sometimes considered indecent; the proper substitute was *limb*. Now racial or ethnic epithets are the scourge; one prominent professor told *U.S. News & World Report* in 1994 that if she used *fuck* in class, no one would bat an eye, but that she would never dare to use any racial epithet in any context.

Today it seems that the taboos against the F-word are weaker than ever. While a few publications still refuse to print *fuck* regardless of the circumstances, the word can be found quite easily in most places. The more literary magazines have printed *fuck* for some time, but now even *Newsweek* and *Time* have used the uncensored word; the publication of the Starr Report in the *New York Times*, and a notable comment from Vice President Cheney in the *Washington Post*, has meant that even the proper papers consider *fuck* fit to print. Even commercial television, though still subject to FCC regulations, is becoming more open in its use.

The unpredictable nature of live television has allowed *fuck* to slip past would-be censors. Kenneth Tynan, then the Director of the National Theatre, was the first to manage this in England, in a November 13, 1965, appearance on the late-night satirical talk show "BBC-3." Asked whether he would stage a play where sexual intercourse was depicted on stage, he replied, "Well, I think so, certainly. I doubt if there are any rational people to whom the word 'fuck' would be particularly diabolical, revolting or totally forbidden. I think that anything which can be be printed or said can also be seen." This provoked a huge reaction in England, with the BBC being forced to apologize and politicians attempting to remove Tynan from his post, remove the head of the BBC from *his* post, and to prosecute Tynan for using obscene words in public. Tynan quickly made a less-than-conciliatory public statement that he "used an old English word in a completely neutral way to illustrate a serious point, just as I would have used it in similar conversation with any group of grown-up people."

There were other such incidents, but the most notorious took place in an interview with the seminal punk band the Sex Pistols on December 1, 1976, conducted by Bill Grundy on Thames Television's *Today* program. First, referring to a large advance the band had received from their record company, guitarist Steve Jones said, "We've fuckin' spent it, ain't we?" As the interview was winding down, Grundy encouraged the band to "say something outrageous." Jones obliged with "You dirty fucker!" to which Grundy replied, "What a clever boy," and Jones casually replied, "What a fucking rotter." Of the next-day newspaper reaction, the singer Elvis Costello later said, "It was a great morning—just to hear people's blood pressure going up and down over it." Grundy was suspended and EMI threatened to drop the band, though others, including Vivienne Westwood, complained of hypocrisy, arguing that it was only the band's image that provoked such a strong response to a word that was in wide use.

The NBC live comedy show "Saturday Night Live" has seen the word used on a number of occasions, perhaps most notably on February 21, 1981. Charles Rocket, playing J. R. Ewing in a sketch based on the TV show "Dallas," said "It's the first time I've ever been shot in my life. I'd like to know who the fuck did it." (Three weeks later, Rocket was fired, though with the show slumping at the time, others in the cast were let go as well.) And on the same show, the musical guest Prince sang "fighting war is such a fucking bore." In 1993 Bono, the lead singer of the rock group U2, used the word during a live broadcast of the Grammy Awards. In sports, powerful microphones have picked up and transmitted various examples, and players have used the word in televised interviews, with differing reactions. In the celebratory rally after the Philadelphia Phillies won the 2008 World Series, second baseman Chase Utley said in front of a packed stadium, "World Champions. World fucking Champions!" But follow-up interviews with viewers—many of them with their children—revealed that most people were excited rather than upset by this.

Fuck in Print

The earliest known publication of *fuck* in the United States appears to be in a legal case, in a fascinating decision. The case, heard in the Supreme Court of Missouri in 1846, concerned a man who had been accused of having sex with a mare, and who successfully sued for slander. The verdict was appealed, and in its rejection of the appeal, the court wrote:

> The slanderous charge was carnal knowledge of a mare, and the word "fuck" was used to convey the imputation. After the verdict for the plaintiff, a motion made in arrest of judgment, for the reason that the word used to convey the slander, was unknown to the English language, and was not understood by those to whom it was spoken.... The motion was overruled, and Edgar appealed.

> Because the modesty of our lexicographers restrains them from publishing obscene words, or from giving the obscene signification to words that may be used without conveying any obscenity, it does not follow that they are not English words, and not understood by those who hear them; or that chaste words may not be applied so as to be understood in an obscene sense by every one who hears them.

In other words, *fuck* was well known and understood, so the fact that it wasn't in dictionaries was irrelevant.

Curiously, this same tack was attempted in another slander case, in one of the very few other examples of *fuck* in nineteenth-century U.S. legal sources, and with the exact same outcome. In an 1865 case in the Supreme Court of Indiana, the court wrote:

Rebecca Kelley sued the appellant in the court below for slander. The words charged are, "I have f--ked Rebecca Kelley one hundred times." "I have screwed Beck Kelley one hundred times." It is claimed that the words charged do not import whoredom, and are not actionable per se. We think otherwise. The word "f--ked," although not to be found in any vocabulary of the English language, is as well understood as any other English word.

Despite these legal examples—and there are really very few in the late nineteenth and early twentieth centuries—it seems that the word may not have been openly printed in a literary source in the United States until 1926, when it appeared once, and seemingly without generating any controversy (the word is still included in the book's tenth printing), in Howard Vincent O'Brien's anonymously published *Wine, Women and War,* his diary of the years 1917–19. It is worth noting that he used it in a figurative sense and was explicitly quoting an Australian soldier (see the 1918 quote at FUCKING *adj.* sense 2).

Fuck is found repeatedly in James Joyce's *Ulysses,* first published in book form in 1922 and circulated through clandestine copies in the United States for some time before a court decision in 1933 allowed the book's legal entry. Judge John Woolsey specifically addressed the obscene words in his verdict: "The words which are criticized as dirty are old Saxon words known to almost all men and, I venture, to many women, and are such words as would be naturally and habitually used, I believe, by the types of folk whose life, physical and mental, Joyce is seeking to describe."

It took far longer for D. H. Lawrence's novel *Lady Chatterley's Lover* to be approved by the courts, partly because of its more frequent use of obscene words, and partly (particularly in England) because of its depiction of an affair between a working-class man and an aristocratic woman. When an American court finally approved its publication in 1959, the judge also discussed the dangerous words. Federal Judge Frederick van Pelt Bryan wrote in his decision: "Four-letter Anglo-Saxon words are used with some frequency...this language understandably will shock the sensitive minded. Be that as it may...the language which shocks, except in a rare instance or two, is not inconsistent with character, situation or theme." The decision was upheld by an appellate court in 1960. At the same time, the English had created a new law, the Obscene Publications Act of 1959, which strengthened the law against pornography, at the same time allowing a publisher to escape prosecution by proving that a given work had literary merit. Penguin published the book in 1960, and the five-day trial, featuring testimony from a number of prominent academic critics, produced a not-guilty verdict. *The Guardian* and *The Observer*, in their coverage, printed "fuck" with no asterisks or dashes.

In 1971 the Supreme Court ruled that *fuck* could be protected political speech in *Cohen* v. *California*. This case overturned a 1968 conviction for "disturbing the peace" against an antiwar protestor who wore a jacket with the words "FUCK THE DRAFT" on it. John Marshall Harlan II noted in his decision that "one man's vulgarity is another's lyric," arguing that a state cannot censor its citizens merely for the sake of civility.

The language writer Hugh Rawson observes that trials of this sort often avoid mentioning the words at issue. After Lenny Bruce's 1963 obscenity trial in Chicago, Bruce described the prosecutor's commenting, "I don't think I have to tell you the term, I think that you recall it...as a word that started with a 'F' and ended with a 'K' and sounded like 'truck.'" A 1981 indecency trial in Maine contained the ruling "that no obscene words should be uttered in court, and that the principal word in question should be referred to simply as 'the word.'" Even in 2009, the U.S. Supreme Court's decision in *FCC* v. *Fox* referred only to "the F-Word or the S-Word" in its summary of the case.

It was not until the 1950s and '60s that *fuck* was frequently printed in full in mainstream fiction and nonfiction, usually in nonliteral senses. Norman Mailer was persuaded to substitute the invented spelling variant "fug" in his first novel, *The Naked and the Dead*, published to great acclaim in 1948; on the other hand, a mere three years later, James Jones was able to use the correctly spelled *fuck* in 1951 in *From Here to Eternity*, for which he won the National Book Award, though the reported 258 examples of *fuck* in the manuscript were cut back to a mere 50 in the final book. Many Americans found both of these novels about World War II shocking, despite the fact that their dialogue accurately reflected the way soldiers really spoke.

With the liberating attitudes toward personal freedom that developed in the 1960s and '70s, the use of *fuck* grew still more. Though upholders of mainstream proprieties still largely frowned on the use of the word, the uninhibited behavior of many of the younger generation forced people to pay attention. Some notable examples of the time include the rise to popularity of the comedian Lenny Bruce, and his many trials for obscenity along the way; the inclusion of *fuck* in a general dictionary, for the first time since 1795; Country Joe leading the throngs at Woodstock in the "fuck cheer" ("Gimme an F!..."); and the inclusion of *fuck*, spelled out in full, in large-circulation periodicals. *Harper's* first used the word—and in a sexual sense, no less—in its issue of April 1968 (cited in this dictionary at FUCK *verb* sense 1.b.).

Fuck also began to appear in some popular music then. There had been occasional examples earlier—a number of surprisingly bawdy blues lyrics exist—but perhaps the most prominent by a major performer was in a cover of the Louis Armstrong song "Ol' Man Mose" by the bandleader Eddy Duchin in 1938. The verse goes, "(We believe) He kicked the bucket and ol' man Mose is dead, / (We believe) Ahh, fuck it! / (We believe) Buck-buck-bucket. / (We believe) He kicked the bucket and ol' man Mose is dead." The pronunciation is extremely clear.

George Carlin's famous "Seven Dirty Words" was not only one of the funniest comedy routines of the era, but it also led to an important Supreme Court decision about obscenity. The routine first appeared on his 1972 album *Class Clown*, in a track entitled "Seven Words You Can Never Say on Television"; the words were *fuck, shit, cunt, cocksucker, motherfucker, piss*, and *tits*. (These words were not in fact banned at the time; the notion was merely a conceit of Carlin's.) An extended version of this monologue, "Filthy Words," appeared on his 1973 album *Occupation: Foole*, and this version was broadcast, uncensored, on the New York radio station WBAI, part of the Pacifica radio group. A man driving with his son heard the routine and complained to the FCC. The FCC, while not sanctioning Pacifica at that time, reserved the right to do so in the future. Pacifica successfully appealed this decision to the U.S. Court of Appeals; the FCC appealed to the Supreme Court, which ruled in favor of the FCC in 1978. That decision, *FCC* v. *Pacifica Foundation*, established the regulation of indecency in American broadcasting. Carlin's routine was acknowledged to be indecent, though not obscene, yet the Court recognized that because of "the pervasive nature of broadcasting," the medium deserved less First Amendment protection than other forms of communication. The FCC was therefore given broad discretion to determine in which contexts material was obscene, and to restrict the broadcasting of such material during hours when children were likely to be listening. In a follow-up case, *FCC* v. *Fox*, decided as this book was going to press in April 2009, the Supreme Court ruled 5–4 that the FCC did have the authority to impose strong fines even for the "fleeting" use of unscripted expletives on TV. This case had been prompted by several large fines the FCC levied against live TV programs where the producers claimed that they could not have anticipated the language of the partipants.

The major newsmagazines, *Time* and *Newsweek*, were also slow to get into the act of using *fuck* in print. *Newsweek* was earlier; the first appearance there was in the issue of October 8, 1984, in an excerpt from Lee Iacocca's memoir in which he recalls a conversation with Henry Ford II: "We've just made a billion eight for the second year in a row. But mark my words, Henry. You may never see a billion eight again. And do you know why? Because you don't know how the fuck we made it in the first place!"

The word seems to have first appeared in *Time* on September 29, 2000, in a remembrance of Canadian Prime Minister Pierre Trudeau: "One memorable afternoon in the House of Commons he sat at his desk while the Tories attacked him, and then, with exaggerated mouth movements, he responded almost silently: 'Fuck off.'" (See the entry for FUDDLE-DUDDLE in this dictionary.)

It took a bit more time for the word to penetrate the pages of the august *The New Yorker*. The editorship of Tina Brown was credited—more usually, faulted—with that journal's frequent use of the word, and though writers did use it with increasing frequency under Ms. Brown, in fact *fuck* appeared there, spelled in full, more than once during the editorship of her predecessor, the puritanical William Shawn. Calvin Trillin quoted a Nebraska farmer: "Goddam fuckin' Jews!…They destroyed everything I ever worked for!" (March 18, 1985), and Bobbie Ann Mason used the word in a short story: "Maybe you have to find out for yourself. Fuck. You can't learn from the past" (June 3, 1985). The current editor, David Remnick, continues to allow the word to appear as necessary, and it is not uncommon in fiction, reportage, or even editorial text.

Major American newspapers were typically slow to include *fuck* for any reason (in Britain, as we have seen, the coverage of the *Lady Chatterley's Lover* case led to the word's appearance in several papers there). The *Los Angeles Times* first used it in 1991, in an article about an attempted coup in Moscow that quoted Gorbachev shouting "Fuck off!" at some conspirators. The *Washington*

Post's first use was in 1992, in a direct quote about the final days of a death-row inmate.

Next came the remarkable appearance of *fuck*, spelled in full, in the pages of the *New York Times* (and many other newspapers). The *Times*'s policies on offensive language are usually quite conservative, often to the extent that articles specifically about obscene words do not provide enough information for the reader to determine what the article is about. But in 1998, having committed itself to printing the Starr Report, the *Times* was obligated to include the money passage on page B6 of its issue of September 12: "Ms. Lewinsky said she wanted two things from the President. The first was contrition: He needed to 'acknowledge...that he helped fuck up my life.'"

Another notable political use led to a prominent appearance of *fuck* in the *Washington Post*. In 2004, Vice President Dick Cheney, exasperated with a political opponent, told him, on the floor of the Senate, to fuck himself. The *Post* ran an article about the encounter on June 25, with more sly wit than one is accustomed to see in political reporting: "The exchange ended when Cheney offered some crass advice. 'Fuck yourself,' said the man who is a heartbeat from the presidency." Though Cheney and the Republican Party were often said to be in favor of civil exchanges—the same day as this encounter, the Senate had passed the Defense of Decency Act—the Vice President defended his statement, claiming that it made him "feel better." The *Post*'s editor personally approved the appearance of the word, on the grounds that Cheney's remark had appeared in public and "not in a casual way," though the paper's ombudsman felt that the "heartbeat" retort was "smart-alecky."

In Britain, the earliest use in Parliament was apparently in 1982, when Labour MP Reg Race referred in the House of Commons to advertisements for prostitutes that read, "Phone them and fuck them." *Hansard*, the official publication of Parliamentary transcripts, rendered the word as "f ***."

In other media, the word has slipped in on occasion, but it seems that in the movie world, no one even tried to have *fuck* uttered on the screen until people were ready for it. The abandonment of the Hays Code, the censorship guidelines agreed to by major motion picture studios, in 1968, effectively allowed the word to be used in studio films, and its first appearance in mainstream movies was in 1970. During a football game in the antiwar black comedy *MASH*, one of the MASH linemen says to an opponent, "All right, bud, your fucking head is coming right off." Also in 1970, *Myra Breckenridge*, a sexually frank film based on Gore Vidal's novel, used the word several times; this film, often regarded as one of the worst ever made, had little influence.

Though 1970 was the first time *fuck* appeared in a major film, it had earlier been used in several avant-garde productions. A 1967 Irish production of Joyce's *Ulysses*, featuring a script taken almost entirely from the book itself, used the word; the film was not allowed to be shown in general release in Ireland until 2000. The 1967 British film *I'll Never Forget What's'isname*, which portrayed a disillusioned advertising executive who drops out of corporate life, also used *fuck* in the dialogue; in the United States the film was denied an MPAA seal of approval because of a scene implying oral sex between the executive and his mistress. And yet again in 1967, D. A. Pennebaker's documentary about Bob Dylan, *Dont Look Back*, shows Dylan drunkenly asking, "Who threw that fucking glass in the street? Who threw it? I'm not going to get fucking blamed for that."

A number of films are regarded as extreme in the number of times *fuck* has been used in them. Until recently, it was very difficult to get more than an impressionistic idea of frequency. But there are now several Web sites devoted to tracking the uses of obscenity in film—usually intended for parents to determine how appropriate a film is for children—and so a more accurate breakdown is possible.

The standout among all mainstream films is, appropriately, the 2005 documentary *Fuck*, a film about the word itself (in which this editor had a minor role), which used a form of *fuck* 824 times in 93 minutes, for an average of 8.86 uses per minute. In second place, and with the highest number of uses in a narrative film, is 1997's *Nil by Mouth*, written and directed by the actor Gary Oldham, about a lower-class family in London, which had 428 *fucks*. Martin Scorsese's 1995 *Casino* rounds out the top three with 398. Other high-ranking films include *Summer of Sam*, *Menace II Society*, and *Goodfellas*. Quentin Tarantino's *Reservoir Dogs* and *Pulp Fiction*, often regarded as exceptionally vulgar, make the list down at numbers 20 and 21, with 269 and 265 *fucks*, respectively.

The F-Word in Titles

It should not be surprising that the appearance of *fuck* in titles, band names, and the like is a relatively recent phenomenon. Kurt Vonnegut's short story "The Big Space Fuck" was published in Harlan Ellison's 1972 anthology *Again, Dangerous Visions*; Vonnegut later claimed that it was "the first story in the history of literature to have 'fuck' in its title." This is not strictly true. The earliest work of any sort with *fuck* in the title is apparently the 1879 erotic work *A New and Gorgeous Pantomime Entitled Harlequin Prince Cherrytop and the Good Fairy Fairfuck, or the Frig, the Fuck and the Fairy* (cited in this dictionary as *Harlequin Prince Cherrytop*). In "proper" literature, Ed Sanders's underground *Fuck You/A Magazine of the Arts*, which began publication in 1962, is likely the earliest. Similarly the poet Douglas Blazek, one of the founders of the "Mimeo Revolution" of self-published poetry, published *Fuck Off Unless You Take Off That Mask* in 1969.

In 1968, the British writer J. G. Ballard published a pamphlet entitled *Why I Want to Fuck Ronald Reagan*, written as a scientific paper analyzing Reagan's psychosexual appeal. When this paper was included as an appendix to his 1970 collection *The Atrocity Exhibition*, Doubleday, Ballard's American publisher, pulped the entire printing.

The practical difficulty of using *fuck* in a title is that most mainstream publications, even today, will not be able to write about it. It is not clear what the intended title is of Greg Araki's 1993 gay-themed film *Totally F ***ed Up*; the title is thus in its own advertising material, but the title may be meant to be spelled without any asterisks. Arthur Neresian's 1997 novel *The Fuck-Up* is perhaps one of the more prominent nonunderground works of this type, but Mark Ravenhill's 1996 play *Shopping and Fucking* was also notable. Shocking for its sexually violent content as well as its title, the play has received various forms of treatment from different publications. When the *New York Times* reviewed a 2005 New York revival, too prominent to ignore, it used *Shopping And* . . . .

The earliest use of *fuck* in the title of a scholarly paper, according to the MLA bibliography, is Roger Luckhurst's "Shut(ting) the Fuck Up: Narrating *Blue Velvet* in the Postmodernist Frame," published in 1989 in the journal *Bête Noire*. The first scholarly paper to be titled "Fuck" exclusively seems to be one by Christopher M. Fairman, a professor at Ohio State, first published in 2006 as the Public Law and Legal Theory Working Paper Series No. 59. The paper analyzes various legal implications of the use of the word.

The F-Word in Dictionaries

The first appearance of *fuck* in a dictionary was in John Florio's *Worlde of Words*, a comprehensive Italian-English dictionary published in 1598—before any monolingual dictionary of English had yet appeared. It was one of five synonyms given to translate the Italian word *fottere*; the others were *jape, sard, swive*, and *occupy*. *Fuck* was first included as a main entry, in its proper alphabetic place, in Stephen Skinner's *Etymologicon Linguae Anglicanae* (1671), a dictionary of English etymology that was written in Latin.

Samuel Johnson's immediate predecessor, Nathan (or Nathaniel) Bailey, listed the word, with a Latin definition, in his 1721 *Universal Etymological English Dictionary*. Bailey's popular 1730 follow-up, the *Dictionarium Britannicum*, contained the curious note that it was "a term used of a goat"; this odd limitation may have been intended to mitigate the inclusion of the word (words inappropriate to humans might be allowable if referring to animals) and not as an indication of actual usage. Samuel Johnson excluded it from his great dictionary in 1755, but he made a conscious decision to omit vulgar words, so the absence of it from his dictionary does not indicate the word's rarity. Still, the word's omission provided one of the great dirty-words-in-dictionaries anecdotes: when complimented by a lady for having left out this and other offensive words, Johnson is said to have replied, "No, Madam, I hope I have not daubed my fingers. I find, however, that you have been looking for them."

The last general dictionary of this era to include *fuck* seems to have been John Ash's *New and Complete Dictionary of the English Language*, first published in 1775, and still containing the word in its 1795 second edition. Ash—a Baptist minister—called it "a low vulgar word," and defined it as "to perform the act of generation, to have to do with a woman." Ash also included *cunt* in both editions of his dictionary, also marked as vulgar and defined as "the female pudendum." After Ash, it was to be 170 years until *fuck* again appeared in a general dictionary.

In the late Victorian era, the great slang dictionary of the time, John Farmer and W. E. Henley's *Dictionary of Slang and Its Analogues*, featured extensive treatments of *cunt* and *fuck* in volumes published in 1891 and 1893, respectively. The entries included compounds, phrases, and numerous dated quotations. Though the volumes were privately published for subscribers only, Farmer's original printer refused to print the second volume of the work after seeing the nature of the contents, and Farmer took him to court to recover the costs of switching printers at such short notice. Despite the claim that the work served a historical and scholarly purpose, the jury, shocked by the extent of the obscene vocabulary, found for the defendant.

Even in the twentieth century the presence of *fuck* in specialized dictionaries has caused problems. The slang lexicographer Eric Partridge included over a dozen F-words in the first edition of his *Dictionary of Slang and Unconventional English*, but he spelled the word "f*ck." In spite of this, his compilation, in that and its various later editions, generated protests to the police, school authorities, and libraries; as late as the 1960s special permission was needed to view it in some libraries. In his etymological dictionary *Origins*, published in 1958, Partridge added a second asterisk to make the word a potentially less offensive "f**k." The missing letters were restored to the *Dictionary of Slang and Unconventional English* in its Supplement of 1967.

Other large general dictionaries cannot be seriously faulted for omitting the word, given the tenor of the times. The next major dictionary to miss its chance was *Webster's Third New International Dictionary* in 1961. Groundbreaking in its approach to slang and colloquial language—for which it was harshly condemned by many critics—the *Third* did include *cunt*, and had set a *fuck* entry into type, but the officers of the G. & C. Merriam Co. vetoed it at the last minute. (The linguist Mario Pei criticized the dictionary's "residual prudishness" in a review.)

Similarly inhibited was Random House, whose 1966 *Random House Dictionary of the English Language* was the other great dictionary of the 1960s. Jess Stein, the editor-in-chief, told the *New York Times* about a meeting he convened with the company's editorial and sales staff to discuss *cunt* and *fuck*: "When I uttered the words, there was a shuffling of feet, and a wave of embarrassment went through the room. That convinced me the words did not belong in the dictionary, though I'm sure I'll be attacked as a prude for the decision." Stein did not have to wait long to be proven right on the last point: a mere two weeks later, on September 30, the *Times*'s own book reviewer wrote, "Unfortunately, a stupid prudery has prevented the inclusion of probably the most widely-used word in the English language. The excuse here, no doubt, is 'good taste'; but in a dictionary of this scope and ambition the omission seems dumb and irresponsible."

Only the previous year, the British *Penguin English Dictionary*, edited by G. N. Garmonsway, had become the first general English dictionary to include *fuck* since Ash's 1795 second edition. The entry—"ludicrously brief," in the words of *OED* editor Robert Burchfield—consisted in its entirety of "(*vulg*) (*of males*) have sexual intercourse (with)." In America the honor of first inclusion fell to the 1969 *American Heritage Dictionary*—ironically, given the otherwise conservative approach that dictionary took to language issues. The treatment was reasonably full, with five verb senses, two noun senses, and adjective and adverb entries. All were labeled "Vulgar."

The words *cunt* and *fuck* had been kept out of the *Oxford English Dictionary*—the *F* entries were edited in the 1890s—though by the time the editors made it to *W* in the 1920s, they decided to enter *windfucker* as a name for the kestrel. Eric Partridge reported a discussion with C. T. Onions, one of the *OED*'s editors, about why the earlier editors had left out *cunt* and *fuck*. Onions: "They considered the two unspeakables to be also unprintables…and although I cannot speak for Craigie, I do myself think them beyond the pale of all decency . . . . I wouldn't have liked my own children to find these words in a volume on my library shelves." Partridge countered by observing that people would never find the words if they didn't already know to look for them, to which Onions grudgingly answered, "Yes, perhaps, perhaps, but I still think the *OED* was right to ban them."

The omission of these words had been objected to at least as early as 1934, when the linguist A. S. C. Ross (now best known for the concept of "U and non-U" language, popularized by Nancy Mitford) reviewed the first *OED Supplement* (1933) in the scholarly journal *Neuphilologische Mitteilungen*. Ross wrote,

> As regards the latter [*i.e.* "obscene" words] there appears to have been a definite policy of omission; it certainly seems regrettable that the perpetuation of a Victorian prudishness (inacceptable [*sic*] in philology beyond all other subjects) should have been allowed to lead to the omission of some of the commonest words in the English language.... Often the words are attested from an early period and their omission from the NED [as the *OED* was then called] has sometimes led to the anomaly of their not appearing in the standard etymological dictionaries either.

Some other comprehensive scholarly dictionaries had included these words. The *Middle English Dictionary* published a full treatment of *cunte* in 1961; *fuck* is not attested in Middle English and thus could not have been included. There are very brief entries for *fuck* and some derivatives in the section of the *Dictionary of the Older Scottish Tongue* that appeared in the late 1940s, but the citations consisted only of bibliographic references, without the quotation text itself, forcing readers to go to the library if they wanted to see the context.

Fuck and *cunt* finally entered the *OED* in 1972 with the publication of the first volume (A–G) of *A Supplement to the Oxford English Dictionary*. When Robert Burchfield accepted the editorship of the Supplements in 1957, he thought that "the time had not yet come" to include the word, but he eventually changed his mind. After consulting scholars around the globe and drafting entries for the words, Burchfield wrote to the Delegates of Oxford University Press that the draft entries were "based on the printed evidence which, though scanty in some centuries, is substantial enough to permit the compilation of articles comparable in quality with those for other words of similar date." And in 1968 the Delegates, as well as the Proctors of the University of Oxford itself, approved the

inclusion of the two words in recognition that "standards of toler-
ance have changed and their omission has for many years, and
more frequently of late, excited critical comment."

Euphemism and Taboo Avoidance

As one can see from the entry for EFF in this book, the use of the
first letter of *fuck* as a euphemism for the word itself arose by the
1920s at the latest. There are earlier precedents for this dodge. In
H.M.S. Pinafore (1878), the librettist Sir W. S. Gilbert alludes to
the use of *damn*:

> Though "Bother it" I may
> Occasionally say,
> I never use a big, big D.

A fascinating—and much earlier—parallel is found in classical
Latin, as David L. Gold has shown in a recent article. In his *Meni-
ppeae*, Marcus Terentius Varro (116–27 BC) writes *psephistis dicite
labdeae.* The sense of the first word in this context is not known, but
the next two words are clear: they are an allusion to the Latin idiom
laecasin dicere "to tell (someone) to go to hell," which literally means
"to tell (someone) to suck," and is based on λαικάζω, a vulgar
Greek verb for *fellate*. (*Labdeae* is the word for *lambda*, the Greek
letter *L*.) An English translation of the Varro quote, then, would be
something like "Tell him to go S himself!"

Of course, all this is not to suggest that the expression "the
F-word" is modeled on a Latin phrase, or even on a Gilbert and
Sullivan comedy. But the two usages illustrate the same device:
the name of the first letter of a vulgar word euphemistically
standing for that word.

The expression *four-letter word* is first found in 1897 and was
well enough established by the 1930s to be used in Cole Porter's
classic lyric "Anything Goes" in 1934: "Good authors, too, who
once used better words/Now only use four-letter words/Writing

prose/Anything goes." (The related expression *four-letter man*, indicating a "man who can be described by a four-letter word [usually *shit*, but sometimes *goof*, *bore*, or *dumb*]" was common in the 1920s.) With both *eff* and *four-letter word* in use in the 1930s, it would not be too surprising if *the F-word* were used at that time as well. However, the earliest example of which the editor is aware is not until the early 1950s, and that was in an academic journal, discussing the publication of *Lady Chatterley's Lover* (see the entry for F-WORD in this dictionary). The later evidence, however, suggests that it was still mainly used as a childish euphemism—another reason to believe that it may have been used earlier, since words such as these are seldom written down.

The use of *the F-word* increased throughout the 1970s and '80s, and eventually the suffix *-word* began to be used freely with the first letter of a word—any word—to be avoided. There are occasional examples from the early 1980s of, for instance, *the L-word* for "lesbian," but this practice did not really peak until the mid- to late-1980s. By this time it was often jocular, as in *the L-word* for "love" or "liberal," or *the T-word* for "taxes," but serious examples were also used: *the N-word* for "nigger." This combining form of the suffix *-word*, finally liberated from association with *fuck*, appeared by itself in general dictionaries by the early 1990s.

The trick of spelling out the word *fuck* is not new. When the singer Britney Spears released a single called "If You Seek Amy," with the song title spelling out "F-U-C-K me," in 2009, it was viewed as shocking, with parents registering complaints and so forth, despite the fact that phrases of this sort have been around for centuries, including, as we have seen, in Shakespeare. In *Ulysses*, James Joyce made the same pun with the bit of doggerel, "If you see Kay. / Tell him he may. / See you in tea. / Tell him from me," thus managing to spell out *cunt* as well. Take that, Britney!

Indeed, the trope is well established among musicians. The blues pianist Memphis Slim recorded a wistful song about his lost girlfriend, called "If You See Kay," in 1963. In 1977, lo-fi pioneer R. Stevie Moore released his "If You See Kay," a lopingly heartbroken revenge song that concludes: "If you see Kay you." The title was used, less wistfully and less heartbrokenly, by the Canadian rock band April Wine, on their 1982 album *Power Play* (sample lyrics: "She had the look of need / Like 'Give it to me'/ I decided I should take a chance"). The pop-punk band Poster Children released a ragged, raucous version on their 1990 *Daisychain Reaction*. The Norwegian punk band Turbonegro released the slick and poppy "If You See Kaye," performed in English, in 2005. Aerosmith used the line in a lyric in their 2006 song "Devil's Got a New Disguise." (In 1991, Van Halen released the album *For Unlawful Carnal Knowledge*, though this was surely not intended to be even remotely subtle.) One of the catchiest recent iterations of this trope comes from the Irish band The Script, which released its "If You See Kay" on MySpace. In a 2009 interview, the band explicitly acknowledged its debt to James Joyce—whom they helpfully identify as "a literary god in Ireland"—noting the use of the gag in *Ulysses*.

In all of these cases, the performers are letting the double-entendre work for them; this is not the case with Britney, whose use of the phrase is not a pun. There is only one possible way to interpret it, since the lyric itself makes no sense in context: "All of the boys and all of the girls are begging to if you seek Amy." The use of *Amy* in this context does seem to be new, though.

Aside from the the use of initial letters, the use of euphemisms for *fuck* itself is also long established. This dictionary includes a number of euphemisms for *fuck* that are used as phonetic substitutions for the word, with *frig* being both early, and also used in a very wide variety of constructions.

As we have seen, when Norman Mailer published *The Naked and the Dead* in 1948, he was persuaded by his publisher to use the spelling *fug*, leading to the story that Tallulah Bankhead (or, in some versions of the anecdote, Dorothy Parker) approached Mailer at a party and said "So you're the young man who can't spell *fuck*." (Of course this spelling was never intended to be any kind of a true mask.)

Another form of avoidance was the use of typographical markers to show that certain letters in a word are to be omitted. The earliest known example of this practice is from 1680, in a poem by John Oldham entitled "Upon the Author of a Play call'd Sodom," where the word *turd* has the vowel replaced by a dash. Richard Ames's 1688 "Satyr Again Man" includes a number of typographically bleeped words, including *bl–d* for 'blood', *w–nds* for 'wounds' (both only when used as oaths; in their normal senses they are written out in the usual way), and *G-d* and *d-mn*. By 1698 we have our first example of the bleeped *fuck*; see the quote at FUCK *v.* sense 1.c. in this dictionary.

Such dashes were common throughout the eighteenth century; by the nineteenth century (if not earlier), asterisks were pressed into service. The 1857 example in this dictionary at FUCKING *adj.* sense 2 is striking in its combination of dashes (to partly obscure the less offensive word *bitch*) and asterisks (to entirely obscure a word that we must conclude is *fucking*).

This Dictionary and Its Policies

Selection of Entries, and Inclusion Policy

This book contains every sense of *fuck*, and every compound word or phrase of which *fuck* is a part, that the editor believes has ever had broad currency in English. It does not contain words meaning 'to have sex' or 'to victimize' that are used, often unconsciously, as euphemisms for *fuck*, such as *lay, screw, shaft*, or *do it*. However, it does include euphemisms for *fuck* that directly suggest, in sound and meaning, the word itself: thus the inclusion of *freaking, foul up, mofo*, and others. These words are typically used as direct replacements for *fuck*.

In earlier editions of this book, priority was given to American English; indeed, in its first edition, forms not found in America were excluded entirely. However, the text is now much more wide-ranging, thanks to the editor's access to the files of the *OED*: uses that are specifically British, Australian, or Irish are included in their own right, and a very large number of quotations have been added from non-American sources to illustrate all entries, not just those associated with a particular national variety. The reader will thus find vastly more British examples (including Welsh and especially Scottish in addition to English), and also quotations from Australia, New Zealand, Ireland, Canada, South Africa, and elsewhere.

Preference has been given to words found in actual use, though the editor did find it necessary to consult other dictionaries or word lists. For earlier uses, where evidence from written sources is sparse, a dictionary quotation may represent a genuine use that is simply unattested elsewhere. But in many cases, words that are found only in dictionaries are joke words, made up as a lark, and there is no way of gauging their true currency; compilers of slang dictionaries put them in because they find such words amusing, or because they can't verify whether the words are truly in use and want to be safe by being completist. For example, the World War II *snafu* gave rise to a number of other words with the *fu* element, including *janfu*, *snefu*, and *tarfu*, and *fubar* and its relations. Certain specialized dictionaries or glossaries of World War II language contain many more examples, but we have no written or spoken evidence of actual use. This suggests that these words were never used seriously, but treated only as jokes. Thus this dictionary does not include *tasfuira* 'things are so fucked up it's really amazing', among others.

The availability of massive full-text databases, as well as Google and other search engines, has, perhaps contrary to expectations, greatly complicated the decision-making process. Even a quick look at, say, www.urbandictionary.com will show that there are very many words or phrases with *fuck* that are not included in this dictionary. Opening the book up to every word or compound for which examples can be found on the Internet would make it very much longer than it is now, with uncertain benefits. The editor has thus done his best to try to determine which of these is most likely to be in truly broad circulation. In general, examples from printed sources have been given preference over online examples. Uses from popular movies or television shows have also received preferred treatment, though even some prominent examples from these genres did not make the cut. Though the song "Uncle Fucka," from the 1999 movie *South Park: Bigger, Longer, and Uncut,* is a brilliant work and won an MTV Movie Award for Best Musical Performance, *uncle fucker* was not included; there was simply no evidence for a broad use of the term.

A partial list of terms that have been excluded includes *clothes-fuck* 'a difficulty in deciding what to wear'; *figure-fucking* 'altering financial documents; "cooking the books"'; *fuck eyes* 'sexually flirtatious glances'; *fuck lips* 'the labia'; *fuckomania* 'rampant sexual desire'; *fuck-stain* 'a foolish or offensive person'; *fuck udders* 'a woman's breasts'; and *fuckwaddery* 'the nature of being a fuckwad; stupidity'.

The editor encourages readers to write in with suggestions for words that are omitted, especially if there is solid evidence for their genuine use, for possible inclusion in future editions.

The Entries
The entries in this book are arranged alphabetically, letter by letter. A word may be shown as a main entry more than once, depending on its use as a noun, verb, adjective, adverb, interjection, or infix (a word, such as *-fucking-*, inserted within another word or set phrase, forming such other words as *absofuckinglutely*).

Within an entry, numbered senses are ordered by the date of the first citation, as are the lettered subsenses within a numbered sense.

This allows the historical development of the senses to be clearly seen.

Phrases using *fuck* or a derivative are listed alphabetically at the end of the main entry; some phrases may be listed as part of a definition in the main body of the entry. Phrases are preceded by the pointing-middle-finger symbol (☞) for clarity.

Cross-references to other words in this volume are given in SMALL CAPITALS. Cross references to phrases are given in *italic* type and specify the main entry word where the phrase may be found.

Certain citations have been placed in square brackets to indicate that the example does not show, or does not clearly show, the use of the word it is meant to illustrate, but provides a parallel or prefiguring use. Examples are the first quotation for CFM, which contains the full form *come fuck me* but not the abbreviation itself; the first two quotations for *fuck the dog* under DOG *noun*, which use "feed" and "walk" instead of *fuck*, with no way to tell whether these were euphemisms or unrelated uses; and *finger-frig*, almost a hundred years earlier than the first actual quotation for FINGER-FUCK.

Field labels, such as *Military* or *Black English* or *British*, describe the group or subculture of people who use the word (not necessarily those to whom the word applies). The choice of labels was made on the basis of the evidence, and it is not intended to be limiting. The presence of a label should not imply that the word is used exclusively by the designated group, or that persons using such words have real ties to the group.

The Examples

Each entry in this book is illustrated with a number of examples of the use of the word in context—quotations from books and magazines, movies or television, the Internet, and sometimes even from speech. These examples, called *citations* (or *cites* for short) by dictionary editors, have several purposes: to demonstrate that a word or sense has actually been in use; to show the length of time it has existed; to show exactly how it has been used; and so forth.

In every case, the first citation given is the earliest one that the editor has been able to find. The last citation is, within reason, the most recent example available. Only a few F-words are truly obsolete and therefore have no recent example. The dates provide important evidence for the use of a word. We may discover that although *fuck around* 'to play or fool around' is recorded only from the early twentieth century, the similar use of *frig* is found in the late eighteenth. Therefore, that sense of *fuck* itself may be just as old but simply unrecorded owing to the vulgarity of the term.

Every example is preceded by its bibliographic source. Most of the sources may be found in a good research library, though some are from manuscripts or other sources kept in the files of the Random House Reference Division or the *Oxford English Dictionary*. The examples taken from speech were collected by the editor, or in some cases by researchers for Random House; the date refers to the year in which the example was actually collected. Online examples can be found in expected places: Usenet quotations are archived at Google Groups; ones from electronic editions of newspapers will be at the Web site of those papers; etc.

The date shown for each citation is the date when we believe the word was actually written or used. This is usually the same as the publication date. Occasionally, when a passage (or the entire book) is known to have been written at an earlier date, that date will be given instead. In most such cases the year of publication is given in parentheses after the title. This is also the case when the quotation was taken from a later edition of a book, but with the expectation that the quotation was present in an earlier edition: The date of the original edition will be given, with the later edition in parentheses after the title. When a book or magazine is quoting an earlier source, the word "in" appears after the date: 1528 in *Notes & Queries*.

Jesse Sheidlower, New York

Introduction to the Third Edition

The F-Word was first published in 1995. There were various extensive changes introduced in the Second Edition of this book, which was published in 1999. Most prominently, the original edition included only F-words that were in use in America; the Second Edition added entries for British and Australian and other uses. It also added a variety of new quotations, including some famous ones that were of interest, and added some words and senses that had been missed.

This Third Edition introduces a vastly larger number of changes. The dictionary text is about twice as large as the Second Edition, and well over 100 new words and senses have been added. A significant number of existing entries have been antedated—that is, earlier examples have been found, showing that a word has been in use for longer than we once thought. All this has been made possible in large part because of the increased availability of online resources. The second major factor is the editor's move to the *Oxford English Dictionary*, and thus his access to its files.

There have been a number of other changes. A broad effort has been made to fix the bibliographic information. Titles have been regularized, and where possible given in their full form. Initials have been added to the names of most authors. Dates assigned to books have been regularized; parenthesized dates have been added to editions of letters or journals, later editions of works, and other cases where the date given for the quotation does not correspond to the publication date of the book in which it was found.

The quotations have been a particular focus of the work. Thousands have been added to this edition. The editor has tried to broaden the range of evidence as much as possible. The geographic range has been expanded, so that, for example, British authors are quoted even for terms that are originally American, and quotations have been added from South Africa, New Zealand, Canada, and elsewhere (a typical practice is to quote from "minority" regions only for terms associated with those regions). A number of uninteresting quotations have been deleted if they could be replaced with better ones from a similar date, and many quotations were added because the editor found them interesting or amusing.

The use of full-text databases has also allowed many existing entries to be expanded or split up. Many entries had parts of speech combined, so that the definition of a word found chiefly as a verb, but with a single noun example, would lump the two uses together. Now, with more noun uses, this use could be split off into its own entry. Examples of this process include CUNT-FUCK *noun*, which previously had only a single quotation from 1998, from a Usenet newsgroup devoted to erotic stories, but has now been expanded into a full-fledged entry, with four quotations covering the range of 1879 to 2002; FUCKWITTED *adjective*, previously part of FUCKWIT *noun* but now on its own; FUGLY *noun*, separated from the adjective; and SPORT FUCK *noun*, upgraded from the verb. Similarly, some entries that were subsumed under others have been elevated. Thus the phrases *fuck 'em if they can't take a joke* and *fuck you and the horse you rode in on* were both in the earlier editions, but merely thrown in with other, less frequent phrases. But it was clear that these should be given individual treatment.

In many other cases, existing entries have been expanded with new senses or parts of speech. The original entry for ASS-FUCK had a single example of 'an instance of victimization' for the noun;

there are now a number of quotations for this sense, as well as a new noun sense 'a despicable person' and a new verb sense 'to victimize'. The noun BUTTFUCKER, previously included under BUTT-FUCK *verb*, is now an entry in its own right, with both the literal sense and the figurative 'despicable person'. The adjective FUCK-FACED, previously only recorded in the sense 'having an ugly face', now has two additional senses, 'tired' and 'drunk; shit-faced'. BFD, in previous editions only present as an interjection, now has a noun equivalent, and the adjective and adverb FUBAR now has a verb.

The bulk of the additions consist of entirely new words. Some are non-American forms that the editor had missed, including the British *eff and blind* under EFF *verb*, FANNY ADAMS, *fuck knows* under FUCK *verb*, and HEADFUCK in senses related to confusion; the Canadian FUDDLE-DUDDLE; the Australian FARK; the Irish FECK. Some are initialisms, many now chiefly associated with the world of online communication, such as FOAD, OMFG, STFU, and especially the now mainstream MILF. But most are simply new or newish developments, or older terms that were rare enough to have been omitted before but for which substantial evidence is now available. A smattering of the many such new entries includes ARTFUCK, F-BOMB, FLAT FUCK, FRAK, *I wouldn't fuck her with your dick* under FUCK *verb*, FUCKABILITY, FUCKFRIEND, FUCK-LESS, FUCK MACHINE, FUCKSHIT, HATE-FUCK *verb*, PIGFUCK, THROAT FUCK, and UNFUCKED.

A small number of entries have been deleted entirely. While there are still examples of words or senses with only one quotation (suggesting that they are not and never have been very common), the decision to remove existing entries of this sort was not undertaken lightly. The deleted examples include *give-a-fuck* 'one's sense of motivation or enthusiasm', an apparently unique variant of the itself rare *give-a-shit*; *fucking* used interjectionally to indicate hesitation, which was perhaps an example of overextrapolation by a dictionary compiler; and *fuck-ox*, a military term for a Vietnamese water buffalo, a further example of which could not be found even in extensive searches of Vietnam War literature. It is possible that additional items could have been removed as well, but a conservative approach seemed best.

Acknowledgments

This book would not have been possible without the help of a large number of people across a long span of time. Of course all errors are my own fault.

For the earlier editions, Bernard W. Kane was indefatigable in providing buckets of useful suggestions; John Simpson generously sent me several citations from the files of the *Oxford English Dictionary*; Fred Shapiro's wizardry with database searches yielded a large number of updatings and important additions to the text; James Rader of Merriam-Webster sent early examples of several terms I had difficulty tracking down. My former colleagues at Random House provided assistance and support of various flavors.

Professor Anatoly Liberman was kind enough to share his detailed researches into the etymology and bibliography of *fuck*. His entry on the word in the *Analytic Dictionary of English Etymology* is by far the most comprehensive treatment of the etymology of *fuck* ever published.

H. Bosley Woolf generously sent me a copy of his privately printed pamphlet *The GI's Favorite Four Letter Word*, the earliest published work devoted solely to our word.

James Lambert, editor of the *Macquarie Book of Slang*, was kind enough to provide extensive citations from Australia and New Zealand in addition to many quotations from often obscure British and American sources. I am grateful for his continued help with this edition. He has been a friend for many years, despite the fact that we have never met in person.

My close friends and colleagues Jonathon Green and Tom Dalzell, slang lexicographers extraordinaire, were extremely generous in every way, personally and professionally. I am as grateful to them for their hospitality over the years as I am for their willingness to share painstakingly collected evidence from their own extensive collections.

For help with certain terms, and for specific editorial advice, I am grateful to Daniel Menaker, Jennifer Dowling, Judy Kaplan, Sarah Burnes, Jeremy Kareken, Charles Levine, Sam Pratt, Alison Biggert, Arnold Zwicky, Barry Popik, William Monahan, Edward Hutchinson, Stephen Berg, Andrew Cohen of *Newsweek*, Aaron Barnhart, Michele Tepper, and the Old and Young Hats of AFU GmbH.

More recently I must thank members of the American Dialect Society mailing list, especially Bill Mullins, Neal Whitman, John Patrick, John Baker, Wilson Gray, and Mark Peters for their detailed suggestions. Michael Adams has been a good friend and a patient colleague; his book *Slang: The People's Poetry* is the best treatment of an unwieldy subject. Adrian Flynn took time away from his studies to hit the library on my behalf. Ben Zimmer has been extremely generous and helpful over the years; along with Fred Shapiro he is the best database plunderer I've ever encountered. Larry Horn, Arnold Zwicky, and Ron Butters gave much useful advice. David Simon corresponded with me about *eye-fuck*, and graciously sent me original shooting scripts of his brilliant show *The Wire*.

I am extremely grateful to my colleagues at the *Oxford English Dictionary*. In particular, I would like to mention Chief Editor John Simpson; Robert Faber, who supported my work on this project more than he had to; Michael Proffitt, for many years of close support and friendship; and Graeme Diamond, with whom

I revised the *OED*'s entries for *fuck* and its relations. It is a rare and humbling pleasure to work in an environment with so many brilliant and dedicated people.

At Oxford University Press, my thanks to Ben Keene, for early editorial support; Damon Zucca and Grace Labatt, for helping bring the project to completion; Jess Lawson, for her production wizardry; Vin Dang for the interior design; Mary Araneo and Steve Cestaro in Production; Purdy for his unstinting publicity efforts; Amy Tiedemann and Kim Craven in Marketing for long-time enthusiasm; and above all to Casper Grathwohl for his approval and support of the book.

Ira Silverberg, my friend and agent (in that order), has been supportive for so long and for so little reason that I can't even begin to express my appreciation.

I received technical support from a number of different sources. Thanks especially to Adam Turoff for extensive help with the XML and XSLT used to produce the book, and for his constant availability to help with complicated issues. A shout-out to all of my colleagues on the Catalyst web framework. Perrin Harkins was extremely generous with his vast knowledge of programming. Paul Steiner at OUP provided ideal support, belying the stereotype of the IT drone. Nonpersonal thanks for some of the underlying technologies go out to Richard Stallman, Larry Wall, and Linus Torvalds, among many others.

This editor, and all students of the F-word, owe an enormous debt to the late Professor Allen Walker Read for his work on the word. Professor Read has made many hugely important contributions to the study of English; he is perhaps best known for his research on *O.K.* But his 1934 article "An Obscenity Symbol" is the pioneering study of the word; without his exhaustive research, we would know far less about this most significant word. His 1974 follow-up, "An Obscenity Symbol After Four Decades," admirably adds forty years of study to our knowledge.

Jonathan Lighter is the greatest slang lexicographer in history. It has been a deep honor to work with him and I continued to be humbled by his astonishing abilities at research, sense division, and defining. There has not been a single entry I have ever worked on that he could not have done better.

And finally, my immense love and gratitude to Sarah Lang, who showed me that I could be happy.

Jesse Sheidlower, New York, March 2009

A

absofuckinglutely *adverb*

absolutely. Compare -FUCKING-, *infix*.

1921 *Notes & Queries* (Nov. 19) 415 [refers to WWI]: The soldier's actual speech…was absolutely impregnated with one word which (to use it as a basis for alliteration) the fastidious frown at as "filthy"…. Words were split up to admit it: "absolutely" became "abso—lutely." **1945** S. J. Baker *Australian Language* 258: Transconti-bloody-nental, abso-f—g-lutely, inde-bloody-pendent. **1970** C. Major *Dictionary of Afro-American Slang* 19: *Absofuckinglutely*: without doubt. **1973** W. T. Huggett *Body Count* ch. viii: That's right, Carlysle, that's abso-fucking-lutely right. **1985** D. Bodey *F.N.G.* 224. "Like, don't it seem like the time has gone fast now?" "Abso-fuckin'-lutely." **1995** *N.Y. Observer* (Apr. 24) 19: "Remember me?"…"Abso-fucking-lutely." **2002** J. Thompson *Wide Blue Yonder* ii. 147: He was nuts. Absofuckinglutely. **2008** *New York Magazine* (Aug. 11) 31: I decided to e-mail Liz Rosenberg, Madonna's publicist since fuh-evah…to see if she would…talk about celebrities and plastic surgery. "Absofuckinlutely," she wrote back.

AMF *interjection*

"*adios* [or *aloha*], mother*f*ucker"; good-bye; the finish. *Jocular*.

1963 in P. Tamony *Motherfucker* 7: "A.M.F…. adios mother fucker,"…"goodbye friend." [**1966** M. Braly *On the Yard* 120: And that's adios mother fuckers.] **1973** McA. Layne *How Audie Murphy Died in Vietnam* (unpaged): *A.M.F.* Adios mother fahckers. **1980** D. J. Cragg *Lexicon Militaris*: *AMF*. Adios (or Aloha) Motherfucker. **1988**

K. Kijewski *Stray Kat Waltz* 286: You're outta here. Just like that. Leaving us behind and everything. Not thinking about us or anything. Just AMF. **2001** R. Martini *Hot Straight & Normal* 17: Alpha Mike Foxtrot—Acronym for "Adios, My Friend." Also seen as initials, "AMF." Other terms may be used for the "M," and "F." **2003** D. Farris *Lie Still* 179: "I will not be able to snatch your ass back from the fire if the GME committee says AMF." "AMF?" "*Adios*, Mutha Fucka."

artfuck *noun*

1. an artistic person, especially one who is elitist or pretentious.

1987 B. E. Ellis *Rules of Attraction* 110: I turn back to our table, with the Art Fucks because they seem less boring. **1999** M. Estep *Soft Maniacs* 121: The way I look, it's hard to tell if I'm some deliberately disheveled successful artfuck or just a down-and-out guy. **2004** J. A. Juarez *Brotherhood of Corruption* 2: Their parents are loaded, so they can afford to be art fucks. Escaping responsibility, if you ask me. **2005** *Houston Press* (June 23) (Nexis): I just think he's one of the most pretentious art fucks I've ever encountered…. He thinks he's some amazing human being and talks down to so many kids.

2. something (especially a piece or style of music) that is pretentiously artistic. Often as *adjective*.

1993 "The Virgin Prunes" (album title): Artfuck: A compilation of rarities. **1997** D. Waller in D. Snowden *Make Music go Bang!* 123: The industrial-strength art-fuck Screamers didn't sound anything like the hippy-hippy shake-shake Nerves. **2001** *Village Voice* (Nov. 27) 64/1: From jackhammer fuzz-romps to well-constructed rapid-fire raveups to art-fuck synth-pop. **2004** C. Eddy in *Village Voice* (Dec. 1) C77: The eight more hipster-oriented units whose current releases are among those happily hyped below may well have a hard time supporting such proudly post-graduate artfuck endeavors through four long years of the ownership society.

ASAFP *adverb*

"*as soon as fucking possible*"; immediately.

1977 P. Tauber *Last Best Hope* 406: It's got to be hand-carried—ASAFP. **1985** J. Hughes *Weird Science* (film): I want you out of here ASAFP! **1990**

P. Munro *Slang U.* 23: *A.S.A.F.P.* as soon as possible, or sooner. **2005** *Variety* (Sept. 19) 73: Tough-as-nails boss Colonel McNulty (Dennis Hopper), a can-do guy who wants stuff done "ASAFP."

ass-fuck *noun*

1. an act of anal copulation.

1940 J. Del Torto *Graffiti Transcript* (Kinsey Institute): Make date for assfuck. **1941** G. Legman in G. V. Henry *Sex Variants* II 1157: *Ass-fuck*...An act of pedication. **1974** "Linda Lovelace" *Diary* 66: He gave me the best ass-fuck I've ever had. **1975** C. Skinner *Carol's Curious Passion* 60: It was no use talking to Bert. For he was carried away with his ass fuck. **1976** J. Johnson *Oriental Festival* 136: I want to give you a tremendous ass fuck. **1981** S. Hite *Hite Report on Male Sexuality* 530: The afterglow of a good ass-fuck can last for days. **2004** T. Bentley *Surrender* 164: Now I just want a three-hour ass-fuck where I give him all my power, he takes it, and takes me to visit God.

2. an instance of cruel victimization; a terrible situation.

1977 P. Schrader *Blue Collar* 14: No way he was gonna take this assfuck forever. **1987** B. Massumi trans. G. Deleuze & F. Guattari *Thousand Plateaus* Foreword x: What got me by during that period was conceiving the history of philosophy as a kind of ass-fuck, or, what amounts to the same thing, an immaculate conception. I imagined myself approaching an author from behind and giving him a child that would indeed be his but would nonetheless be monstrous. **2005** D. H. Wilson *Pseudo-City* 209: You called life an assfuck. **2008** *Gawker* (Oct. 31) (online): Apparently, they hadn't been paying insurance premiums either and people who went to the doctor in November or December were being denied their claims because they had no idea they weren't insured any longer. One big giant ass fuck, basically.

3. a despicable person.

2000 *S.F. Weekly* (Mar. 1) (Nexis): So thank you SF Weekly for giving this stupid ass fuck of a human the time for this story. **2003** E. Shade *Eyesores* 127: I pushed Shitwad into a sand trap and kicked sand in his face. I called him a dirty pissant little ass-fuck. **2004** "Minister Faust" *Coyote Kings of the Space-Age Bachelor Pad* 362: Next time I tell you ass-fucks what I want done, I want it done, and I want it done right. **2007** B. Frazer *Hyper-Chondriac* 98: I'm surprised this Bikram assfuck allows anyone to even use the temperature of 105 degrees without winding up in court.

ass-fuck *verb*

1. to engage in anal copulation [with].

[**1866** *Romance of Lust* IV 361: We had not as yet...indulged even in bottom-fucking the women.] **1940** J. Del Torto *Graffiti Transcript* (Kinsey Institute): Want to be assfucked. **1941** G. Legman in G. V. Henry *Sex Variants* II 1157: *Ass-fuck*...To pedicate. **1971** D. Rader *Government Inspected Meat* 105: Get ass-fucked like a bender by a butching lover. **1974–77** L. Heinemann *Close Quarters* 184: She would...ass-fuck. **1984** W. D. Ehrhart *Marking Time* 66: Pam, that old boyfriend of yours—you...even ass-fuck the guy! **1992** Madonna *Sex* (unpaged): That's what ass-fucking is all about. It's the most pleasurable way to get fucked. **1998** *Sick Puppy Comix* (No. 8) (Sydney, Australia) 21: You gotta write about sweet, tender little girlies getting arsefucked like cheap little whores! **2005** "Noire" *G-Spot* 36: He held me down and ass-fucked me until I thought I would die.

2. to victimize cruelly.

1980 *Samisdat* XVII. 75: Since "world order" has traditionally consisted of the haves alternately plundering and ass-fucking the have-nots unchallenged, we shall not miss it. **1995** H. Stern *Miss America* 433: I'm getting the worst ass fucking in history. It's happening in front of the world. **1998** E. Reid *If I Don't Six* 43: There's always someone out to ass-fuck you. Watch out for yourself. **2006** S. M. Stirling *Meeting at Corvallis* 471: *You* got greedy, and yeah, *we* got collectively ass-fucked. **2007** P. Morris *Guardians* viii. 41: That's what happened with the Preznit and Saddam Hussein, and we all know who wound up getting assfucked on that particular occasion.

B

batfuck *adjective & adverb*
crazy. Cf. *batshit.*

1977 F. Stanford *Battlefield where the Moon says I Love You* in I. Reed *From Totems to Hip-Hop* (2003) 330: While you're at it tell her she's bat fuck too. **1991** D. Grinstead *Promises of Freedom* 302: [He] got a Marine killed because he set up a patrol wrong; then the major went batfuck in another crisis. **2005** S. Monette *Mélusine* 423: I needed to start walking again. It was either that or go batfuck nuts.

beans and motherfuckers, see under MOTHERFUCKER.

bearfuck *noun*
Military. a confused or disappointing undertaking.

1983 K. Miller *Tiger the Lurp Dog* 92 [refers to Vietnam War]: The mission turned out to be another disappointing bearfuck. **2005** D. De-Frain *Salt Palace* viii. 80: I was in Palermo for most of mine. F.I.G.M.O., you know? A real bear-fuck start-to-end, if you know what I mean.

bends and motherfuckers, see under MOTHERFUCKER.

BFD *noun* [see BFD, *interjection*]
something important; a big deal.—usually in negative contexts.

1992 H. Childress *Reality Bites* (film script) 75: *Lelaina.* I'm only taking this [money] so you won't get in trouble—And it's just a loan, okay? *Patty*. Cool your pits—It's not a B.F.D. You can have it. **2000** *Out* (Aug.) 30: In 1981...an STD...was not a BFD. **2008** S. King *Duma Key* 157: I tell you what, Eddie, if this is such a BFD to you, then *you* confront him!

BFD *interjection* [*b*ig *f*ucking (or *f*at) *d*eal]
"so what?" "who cares?"

1971 H. Dahlskog *Dictionary of Contemporary & Colloquial Usage* 7: *BFD, b*ig *f*at *d*eal, an ironic comment meaning "What's so great about that?" **1981** J. Harrison *Warlock* 16: "You were thinking about sex." "B.F.D., Sherlock." **1988** J. Brown & C. Coffey *Earth Girls Are Easy* (film): "There's a UFO in my pool. A *UFO*." "BFD." **1988** P. Fonda, on *Unauthorized Biography* (Fox-TV): He was very angry that I had destroyed his honeymoon—*BFD!* **1992** J. Mowry *Way Past Cool* 12: "I the first, 'member?" "BFD!" **2003** J. Cantor *Great Neck* 552: And if they find me, sweetie, BFD, huh?

BFE *noun* [*B*umfuck (or *B*umblefuck), *E*gypt]
Military & Students. a very remote place; the middle of nowhere.

1989 P. Munro *U.C.L.A. Slang* 20: Troy...lives out in B.F.E....*Bum Fuck, Egypt*. **1991** Student slang survey: *BFE*—out in the middle of nowhere...Bumblefuck, Egypt. **1997** Student slang survey: Faraway place... in *b.f.e.* **2005** *N.Y. Times* (June 1) B6: Most characters in "BFE" (the title is an abbreviation of a vulgar slang term for the middle of nowhere)...try to be positive.

Bubblefuck *noun* [alteration of BUMBLEFUCK]
a very remote place; BUMBLEFUCK. Usually used with *West*.

1993 "Fat Joe" *Another Wild Nigga from the Bronx* (rap song): I'm from the West Bubblefuck so fasten your seatbelts and buckle up. **1993** *Re: Not all heterosexuals...* on Usenet newsgroup alt.homosexual (Dec. 31): I GO TO THE VILLAGE ANYTIME I FEEL LIKE IT AND YOU CAN STAY OVER THERE IN WEST BUBBLEFUCK. **1999** "Slick Rick" *2 Way Street* (rap song): Well I shot some there, then I copped some beer. And did a show up in West Bubblefuck somewhere. **2004** "Black Artemis" *Explicit Content* 79: I just know every other label's out searching from here to Bubblefuck for the female

Eminem. **2007** V. M. Stringer *Dirty Red* 79: They sure knew how to pick prison locations, out in the middle of West Bubblefuck. **2007** D. Stumpf *Confessions of a Wall Street Shoeshine Boy* 25: Other guys I knew who went into journalism had to spend five years grinding out the police blotter in West Bubblefuck.

buddy-fuck *verb*

Especially *Military.* to impose upon or betray (a close friend). Hence **buddy-fucker, buddy-fucking,** and as *noun.* Compare FUCK-YOUR-BUDDY WEEK.

1966 *Folk-Speech* (Indiana University Folklore Archives): Denotes asking a friend for money. *Buddy-fuck.* **1968** C. Baker et al. *College Undergraduate Slang Study* 89: *Buddy fucker, play.* Take someone else's date away. *Buddy-fuck.* Take someone else's date away. **1970** College student, age 21: At Fort Gordon [Ga.] last year I kept hearing *buddy-fucker.* It's a guy who turns around and shafts people. **1972** College student, age 25: You *buddy-fuck* a guy like if you start going out with his girl without telling him. *Buddy-fucking* means letting somebody down or ripping them off. **1986** D. Tate *Bravo Burning* 161: Wash your mouth out...buddyfucker. **1993** R. Shilts *Conduct Unbecoming* 201: Everybody talked about the "buddy-fuckers" as those who turned in their friends were called. **2003** D. Lipsky *Absolutely American* iii. 237: *Blue Falcon* is a polite way to invoke the initials BF—a buddy fuck. It's about the lowest form of behavior Huck can imagine.

BUFF *noun* [*b*ig *u*gly (*f*at) *f*uck(er)]

U.S. Air Force. a Boeing B-52 Stratofortress. Also **BUF.**

1968 J. Broughton *Thud Ridge* 32: BUF stands for big ugly fellows in polite conversation, but is suitably amplified in [fighter pilot] conversation....The Strategic Air Command general... issued an edict that the B-52 "Stratofortress" was not to be referred to as a BUF. **1972** in J.C. Pratt *Vietnam Voices* 510: 6 "Bufs" came in and rippled that road. **1972** Bob Hope at U.S. Air Force base in Thailand, on *CBS Evening News* (Dec. 22): This is the home of the B-52s. Also known as BUFFs—big ugly friendly fellows [laughter]. **1981** *Time* (Mar. 16) 8: To air crews the B-52 is known as BUFF, a fairly loving acronym that stands for Big Ugly Fat Fellow. **1985** W. J. Boyne & S. L. Thompson *Wild Blue* 517: *The BUFFs*—Big Ugly Fat

Fuckers to the crews, Big Ugly Fat Fellows to the press. **1990** D. Poyer *Gulf* 47: Got a wing of fifty Buffs movin' in. **1991** *Newsweek* (Feb. 18) 46/3: B-52 navigator Lt. David Rey compares the feeling of riding in the BUFF to going over an endless series of speed bumps. "Flying it is very tiring." **2007** *Atlantic Monthly* (Sept.) 91/2: This was in early 2002, during Operation Anaconda, and he was flying a B-52 Stratofortress—or BUFF ("Big Ugly Fat Fucker"), as pilots call that hall-of-fame bomber, which made its debut in Vietnam.

buffy *noun* [respelling of *BUFE*, for *b*ig *u*gly *f*ucking *e*lephant or variants]

Military. a large ceramic elephant, commonly sold in South Vietnam as a souvenir. *Jocular.*

1973 *N.Y. Post* (Jan. 15) 29: A buffy (rhymes with stuffy) is an enormous, glazed ceramic elephant....The name derives from the acronym b-u-f-e, for bloody useless foul-word elephant. **1980** D. J. Cragg *Lexicon Militaris* 55: *Buffie.* From the acronym BUFE, *B*ig *U*gly *F*ucking *E*lephants. *Buffies* were large ceramic elephants produced in vast quantities by South Vietnamese craftsmen for sale to Americans. **1982** J. Cain *Commandos* 343: He took the roll of bills stuffed inside the white, ceramic "buffy" elephant. **1991** L. Trotta *Fighting for Air* 98: Shipping Bufes home was as much a cliché as sending pink grapefruit from Florida.

bufu *noun* [from *bu*tt-*fu*cker (or *bu*tt-*fu*cking)]
1.a. a homosexual man. Also as *adjective.* [Pronounced "Boo-foo."]

1982 F. Zappa *Valley Girl* (pop. song): Like my English teacher...He's like Mr. Bufu...He like flirts with all the guys in the class. **1982** L. Pond *Valley Girls' Guide* 50: Any dude who'd wear designer jeans *must* be bu-fu, right? **1986** C. Eble *Campus Slang* (Oct.) 4: *Mo*—a homosexual or someone who acts like one....Also *Bufu.* **1989** P. Munro *U.C.L.A. Slang* 25: He is so feminine, you can tell he's a bufu. **2005** *Homosexuality IS a Disease!* on *ADGBC Forums* (Nov. 23) (online): I think you underestimate boofoos['] wileyness.

b. homosexual anal intercourse.

1982 *The Tech* (Massachusetts Institute of Technology) (Oct. 8) 4/2: It talked about bufu and mayonnaise and cock rings and all sorts of neat stuff. **1995** "Impotent Sea Snakes" *Chicks with Dicks* (pop. song): A penis-totin' homo/With some bufu on the mind. **2002** D. Anderson *Sex Tips For Gay Guys* 103: A bufu buddy is your basic steady lay. **2008** *Death or Boofoo* on *eBaum's World* (online): "You may pick one of two things death, or boofoo." The first guy not knowing what boofoo is says "okay I pick boofoo." The next thing he knows he is taken into a tent and is raped by a male indian.

2.= BUMFUCK.

1995 *Help Finding Chicago Area Shows* on Usenet newsgroup rec. arts.marching.band.high-school (Oct. 14): I'm down here in Bufu, Missouri going to school. **2000** *Re: Spam help* on Usenet newsgroup 24hoursupport.helpdesk (July 7): I'm sure they're forging headers and bouncing off some inept admin's server in bufu someplace. **2007** *Appliance repair?????* on *Midwest F-Body Association Forum* (June 18): If you all...moved close to where I live you wouldn't have these problems but when you live in bufu I can't help ya.

bugfuck *adjective*

Chiefly *Military*. insane; crazy.

1970 D. Ponicsan *Last Detail* 74: You two bastards are trying to drive me bug-fuck in the head, right? **1971** T. Mayer *Weary Falcon* 11: If Charles doesn't get you, you stand a fine chance of going bug-fuck. **1973** U.S. Navy veteran, age *ca*28: When you go nuts you go *bugfuck*. **1975** S.P. Smith *American Boys* 130 [refers to *ca*1968]: May dead, Irwin dead, Brady bugfuck. **1979** J. Morris *War Story* 161: My team would go bugfuck when I came back suggesting that we start bayonet drill. **1983** W. D. Ehrhart *Vietnam to Perkasie* 199 [refers to Vietnam War]: I was gettin' bug-fuck sittin' around the CP all the time. **1987** D. Sherman *Main Force* 83 [refers to 1966]: We figured you must be going bug-fuck by now, so I came to give you a ride back to Camp Apache. **1991** H. Nelson & M. A. Gonzales *Bring Noise* 167: Law enforcement officials across the country went bug-fuck. **1993** W. Gibson *Virtual Light* 25: Then Sgt. Valdez went posttraumatic in stone bugfuck fashion, walking into a downtown tavern and clipping both kneecaps off a known pedophile. **2007** A. Theroux *Laura Warholic* xlvii. 790: But now she seemed utterly bugfuck, bewildered and unhinged.

9

bugfucker *noun*

a man with a ridiculously small penis; (*hence*) a contemptible person.

> **1973** *Zap Comix* (No. 6) (unpaged): Needle Dick the Bug Fucker. **1977** J. Sayles *Union Dues* 20: "Hey, Needledick, check anybody's oil lately?" "Needledick the Bug-Fucker!" **1966–80** J. McAleer & B. Dickson *Unit Pride* 345: Then that dirty bohemian bug-fucker...puts the screws to us. **1990** A. Steele *Clarke County, Space* 102: Screw that...I'm the only judge and jury you're getting here, bugfucker.

bull fuck *noun*

cream gravy (sometimes as a thick stew) or custard, fancied to resemble the semen of a bull.

> [**1942** L. V. Berrey & M. Van den Bark *American Thesaurus of Slang* 100: Gravy: *Bull shit, come,...gism*]. **1961** E. Partridge *Dictionary of Slang & Unconventional English* (ed. 5) 1019: *Bull-fuck.* Custard: Canadian railroad-construction crews: since *ca*1910. **1966–67** in *Dictionary of American Regional English* I 445 [in sense "cream gravy"]. **1971** C. C. Adams *Boontling* 180: *Bull fuck*...A thick gravy containing chopped meat. **1991** A. R. Killingbeck *U.S. Army Privates, Sergeants, Fire & Smoke* 40 [refers to 1953]: "Make a bullfuck."...I watched the stew become thicker. "Soldier, that is what is known as a bullfuck."

Bumblefuck *noun* [alteration of BUMFUCK]

a very remote place. *Jocular.*

> **1989** P. Munro *U.C.L.A. Slang* 26: *Bumblefuck*...any faraway little town. **1990** U.S. student slang survey: *Bumblefuck*—a word used to describe a location that is very far away or out in the country. "I can't believe we drove all the way to Bumblefuck to go to this party." **1991** R. Spears *Slang & Euphemism* (abridged edition 2) 62: *Bumblefuck*...a primitive and rural place; podunk. **1999** S. Turow *Personal Injuries* 23: Like two goofs from East Bumblefuck, Mort and I put all the pieces together. **2005** J. Mitchard *Breakdown Lane* 63: He can't spend too much, because, though he practices law where he lives now, he doesn't make a lot because he basically lives in Bumblefuck, Egypt.

bumblefuck *noun*

a bumbling person; a fool.

1997 S. Shem *Mount Misery* vii. 204: "My two older kids always called me a 'bumblefuck'." "What's a bumblefuck?" "A slow, overly cautious driver." **2004** S. Grafton *R is for Ricochet* xiii. 139: "I can help with that," I said, mentally cursing the bumblefuck FBI agent who jumped the gun on us. **2008** A. Davies *Mine All Mine* 217: I can get you past the primary systems, but then what are you two bumblefucks going to do?

Bumfuck *noun*

Military & Students. a very remote place.—used with a placename, esp. in **Bumfuck, Egypt.** Also **Bumfuckistan.** *Jocular.* See also BFE, BUMBLEFUCK.

1972 Sgt. E-6, U.S. Army: They probably sent those records out to Bumfuck, Egypt. **1974** P. Kingry *Monk & Marines* 31: When they asked... whether he would...volunteer for Vietnam, he said he would volunteer for Bumfuk, Egypt, first! **1983** C. Eble *Campus Slang* (Nov.) 1: *Bumfuck*— the worst place: We had to park in Bumfuck, Egypt. **1986** J. Cain *Suicide Squad* 20: Together, they'll come up with some place beyond Bumfuck, Egypt, to send my sorry ass. **1999** N. Roberts *Inner Harbor* xx. 319: I don't have all day to hang around this bumfuck town. **2001** T. II. Culley *Immortal Class* iv. 84: I could see five or six enormous radio towers...like the antennae of the Death Star—very bizarre, very bum-fuck Florida, really. **2006** C. Langston *Bicoastal Babe* vi. 46: It's one thing to smoke the house in a white Chanel pantsuit, but it's another thing to imagine the housewives in Bumfuck, Ohio, trying to copy the same look at their local Wal-Mart. **2006** J. P. Othmer *Futurist* 12: Eastern Bumfuckistan. **2008** *New York Magazine* (June 2) 40/1: I am from Bumfuck, France, okay?... I wanted to kill myself...because nothing happened. So I moved to Paris.

bumfuck *noun*

1. an act of anal intercourse.

1879 *Harlequin Prince Cherrytop* 4: Crumb fuck, bum fuck, not another peaceful minute. **1996** *Face* (Apr.) 3/3 (table): Fancy a blow-job in Zaire or a bum-fuck in Bangladesh? Tough. As our guide to prohibited sexual practices shows, what turns you on can turn off the authorities and land you in a rather unpleasant prison cell. **2002** R. Coover *Adventures of Lucky Pierre* 145: A rush of speeded-up highlights from old movies—rapes and seductions, birchings, bumfucks, facials, and fistings.

2. a despicable person; an idiot; wretch.

1979 *Easyriders* (Dec.) 6: A pretty crafty way...to get us bumfucks to read your rag cover to cover. **1981** *Easyriders* (Oct.) 47: Cut loose some of those bumfuck, hardluck losers. **2000** R. Bingham *Lightning on Sun* 116: Dwayne grew more agitated. He didn't like the sound of this bum-fuck country cracker knocking his vehicle. **2005** S. Amick *Lake, River & Other Lake* viii. 42: As far as Mark could tell, there were three types of outsiders you could be if you didn't happen to get born and die in Weneshkeen, like the rest of these bumfucks his dad seemed to want to fit in with.

bumfuck *verb*

to have anal intercourse with. Hence **bumfucker**, *noun*.

*ca***1866** *Romance of Lust* 269: The very fine bum-fucking his adorable wife had the art of giving him. **1880** *Pearl* (May): My ridicule of his ignorance made him quite ashamed of his want of knowledge, especially when I introduced him to the delights of bum-fucking, and he faithfully promised me that when Her Ladyship returned, he would insist upon his marital rights over every part of her person. *ca***1890** *My Secret Life* VIII. iv.: She didn't hesitate to say she should like to be bum-fucked again. "Just to try if there is any real pleasure in it." *ca***1890** *My Secret Life* VIII. xi.: In after years she was the most complacent creature, and did with me everything excepting bum fucking. **1967** N. Mailer *Why Are We in Vietnam?*: You... been bum fucking the wrong cunt. **1969** P. Louÿs *Mother's Three Daughters* 77: You can bum-fuck her in any posture of your choice; you can come in her mouth. **1973** T. Pynchon *Gravity's Rainbow* 547: His name was Frank, his hair curled away from his face, his eyes were rather sharp but pleasant, he stole from American Army depots, he bum-fucked me and when he came inside me, so did I. **1975** *Ribald* (Sydney, Australia) (May 29) 10: Titles included "Tongue Teacher"; "The Bumfuckers"; "The House of the Golden Showers." **1993** *Saturday Night* (Toronto) (July–Aug.) 35/2: He says he remembers being "bum-fucked" by an "uncle" when he was four "but it was no big deal, the sort of thing all kids go through." **1996** *Vertigo* (Sydney, Australia) (No. 3) 12: Anal intercourse: buggery, sodomy, arse-fucking, bum-fucking. **2002** J. W. Nichol *Midnight Cab* 112: Did you pull out your wee-wee? Did you go all wet? Did you try to bum-fuck that boy?

Buttfuck *noun*

a very remote place.—usually used with a placename. *Jocular.* See also BFE, BUMBLEFUCK.

1999 *Independent* (London) (May 2): All Americans will tell you at first meeting where they come from and who their parents were, even if it's (a) Buttfuck, South Dakota and (b) brothel-keepers. **2005** *The Pitch* (Kansas City) (Nov. 3): The 80-second commute from his manse in West, West Buttfuck, Missouri, to downtown St. Louis. **2006** *Observer* (July 16) (Music Mag.) 29: If Timberlake stood on a musical precipice last time around, trying to convince the world he was more than some Buttfuck, Tennessee boy-band soon-to-be-has-been, he stands on even more of one now with FutureSex.

butt-fuck *noun*

1. an act of anal copulation.

1971 H. Dahlskog *Dictionary of Contemporary & Colloquial Usage* 11: *Butt fuck, v....*To engage in anal intercourse.—[also] *n.* **1981** *National Lampoon* (Apr.) 39: Let's go to my place for brunch and a buttfuck. **1997** *N.Y. Press* (Aug. 27) 18: "I need a buttfuck *now!*" screamed an overpierced male in fluorescent green Speedos. **2002** I. Welsh *Porno* 374: It hits me like an iron fist in the chest that in this global communications village somehow, in some way, my father's going to see me getting a butt-fuck.

2. an instance of victimization; an unfortunate event.

1986 L. Heinemann *Paco's Story* 128: Iwo Jima was a sloppy, bloody butt-fuck. **2000** R. Meltzer *Whore Just Like Rest* 136: At times it was like being the lone mocker in a room full of newsfolks cheerleading Reagan's buttfuck of Grenada. **2004** C. Hiaasen *Skinny Dip* 256: He...could smell a butt fuck coming a mile away, and he'd never stand still for it.

butt-fuck *verb*

1. to copulate with anally. Also in extended use. Compare earlier BUTTFUCKER.

1971 D. Rader *Government Inspected Meat* 72: I liked to get buttfucked. **1975** J. Wambaugh *Choirboys* xii. 296: I hear when Carolina was living with that Greek bartender he used to butt-fuck her all the time. **1976** J. Vasco *Three-Hole Girl* 186: It hurts so good. Oh, you butt-fuck me so good! **1979** H. Crews *Blood & Grits* 122: Said if I'd butt-fuck him, he'd take me out there on the train and innerduce me. **1983** R. Eilert *For Self & Country* 272 [refers to 1968]: You're butt-fucking each other then. **1985** D. Dye *Run Between the Raindrops* 129: Their...buddy has just been butt-fucked by a B-40 [rocket] or some such nonsense. **1990** D. Poyer *Gulf* 186: The warriors grab the first missionary...[and] butt-fuck him. **1997** A. Bourdain *Chef's Night Out* in K. Williamson *Rovers Return* (1998) 134: I felt like I had suddenly and inexplicably, put on a fluffy crepe and organza cocktail dress, a rubber clown nose, roller skates, wheeled out into the center of Times Square, and allowed myself to get butt-fucked by a procession of crack-heads and circus freaks. **2001** M. Spitz *We Got the Neutron Bomb* 112: I have gotten butt-fucked, but never in jail. I did it on the street for the money. **2004** T. Bentley *Surrender* 13: Butt-fucking is more intimate than pussy-fucking.

2. to victimize.

1979 *Maledicta* III 55: Males in particular...who have been denied promotion, given low grades...been fired, jilted [etc.]...commonly relate that they have been *screwed, fucked,...butt-fucked*...and so on. **1981** J. Wambaugh *Glitter Dome* 240: He'll be back to being butt-fucked by those bogus producers. **1982** J. M. Del Vecchio *13th Valley* 491: Gettin butt-fucked. **1988** J. Stuart *Die Hard* (film): I'm not the one who just got buttfucked on national TV. **1999** D. Mitchell *Ghostwritten* 221: If he... chooses to sell us up the river, we will be royally butt-fucked from here to Windsor. **2007** R. N. Patterson *Exile* 177: The Zionists have been buttfucking the Palestinians for the last three generations.

buttfucker *noun*

1. a person who engages in anal copulation.

1962–68 B. Jackson *In the Life* 324: Everybody was "Old Butt-Fucker" to him. **1990** A. Parfrey *Apocalypse Culture* (revised edition) 203: With all the buttfuckers and drug addicts having cival rights when they have aids; this makes the other 50% of the country half a citizen; we have no rights. **1995** *New York Press* (Mar. 8) 67: Dr. Jack Morin, author of the Buttfucker's Bible, *Anal Pleasure and Health*. **2005** *Exit* (South Africa) (Feb.) 26/2 (advt.): Primrose Wanted: Active butt-fucker 18–40 GM/Bi VWE no hang-ups for 3somes with GWMs 35/45 our place.

2. a despicable person.

1973 H. S. Thompson *Letter* (Oct. 19) in *Fear & Loathing in America* (2000) 552: How many more mesas will you have to sell to those corporate butt-fuckers at The Institute? **1999** T. Parker et al. *South Park* (film script) 137: Ay! Don't call me fat, buttfucker. **2008** J. Strong *Drawn from Life* 90: "Well, what would you know, buttfucker?" Mac said. It was one of their routines. Pete came back with, "Well, what would you know, muffdiver?" "Well, what would you know, horsedick?"

C

---

celebrity-fucker *noun*

a person, typically a young woman, who engages in promiscuous sexual intercourse with filmstars or other celebrities; (*broadly*) a hanger-on among celebrities. Compare STARFUCKER.

1968 T. Wolfe *Electric Kool-Aid Acid Test* 224: "You need all the big names you can get, to get the crowd out." "Well, that's what you get for being celebrity fuckers." **1969** J. Susann *Love Machine* 124: Falling all over the guest star. She's living up to her title: the Celebrity Fucker. **1970** J. Bouton *Ball Four* 218: A stew [*i.e.* stewardess] can come under the heading of class stuff, or table pussy, in comparison with some of the other creatures who are camp-followers or celebrity-fuckers. **1972** R. A. Wilson *Playboy's Book of Forbidden Words* s.v. *plaster-casters*: A celebrity-fucker (the word was coined by writer-editor John Wilcock) is a young woman who will fuck anybody as long as he's famous. **1974** P. K. Dick *Flow My Tears, the Policeman Said* 53: Do you think I slept with them because they were famous? Do you think I'm a CF, a celebrity fucker? **1986** R. Campbell *In La-La Land* 232: I thought he was just a celebrity fucker, you know. **1993** R. Watson *Niagara* 22: Not women on the rebound, not women punishing their husbands, not women trying to make their boyfriends jealous, not celebrity fuckers, not women seeking publicity. **1997** G. Plimpton *Truman Capote* 269: She [*sc.* Lillian Hellman] was always such a celebrity fucker. **2004** *New York Observer* (Nov. 24) 1: I'd hate to see it go in for more interviews, author photographs, publishing news, even the gossip—anything that cuts down on anything devoted to the review of books.... I hope it won't go that way, but the whole culture is going that way, in a celebrity-fucker direction.

CFM *adjective* [come *fuck me*]

(of an article of clothing, especially shoes) intended to invite sexual advances. Also as *noun*, a sexually provocative item of clothing. Compare FUCK-ME, *adjective*.

[**1972** B. Rodgers *Queens' Vernacular* 53: *Come fuck-me's*...overly tight pants.] **1990** P. Munro *Slang U* 56: All her other clothes were preppy, but she had a C.F.M. skirt on. **1998** Personal letter to editor (Aug. 26): Out west, sexy boots worn by ladies are known as CFMs. **1998** *Revised: Svengali*, on Usenet newsgroup alt.tv.x-files.creative: Her legs ...were nicely highlighted by the type of shoes Scully had once jokingly referred to as CFM shoes. **2001** B. Thacker *Rule No. 5—No Sex on the Bus* 176: They would spend six months standing in bars with their CFM shirt on. **2002** *Spectator* (May 25) 18: The bride had forsaken her patent-leather, white-and-lilac "cfm" shoes with the six-inch heels in favour of Nike "air-heels" in which she danced enthusiastically. **2005** J. Coburn *Reinventing Mona* 113: The group burst into wild applause when Violet stumbled on her five-inch CFM heels and momentarily lost her balance.

charity fuck *noun*

= MERCY FUCK.

1978 J. D. Macdonald *Empty Copper Sea* 47: He described the awkward union which he terms "the charity fuck." **1986** P. Anderson *Lords of the Earth* 369: I don't want your charity... That's what it's called, you know. A charity fuck. **1993** J. Varley *Steel Beach* 344: If there's a worse kind of sex than the charity fuck, I haven't heard about it. **2001** A. Wall *School of Night* 268: I sort of stumbled into her. I reckon it must have been a charity fuck, to be honest. **2005** M. Musto in *Village Voice* (Jan. 11) (Nexis): Worst Partygoer: A nebbish who cranes his head to find someone better, when you were only talking to him as a charity fuck anyway.

chicken-fucker *noun*

a depraved or disgusting fellow.—usually used with *baldheaded*. Also: a man who prefers to copulate with boys. [The 1984 quotation is euphemistic.]

1953 in G. Legman *Rationale of Dirty Joke* 20: Suddenly two bald-headed men enter, and the parrot says, "You two chicken-fuckers come out in the hen-house with me." **1970** M. Mirsky *Proceedings of the Rabble* 159: "Chicken fuckers!" shouted the Maine men. Taking up their own guns, they began picking off Mississippi dogs. **1976–79** H. G. Duncan & W. T. Moore *Green Side Out* 276 [refers to *ca*1960]: All right ya bald-headed chicken fuckers, I want this area policed the fuck up. **1967–80** J. McAleer & B. Dickson *Unit Pride* 387 [refers to Korean War]: Heave in the first shovelful...and run like a baldheaded chicken-fucker. **1984** S. Terkel *"Good War"* 397 [refers to WWII]: "I'm gonna have you shot."... "You baldheaded so-and-so, go ahead and shoot." **2002** R. B. Parker *Widow's Walk* xxxii. 163: "Nathan Smith was a serious chickenfucker."... "He was drawn to young boys?" "Early adolescent when he could get them."

clusterfuck *noun*

1. an orgy.

1965 *East Village Other* (Oct.) 2/3: As soon as they legalize "pornies" I'll be the first producer to hit the neighborhood theatres with my now in progress epic film entitled "Mongolian Cluster Fuck!" **1967–68** N. von Hoffman *We Are the People Our Parents Warned Us Against* 182: Oh, those big cluster fucks! I can't stand them. **1968** "A. D'Arcangelo" *Homosexual Handbook* 115: You may see many of the people at your "do" only at other "cluster fucks," having nothing in common with them but a taste for orgies. **1969** G. D. Bartell *Group Sex* 134: One advantage of open versus closed swinging, according to most of our informants, is the possiblity of "three-on-one" or "gang bang" (sometimes called "clusterfuck") activity. **1972** R.A. Wilson *Playboy's Book of Forbidden Words* 69: *Cluster Fuck*—Two men copulating simultaneously with the same woman. **1975** G. Legman *No Laughing Matter* 754: The cheap hippie "group-grope" and "cluster-fuck." **1977** *National Lampoon* (Aug.) 50: Well, they're usually pretty wrapped up in a cluster-fuck with the photo models. **1986** J. Ellroy *Suicide Hill* 699: I'm startin' to feel like the bottom man in a Mongolian cluster fuck. **2001** J. Ellroy *Cold Six Thousand* xxi. 115: Pete saw cartoons and FBI text. Hate and smut—a coon named Bayard Rustin—a queer cluster-fuck.

2. *Military.* a bungled or confused undertaking or situation; mess; (*also*) a disorganized group of individuals.

1969 in B. E. Holley *Vietnam* (1993) 143: These are the screwups that the American public rarely hears about. They happen often enough over here that we have a term for them—"cluster-fuck". **1974** New York City man, age 27: A clusterfuck was a big expression in [the N.Y. National Guard] in 1969. It meant any time people were standing around outside of a regular formation. They'd say, "What the hell is this clusterfuck?" "Break up this clusterfuck." **1982** J. M. Del Vecchio *13th Valley* 42: This place looks like a giant clusterfuck. *Ibid.* 137: We gonna get this clusterfuck up in the air? **1983** K. Miller *Lurp Dog* 222 [refers to Vietnam War]: Shame to piss up a clusterfuck target like this. **1985** D. Dye *Run Between the Raindrops* 42: The rest is up for grabs. This place is a cluster-fuck. **1986** J. Thacker *Finally the Pawn* 135 [refers to 1970]: What you're going to have is an A number one clusterfuck. **1986** J. C. Stinson & J. Carabatsos *Heartbreak Ridge* 146: "What's your assessment of this alert?"…"It's a clusterfuck!…marines should be fighting, not…filling out request forms for equipment they should already have, Sir." **1988** P. J. O'Rourke *Holidays in Hell* 218: "Mongolian Cluster Fuck" is the technical term journalists use for a preplanned, wholly scripted, news-free event. **1991** D. Simon *Homicide* 82: Allowing a herd of new recruits to graze through a crime scene had all the makings of what detectives and military men like to call a clusterfuck. **1999** C. Brookmyre *One Fine Day in Middle of Night* 136: This whole op is from page one of the cluster-fuck recipe book. **2006** *New York Magazine* (Apr. 17) 36/1: Says one bitter paparazzo: "The whole thing was a giant cluster-fuck, a total waste of time."

3. Originally *Military.* a bungler; idiot.

*a*1987 C. Bunch & A. Cole *Reckoning for Kings* 284 [refers to Vietnam War]: He's a clusterfuck. **2006** A. Davies *Goodbye Lemon* ii. 115: That clusterfuck Musser gets sixty grand a year up and down a goddamn telephone pole. He didn't get that job because he's a supergenius either.

cluster-fuck *verb*

1. to participate in an orgy; (also) to gang bang.

1971 J. F. Hunter *Gay Insider* vii. 134: In the bird sanctuary…you can cluster-fuck with relative impunity. **2002** J. Ashbless *Divine Torment* (2007) 131: I've tried to tone it down, to make do with the lighter stuff. But it doesn't give me a rush the way being cluster-fucked in a latrine does. **2003** C. McCann *Dancer* 243: Fucking in the rest rooms and fucking in the baths, fist-fucking, toe-fucking, finger-fucking, cluster-fucking, not to mention rimming, a regular fuckfest.

2.a. Originally *Military.* to congregate or behave in a disorganized manner.

1983 W. D. Ehrhart *Vietnam to Perkasie* 162 [refers to 1967]: All those amtracs clusterfuckin' around the CP yesterday—Charlie knew somethin' was up. **1999** M. Foley *Have a Nice Day* xxii. 277: It was the worst Pay-Per-View match that I have ever been in, and the fans knew it.... I got that same feeling in Orlando that night as we cluster fucked to a symphony of silence, but I waited on the ring apron until the feeling went away.

b. to victimize; to doom; (also) to make confused or disorganized.

1996 R. Marcinko & J. Weisman *Green Team* 310: The schedule I'd carefully calculated was now OBE—in other words, Overtaken By Events—and we were clusterfucked. **2000** K. W. Nolan *Ripcord* 429: Everybody just went in their own direction.... We became totally clusterfucked. **2001** J. L. Burke *Bitterroot* 141: The shorter version is I got cluster-fucked eight ways from breakfast and that broad is living on a horse ranch bought with my money. **2001** O. West *Sharkman Six* 47: Sir, this is going to get clusterfucked, we don't play it right. If the press gets hold of this, we're dead. **2007** J. L. Burke *Tin Roof Blowdown* v. 30: This lamebrain not only outsmarted you, he cluster-fucked you six ways from breakfast. **2007** P. F. Hamilton *Dreaming Void* 180: Is it a bunch of crap, or are we all going to get cluster-fucked by the Void?

cunt-fuck *noun*

a sexual act involving the vagina, esp. an act of heterosexual vaginal intercourse.

1879 *Harlequin Prince Cherrytop* 4: Cunt fuck, front tuck, he shall never once begin it. **1967** N. Mailer *Why Are We in Vietnam?* 155: Walk in on them in an unlocked bathroom and you can have a two minute red-hot steaming ass blubber wet slap-dizzy oceanic cunt fuck. **1998** *Nubile Treat,* on Usenet newsgroup alt.sex.stories (Oct. 1): It was a first-class cunt-fuck, and they dug it as much as the ass-fuck they'd seen before. **2002** B. McAvera *Yo! Picasso!* 55: Oh I know he's not great in the cunt-fuck department...never was...but it doesn't really matter.

cunt-fuck *verb*

to engage in any form of sexual activity involving the vagina, esp. to engage in heterosexual vaginal intercourse (with).

*ca*1890 *My Secret Life* IX. vi.: It was at a time of my life when straight forward cunt fucking was all I cared about. 1908 *Way of a Man with a Maid* 151: Alice and Connie flew into each others' arms—too excited to rush to the couch, they fell on the soft thick carpet and madly cunt-fucked each other till their feelings were relieved. 1966 A. Wainhouse & R. Seaver trans. Marquis de Sade *120 Days of Sodom* 634: The Duc cunt-fucks one servant and Rosette at the orgies and ass-fucks the same servant, ass-fucks Rosette too. 1990 *Footlicker* 80: I can't cuntfuck with men. Won't ever again. 1994 N. Baker *Fermata* 135: Smiling again at the traffic because they couldn't know the supreme full-pelvic cuntfucking she was giving herself. 2003 R. Gordon *Undying Lust* 106: "A right little slut," Rod rejoined, his swinging balls meeting Mick's as he cunt-fucked Wendy.

D

deck *noun*
In phrase:
☞ **fuck the deck**, *U.S. Marine Corps.* to perform push-ups on command.

> **1983** W. D. Ehrhart *Vietnam to Perkasie* 32 [refers to 1966]: Fuck the deck, piggy!...Push-ups!

DILLIGAF *interjection*
"do I look like I give a fuck?"

> **1973** S. A. Rowan *They Wouldn't Let Us Die* (ed. 2) 27: We had a guy named Dilligaf—DILLIGAF—Do I Look Like I Give A Fuck? And that was his attitude; so Dilligaf was his name. The favorite [North Vietnamese] guard of all. **1996** D. Underhill & H. Curtis *Miramichi Dictionary: Diligaf.* Famous bar in the village of Blackville, about twenty miles south of Miramichi City. Translated, Dilligaf means: Does It Look Like I Give a F---. **2007** S. Hyde *Darkside Zodiac at Work* 157: A T-shirt with the...logo, DILLIGAF (Do I look like I Give a F@?%?).

dog *noun*
In phrase:
☞ **fuck** [or occasionally **screw** or **finger**] **the dog**

1. to loaf on the job, especially while pretending to be hard at work; fool around; idle; waste time. [The 1918 and 1919 quotations presumably euphemize this expression.]

[**1918** in M. Sullivan *Our Times* V 328: *F.T.D.*: Feeding the dog. The supposed occupation of a soldier who is killing time.] [**1919** H.S. Warren *9th Co.* 35: The Engineer's Dictionary...*Walking the dog*—Soldiering on the job. When one is caught at it he is said to have stepped on the puppy's tail.] **1935** J. Conroy *World to Win* 201: One of the first things you gotta learn when you're f—n' the dog...is t' look like you're workin' hard enough t' make yer butt blossom like a rose. Rattle templets, beat with a hammer on a beam, but do *somethin'*. If the boss ketches you f—n' the dog while you're helpin' me, he'll eat *me* up blood raw. **1939** A. C. Bessie *Men in Battle* 331: They were "fucking the dog," spending what money they had. **1942** L. V. Berrey & M. Van den Bark *American Thesaurus of Slang* 490: Fuck the dog, to loaf on the job. **1948** W. Guthrie *Born to Win* 19: I'll do all I can to stay alive and argufying, alive and kicking, alive and flurking the dog. **1954** *International Journal of Psycho-Analysis* XXXV 351: This was followed by a four-month period of "finking," "fucking the dog," characterized by drinking, missed hours, tardiness, and "sponging" on mother. **1962** E. Stephens *Blow Negative* 54: Those apes are screwing the dog all day long up there. **1967** W. Crawford *Gresham's War* 125: "And meantime?" "Frick the dog, I reckon." **1967** K. Kolb *Getting Straight* 70: Until you said that, I thought you'd been screwing the dog on this project. **1977** J. Sayles *Union Dues* 58: You let me catch you fuckin the dog again, so help me, you'll be some sorry characters. **1978** T. Alibrandi *Killshot* 146: "You bet our entire stake on this one match?" "You got it, kid. No sense fucking the dog. We came to gamble, remember?" **1984** K. Weaver *Texas Crude* 93: *Fuckin' the dog and sellin' the pups*. Wasting time and loafing on the job. **1986** J. C. Stinson & J. Carabatsos *Heartbreak Ridge* 125: You hotshots are "fingering the dog" and you wind up killin' every swinging dick in this platoon. **2003** M. Atwood *Oryx & Crake* 328: Now quit fucking the dog and let us in.

2. to bungle; blunder.

1962 J. O. Killens *Then We Heard the Thunder* 144 [refers to WWII]: Saunders, I don't know what I'm going to do with you...You've gone and fucked the dog again. **1985** J. T. Heywood *Taxi Dancer* 34: But he had "screwed the dog by the numbers." He had failed to conserve fuel and he had forgotten about their bombs. **1998** Graydon Carter, in *N.Y. Press* (Oct. 21) 17: I gave you the opportunity of a lifetime and you fucked the dog. **2005** A. Miller *Coast of Akron* 313: Last time I was here, the Indians fucked the dog during the '97 World Series.

dogfuck *noun*

trouble.—used with *the*.

1978 W. Groom *Better Times Than These* 30: We're really in the dogfuck now.

dogfuck *verb*

to engage in copulation with a male partner entering from the rear, especially anally.

1967–80 E. Folb *Runnin' Down Some Lines* 235: *Dog fuck.* Engage in anal intercourse. **1981** L. Bangs in *Psychotic Reactions* (1987) 348: When they were done dogfucking they sprawled back awhile to rest and pant. **1986** in R. Chapman *New Dictionary of American Slang:* Including how to 69 and dogfuck. **2008** *Deadspin.com* (July 11): If I were an Arizona State fan and I wanted to go double agent as a way to get my team fired up? The banner sounds like a pretty good plan. Personally, I'd go with, "Hey Dawgs, Herschel is dog-fucking your wife right now. Enjoy Tempe."

double fuck *noun*

an act of intercourse in which two people simultaneously copulate with a third person.

ca1866 *Romance of Lust* 218: Bringing his stiff-standing prick against the root of mine, pressing it well down, he gently shoved forward, and gradually sheathed himself within the well-stretched and capacious orbit of my aunt, who winced a little in pretended pain, but who, by the grip she immediately gave to the double fuck within her, showed how much gratified she was. **ca1890** *My Secret Life* VIII. iii.: I thought of the double fuck without the washing, of the prick in my mouth, and then felt ashamed.— "I must have been screwed and so excited that I did not know what I was about, I shall never do that again, and hope he won't tell Sarah." **1998** *Suzifest '98*, on Usenet newsgroup alt.sex.stories.moderated (Oct. 26): Todd and James were going to give Suzi an old fashioned double-fuck.... They would "double-fuck" her from behind...a cock in her pussy, with another stuffed up her ass. **2007** K. Rockwood *Very Private Secretary* 81: He doubted if Mona desired such a double-fuck and, he strongly suspected, he wouldn't be capable of it anyway.

double-fuck *verb*

1.a. (used as an imprecation or oath); God damn.—an emphatic form of FUCK, *verb*, definition 4a.

1966 R. Fariña *Been Down So Long* 244: Double-fuck the letter. **1971** J. Sandford *Down & Out in Britain* 49: "Fuck you!" shouts the bearded man by the hot plate. "Double fuck you!" shouts another man back. **1997** A. Hoffman *Here on Earth* 37: As usual, the thoroughbred looks right through him. "Fuck you too." Hollis is astounded at how damn haughty a horse can be. "Double fuck you." **2002** J. McGahern *That They May Face Rising Sun* 75: At the foot of the ladders Patrick Ryan was slumped low but his breathing was growing easier. "Double fuck those for fucken cunts of bees," he cried out. **2004** *N.Y. Observer* (Jan. 26) 2: Fuck South Dakota. Fuck New Mexico. Double-fuck Oregon. **2006** C. Adrian *Children's Hospital* 66: A few things her brother might have said ran through her head—Double-fuck you, bitch!

b. (used as an emphatic form of FUCK, *verb*, in other senses).

1982 A. Lane & W. Crawford *Vals* (film script for 'Valley Girls') (rev. draft) 78: Then fuck off! Yeah...double fuck off!!! **1991** M. R. Zubro *Sorry Now?* 4: "Double and triple fuck," Buck swore. **1998** *Dallas Observer* (May 14) (Nexis): The way I've always been musically is very selfish—I could only do what I like. I can't sit there and go, "Oh, I think people will like this," because you're kind of double-fucked. You don't like what you're doing, and people don't like it, then you got nothing. **2006** *Adweek* (Feb. 13) (Nexis): God, did I double-fuck that one up: overwritten, overproduced, over-not-funny, over-not-relevant, overboring, overstupid—over-everything, except over-good. **2007** S. King *Blaze* 348: I knew I was fucked, double-fucked, I was dead-ass-fucked in the pouring rain.

2. to engage in a DOUBLE FUCK (with).

1984 B. Baker *Sally's Anal Punishment* 161: His brain buzzed with the ecstatic wonder of doublefucking both women. **1995** *Sydney Star Reporter* (Australia) (Nov. 9) 30 [personal ad]: Seek submissive guy to 30 to be double fucked & abused. **1998** (quotation at DOUBLE FUCK, *noun*). **2001** *Playboy* (Feb.) 41: Later she asked to be "double fucked" with me in her vagina and my friend in her ass.

double-fucking *adjective*

= FUCKING, *adjective.*—used for emphasis.

1929 R. Graves *Good-Bye to All That* 79 [refers to 1917]: The Bandmaster, who was squeamish, reported it as: "Sir, he called me a double-effing c—." **1945** in *Verbatim* (Autumn, 1989) 6: *Double [fucking]*...Embellished or emphatic [form] of *fxxxing.* **1991** M. Tolkin *Rapture* (film): No double-fuckin' *way* would I stop. **2007** C. Adair *White Heat* 137: Damn, and double-fucking damn. That trail was now cold. No fingerprints on file, no form of ID.

drug-fucked *adjective*

Originally *Australian.* intoxicated by drugs. Compare FUCKED, *adjective,* definition 1.

1991 *Arena* (Sydney) (No. 8) 13: When you're that drug-fucked, a piece of navel lint can have occult significance. **1996** *Catalog* (Summer Extra) 9: Drew Barrymore...the world's wildest drug-fucked child starlet. **1996** *Capital Q Weekly* (Sydney) (Mar. 29) 11: Three hundred drug-fucked and horny gay men. **1997** *Rants* (Sydney) (Oct. 23): Fuck you, yer dumb drug-fucked bitch! **2001** *AXM* (Aug.) 126/2: Closer to Heaven, although popular by word of mouth—especially with the brilliant Frances Barber as the drug-fucked club diva "Billie"—had not done too well with the critics. **2007** *New Yorker* (Dec. 17) 40/3: 1974. Bowie was absolutely drug-fucked. That's when he was living on peppers and milk.

dry fuck *noun*

1. a simulated act of copulation, usually while fully clothed.

1938 H. Miller *Tropic of Capricorn* 104: Maybe you'll...get a dry fuck. **1965** J. Trimble *5000 Adult Sex Words & Phrases* 68: *Dry Fuck*... The act of two lovers rubbing up against each other while clothed and in public, as while dancing, etc., which results in great excitation and, in some cases, orgasm. **1970** E. E. Landy *Underground Dictionary* 71: *Dry Fuck...n.* The simulated act of sexual intercourse with clothes on. **1971** B. B. Johnson *Blues for Sister* 101: A professional virgin...The kind that always denied you penetration. A dry fuck. **1975** T. Williams *Memoirs* 27: They would give her what was then called "a dry fuck." **1981** S. Hochman

Playing Tahoe 124: Rev was the kind of guy you fell for in high school on a dry fuck in the back of a Chevrolet. **2003** L. Begley *Shipwreck* 58: Let's take our clothes off. She shook her head vehemently. I got the point. She wanted a dry fuck.

2. something that is exceedingly tedious or disappointing.

1945 in T. Williams *Letters* 177: If only Margo could get something of this quality into "The Project."...It is a dry fuck, really! **1972** Gram Parsons in B. Fong-Torres *Hickory Wind* 5: I've some sort of "rep" for starting what (I think) has turned out t'be pretty much of a "country-rock" (ugh!) plastic dry-fuck. **1998** S. Firestone *Airless Spaces* 58: It was a dry fuck, every word painful and laborious. **2005** D. DeFrain *Salt Palace* 82: "Was a bit of a dry fuck really, all that." "What? The Church?" I say.

dry-fuck *verb* [compare earlier synonym *dry-bob*]
to simulate sexual intercourse without penetration; to engage in a DRY FUCK with. Also used figuratively.

[**1935** J. O'Hara in *Selected Letters* 106: Write something...that will help you get rid of the bitterness you must have stored up against all those patronizing cheap bastards in that dry-fucked excrescence on Sharp Mountain.] *ca*1937 in T. Atkinson *Dirty Comics* 106: Try to dry-fuck the hostess who is the big shot's sweetie. **1938** "Justinian" *Americana Sexualis* 20: *Dry-Fuck.v.* To rub stomach, thighs, and genitals together in an erotic manner while dancing. Popular in collegiate circles...U.S., 1925—. **1954** C. Himes *Third Generation* 243: Now seeing him in the arms of a sweet young girl she was scalded with jealousy. "What kind of dryfucking shit is this?" she screamed. **1958–59** L. Lipton *Holy Barbarians* 156: As long ago as the twenties dancing was considered "dry fucking" by the *cognoscenti* who regarded it as something for sub-teenagers only. **1965** D. A. Ward & G. G. Kassebaum *Women's Prison* 99: That's more or less a *bulldagger's*... kick, this dry fucking. **1969** J. Briley *Traitors* 133: They had had a spell of intense sessions holding hands in the library and dry-fucking against the back wall of her sorority. **1970** E. E. Landy *Underground Dictionary* 71: *Dry fuck*...Go through the motions of sexual intercourse without entering the vagina, usually with clothes on. **1982** C. Bukowski *Ham on Rye* (2001) xxv. 111: You ought to try dry-fucking, Morrie, it's great! **1983**

E. Dodge *Dau* 110: They dry-fucked in the pre-dawn darkness. **1991** D. Jenkins *Gotta Play Hurt* 37: Heike... dry-fucked the rear fender. **2000** *Seattle Weekly* (Jan. 20) (Nexis): A dreadlocked couple is dry-fucking. **2000** A. L. Kennedy *Everything You Need* 361: The mutter and jump of manuscripts as they jerked off their watery efforts inside his mind, as they wasted his intelligence, as they dry-fucked his privacy.

duck *noun*

In phrase:

☞ **fuck the duck**, to loaf; *fuck the dog* under DOG. See also *fuck a duck* under FUCK *verb*.

1968–77 M. Herr *Dispatches* 57: I met a man in the Cav who'd been "fucking the duck" one afternoon, sound asleep in a huge tent. **1978** H. Selby *Requiem for a Dream* 31: Well let's stop fucking the duck and figure out how we can pick up the bread. **1979** L. Heinmann, in *TriQuarterly* (Spring) 180 [refers to Vietnam War]: He was taking one of his famous naps—fucking the duck, we called it.

dumbfuck *noun*

a contemptibly stupid person. Also as *adjective*.

1946–50 J. Jones *From Here to Eternity* 531 [refers to 1941]: Shut up you dumb fuck Turniphead you. **1966** *Folk Speech* (Indiana University Folklore Archives): Denoting someone's stupidity. *Dumb fuck.* **1970–71** J. Rubenstein *City Police* 427: You know why that dumb-fuck sergeant has Smith drive him? **1973** *TULIPQ* (coll. B.K. Dumas): Dingbat; super dumb fuck. **1980** P. Conroy *Lords of Discipline* 150: I want you to rack that chin into your beady, ugly neck, dumbfuck. *a***1987** C. Bunch & A. Cole *Reckoning for Kings* 151: Of all the dumb-fuck things to do. **1991** G. Dyer *But Beautiful* 46: The English bitch yelling, the cops yelling too.—Lemme get at this dumb-fuck. **1998** *Sick Puppy Comix* (Sydney, Australia) (No. 8) 18: It's not a demon it's nicotine you dumb fuck! **2000** R. Barger et al. *Hell's Angel* iv. 61: The dumb-fuck politicians didn't even consider that's how the everyday person controls their car. **2007** A. Bay *Embrace the Suck* 38: Puzzle Palace, a high-security or intelligence site, or a headquarters located in a high-security area... Usually a derogatory term. ("What do those dumbfucks at the Puzzle Palace say now?"). **2007** J. Hayes *Precious Blood* 122: In the future, try and watch just who the fuck you're pointing your dumb-fuck cadet fingers at!

Dutch fuck *noun*

an act of lighting one cigarette from another.

1948 E. Partridge *Dictionary of Slang & Unconventional English* (ed. 3) 1039: *Dutch f **k*. Lighting one cigarette from another. Forces': 1940 +. **1974** New York City man, age 23: A Dutch fuck is when you light someone's cigarette with your own. **1993** J. Meades *Pompey* 457: She flinched ever after at the light of lighters, matches, the intimacy of shared flame; even a Dutch fuck frightened her. **1997** A. MacAndrew *Bits of String* 151: "Give us a light, Harry please."..."It'll have to be a Dutch fuck," Harry answered, handing over his cigarette.

E

eff or **F**

1. (a partial euphemism for) FUCK in various senses and parts of speech.

1929 R. Graves *Good-Bye to All That* 79 [refers to 1917]: The Bandmaster, who was squeamish, reported it as: "Sir, he called me a double-effing c——." **1931** E. E. Cummings *I Sing of Olaf Glad and Big*: I will not kiss your f.ing flag. **1931** J. Hanley *Boy* 252: Tell the effin bosun there's only the crew's stuff here now. **1945** E. Hemingway *Letter* (Apr. 2) in *Selected Letters* (1981) 579: You'll hear I'm a phony, a liar, a coward, maybe even a Man of Honor. Just tell them to Eff off. **1950** E. Hemingway *Across the River and into the Trees* 78: "Eff Florence," the Colonel said. *Ibid.* 173: You would eff-off, discreetly. **1959** B. Cochrell *Barren Beaches of Hell* 130: They've come closer to solving the recreation problem than anyone else in this effing division. **1961** J.A. Williams *Night Song* 152: "Eff you, man," Yards said. **1961** H. Ellison *Memos from Purgatory* 43: Turn that effin' thing off before I put a fist through it. **1965** R. Hardman *Chaplains Raid* 34: An effing chaplain's assistant! **1965** N. Simon *Odd Couple* III: "We're all out of Corn Flakes. F.U." It took me three hours to figure out that F.U. was Felix Ungar. It's not your fault, Felix. It's a rotten combination. **1967** D. Taggart *Reunion* 189: You effin well know it. **1970** E. E. Landy *Underground Dictionary* 76: *F. you*—Fuck you. *Ibid.* 77: *F—ing* v. Fucking; having sexual intercourse. *Ibid.* 78: *F—ing around*... Goofing off. **1973** W. Overgard *Pieces of a Hero* 61: Where in the effin hell have you been? **1977** *N.Y. Post* (Mar. 18) 37: With the language sensitivity of one who knows what will and will not get on TV he later asked:

"Am I being effed around, or not?" He actually said "effed." *a*1984 in W. Terry *Bloods* 127: What the F was I there for? **1987** *Newsweek* (Mar. 23) 58: Don't F with him. *Ibid.* 63: He says he F'd you up. *Ibid.* 65: Stay the F out of the way. *Ibid.* 73: He said *F* the doctors. **1991** L. Bing *Do or Die* iv. 81: I looked crazy back at him, and I said, "Eff, yo' set and eff yo' dead homeboys." **1993** *Washington Post* (Sept. 3) A8: What the f are you doing here? **1998** N. Hornby *About a Boy* viii. 52: "You should've told her to ..."—she looked around to see whether Marcus, the strange kid they were apparently stuck with for the day, was still listening—"...to eff off." **2008** *Entertainment Weekly* (Dec. 19) 31: Charlie "Slim" Hendrick, a don't-eff-with-me ex-con, returns home to find that his sweetie has moved on and his bitter brother has gambling debts.

2. *British.* to use the word "fuck"; chiefly in phrase: ☞ **to eff and blind** to swear frequently; to use strong language.

1943 M. Harrison *Reported Safe Arrival* 31: They'd eff and blind till yer ear-'oles started ter frizzle. **1959** A. Wesker *Chicken Soup with Barley* i. ii: He started effing and blinding and threw their books on the floor. **1965** J. Gaskell *Fabulous Heroine* 50: He would argue and eff in an intellectual ecstasy all afternoon. **1977** J. Rosenthal *Spend, Spend, Spend* in *Bar Mitzvah Boy & Other Television Plays* (1987) 178: *First Woman*: Well, they haven't the time really, fair's fair. It's a full-time job is boozing all day. *Second Woman*: I believe they were paralytic in the Miners Arms. Effing and blinding. You'd think they'd ban them ... but they won't. *First Woman*: Mrs Danby said the police were round to them three o'clock this morning. Disturbing the peace. **1981** W. Foley *Back to Forest* in *Forest Trilogy* (1992) 309: In winter he effed and blinded the queueing customers who were making life hard for him and his assistant fryer. **1989** J. Galloway *Trick is to Keep Breathing* (1991) 26: A man and a woman shouting, effing and blinding and the little girl starts screaming. **1995** M. Amis *Information* 48: Even the Asians and West Indians who lived there had somehow become saxonized—they loped and leered, they peed, veed, queued, effed and blinded, just like the locals. **1999** L. Hird *Born Free* xiv. 109: A bairn starts screaming up the back and I hear the mother effing away, smacking it. **2003** C. Birch *Turn Again Home* iii. 47: She'd turned up at Edmund and Isabel's blind drunk in the middle of the afternoon. Disgusting! Effing and blinding she was in front of the children.

em-eff variant of M.F.

eye-fuck *verb*

to gaze at lecherously; ogle. Also: (especially *Military*) to stare at, especially with hostility; (*hence, Military*) to look around.

1916 H. N. Cary *Slang of Venery* I 79: *Eye Fuck*—To stare and leer at a woman. **1971** P. Barnes *Pawns* 69: The DI's have picked out the recruits who don't look sharp, who fall behind in the runs, or are caught "eye-fucking." ("Eye-fucking" is a heinous crime in Marine Corps boot camp. It consists of moving one's eyeballs to the side while standing at attention.) **1972** B. Rodgers *Queens' Vernacular* 77: *Eye fuck* (late '60s)...to stare holes through someone. **1980** M. Baker *Nam* 36: Smokey catches the dude looking at him out of the corner of his eye. He says, "Are you eye-fucking me, boy? I don't want your scuzzy eyes looking at me." **1980** J. DiFusco et al. *Tracers* 12: While maggots are at attention, they will not talk, they will not eye-fuck the area, they will listen to me and only me! **1983** W. D. Ehrhart *Vietnam to Perkasie* 30 [refers to 1966]: You will not talk. You will not eye-fuck the area. *Ibid.* 32: You eye-fuckin' me, sweetpea? You wanna fuck me, scum? **1988** J. Norst *Colors* 17: Killer Bee...was... eye-fucking McGavin. **1991** J. T. Ward *Dear Mom* 5 [refers to 1968]: You will stand at attention, eyes forward. I don't want you eyefucking me or the area. **1991** D. Simon *Homicide* 260: And damned if he didn't always come back with some pieces of information about the dead man. Any other detective would get eyefucked and maybe cursed, but Worden somehow managed to take the corner boys beyond that. **1997** D. Simon & E. Burns *Corner* 16: Three of the plainclothesmen stand over them, shouting; a fourth stands in the street, eyefucking the crews on the Mount Street corners. **2000** E. Reid *Midnight Sun* 29: Her boyfriend, a tattooed biker, stood nearby...making sure we weren't eyefucking her. **2008** A. Davies *Mine All Mine* 155: The daughters of tourists in their sherbet-colored minis getting eyefucked by vendedores.

F

F variant of EFF.

face-fuck *verb*

~ MOUTH-FUCK. Hence **face-fucker** *noun*.

1972 "Coop" *Sexy Southern Boy* 66: He was lying on his back now, letting me do all the work, just enjoying it, rather than face-fucking me, like he'd done the first time. *a***1980** *About Time: Anthology of California Prison Writing* 19: One million days filled with cumdrunk bitches who facefuck and rimshot and tonguebathe. **1983** R. N. Boyd *Joint Sissies* in *Sex behind Bars* (1984) 56: Gary was a real face-fucker; it was hard to catch my breath while doing him. **1990** S. Morgan *Homeboy* xlvi. 277: Billy had grabbed Magdalena by the hair and lifted her around and slammed her up against the cage's wire mesh, which he clutched to facefuck her. **1999** R. T. Davies *Queer as Folk: Scripts* (Episode 4) 113 (stage direction): Quickly, Stuart gets Nathan on to his knees, facefucks him With one hand on the back of Nathan's head, Stuart reaches out to balance himself. **2006** R. Kick *Everything You Know about Sex is Wrong* 120/2: They want to open their throat, get facefucked, and swallow a load of cum.

fan-fucking-tastic *adjective*

wonderful; fantastic. See -FUCKING-, *infix*, for related forms.

1970 T. Southern *Blue Movie* 108: Tony was delighted. "Fanfucking-tastic!" **1971** *National Lampoon* (Aug.) 26: Just groove on those colors! Fan-fucking-tastic! **1976** A. Schroeder *Shaking It Rough*

78: "Fan-fucking-tastic!" Corso whistles in astonishment. **1977** D. Bredes *Hard Feelings* 42: He said "Fan-fucking-tastic!" over and over. **1981** R. Graziano & R. Corsel *Somebody Down Here Likes Me Too* 156: Frankie...is fanfuckintastic! **1988** M. Atwood *Cat's Eye* 298: Fan-fuckin'-tastic. **1989** C. Hiaasen *Skin Tight* xxiii. 248: "Swell," said Murdock. "That means it's only what?—another four, five hours in the mud. Fanfuckingtastic. By then it'll be good and dark too." **1993** M. Crichton *Disclosure* i. 56: I am pleased to report...that as of half an hour ago, The Corridor is fan-fucking-*tastic*. **2004** J. Moore *Dot.homme* xiv. 171: "Isn't this fan-fucking-tastic, Jess!" she'd shrieked above the music, spinning me around until I felt utterly sick.

fanny *verb*

British. (a euphemism for FUCK AROUND *verb*). Usually as **fanny about.**

1971 J. Leasor *Love-All* iv. 62: We haven't much time to fanny about. **1996** P. Gregory *Perfectly Correct* 246: I'm not accustomed to being fannied about. I don't like this will-you won't-you stuff, Lou. You said you'd come for the weekend and I want you there with me. **2000** M. Gayle *Turning Thirty* xxxix. 159: That's three years wasted. Three years! If I hadn't spent all that time fannying around in lecture halls I'd be twenty-seven now instead of thirty! **2004** *Independent* (Apr. 8) (Review section) 13/1: I took the family to Cowley Manor in Gloucestershire at the weekend, and having fannied around for 20 minutes in London deciding what to pack, eventually decided to go in what I was wearing. **2008** *Guardian* (Aug. 30) 7: It is time to end the British habit of fannying about with Olympic football.

Fanny Adams *verb* [euphemism for FUCK ALL *noun*, after *Fanny Adams*, young English girl murdered in 1867]

British = FUCK ALL *noun*. Usually used with *sweet*.

1919 W. H. Downing *Digger Dialect* 22: F.A., 'Fanny Adams', or 'Sweet Fanny Adams'—nothing; vacuity. **1930** J. Brophy & E. Partridge *Songs & Slang of the British Soldier* 123: F.A. Sometimes lengthened into Sweet F.A. or bowdlerized into Sweet Fanny Adams. Used to mean 'nothing' where something was expected. **1949** J. R. Cole *It was so Late* 61: What do they do? Sweet Fanny Adams! **1958** B. Behan *Borstal Boy* 15: You'll order sweet fanny adams from outside, and never you mind the regulations, I'll regulate you. **1978** B. Ashley *Kind of Wild Justice* (2002) 92: There was sweet Fanny Adams around here, only mud and slippery wood, and stink. **1983** J. H. Heminway *No Man's Land* 5: I was no ruddy star and I knew sweet Fanny Adams about acting, but I did have fun. **1990** M. Leigh *Life is Sweet* in *Naked & Other Screenplays* (1995) 145: So what you been doin' all mornin'? Sweet Fanny Adams, as usual. **1999** S. Perera *Haven't Stopped Dancing Yet* xiv. 186: "You sound like my mum." "And you're going to end up like her: working your fingers to the bone for sweet Fanny Adams." **2002** J. Diski *Stranger on a Train* 112: You're completely drunk, you are drunk as a horse's arse and you know sweet fanny adams about the little people. You are a fraud.

fark *verb*

Chiefly *Australian*. (a partial euphemism, in various senses, parts of speech, and derived forms, for) FUCK.

1971 J. Hibberd *Stretch of the Imagination* 23: (He continues [gardening] for a while, then stops suddenly, in pain and bent over at a fixed angle at the hips.) Faaarrk. **1983** D. Foster *Plumbum* ii. 56: "When it comes to drumming, you'd make a good panel beater." "Farkin' hell!" **1992** *Picture* (Sydney) (Feb. 5) 26/1: Experts reckon that now our bastard drought has broken, roaches will breed like buggery and we'll stand no farkin' chance. **1994** *Picture* (Sydney) (Feb. 5) 14/2: And if this year's show is anything to go by, that'll be a dead farkin' cert. **1996** *Tracks* (Sydney) (June) 51/2: Faark! (Sorry, I had to say that 'cause this word is a major part of Australian surfer's dialect.) **1998** *Hairball Goulash* (Wodonga, NSW) 26: They did walk and they di[d] see in each other that words could not express how beautiful these dirty grotty streets in this farked up hostile world looked to them... **1998** *Hairball Goulash* (Wodonga, NSW) 26: Tanith, and her typewriter put this zine together, and it is so farken cool. **2001** *Touch* (Dec.) 127/1: So Touch Magazine is back. Thank fuck. It's about farking time that the best magazine made its late but welcome spectacular entrance on the market. **2003** K. Kuitenbrouwer *Way Up* iv. 62: Jane Rae, Joanie and I went for a walk so we could smoke up, farking freezing.

35

F-bomb *noun*

the word FUCK or one of its variants or compounds, esp. with refer-ence to it as a shocking or inappropriate term. Often in **to drop the F-bomb**.

1988 *Newsday* (New York) (Aug. 11) i. 144/3: That was when I used to use the F-bomb. **1991** *Boston Globe* (Jan. 11) (Sports section) 31: It looked like I was calling him everything in the book.... I dropped the F-bomb a few times. **1995** *Denver Post* (June 11) B 10/3: I tried not to say any F-bombs with my mom there. **2000** *Sporting News* (Oct. 23) 54: 4... Times (at least) lip readers with an aversion to the f-bomb would have blushed if they watched Games 3 and 4 of the NLCS. **2002** A. St. John in *Village Voice* (Aug. 28) 159/4: When he got a questionable call late in the fifth set against Hewitt, he launched an atypical F-bomb on the umpire and promptly pissed away what was left of the match. **2006** *Philadelphia Inquirer* (May 7) B4/5: Two years ago, Vice President Cheney dropped the f-bomb on Sen. Patrick Leahy on the Senate floor, then defiantly said, "I feel better now." **2008** *Sports Illustrated* (Dec. 19) 16: Of course, with no restrictor plates on anyone's mouth, the language can get hotter than a brake pad at Martinsville—Stewart's f bomb-laden exchange with crew chief Greg Zipadelli at Indy in July being Exhibit A.

feck *verb*

Irish. (a partial euphemism, in various senses, parts of speech, and derived forms, for) FUCK. [Popularized on the *Father Ted* TV series.]

1980 "H. Leonard" *Life* I. 24 Feck off, that's not yours. **1989** H. Leon-ard *Out After Dark*: I went on clinging to the wall until old Fanning made feck-off gestures of great savagery. **1993** D. Purcell *Falling for a Dancer*: "Fecker," said Hazel passionately. "That's all he is, a fecker. I can't stand the sight of him." **1995** P. Boland *Tales from a City Farmyard*: Some little feck-er of a kid pinched the bum off me. **1998** M. McDonagh *Beauty Queen of Leenane* (play): Feck! **1999** F. McCourt *'Tis* xvii. 136: He's over by the coal range with a mug of tea and all he does is smoke cigarettes and cough till he's weak, clutching at himself and laughing, These feckin' fags will kill me in the end. **2003** J. Mullaney *We'll be Back* 33: It's a dangerous path to go down, but what the feck do I know? I'm only a football fan who's dropped out of the rat race with ill health.

fed up *adjective*

In phrase:

🕮 **fed up, fucked up, and far from home**, *Military*. disgusted, helpless, and far from one's home. Compare *fucked [up] and far from home* under FUCK, *verb*.

1936 E. Partridge *Dictionary of Slang & Unconventional English* 269: In the [First World War], a military [catch phrase] ran, *fed up, f **ked up, and far from home*. **1977** P. Caputo *Rumor of War* 93 [refers to 1965]: The Marines are all in the same state of mind as I, "fed-up, fucked-up, and far from home." **1979–81** C. Buckley *Steaming to Bamboola* 207: "Fucked up, fed up, and far away from home," he snorted. **1984** E. Partridge *Dictionary of Slang & Unconventional English* (ed. 8) 383: *Fed-up, fucked up, and far from home*...still being used by the WWI Tommies' soldier-grandsons, 1970s. **1984** A. Burgess *Enderby's Dark Lady* 84: Fed up, fucked up and far from home. **1998** A. Sillitoe *Broken Chariot* 98: When the six hundred men were moved from place to place, an exercise of seeming pointlessness, all complained at being fed up, fucked up, and far from home.

ferk *verb*

(a partial euphemism for) FUCK in various senses and parts of speech. Sometimes *jocular*.

*ca***1929** *Collection of Sea Songs* 43: Perkin you're shirkin your ferkin. **1945** T. Lea *Peleliu Landing* 15: It's the ferking night time I don't like, when them little ferkers come sneakin' into your lap. **1946–51** J. Jones *From Here to Eternity* ch. xxi [refers to *ca*1940]: Ah, what's the difference? They all the ferkin same. Five cents of one, a nickel of the other. **1965** in G. Legman *New Limerick* 4: He jerked 'em, and ferked 'em. **1977** J. Hersey *Walnut Door* 56: She raved for several hours, keening most of her threnody not at Macaboy, whom she addressed exclusively as *you ferking shithead*, but at her dear dead daddy. **2007** K. Tout *By Tank* 87: Bloody SS. Shit on you, rotten buggers. Shooting our colonel. Why don't you ferk off back home and shoot bleeding Hitler.

fiddlefuck *verb*

to play or fiddle about; FUCK AROUND.—usually used with *around*. Also (in 1974 quotation) as *noun*.

1949 W.S. Burroughs *Letter* (Jan. 16) in *Letters of William S. Burroughs* (1993) 35: When his neglect takes the form of deserting her without funds (what money she has did not come from him), and expecting me to take over until such time as he gets tired of fiddle fucking around N.Y. and decides to come down here, it ceases to be a personal matter between him and his wife. **1974** R. Stone *Dog Soldiers* 321: Some of you birds think I'm down here to play fiddle fuck around. **1973–77** J. Jones *Whistle* 506 [refers to WWII]: It was strange, all right, and he didn't fiddlefuck around. **1979** J. Hurling *Boomers* 84: I'm not going to fiddle-fuck around 'til those pricks come out of the office. **1985** D. Dye *Run Between the Raindrops* 192: Can't fiddle-fuck around on the perimeter. **1990** G. G. Liddy *Monkey Handlers* xix. 322: Better to get ahead than fiddle-fuck along like this. **2002** *New Yorker* (July 15) 73/3: She was all reticence and demurrals—no drink, no dinner, no nothing.... The mournful fraülein desired them to stop fiddle-fucking, order dinner or go away. **2008** *Guardian* (Feb. 16) (Saturday Comment section) 32/3: But we'll let an editor fiddlefuck all over with it [*sc.* a novel].

In phrase:

☞ **be fiddlefucked** to be damned.

1976 P. Atlee *Last Domino Contract* 52: This is Korea's nuclear reactor one...and I'll be fiddle-fucked if I understand why it hasn't fallen down yet.

fiddlefucking *adjective*

= FUCKING, *adjective*.

1974 P. Roth *My Life as a Man* 19: I guaranfuckingtee you gentlemen, not one swingin' dick will be leavin' this fiddlefuckin' area to so much as chew on a nanny goat's tittie.

fiddler's fuck *noun*

a damn; FUCK *noun*, definition 2.a.; in phrase: ☞ **not make a fiddler's fuck**, not make any difference. [The 1932 quotation is euphemistic.]

1932 V. F. Nelson *Prison Days & Nights* 25: We could all rot to death, and they wouldn't give a fiddler's so-and-so for us. **1961** H. Selby *Room* 187: They ain't worth a fiddlers fuck. **1973** W. Crawford *Stryker* 91: I don't give a fiddler's fuck about jurisdictional disputes, ace. **1976** P. Atlee *Last Domino Contract* 175: A shamed patriot…ain't worth a fiddler's fuck. **1978** H. Selby *Requiem for a Dream* 183: Why didn't make a fiddler's fuck. **1979** G. Wolff *Duke of Deception* 236: I didn't care a fiddler's fuck where my father was. **1984** W. J. Caunitz *One Police Plaza* 22: I don't give a fiddler's fuck what the Forensic boys like. **2000** T. Robbins *Fierce Invalids Home from Hot Climates* 87: You come along on your bleeding errand, oblivious, unmindful, not caring a fiddler's fuck, and fall into it, just bloody stumble into it, roses and whistles.

fiddly-fuck *noun*

= FIDDLER'S FUCK.

1973 New York City man, age 25: Do you think I give a fiddly-fuck? **1992** S. King *Dolores Claiborne* (1993) 62: I didn't know what'd happen to her or who would take care of her, but right then I didn't care a fiddlyfuck.

In phrase:

☞ **play fiddly-fuck**, to fool around.

1964–66 R. Stone *Hall of Mirrors* 305: I didn't come out to play fiddly fuck. **2001** S. King *Dreamcatcher* xiii. 453: We don't think they will come again, or at least not for awhile. They played fiddly-fuck for half a century before getting this far. **2006** S. King *Lisey's Story* 289: He was coming around and you were still out there playin fiddly-fuck in the shed.

fifteen fucker *noun*

Army. punishment under Article 15 of the Army Code of Conduct.

1981–89 R. Atkinson *Long Gray Line* 295: Each of them was repri manded, fined $300, and given an Article 15—an administrative punishment known within the ranks as a Fifteen Fucker—"for conduct totally unbecoming an officer." **2004** P. Maslowski *Looking for a Hero* iii. 73: At 6:00 am on May 1 Joe missed reveille formation, resulting in a Fifteen Fucker that sentenced him to forfeit $163 for one month.

FIGMO ["*fuck it, got my orders*," with variations] *interjection & adjective*

Military. (used as an expression of contempt or dismissal). Also **FUIGMO.** Compare FUJIGMO. *Jocular.*

1962 F. Harvey *Strike Command* 101: Everybody in the Air Force is familiar with the expression a man about to ship out to some new duty station gives those about him who have some insane notion that they'll get some useful work out of him. It is "FIGMO!"…the expression which… [he] delivers at his new duty station…is FIGMO spelled backward, or OMGIF! **1968** J.D. Houston *Between Battles* 212: Once he knows [he is scheduled to rotate], he goes FUIGMO—fuck u, I got my orders. At the PX he buys a FUIGMO button. **1969** C. C. Moskos *American Enlisted Man* 144: Rather, the attitude is typically, "I've done my time, let the others do theirs." Or, as put in the soldier's vernacular, he is waiting to make the final entry on his "FIGMO" chart—fuck it, got my orders (to return to the United States). **1969** *Current Slang I & II* 32: *Figmo*…"forget it, I've got my orders."—Air Force Academy cadets. **1983** J. Groen & D. Groen *Huey* 102 [refers to 1971]: Roger and John were among the few remaining…who were not figmo (fuck it, got my orders). *Ibid.* 105: You're figmo…I'll send them. **2005** D. DeFrain *Salt Palace* viii. 80: I was in Palermo for most of mine. F.I.G.M.O., you know?

fingerfuck *noun*

an act of masturbation of the vagina or anus.

[**1884** *Randiana* 31: The easy transition from a kiss to a feel, from a feel to a finger frig, and eventually by a more natural sequence to a gentle insertion of the jock.] **1970** E. E. Landy *Underground Dictionary* 77: *Finger fuck…n.* Stimulation of the female sex organs with the finger. **1978** J. Webb *Fields of Fire* 228: This bastard wants to kill me for a damn fingerfuck. **1999** S. Rushdie *Ground beneath her Feet* xiv. 443: Sometimes she lazily played at adolescent sex, all finger-fucks and blow-jobs; more often she just came at you like Octopussy, all arms and legs and whoops-a-daisy. **2005** "Noire" *Candy Licker* viii. 78: I told them all about the finger fuck he gave me on the dance floor.

fingerfuck *verb*

to masturbate the vagina or anus [of].

*a***1793** R. Burns *Merry Muses* 29: She m—s like reek thro' a' the week,/ But finger f—s on Sunday, O. *ca***1866** *Romance of Lust* 197: Anything but finger-fucking. *a***1890–91** J. S. Farmer & W. E. Henley *Slang & Its Analogues* II 398: *Finger-fucking*…masturbation (said of women only).

1916 H. N. Cary *Slang of Venery* I 84: *Finger fucking*—to induce a sexual spasm in a woman by digitation. **1921** in E. Cray *Erotic Muse* 195: There she saw her lovin' boy/finger-fucking Nellie Bly. **1945–48** *Marianas Collection* (unpaged): I started finger fucking myself. **1964** in H. Huncke *Huncke's Journal* 4: Licking—eating—jerking off and finger fucking. **1965** C. Bukowski *Letter* (Feb.–Mar.) in *Screams from Balcony: Selected Letters* (1998) 135: Who knows about the boss finger-fucking the secretary in the stock room? **1968** P. Roth *Portnoy's Complaint* 143: She wants you to finger-fuck her *shikse* cunt till she faints. **1970** R. Byrne *Memories non-Jewish Childhood* 157: I get tired of finger-fucking Wanda Farney all the time. **1970** G. Cain *Blueschild Baby* 53: Boy and girl flirting in hall shadowkiss and finger fuck. **1971** H. Dahlskog *Dictionary of Contemporary & Colloquial Usage* 23: *Fingerfuck, v. Vulgar.* To arouse (someone) sexually by vaginal or rectal stimulation with the finger. **1976** J. Johnson *Oriental Festival* 139: I'm gonna…slip my finger inside your hot ass.…Maybe I should give you a little finger fucking. **1983** *Playboy* (Aug.) 88: He claims that he is obsessed with sex, that he has done it with animals, that he's finger-fucked his cat. **1991** M. Dibdin *Dirty Tricks* (1992) 103: Despite her frantic pleas I refused to go any further than finger-fucking until she had signed on the dotted line. **1996** *Village Voice* (N.Y.C.) (Apr. 23) 74: Then he finger-fucks her on a roller coaster. **2000** *New Yorker* (Sept. 4) 48/3: Then you got guys standing around…talking about how they finger-fucked you and your yin-yang made their hands smell like tuna fish. **2007** J. McCourt *Now Voyagers* xi. 512: "Finger-fuck me then, you heavenly boy-man," she brayed to be heard in the hall.

fist-fuck *verb*

Especially *Homosexuals,* to insert the hand into the rectum or vagina for sexual stimulation. Also as *noun.*

[**1971** (see quote at FIST-FUCKING *noun* definition 2).] **1972** B. Rodgers *Queens' Vernacular* 81: *Fist fuck.* The extended process of inserting a fist to the elbow anally. **1978** R. Price *Ladies' Man* 224: That guy's into getting fist fucked…right up the ass. Right up to the elbow. Can you believe that? **1978** L. Kramer *Faggots* 216: You probably still want me to fist-fuck you, don't you?…. I could never understand why you liked to get fist-fucked and don't like to get regular fucked. **1984** H. Gould *Cocktail* 91: He liked to put on mesh stockings…and get fist-fucked. **1991** J. Barth *Last Voyage of Somebody the Sailor* 368: He aspired one day to fist-fuck Sindbad the

Sailor in his half an ass. **1995** *New Statesman* (Aug. 4) 41: Each month's curse earned her a beating on the bedpost, a fistfuck for failure, exposure on the platform at the march past. **1995** *Village Voice* (N.Y.C.) (Dec. 12) 31: For a grand finale she got fistfucked by a ring-wearing "gypsy" lady while deep-throating a 13-inch dick. **2002** W. Self *Dorian* x. 144: "His gut," he said of one patient, "was punctured by some guy fist-fucking him."

fist-fucker *noun*

1. a man or boy who is a frequent masturbator.—used contemptuously.

> **1962** J. O. Killens *Then We Heard the Thunder* 168 [refers to WWII]: Corporal Solly, you old-fashioned fist-fucker, why don't you come out of that orderly room and get some air in your ass sometimes? **1969** H. S. Thompson *Letter* (Dec. 6) in *Fear & Loathing in America* (2000) 223: Never, under any circumstances, have I been shit on so totally as I was in the course of this Playboy /Killy thing. That whole goddamn magazine is a conspiracy of anemic masturbators....scurvy fist-fuckers to the last man. **1974** E. Thompson *Tattoo* 111: I feel plumb sorry for you poor Wichita fistfuckers...got nothin to fuck there but their fists. **1984** A. R. Sample *Racehoss* 266 [refers to 1960s]: Nelly Nuthin, Proud Walker, Bow Wow, and Fistfucker were...dunces. **2006** U. Chatterjee *Weight Loss* 150: Spilling his precious seed six times a day like a fourteen-year-old fistfucker.

2. *Homosexuals.* a practitioner of FIST-FUCKING, definition 2.

> **1972** B. Rodgers *Queens' Vernacular* 81: *Fist fuckers*...those who practice fist fucking. **1973** *Oui* (July) 73: Fist Fuckers of America: Their clenched-fist gestures are often an internal expression. **1985** J. Dillinger *Adrenaline* 213: How about *Fistfucker Beach?* **1993** *Folio* (Oct. 15) 57: The organizers [of a gay-rights march in Washington, D.C.] didn't want the Fist Fuckers of America marching down Pennsylvania Avenue. **1999** "Eurydice" *Satyricon USA* 94: The natives patronize corsetries, boutiques that sell Würtenburg wheels, Victorian parlors, Edwardian attics, "handballing soirées," "electroplay charity fund-raisings." The streets brim with Gender Variant Folk, Granddaddies and G-spot Mommies, bulldaggers, adult babies, PVC boy-toys and sex-maids, and infinite combinations thereof (top-femme-hookers, butch-bottom-cocksuckers, androgynous leather

doggies, radical bi fistfuckers). **2008** J. D. Lichtenberg *Sensuality & Sexuality across Divide of Shame* 12: He reported a dream in which a clear stand-in for me was identified as a fist fucker.

3. a despicable or contemptible fellow.

1977 in H.S. Thompson *Shark Hunt* 602: If that treacherous fist-fucker ever comes back to life, he'll wish we'd had the good sense to nail him up on a frozen telephone pole.

fist-fucking *noun*

1. male masturbation.

*ca***1890** *My Secret Life* VI. i.: All day spite of the relief I had given myself by fist fucking, I was as lewd as I could be, mad to see more of her. *ca***890–91** J. S. Farmer & W. E. Henley *Slang & Its Analogues* II 402: *Fist-fucking* masturbation. **1916** H. N. Cary *Slang of Venery* I 85: *Fist fucking*—masturbation.

2. Especially *Homosexuals.* insertion of the hand into the rectum or vagina for sexual stimulation.

1971 J. F. Hunter *Gay Insider* iii. 36: Kim, when worked up, did like rough treatment. He specifically wanted to be plowed hard, preliminary to fist fucking. **1972** (quotation at FIST-FUCKER, definition 2). **1973** *Oui* (July) 75: We spent some time discussing fist fucking ("it can be dangerous"). **1981** *Film Comment* (May) 21: Oriental beheadings and Occidental gay fistfuckings. **1984** R. J. Avrech & B. De Palma *Body Double* (film): No animal acts, no fist-fucking, and absolutely no coming in my face. **1988** R. Shilts *And the Band Played On* II. ii. 24: "It looks like that guy has his arm up the other guy's ass." "He does have an arm up his ass"...."That's fist-fucking," the psychologist said. **1989** S. Chapple & D. Talbot *Burning Desires* 260: Videos that did not stop at fist-fucking. **1992** *Whole Earth Review* (June 22) 94: "Is 'perineal massage' really fist fucking?"..."Of course."...A hand going inside my pussy is...exciting. **1997** L. Yablonsky *Story of Junk* 39: Her specialty was gay male erotica; the idea of fist-fucking gave her a charge. **2001** P. Burston *Shameless* viii. 114: Dressing up in drag? Fist fucking? He already knew that David found his father attractive. What if the E turned his father into a sex maniac? Would he be able to resist David's advances?

flak

Military Aviation. (a jocular euphemism for) FUCK.

1961 G. Forbes *Goodbye to Some* 120 [refers to WWII]: The 38's will get the flak out of there. **1963** E. M. Miller *Exile* 57: "Flak you, fellows," he said as the door slammed.

flat fuck *noun & verb*

among lesbians: a sexual act in which two women lie prone face to face and rub and stimulate each other; (*as verb*) to perform this act.

*ca***1890** *My Secret Life* IX. vii.: French women were much more free spoken than the English, who mostly said they disliked to touch another woman's cunt, which I believed was a lie. One or two only, said they'd had a flat fuck with a friend, and what harm was there? *ca***1890** *My Secret Life* IX. ix.: Putting them on the top of each other I wanted them to flat fuck—Nelly refused, tho Sophy was ready for it, half screwed when she came and more so now, for I'd taken a bottle of gin with me. However they laid belly on belly with thighs wide apart, their mottes touching, cunt wigs entwining, but clitoris did not touch clitoris. **1970** R. Blake *Porno Movies* 169: She got to opening up the other girl's pussy and they did a flat fuck together. **1980** *Maledicta* IV. 197: This practice may best be seen amongst lesbians...who prefer soixante-neuf to a flat fuck. **1998** S. Waters *Tipping Velvet* xviii. 415: "I said," came a girl's voice, "'I only does that sort of thing, sir, with my friends.' 'Emily Pettinger,' he said, 'said you let her flat fuck you for an hour and a half'—which is a lie, but anyway, 'Flat fucking is one thing, sir,' I said, 'and this quite another. If you want me to — her'"—here she must have made a gesture—"'you shall have to pay me for it, rather dear.'"

flipping *adjective & adverb*

Chiefly *British*. (a euphemism for) FUCKING *adjective & adverb*.

1911 D. H. Lawrence *White Peacock* II. ix. 347: Ain't it flippin' ot? **1948** C. Day Lewis *Otterbury Incident* i. 2: Flipping heroes, ain't we all? **1957** J. Kerouac *Letter* (Mar. 19) in *Selected Letters 1957–69* 14: In the original version there was no flipping confession and everyone read it and naturally

didn't miss it. **1959** *Spectator* (Nov. 20) 713/3: While terms of approval…
change rapidly with the fashion, terms of disapproval (blinking…flippin'
awful…) show very little alteration. **1987** R. Curtis & B. Elton *Blackadder
the Third* in R. Curtis et al. *Black-Adder* 311/2: Mysterious Northern beauty,
Miss Amy Hardwood, comes to London and spends flipping great wodges
of cash. **2002** N. Walker *Blackbox* 180: Dan told him to mind his own
flipping business.

flying *adjective*
In phrases:
☞ **flying fuck**, a damn; the least bit.—usually used in negative, with
give. Also in euphemistic variants.

[*a***1850** (see quotation at FUCK, *noun*, definition 1a). **1946–51** J. Jones
From Here to Eternity [refers to 1941]: I don't give a flyin' fuck. **1953**
C. Brossard *Bold Saboteurs* 30: They did not give a flying hoot. **1956**
H. Ellison *Deadly Streets* 190: Tony didn't give a flying damn. **1967** in
H. Ellison *Sex Misspelled* 154: I…don't give a flying *shit* what time you
were behind your desk. **1973** R. M. Brown *Rubyfruit Jungle* 67: I don't
give a flying fuck what you do. **1974** V. C. Strasburger *Rounding Third &
Heading Home* 12: Who gives a flying fuck, Junior? **1980** P. Conroy *Lords
of Discipline* 297: He wouldn't have given a flying crap about this city. **1984**
W. D. Ehrhart *Marking Time* 19: Most…weren't worth a flying fuck. **1985**
K. Finkelman *Head Office* (film): He doesn't give a flying shit about Stead-
man's position. **1992** M. Crichton *Rising Sun* 227: Older people don't give
a flying fuck, John. **1995** E. White *Skinned Alive* 9: He didn't give a flying
fuck about the Crowd. **1997** A. Proulx in *New Yorker* (Oct. 13) 79: And
I don't give a flyin fuck. **2005** M. H. Smith *Delicious* xi. 152: He didn't give
a flying fuck about the Bellagio's water fountain.

☞ **[go] take a flying fuck**, get away! go to hell! Also in euphemistic and elaborated variants, especially **take a flying fuck at a
rolling donut.**

1926 L. H. Nason *Chevrons* 73 [refers to 1918]: Me, I'd tell 'em to
take a flyin' fling at the moon. **1929–30** J. Dos Passos *42nd Parallel* 271:
I hadn't the nerve/to…tell/them all to go take a flying/Rimbaud/at the
moon. **1932** Miller & Burnett *Scarface* (film): "They said you could take a

flyin' —" "That's enough of that!" **1934** W. Saroyan in J. North *New Masses* (1969) 93: I didn't obey my mother or my teachers and I told the whole world to take a flying you-know-what. **1935** J. Conroy *World to Win* 64: Go take a flyin' jump at a gallopin' goose for all o' me. **1936** S. Kingsley *Dead End* 706: Well, go take a flyin' jump at ta moon! **1938** J. O'Hara in *Selected Letters* 140: I say go take a flying fuck at a galloping r—ster. **1939** B. Appel *Power-House* 165: If this's the *Hamilton Dectective Agency* it can take a flyin' trip to the moon. **1941** C. Brackett & B. Wilder *Ball of Fire* (film): Tell the D.A. to take a flyin' jump for himself. **1944** B. Stiles *Serenade to the Big Bird* 105: You can take a flying one at a rolling one. **1949** A. I. Bezzerides *Thieves' Market* 122: He can go take a flying frig at himself. **1949** R. Pirosh *Battleground* (film) [refers to WWII]: Tell him to take a flyin' leap at a rollin' doughnut. **1952** C. Himes *Stone* 238: How would you like to take a flying frig at yourself? **1961** J. Brosnan *Pennant Race* 48: Brosnan, you take a flying leap at my —. **1962** J. O. Killens *Then We Heard the Thunder* 415: And you and your colored problems can take a flying frig at the moon. **1966** "T. Pendleton" *Iron Orchard* 40: You take a flyin' bite at my ass! **1968** G. Swarthout *Loveland* 169: "Go take a flying jump at a rolling doughnut!" I hollered. **1968** K. Vonnegut *Slaughterhouse-Five* 147 [ref. to WWII]: Go take a flying fuck at a rolling doughnut....Go take a flying fuck at the moon. **1971** L. Cameron *First Blood* 119: Why don't you go take a flying fuck at a rolling doughnut? **1972** R. A. Wilson *Playboy's Book of Forbidden Words* 107: Take a flying Philadelphia fuck in [*sic*] a rolling doughnut. **1972** *Rowan & Martin's Laugh-In* (NBC-TV): I told him to go take a flying leap. **1977** M. Torres in R. P. Rettig et al. *Manny* iv. 115/2: Why don't you take a flying fuck at Mickey Mouse? **1979** J. Hurling *Boomers* 13: I...just told him to take a flyin' fuck at a rollin' doughnut. **1979** W. P. McGivern *Soldiers of '44* 185 [refers to WWII]: Why don't you take a flying fuck at a rolling doughnut? **1966–80** J. McAleer & B. Dickson *Unit Pride* 117: Go take a flyin' fuck at a rollin' doughnut. *Ibid.* 408: You go take a flyin' fuck at the moon. **1983** S. King *Christine* 296: Tell him to take a flying fuck at a rolling doughnut. **1985** J. Briskin *Too Much Too Soon* 264: Tell 'em to go take a flying fuck. **1988** D. DeLillo *Libra* 93: Take a flying fuck at the moon. **1995** A. J. Holt *Watch Me* 204: I told the Narc to take a flying fuck at himself. **ca1999** F. Darabont *Green Mile* (film script) 99: No salesmen in the middle of the night!... Tell them to take a flying fuck. **2005** M. H. Smith *Delicious* 219: He struggled to repress his burning desire to tell this fat Samoan asshole to take a flying fuck at a rolling donut. Instead, he held up his hands.

FNG *noun* [*fucking new guy*]

Especially *Military.* a person who is a newly arrived member, especially of a combat unit. [Most quotations refer to the Vietnam War.]

1966 *N.Y. Times Magazine* (Oct. 30) 104: F.N.G. designates a "foolish new guy." **1966** E. Shepard *Doom Pussy* 217: Major Nails says several FNGs believe it. **1972** T. O'Brien *Combat Zone* 73: Look, FNG, I don't want to scare you. **1980** M. Baker *Nam* 54: Who the hell was I? This rather quiet, slightly older FNG. **1983** L. Van Devanter & C. Morgan *Home Before Morning* 80: "And what's an FNG?" "What else?...A Fucking New Guy." **1983** J. Groen & D. Groen *Huey* 7: Rather than look like FNGs, fucking new guys, including officers, suffered their anxieties quietly. **1985** J. McDonough *Platoon Leader* 65: Despite...his disdain for new guys ("FNGs" he would mutter under his breath),...he was the most respected member of the platoon. **1995** *Newsweek* (May 8) 8: *FNG*. F—ing New Guy; the latest crew hire. **2000** A. Bourdain *Kitchen Confidential* 226: Externs from culinary school, working for free as a "learning experience"—which by itself translates to "lots of work and no money"—are quickly tagged as *FNG* (Fucking New Guy), or *Mel* for *mal carne* (bad meat). **2004** *Observer* (Apr. 18) 21: More than half the girls don't last a day. New staff are referred to as FNGs—Fucking New Guys—until they sort themselves out.

FO *noun & verb*

Especially *Military.* = FUCK-OFF, *noun & verb.*

1945 *American Speech* (Dec.) 262: F.O., to avoid work. **1948** *N.Y. Folklore Quarterly* (Spring) 20. **1957** E. Brown *Locust Fire* 14a [refers to WWII]: I'm an R.O., you F.O. **1974** V. C. Strasburger *Rounding Third & Heading Home* 132: F.O., Carter. **1983** J. Groen & D. Groen *Huey* 98: "Just CA for a few months and then FO." Cover your ass and then fuck off. **1988** O. Clark *Diaries* (1998) p. lxxvi, Nikki Waymouth flaunting her mammories—"Well, that's it, you can all F.O. now."

FOAD *interjection* [see FUCK OFF *verb* definition 1]

"*Fuck Off And Die.*"

1987 "Broken Bones" (title of rock album): F.O.A.D. **1993** *IMHO - HELP!* on Usenet newsgroup alt.business.multi-level (Dec. 4), citing *The BBS_USER Unofficial Acronym List v1.9*: FOAD - F *** Off And

Die. **2004** *AutoWeek* (Nov. 8) 32: Public sentiment that so far is running 10-to-1 opposed, judging by public comment on NHTSA's website…. Another comment was more succinct: "FOAD." **2005** *The Sun* (London) (June 21) (Nexis): Shocked Niall Farrell was appalled to receive the four-letter tirade—contained in the acronym FOAD—which was first spotted by his 15-year-old daughter Mairead.

force-fuck *verb*

Especially *Politics*. to rape. Also figurative.

    1972 B. Rodgers *Queens' Vernacular* 90: *Force-fuck*…to rape a man's anus. **1976** T. Teal trans. *Suzanne Brogger's Deliver Us from Love* 122: All the women who copulate to keep peace in the house are the victims of rape. All our grandmothers who just "let it happen" were essentially force-fucked all their lives. **1987** *Nation* (May 30) 722: MacKinnon's bluster is stunning….Since women are presumed "force-fucked," sexuality is presented in the light of Marx's theory of work. **1992** P. Hamill in *Playboy* (Jan. 1993) 138: According to Dworkin, all women are "force-fucked," either directly through the crime of rape or by the male power of mass media, by male economic power or by the male version of the law.

forget *verb*

Originally *Black English*. to hell with; damn; FUCK, *verb*, definition 4a.

    1969 *Elementary English* XLVI 495: F'get you, honky! **1983** *Reader's Digest Success with Words* 85: Black English…*forget it* = "emphatic phrase expressing negation, denial, refutation." **1980–89** J. E. Cheshire *Home Boy* 105: Forget you, shit-for-brains. **1990** *Simpsons* (Fox-TV): Forget you, pal! Thanks for nothin'! **1995** (see quotation at FUCK-YOU MONEY). **1997** M. Groening et al. *The Simpsons: Complete Guide* 117/1: *Krusty*. Now boys, ah, the network has a problem with some of your lyrics. Would you mind changing them for the show? *Anthony*. Forget you, clown. **2003** *Gazette* (Montreal) (Feb. 20) A4/3: I thought, "(Forget) this, I'd rather be written about than doing the writing."

fork *verb*

to hell with; damn; FUCK, *verb*, definition 4a.

    1954–60 H. Wentworth & S. B. Flexner *Dictionary of American Slang*: *Fork You*…Euphemism for *fuck you*. **1972** B. Rodgers *Queens' Vernacular*

88: *Camp*: "Fork you, Rose, we're doing it *my* way!" *a*1990 B. Raspberry in A. Parfrey *Apocalypse Culture* (1990) (rev. ed.) 241: If you really thought white people are trying to force you to use these things [*sc.* drugs]—you don't like white people, and you don't want 'em to do it—fork them! Tell 'em to go to hell! **1997** A. Neiderman *Dark* 251: "Go fork yourself," he said. Maggie smiled with confusion.

fouled-up *adjective*

Originally *Navy & U.S. Marine Corps.* confused, chaotic, or disorganized; (*broadly*) mistaken; (*also*) stupid or worthless. [Frequently regarded as a euphemism for FUCKED UP.]

1942 *Time* (June 15): The Army has a laconic term for chronic befuddlement: *snafu*, situation normal; all fouled up. **1942** *Leatherneck* (Nov.) 145: *Fouled Up*—mixed up, confuoed. **1942** *Yank* (Nov. 11) 4: Navy [slang]… *Foul*, or *foul up*—Trouble or being in trouble or to get someone in trouble. Thus, if a sailor gets all fouled up with a skirt, he's got babe trouble. **1943** *Saturday Evening Post* (Mar. 20) 86: Those knuckleheads are all fouled up. **1944** P. Kendall *Service Slang* 23: *All fouled up…* messed up. **1945** in *California Folk Quarterly* V (1946) 390: *Fouled up like an ensign's sea bag* is the commonest [U.S. Navy simile]. **1940–46** McPeak *Navy Slang Manuscript*: You're as fouled up as a man overboard in dry dock…as a mess-cook drawing small stores…as a marine at fire drill. **1947** J. C. Higgins *Railroaded* (film): Somebody's all fouled up! **1948** W. Manone & P. Vandervoort *Trumpet on the Wing* 157: Aw, I don't want to go out to ol' Cali-fouled up-ornia and mess with those square people out there. **1949** Grayson & Andrews *I Married a Communist* (film): We're trying to get some sense into a fouled-up situation while there's still time. **1956** M. M. Boatner *Military Customs & Traditions* 125: *Fire Call.* A confused situation or formation. "All fouled up like a fire Call." **1960** C. Simak *Worlds* 43: It was all just this side of crazy, anyhow. No matter how fouled up it was, Steen seemed satisfied. **1964** H. Rhodes *Chosen Few* 57: I've been in this fouled-up place for almost four years straight now and I don't think I can or want to get used to it. **1967** W. Crawford *Gresham's War* 7 [refers to Korean War]: I called him Goat, for fouled-up like Hogan's goat, which he was. **1968** W.C. Anderson *Gooney Bird* 124: The whole thing is insanity. More fouled up than an Ethiopian fire drill. **1967–69** Foster & Stoddard *Pops* 1: I've always wanted to write down what I know about the times in New Orleans. Some of the books are fouled up on it and some of the guys weren't telling the truth. **1977** R. S. Parker *Effective Decisions* 2: Some cynics might say, "It's all society's fault. That's the real reason our lives are all fouled up." **1981** J. Ehrlichman *Witness to Power* 21: Wooley earned a reputation for running the most fouled-up ticket and credential operation in modern Republican history. **1984** L. Fawcett & B. J. Greenwood *UFO Cover-Up* v. 76: Was it a fouled up administrative effort or was the Coast Guard suppressing information? Or was it both? **1992** R. Price *Blue Calhoun* 28: In my fouled up head, I thought that would hurt her even worse. **1998** *Total Football* (Aug.) 93/1: Colombia, the most fouled-up country in the footballing firmament, managed to forget its fear just enough to knock Tunisia out of the World Cup. **2000** B. Blech *Complete Idiot's Guide to Learning Yiddish* 19: That was truly making a *mishmash*, a real fouled-up state of things, of the word *mishmash*. **2006** P. Anthony *Stork Naked* 154: Demon Xanth would lose, and Stymy would remain a hopelessly fouled-up low-echelon stork.

foul-up *noun*

1. Originally *Navy & U.S. Marine Corps.* a blunder leading to a state of confusion or inefficiency; (*also*) a state of confusion brought about by ineptitude or inefficiency; (*also*) a mechanical malfunction. [Frequently regarded as a euphemism for FUCK-UP, definition 1.]

1943 in R. Sherrod *Tarawa* 82: Orders...never came because of the radio foul-up. **1944** *Newsweek* (Feb. 7) 61: *Janfu*: Joint Army-Navy foul-up. *Jaafu*: Joint Anglo-American foul-up. **1945** J. Bryan *Carrier* 139: There's been a foul-up. **1958** J. Thompson *Getaway* (1994) vii. 80: Checkroom attendants were always losing things.... Nothing ever happened, naturally, to a two-dollar suitcase with a few bucks worth of clothes in it. But let the bag contain something hot—money or jewelry or narcotics, or part of a dismembered corpse—and sure as shootin' there was a foul-up. **1958** A. Hailey & J. Castle *Runway Zero-Eight* 109: There's a foul-up on the phones in the press room. **1959** R. G. Fuller *Danger! Marines at Work* 143: "That's the history of the rock, doll," she was told. "Always a foul-up somewhere." **1971** M. Dibner *Trouble with Heroes* 44: The foul-up was especially galling to this bunch because ten days earlier the landing had been smooth and undetected. **1986** F. Walton *Once They Were Eagles*

8: There he ran into a bureaucratic foulup: he couldn't get back into the Marine Corps. **1991** G. Burn *Alma Cogan* ix. 190: I had worked the script up over many weeks with my parents... (I had to get it right first time; there was no overdubbing; any foul-up was going to cost them money). **2000** J. Simpson *Mad World, My Masters* viii. 275: Receive an emollient letter from Alastair Campbell. Not an apology, certainly, but then I didn't expect one: governments never apologize. But he's sorry it happened, and I get the impression he feels it was all a foul-up from their side. **2006** A. J. Zerries *Lost Van Gogh* 180: I never showed up at the school district office to sign the employment papers. A foul-up in the system delayed our benefits from the government.

2. Especially *Military.* a bungler or misfit. [Frequently regarded as a euphemism for FUCK-UP, definition 2.]

> **1945** in M. Chennault *Up Sun!* 136: I know what you foulups were up to. **1954–60** II. Wentworth & S. B. Flexner *Dictionary of American Slang: Foulup...* A person who makes frequent blunders. **1964** J. Pearl *Stockade* 70: I should have known better than to trust that foul-up Larkin. **1965** S. Linakis *In Spring the War Ended* 293: These foul-ups are kids mostly. **1966** P. Derrig *Pride of the Green Berets* 144: Even if he is a short-timer we can't afford even one foul-up in the outfit. **1978** H. Berry *Make the Kaiser Dance* 361: The CO would have the dental officer make out a form saying that Lieutenant Foulup needed a lot of work on his teeth. **1987** D. da Cruz *Boot* 49: You're the worst bunch of foul-ups it's ever been my misfortune to have inflicted on me. **1995** R. Didinger *Game Plans for Success* 130: Hey, this guy is a foul-up. We can't trust him. **2006** J. Lutz *Chill of Night* 44: "She's a foul-up?" "More a don't-give-a-damn type. Mind of her own."

foul up *verb*

1. Originally *Navy & U.S. Marine Corps. transitive.* to bring into confusion; mix up; confound; botch; ruin; in phrase: ☞ **foul up the detail,** *Military.* to bungle. [Frequently regarded as a euphemism for FUCK UP, definition 1.]

> **1942** (quotation at FOULED-UP). **1943** in R. R. Rea *Wings of Gold* (1987) 76: I fouled up a navigation quiz completely. **1944** F. Wakeman *Shore Leave* 21: You know damn well she's in Hartford, making those

Pratt-Whitney engines you foul up. **1946** S. Wilson *Voyage to Somewhere* 108: They've just fouled up the mails. I don't doubt she's writing. **1949** A. I. Bezzerides *Thieves' Market* 198: She's always fouling us up. **1949** "R. MacDonald" *Moving Target* 82: I'm fouled up. Why should I foul you up? **1952** L. Uris *Battle Cry* 132 [refers to WWII]: You guys have been fouling up field problems like a Chinese firedrill. **1953** Brackett, Reisch & Breen *Niagara* (film): It'll be all right if I don't foul it up. **1953** H. G. Felsen *Street Rod* 83: We'd clobber the first guy that fouled us up by racing or being reckless on the roads. **1955** J. McGovern *Fräulein* 170: You're in charge here, and I never try to foul you up. **1957** A. Myrer *Big War* 150 [refers to WWII]: Somebody fouled up the detail, that's for sure. **1958** W. B. Plageman *Steel Cocoon* 55: A guy like that is a jinx. He could foul us all up. Don't you see that? *Ibid.* 165: He fouled it up!…We almost had it, just perfect, and he fouled it up! **1958** L. F. Cooley *Run for Home* 343: The sonuvabitch nearly fouled up the whole detail. **1966** Rose *The Russians Are Coming!* (film): You're gonna foul up the whole detail! **1966** J. Christopher *Little People* 179: And you're determined to foul it up if you can. **1971** N. Capaldi *Art of Deception* 95: He might easily fit both categories and hence foul up the classification again. **1971** K. W. Keith *Long Line Rider* 91: He put black pepper behin' 'em to foul up the dogs. **1971** J. N. Rowe *Five Years to Freedom* 402: My screwed-up additions to the map had done some good, even if they hadn't fouled Charlie up completely. **1989** C. Stoll *Cuckoo's Egg* 275: By 11:30, I'd fouled up two programs— what had worked an hour ago wasn't working now. **1996** K. Hafner & M. Lyon 181: To all but the initiated the scenarios book was fairly incomprehensible, and it was easy to foul up the system. **2001** J. Picoult *Salem Falls* 292: As laboratory technician, Arthur Quince had enough trouble trying to keep afloat at Duncan Pharmaceuticals without investigators coming along to foul up the rhythm of his day.

2. Originally *Navy & U.S. Marine Corps. intransitive.* to become confused, especially to blunder into or cause trouble; fail through confusion or ineptitude; go wrong or awry. [Frequently regarded as a euphemism for FUCK UP, definition 4.]

1944 *New Yorker* (May 6) 26: Look how we fouled up on maneuvers. **1946** S. Wilson *Voyage to Somewhere* 197: Pretty soon all the crew will know that to get a transfer, all they have to do is foul up. **1951** J. Kerouac *On the Road: The Original Scroll* (2007) 141: When Neal came out Justin gave him one more chance. But Neal fouled up again. **1954** E. Hunter *Blackboard Jungle* 27: They'd come to within a term of graduation, and they...didn't want to get thrown out of school for fouling up at this late stage of the game. **1956** M. Wolff *Big Nickelodeon* 243: You fouled up and the old man came and took the kid. **1958** in R. Schwitzgebel *Streetcorner Research* 21: We want to know why kids foul up and why they do the other things they do. **1964** R. Newhafer *Last Tallyho* 135: If anything fouls up, he wants to be there. **1965** S. Linakis *In Spring the War Ended* 292: I don't like to see a G.I. foul up. **1970** T. Thackrey *Thief* 295: Only my tipsters had fouled up again. **1978** J. Lee *13th Hour* 21: If anything can foul up, it will. **1972–79** T. Wolfe *Right Stuff* 265: Please, dear God, don't let me foul up. **1985** M. Atwood *Handmaid's Tale* 176: The system had fouled up before, but a few phone calls usually straightened it out. **1992** *Spectator* (Dec. 19) 33/1: I couldn't understand what he was saying, but I could see he was nervous. He fouled up several times, and each time he got more upset. **2004** I. Johansen *Blind Alley* 320: You shouldn't forget. You fouled up.... Maybe you'll learn something from it.

four Fs *noun* [partially punning on *4F*, draft status for a person physically unfit to serve]

a motto for sexual behavior: "find 'em, fool 'em, fuck 'em, and forget 'em." Also variants. Also as **fuck 'em and forget 'em** (with variants) without *four Fs*.

[**1934** L. Berg *Prison Nurse* 29: No one ever got rich letting suckers keep their dough. My motto is "find them, fool them, and forget them!"] [**1941** Macaulay & Wald *Manpower* (film): You're talkin' to the guy who finds 'em, feeds 'em and forgets 'em.] *a***1942** in A. B. Hollingshead *Elmtown's Youth* 422: The five F's —"find 'em, feed 'em, feel 'em, f— 'em, forget 'em." **1953** L. V. Berrey & M. Van den Bark *American Thesaurus of Slang* (ed. 2) 325: *The four F's*, high-pressure romancing—find 'em, fool 'em, frig 'em, and forget 'em. *a***1961** E. Partridge *Dictionary of Slang & Unconventional English* (ed. 5) 1096: *Four F method, the*. This is the lower-deck's allusive synonym (C.20) of its sexual motto, *find, feel, f**k and forget*, itself current since *ca*1890. **1965** *Playboy* (Nov.) 67: The Four F's. **1966** S. Harris & L. Freeman *Lords of Hell* 30: What a sportsman mean when he say weaving the four F's is—you got to find you chick and you got to fool her and you got to frig her and forget her! **1974** J. Lahr *Hot to Trot* 7: Melish, baby, the Four F's are forever....find 'em. Feel 'em. Fuck 'em. Forget 'em. **1978** S. Kopp *End to Innocence* 58: I aspired to the macho four Fs of my generation: find 'em, feel 'em, fuck 'em and forget 'em. **1978** W. Brown *Tragic Magic* 23: He could find them, fool them, feel them, fuck them, and forget them with exceptional agility. **1986** J. Ciardi *Good Words* 118: *Find 'em, fool 'em, fuck 'em, and forget 'em.*...I was first drilled to these orders in WWII and received them as essential GI pitch. **2006** L. Pitts *Becoming Dad* 196: Don't let any one of them tie you down. Follow the "four F's": find 'em, feel 'em, fuck 'em, forget 'em.

fox *noun*

In phrase:

☞ **hotter than a fresh-fucked fox in a forest fire**, extremely hot (in any sense). *Jocular.*

*ca*1950 in T. Atkinson *Dirty Comics* 197: Betty! This guy's got me hotter than a fresh fucked fox in a forest fire. **1973** *TULIPQ* (coll. B.K. Dumas): Horny...Hotter than a fresh-fucked fox in a forest fire. **1974** E. Thompson *Tattoo* 264 [refers to 1940s]: It's a bitch down there. Hotter than a fresh fucked fox in a forest fire. **1974** R. Blount *3 Bricks Shy* 307: I'm hotter than a freshly fucked fox in a forest fire. **1977** S. Gaines *Discotheque* 268: It's hotter in here than a fresh fucked fox in a forest fire. **1980** J. Ciardi *Browser's Dictionary* 41: Hot as a fresh fucked fox in a forest fire. **1988** D. Dye *Outrage* 125: Locker room wisdom held churchmen's daughters were "hotter'n a freshly fucked fox in a forest fire." **1997** E. Little *Another Day in Paradise* 14: The cops are looking all over for ya, you're hotter than a freshly fucked fox in a forest fire. **2006** C. Grabenstein *Slay Ride* 313: These bastards are going to swing around and start shooting at you the second you pull in. It'll be hotter than a fresh-fucked fox in a forest fire. Copy?

fox around *verb*

(used as a euphemism for FUCK AROUND, *verb*, sense 2).

1938 R. Chandler *Big Sleep* 108: So all you did was not report a murder that happened last night and then spend today foxing around so that this kid of Geiger's could commit a second murder this evening. **1998** B. R. Johnson *Woman Who Knew too Much* 44: I saw him foxing around out there, messing with some kind of gizmo he had by the river behind his house.

frak

(a partial euphemism for) FUCK, in various senses and parts of speech. [Coined on, and chiefly associated with, the television show *Battlestar Galactica*. In the Original Series (1978), used exclusively as an interjection; in the Reimagined Series (2003–2009), used more broadly as a euphemism for many forms of FUCK, both figurative and literal. Spelled *frack* in Original Series scripts, *frak* in the Reimagined Series, apparently because the producers wanted it to literally be a four-letter word.]

1978 *Ultimate Weapon* (Battlestar Galactica shooting script) (Sept. 14 reshoot) 13: STARBUCK'S COCKPIT...*He is furious.* STARBUCK Frack! **1978** *Galactica Terminology Sheet* (Battlestar Galactica Writers Guide, Universal City Studios) (Oct. 2); Frack!—an expletive. **1978** *Hand of God* (Battlestar Galactica shooting script) (undated) 38:*Starbuck turns to his right and we see a Cylon fighter fly past extremely close.* STARBUCK Oh...frack! **2005** *Hand of God* in *Battlestar Galactica* (Sci Fi Channel) (Mar. 11): We are well and truly frakked. **2006** *Scar* in *Battlestar Galactica* (Sci Fi Channel) (Feb. 3): I guaran-frakkin-tee you, I will put you down this time for good. **2006** *Lay Down Your Burdens, Part II* in *Battlestar Galactica* (Sci Fi Channel) (Mar. 10): You're not still trakkin' Dualla are ya? **2006** *Entertainment Weekly* (Sept. 29) 32: And it will be used to express rage after a high-ranking officer (nope, we ain't tellin') drives a pen into the neck of tortured traitor Gaius Baltar (James Callis) and screams "MOTHERFRAKKER!" **2007** *Crossroads, Part I* in *Battlestar Galactica* (Sci Fi Channel) (Mar. 18): You know this game's got frak-all to do with the real thing, right? **2009** *Calgary Herald* (Jan. 16) (Swerve section) 16: Be sure to take in the one-hour clip show that precedes the premiere for a refresher on what the frak is going on. Well, on most of what's going on; after all, this is *Lost* and what fun would it be to have all the answers?

frap [formed from FRAPPING]

(used as a euphemism for FUCK in various senses and parts of speech).

1980 G. Benford *Timescape* 100: And frap, you should see the antiburglar network. **1992** C. Eble *Campus Slang* (Fall) 3: What the frap is going on? **1998** *Washington Post* (Apr. 29) D4: "Frap," a way to curse without cursing ("Boy, I really frapped that up."). *Ibid. Off-brand frap...*"a lame girl." **2007** W. B. Scott et al. *Space Wars* 38: She and her boss didn't give a flyin' frap about space.

frapping *adjective*

Military. (a partial euphemism for) FUCKING, *adjective.*

    1968 W.C. Anderson *Gooney Bird* 76: We'll let a whole frapping regiment get away before we'll risk hitting one old lady in sneakers. **1970** *N.Y. Times* (Apr. 19) 1: And finally in desperation: "What's the frappin' altitude?" **1972** W.C. Anderson *Hurricane* 196: And the poor frapping navy! **1973** M. Collins *Carrying the Fire* 334: Yeah, but the frapping thing bombed out again. **1989** M. Berent *Rolling Thunder* 133: That frapping Dash-K is shooting out our cover by the frapping roots. **1991** *Soldier of Fortune* (Dec.) 48/1: I need a frapping medic like I need a hole in the head. **1994** J. Lovell & J. Kluger *Apollo 13* vi. 167: "What's the frappin' attitude?" Lovell asked. **2007** K. W. Fields *Rescue of Streetcar 304* 148: "I'm still alive, you frapping mothers," I mumbled out loud. I felt macho, but thought, *this is not real. It's too much like a frapping movie.*

freaking *adjective & adverb*

(a partial euphemism for) FUCKING, *adjective & adverb.*

    1928 M. Bodenheim *Georgie May* 9: Oh yuh cain't catch o-on to thuh freakin' Mistah Stave an' Chain. *Ibid.* 70: Ah hate the hull, freaking pack uh you. **1955** *Harper's* (Mar.) 35: Open the Freaking Door, Joe. **1961** G. Garrett *Which Ones Are the Enemy* 16: Not freaking likely. **1965** R. Hardman *Chaplains Raid* 1: A great big freaking disaster! **1972** C. Gaines *Stay Hungry* 152: He's freaking Superman is who he is. **1972–76** C. Durden *No Bugles, No Drums* 9: It's too freakin' late now. **1978** W. Wharton *Birdy* 276: It's like my freaking body has some kind of controls all its own. **1972–79** T. Wolfe *Right Stuff* 6: It was a struggle to move twenty feet in this freaking muck. **1982** *Flash* (Dec.) 10: Have you gone freakin' bananas? **1989** U.S. Navy officers, on *Prime News* (CNN-TV) (Jan. 5): "He's got a missile off!" "Freakin' right!" **1998** *Esquire* (Mar.) 148: Enough already with all the theory and dice games and analysts. Let's buy some freakin' stocks. **2005** *GQ* (Sept.) 196/3: You will be a guinea pig, but you will freaking love it.

frell

(a partial euphemism for) FUCK, in various senses and parts of speech. [Coined on, and chiefly associated with, the television show *Farscape*.]

1999 *Farscape* (Sci Fi Channel) (June 18): *John*: Well, gotta give me a clue here, Aeryn. Is this something new, or is this just your usual PMS, Peacekeeper military sh— *Aeryn*: Frell you. **2000** *Farscape* (Sci Fi Channel) (Aug. 4): *Dregon*: Because of all the days before it hurts. The good days when you're in love. It's too bad you can't get back to at least tell Crichton how you feel. *Aeryn*: What difference would it make? He's a frelling statue. *Dregon*: But he can hear, he can see, he'll know Aeryn, at least he'll know. **2001** *Farscape* (Sci Fi Channel) (Mar. 23): Work, frell you, work! *Ibid.* Frell me dead. **2002** *TV Zone* (No. 157) 82/1: If networks want to frell with the fans, then so be it. Let them continue to make mind-numbing drivel of TV shows like daily Soap Operas where the dumb and dumber will continue to tune in to watch absolutely no character development or true emotions. **2003** *Farscape* (Sci Fi Channel) (Feb. 28): Taken her back to my ship, frelled her, and made babies. **2003** *Horn Book Mag.* (July/Aug.) 503: We worked our frelling tails off for a whole year. **2003** *Farscape* (Sci Fi Channel) (Mar. 14): "You are so self-righteous! I have used all my skills, all my resources, for one perfect chance at peace. And because of you, it is gone! And I am…" "Frelled. Screwed. Raped."

French fuck *noun*

an act of rubbing the penis between a woman's breasts. Also as *verb*. Compare TIT-FUCK.

1938 "Justinian" *Americana Sexualis* 22: *French Fuck*. n. A form of sexual activity in which the male sits astride the recumbent female and achieves sexual orgasm by rubbing his penis between her breasts, while concomitantly effecting her orgasm by digital stimulation of her vaginal area. Br. & U.S., C. 19-20. **1974** U.S. graduate student: A…French fuck is when you rub your dick between her breasts. It's also called a *muscle fuck*. [Heard in Arkansas, *ca*1970.] **1997** *Jacob's Paradise (FFF, FFFM, teen)* on Usenet newsgroup alt.sex.stories (May 3): Jake decided he wanted to suck Amy's huge tits. He did this for about 5 minutes, until they were both aroused again, then he started to French fuck her while he fingerfucked her cunt.

frick

(a partial euphemism for) FUCK in various senses and parts of speech, esp. as **fricking** adjective.

1936 E. Partridge Dictionary of Slang & Unconventional English 982: Fricking. A s. euphemism for f**king, adj.: C.20 On or ex frigging, adj. **1942** J. Aldridge Signed with Their Honor 234: I wonder where those frickin' Jerries are. **1952** M. Cooper Sironia, Texas II. 1391: If you ever so much as thinks 'bout tellin' dat frickin' Night Chief anything, you goner get such a bust in de mouf my fist'll end up in yo' stummuck. **1967** W. Crawford Gresham's War 125: "And meantime?" "Frick the dog, I reckon." **1970** New York Magazine (Mar. 30) 32/2: "Frickin' kids.... Those frickin' kids." Frank never swears. **1970** in P. Heller In This Corner 237: That fricking bum. **1976** C. Rosen Mile Above the Rim 40: Jesus H. Keerist! What a fricken ball club! **1977** N. Dowd Slap Shot (film): Grab your frickin' gear and get goin'. **1986** L.A. Law (NBC-TV): You got a problem with that, you go live in the frickin' Soviet Union! **1987** U.S. college professor, age ca65: In Albany [N.Y., ca1934] we used frickin' a lot. Certainly more than friggin': "That frickin' son of a bitch!" **1988** J. F. Powers Wheat that Springeth Green 234: Well, I'll be fricked. **1989** CBS Summer Playhouse (CBS-TV): Who do you think you are? Attila the Hun? Jack the fricking Ripper? **1989** 21 Jump St. (Fox-TV): Absofrickin'lutely! We're talking total obliteration. **1992** N. Baker Vox 56: I get so fricking horny. **1998** Sick Puppy Comix (Sydney, Australia) (No. 7) 2: Maybe things will change now that I've got this frickin' hi-tech e-mail address. **2001** New York Magazine (Apr. 2) 15/4: One hundred thousand [New Yorkers] are waiting for some snotty salesgirl in Bergdorf's, 100,000 are on hold with NYNEX, or Verizon or AT&T or Lucent or whatever the frick the company is called now,…and the rest are stuck in traffic. **2001** FHM (Feb.) 120/1: ["]In American Pie, you utter the infamous line, "One time at band camp, I stuck a flute in my pussy!"—were you embarrassed at all at saying it?["] ["]God no! I fricking loved that script as soon as I got it.["] **2004** N. Flynn Another Bullshit Night in Suck City iii. 205: By morning it all will be gone—no inside no outside, no cardboard box no mansion, no birth no death, no container no contained, a Zen koan, a frikkin riddle. **2009** *Scrubs* (ABC-TV) (Feb. 3): "You know what? Frick them!" "Frick them? I'm one of them!" "But they're acting like a bunch of frick-heads. Sorry about all the f-bombs."

frig *noun*

1. an instance of masturbation.

1786 R. Burns in J. S. Farmer *Merry Songs* IV 282: Defrauds her wi' a frig or dry-bob. *ca*1890 *My Secret Life* V. viii. 171: I pulled out my prick and with two or three frigs spent in a spasm of pain and pleasure. *ca*1890 *My Secret Life* XI. xi.: A frig in a summer house. A frig in a grotto.

2. an act of copulation.

1888 *Stag Party* 62: What is the difference between a flag and a frig? One is bunting, the other is cunting. **1927** *Immortalia* 14: 'Twas a frig to a finish.

3. a damn; FUCK, *noun*, definition 3a.

1954–55 M. McCarthy *Charmed Life* 66: This is ridiculous....I don't give a frig about Sinnot's heredity. **1968** A. Myrer *Eagle* 61: Ain't worth a frig. **1988** J. Collins *Rock Star* 328: I don't give a frig. **2002** J. McGahern *That They May Face Rising Sun* (2003) 119: "If the thing was to break down now we'd be able to get up what's left with the forks." "What about my poor meadows?" "You wouldn't care a frig."

4. (a partial euphemism for) *the fuck* definition 1, under FUCK, *noun*.

1944 A. Kapelner *Lonely Boy Blues* 91: And who the frig is Sam Duncan? **1948** I. Wolfert *Act of Love* 239: Here the frig we go again. **1964** C. Howe *Valley of Fire* 98: Leave him the frig alone. **1978** R. De Christoforo *Grease* 96: And who the frig are you? **1997** A. Khan-Din *East is East* (rev. ed.) ii. v. 71: Who the frig do you think you are coming in here telling me my house isn't good enough for your daughters.

frig *verb*

1. [a specialization of the obsolete Standard English sense 'to rub or chafe'] to masturbate.

1598 J. Florio *Worlde of Wordes* 139/1: *Fricciare*...to frig, to wriggle, to tickle. *ca*1650 in J. Wardroper *Love & Drollery* (1969) 197: And lest her sire should not thrust home/She frigged her father in her mother's womb. **1680** Lord Rochester in *Oxford English Dictionary Supp.*: Poor pensive lover, in this place, Would Frigg upon his Mothers Face. *ca*1684 in Ashbee *Biblio.* II 333: All the rest pull out their dildoes and frigg in point of honour. *ca*1730 in E. J. Burford *Bawdy Verse* (1983) 254: *You* know, at fifty-five,/A man can only *frigg* her! **1734** in G. Legman *No Laughing Matter* (1975) III 18: Assembled, and Frigged upon the Test Platter. *ca*1716–46 in J. S. Farmer & W. E. Henley *Slang & Its Analogues* III 74: So to a House of office...a School-Boy does repair, To...fr— his P— there. **1785** F. Grose *Classical Dictionary of the Vulgar Tongue: To frig.* To be guilty of the crime of self-pollution. **1835** in J. E. Valle *Rocks & Shoals* (1980) 167: *Question.* Did you ever frig Lt. Burns? *A.* Yes— *Q.* How often? *A.* five or six times. **1865** Capt. E. Sellon *New Epicurean* 13: I frigged and kissed their fragrant cunnies. *ca*1866 *Romance of Lust* 27: Fortunately, I had never frigged myself. **1879** *Harlequin Prince Cherrytop* 29: Better frig, howe'er the mind it shocks,/Than from promiscuous fucking catch the pox. **1909** J. Joyce in *Selected Letters* 182: You... frigged me slowly till I came off through your fingers. **1940** J. Del Torto *Graffiti Transcript* (Kinsey Institute): My finger against his asshole....I pushed it up and began to frig him. **1957** A. Myrer *Big War* 361 [refers to WWII]: There'll be no friggin' in the riggin'...and no poopin' on the poop-deck. **1968** "A. D'Arcangelo" *Homosexual Handbook* 209: While you're approaching from the rear, you can reach around and frig her clitoris with a free hand. **1970** Peters *Sex Newspapers* 4: I began frigging myself even harder. **2002** R. Williams *Sing yer Heart out for Lads* ii. 65: Barry I'd give Posh Spice a fucking good seeing to I would. Fuck her till she screams. I'd strip off all her clothes, her damp and sticky knickers, I'd lay her down on the floor, frig her pussy with my finger, rubbing away at her clit, till she had an orgasm. Then I'd give her a fuck, long lingering fuck.

2.a. to copulate; (*hence*) to copulate with. [The earliest quotations—variants of the same ribald song—involve word play on the obsolete Standard English sense 'to move about restlessly; wiggle', and suggest that the current sense arose as a euphemism; note that as early as *ca*1650 the word seems to have been regarded as coarse and to be avoided.]

*ca*1610 in E. J. Burford *Bawdy Verse* (1983) 65: Faine woulde I try how I could frig/Up and downe, up and downe, up and downe,/Fain would I try how I could Caper. *ca*1650 in J. Wardroper *Love & Drollery* (1969) 186: Fain would I go both up and down…/No child is fonder of the gig/ Than I to dance a merry jig./Fain would I try how I could —. *ca*1684 in H. N. Cary *Sexual Vocabulary* II: You frigg as though you were afraid to hurt. 1865 Capt. E. Sellon *New Epicurean* 19: I had flung her on her back on the hay and was frigging away at her maidenhead. 1888 *Stag Party* 71: Why is the firing of an outhouse like flies frigging? It is arson on a small scale. *ca*1889 E. Field *Boastful Yak*: She would have been frigged, but he re-neagued. 1918–19 in M. B. Carey, Jr. *Mlle. from Armentières* II (unpaged): The first Division is having a time,/Frigging the Fraus along the Rhine. 1916–22 H. N. Cary *Sexual Vocabulary* I under *copulation*: *Frigging like a mink.* To perform with vigor. *frigging like a rabbit.* To have great capacity. 1922 H.L. Mencken in T. P. Riggio *Dreiser-Mencken Letters* II 463: But frigging, as you must know, is invariably unlawful, save under ecclesiastical permit. 1922 T. F. Lawrence *The Mint* (1955) 155: [It sounded] like a pack of skeletons frigging on a tin roof. 1927 in E. Wilson *Twenties* 413: Story about the fellow whose girl kept on eatin' an apple all the time he was friggin' her. 1927 *Immortalia* 32: The Khan would rather frig than fight. 1930 *Lyra Ebriosa* 12: We'll go over and do some friggin';/Dollar and a half will pay your fee. 1934 in V. Randolph *Pissing in Snow* 88: She was better frigging than the other girl, so he diddled her twice. 1938 "Justinian" *Americana Sexualis* 23: *Frig (Frick).* v. To copulate with….Often used as euphemistic expletive for the phrase "Fuck it!" 1942 W. L. McAtee *Supplement to Grant Co.* 4 [refers to 1890s]: *Frig,* v., copulate. 1942 in G. Legman *Limerick* (1954) 18: A young wife…/Preferred frigging to going to mass. 1944 in P. Smith *Letters from Father* 426: He would "frig" her himself. 1951 W. Styron *Lie down in Darkness* (1992) vii. 389: Christine say she want to frig wid me. 1969 R. Jessup *Sailor* 6: Better than you, letting him come up here while I'm at work and frigging from morning til night, probably. 1998 S. Waters *Tipping Velvet* xii. 267: I had not *fucked* her, we had not *frigged*.

b. (used as an expletive); "screw"; to hell with; (*hence*) to disregard utterly. [Frequently regarded as a partial euphemism for FUCK, *verb*, definition 2a.]

1879 *Pearl* 103: Two prisoners were brought in…. The Sergeant requested orders regarding them. The Major merrily answered: "Oh, take them away and frig them!" **1905** in J. Joyce *Letters* II. 104: Cosgrave says it's unfair for you to frig the one idea about love which he had before he met you, and say "You have educated him too much." **1929–35** J. T. Farrell *Judgment Day* 629: Phrigg you, Catherine! **1936** S. Kingsley *Dead End* 691: *Spit. Frig you! Drina...* I'll crack you... you talk like that! **1938** J. O'Hara *Hope of Heaven* 131: Frig dat. **1940** L. Zinberg *Walk Hard, Talk Loud* 133: Aw, frig it, if I hadn't been expecting a fight... it wouldn't of happened. **1946** W. L. Gresham *Nightmare Alley* 20: Frig him, the Bible-spouting bastard. **1948** I. Wolfert *Act of Love* 155: Frig them. *Ibid.* 399: The Navy was still saying, Frig you Joe, I'm okay. **1949** A. I. Bezzerides *Thieves' Market* 23: Frig Mom, let her try to stop me. **1953** W. Manchester *City of Anger* 116: Frig trouble, I always say. Better frig it before it frigs you. **1956** G. Metalious *Peyton Place* 358: "Frig you," said Kenny hostilely. **1965** C. Himes *Cotton comes to Harlem* (1988) xiv. 98: Deke looked up at him as though from a great distance. He looked as though he didn't care about anything any more. "Frig you," he said. **1970** M. Gattzden *Black Vendetta* 102: Let's frig it. **1980** J. McAleer & B. Dickson *Unit Pride* 96: Frig 'em all and their mothers too. All but six and leave them for pallbearers. **1982** P. Redmond *Brookside* ((Mersey TV transmission script) Episode 6.) 21: *Bongo.* We could always go down town. *Ducksie.* Frig that. Too bleedin' cold. **1992** J. Cartwright *Rise & Fall of Little Voice* i. 9: When am I this morning, the Okay Corral or what? Frig me. Don't put loads of bloody sugar in yours an all.

c. to cheat. [Frequently regarded as a partial euphemism for FUCK, *verb*, definition 4a.]

[*ca*1684 in Ashbee *Biblio.* II 339: I'll then invade and bugger all the Gods/And drain the spring of their immortal cods,/Then make them rub their arses till they cry,/You've frigged us out of immortality.] **1928** *American Speech* III (Feb.) 219: *Frig.* To trick, to take advantage of. "They frigged me out of the last bottle of Scotch!" **1935** J. Conroy *World to Win* 209: They'll frig themselves and ever'body else out of a job. **1945** in S. J. Perelman *Don't Tread on Me* 60: I don't use a literary agent, but I probably should, because I have been frigged time and again by publishers. **1952** H. Grey *Hoods* 88: He's the kind of guy who talks through both sides of his mouth and whistles "I frig you truly."

3. to trifle or fool about.—used with *with, about,* or *around*. [Frequently regarded as a partial euphemism for FUCK, *verb*, definition 5.]

1785 F. Grose *Classical Dictionary of the Vulgar Tongue*: *To frig*. ...
Frigging is also used figuratively for trifling. **1811** in F. W.
Howay *Voyage of the New Hazard* (1938) 15: Staying jib-boom; loosing and handing sails over; getting boat on the quarter and frigging about all the afternoon. **ca1900** in *English Dialect Dictionary*: I can do nothing while you keep frigging about. **1928** C. McKay *Banjo* 241: Don't think I like frigging round officials. I hate it. **1930** T. Fredenburgh *Soldiers March!* 151 [refers to 1918]: What the hell do you want, frigging around that echelon? **1933** J. Masefield *Conway* 211 [refers to 1891]: *Frig about*, to fool around. **1940** E. Hemingway *For Whom the Bell Tolls* 272: We do not let the gypsy nor others frig with it. **1946** J. H. Burns *Gallery* 301: Untying his shoelaces and frigging with the buckles on his boots. **1949** H. Ellson *Tomboy* 127: Do you let any punk in the mob frig around with you? **1952** H. Grey *Hoods* 225: No friggin' around. **1954** B. Schulberg *On the Waterfront* 11: I worked too hard for what I got to frig around with a cheese-eater. Know what I mean? **1961** A. J. Roth *Shame of Wounds* 34: Now if you was in my gang, we'd fix Nolan for you. He don't frig around with none of us. **1962** R. Dougherty *Commissioner* 187: You go in there—no friggin' around. **1975** J. Gould *Maine Lingo* 102: *Frig*. A word with four-letter nuance almost everywhere except Maine. Here, it means fiddle around, dawdle, fidget, fuss, fondle idly, putter. A Maine lady of unimpeachable gentility once described her late husband as nervous and ill at ease in public, and said he would sit "*frigging* with his necktie." **1988** M. Bail *Holden's Performance* 113: You can't frig around with nature. **2001** A. Wheatle *East of Acre Lane* 4: Don't frig about, Chaks, you'll get de t'ings back, no worries.

In phrase:

☞ **go frig [yourself]!** get away! go to hell!

   1936 S. Kingsley *Dead End* 726: Ah, go frig! **1946** W. L. Gresham *Nightmare Alley* 47: Go frig a rubber duck. **1951** W. J. Sheldon *Troubling of a Star* 20: Tell the bastard to go frig himself. **1961** A. J. Roth *Shame of Wounds* 213: They stared at each other for several seconds. Then Red lowered his eyes and muttered uneasily. "Aw, go frig yourself." **1984** T. Robbins *Jitterbug Perfume* 48: You have strayed from your kingdom, Your Majesty. I am not subject to your authority. In fact, go frig yourself. **2000** J. Brady *Marines of Autumn* 200: Izzo told them to go frig themselves.

frigger *noun*

1. a person who frigs.

1659 G. Torriano *Vocabolario Italiano & Inglese: Frugatoio…*a frigger, a clown, a wriggler up and down. **1879** *Harlequin Prince Cherrytop* 12: Such cheek from a half-hung selfish frigger. *ca***1890** *My Secret Life* VIII. ix.: She was a wonderful frigger.—Her masturbation was most delicate and fetching (some women never can frig).

2. (a partial euphemism for) FUCKER, definition 2.

1953 W. Manchester *City of Anger* 145: That bastard… that no good frigger. **1989** *Viz* (Oct.–Nov.) 24/2 (in cartoon): Fuck! It's deed! Hey! It is n'all! Eh? It was alreet when I wrapped the frigger up this mornin'. **2002** J. McGahern *That They May Face Rising Sun* (2003) 260: Don't be standing up for him, Kate…. Give him an inch and the frigger will build nests in your ears.

frigging *adjective & adverb*

contemptible or despicable; damned; (often used with reduced force for emphasis). Also as infix. [Perhaps originally derived from literal phrases such as *frigging youngster, frigging madman,* etc., used opprobriously; now usually regarded as a partial euphemism for FUCKING.]

*a***1890–93** J. S. Farmer & W. E. Henley *Slang & Its Analogues* III 74: *Frigging…Adj. and adv.* (vulgar).—An expletive of intensification. Thus *frigging bad*—"bloody" bad; a *frigging idiot*—an absolute fool. **1929–30** J. Dos Passos *42nd Parallel* 55: If people only realized how friggin' easy it would be. *Ibid.* 89: I told 'em I was a friggin' bookagent to get into the damn town. **1943** in P. Smith *Letters from Father* 332: It was a "friggen" swell party. **1944** F. Wakeman *Shore Leave* 10: It took me three more weeks to get off that frigging island. **1947** W. Motley *Knock on Any Door* 194: I'm no friggin' good. **1948** I. Wolfert *Act of Love* 136: On your feet, you friggin' volunteers. **1949** A. I. Bezzerides *Thieves' Market* 3: You're frigging right, Pa. **1947–52** R. Ellison *Invisible Man* 192: A frigging eight-day wonder. **1954** F. I. Gwaltney *Heaven & Hell* 264 [refers to WWII]: That would be oh-friggen-kay with me. **1956** G. Metalious *Peyton Place* 93: Where's the friggin' bottle? **1957** Mayfield *Hit* 89: "Is he the only one who can drive this friggin' car?" squealed Frank. **1968** P. Larkin *Letter* (Aug. 19) in A. Thwaite *Selected Letters of Philip Larkin* (1992) 403: Your whacking great book on Stalin's purges came this afternoon; I began putting my nose in it as a change from writing my frigging annual report. **1974** M. Cherry *On High Steel* 160: So friggin' what? **1980** J. Carroll *Land of Laughs* 22: I got the friggin' renewal already. **1986** *Newsweek* (Jul. 28) 26: I said, "Give me a break, this ain't no frigging war." **1989** *Tour of Duty* (CBS-TV): There ain't no friggin' justice! **1991** R. Marcinko & J. Weisman *Rogue Warrior* 63: I don't frigging believe it. **1992** N. Cohn *Heart of World* 9: Straight off the friggin' boats. **1995** C. D. Short *Shining Shining Path* iii. 57: The wonderful weather was holding and every single aspect was going so ab, so, frigging, lutely, *perfect*. **2001** C. Palahniuk *Choke* ii. 12: All these people you think are a big joke. Go ahead and frigging laugh your frigging head off.

frigging-A *interjection*

(a partial euphemism for) FUCKING-A.

1966 J. Kerouac in *Evergreen Review* X. 84/2: I heard somebody say to another guy :- "*Le roi n'est pas amusez*." (The king is not amused.) ("You frigging A!" I shoulda yelled out the window.) **1971** Jacobs & Casey *Grease* 13: DANNY. Is that all you ever think about, Sonny? SONNY.... Friggin'-A! **1973** W. Crawford *Stryker* 41: You're friggin-A-well right I would have. **1979** W. P. McGivern *Soldiers of '44* 139 [refers to WWII]: "So you know what I'm thinking."..."Frigging A." **1984** in W. Safire *You Could Look It Up* 120: A euphemism from my adolescence, like "Friggin'-A, I'm going." **1992** C. Sellers *World Ablaze* 149: "Frigging-A right!" Sloan yelled, and stood up to empty his clip at the enemy's flank.

frig off *verb*

1. to masturbate to orgasm.

1909 J. Joyce in *Selected Letters* 191: Do you frig yourself off first? **1955** "Thirty-Five" *The Argot: Frig up* To mess up (euphemism),...In literal sense, *to frig oneself off*, to masturbate. **1979** *American Speech* LI 22 [refers to ca1950]: *Frig* and *frig off*.

2. to go away; go to hell.—used imperatively. [Regarded as a partial euphemism for FUCK OFF, definition 1.]

> **1961** A.J. Roth *Shame of Wounds* 141: "Go on, frig off," Red's scowl dared him. "See how far you get by yourself." **1965** in *Oxford English Dictionary Supp.*: "Frig off," he said, swinging towards the door.

frig-up *noun*

(a partial euphemism for) FUCK-UP, definitions 1 & 2.

> **1941** S. J. Baker *Dict. Australian Slang* 30: *Frigg-up*, a confusion, muddle. **1948** I. Shaw *Young Lions* 542: You're the frig-ups of the Army. **1954** F. I. Gwaltney *Heaven & Hell* 15 [refers to WWII]: Hell no! I ain't no frigup. *Ibid.* 18: They're frigups, sure, but they ain't jailbirds. **1992** J. Cartwright *Rise & Fall of Little Voice* 45: I've just been involved with the worst...frig-up in Mari's history.

frig up *verb*

1. (a partial euphemism for) FUCK UP, definition 1.

> **1933** in J. Dos Passos *14th Chronicle* 428: All my plans for work are frigged up for fair, too. **1937** J. Weidman *I Can Get It for You Wholesale* 60: Something's frigged up around here! **1942** S.J. Baker *Australian Language* 267: It is common in English for *up* to be added in a verbal sense, thus *mess up, rust up, knock up,* and even for certain nounal forms to emerge.... Thus we have...*frigg-up* or *muck-up*, a confusion, a row or argument.] **1954** F.I. Gwaltney *Heaven & Hell* 26: When they frigup [*sic*] here, they ain't no place to send 'em except home in a box. *a*1966 S.J. Baker *Australian Language* (ed. 2) 217: *Frig up*, to mar. **1985** L. Choyce *Why I Live Where I Live* in *Avalanche Ocean* (1987) iii. viii. 166: The warm weather had frigged up any possibility of decent snowmobiling. **1992** S. King *Dolores Claiborne* 62: The person in charge isn't there to frig it up.

2. (a partial euphemism for) FUCK UP, definition 2a.

> **1948** I. Shaw *Young Lions* 595: Every day they bury a thousand like you, and the guys like me, who never frigged up, go over the lists and send up a thousand more. **1953** "F. Paley" *Rumble on the Docks* 257: The Stompers are saying that only a Digger could frig up like that. *a*1981 in

S. King *Bachman* 470: No, I frigged up. **2001** L.E. Modesitt *Octagonal Raven* 463: You've frigged up bad.

fsck [after *fsck*, the name of a command on the Unix operating system that checks and repairs disk errors, from *file*system *check*] *Computing.* (a partial euphemism for) FUCK, in various senses and parts of speech.

1992 *Re: IIGS RGB Out of Focus* on Usenet newsgroup comp.sys.apple2 (Apr. 3): Caveat: I learned about fscking around inside equipment like this (high voltage) as a kid, from my dad.... You can easily kill yourself, even with the power cord unplugged. **1992** *Re: Pickup Lines* on Usenet newsgroup soc.singles (July 12): Wanna fsck? **1995** *Re: Slight flame from Linux user* on Usenet newsgroup comp.unix.bsd.freebsd misc (June 7): Now what the fuck am I meant to do? **2006** *Around The Water Cooler: Best comment thread roundup* on *Lifehacker* (online) (Dec. 11): Okay, that right there is fscking HOT.

FTA *interjection*
Army. "*f*uck *t*he *A*rmy."

1958 "D. Harde" *Lusty Limericks* 44: Marching Song of the F.T.A. (Fuck The Army). **1963** T. Doulis *Path for our Valor* 32: "And what does FTA stand for, Specialist?"... "Sir...excuse me....The initials stand for Fuck the Army." **1969** *N.Y. Times Magazine* (May 18) 122: Some of the blacks gave the closed-fist militant salute and several soldiers shouted "F.T.A."—initials which recruiting sergeants insist stand for "Fun, Travel, and Adventure" but which most soldiers recognize as a suggestion of what should be done to the Army. **1970** W. Just *Military Men* 67: The slogan is F.T.A., which means Fuck the Army. **1984** R. Riggan *Free Fire Zone* 109: New helmet covers with none of that FTA stuff written in ballpoint pen on them. **1989** D. Hackworth & J. Sherman *About Face* xix. 656: One of the RTOs in Slater's Operations shop had the letters "FTA" printed boldly on his helmet cover in two-inch-high letters. *a***2007** S. Estes *Ask & Tell* v. 144: There was this whole bad attitude thing about the military, you know, "FTA: Fuck the Army." Scratch it on the walls, write it on the latrines, FTA, FTA, FTA.

FTL *interjection*
"*f*uck *t*he *l*aw."

> **1992** *New Yorker* (May 18) 28: The graffiti on the walls everywhere said "F.T.L."—I was told that it stood for "Fuck the Law." **1995** H. Rawson *Dictionary of Euphemisms* (rev. ed.) 157: Kids still write "FTL" on walls instead of "Fuck The Law." **1996** M. B. Hunt *Sociolinguistics of Tagging & Chicano Gang Graffiti* (Ph.D. Diss., Univ. Southern California) 94: *FTL*—Fuck the Law.

FTN *interjection*
Navy. "*f*uck *t*he *N*avy."

> **1982** F. Mosco *Whitemoon Crisis* (2004) 47: Says right there under the anchor, FTN. That means, Fuck the Navy. **1992** M. Sprouse *Sabotage in American Workplace* 74: One guy was constantly harassed and attacked, especially after he carved FTN (fuck the Navy) in his forearm. **2004** C. Burke *Camp All-American, Hanoi Jane, and the High-and-Tight* 245: FTN: fuck the Navy (an FTN space is a small space in a ship where a sailor can hide from officers).

FTW *interjection*
"*f*uck *t*he *w*orld."

> **1968** *Psychiatry & Social Science Review* II. 16: Fuck the world (FTW) is their motto and that they have done since their California founding in the early 1950's. **1972** R.A. Wilson *Playboy's Book of Forbidden Words* 113: *F.T.W.* A slogan of Hell's Angels...meaning *fuck the world.* **1981** *Easyriders* (Oct.) 68: F.T.W. **1991** D. Gaines *Teenage Wasteland* iii. 67: Joe grabs my arm and draws a tattoo: an iron cross with a snake in the center in purple felt pen; "F.T.W." on the top, "M.O.D." on the bottom. He explains as he retraces his artwork on my arm. "Fuck the World" and "Method of Destruction." **1995** S. Moore *In the Cut* 111: I saw the letters FTW tattooed crudely on the boy's arm. **2004** J. Meno *Hairstyles of Damned* 203: They were your typical stoners, one with a black baseball bat that read "F.T.W."—which stood for Fuck the World.

fubar *adjective* ["*f*ucked *u*p *b*eyond *a*ll *r*ecognition"; suggested by SNAFU, definition 1]

1. Originally *Military*. thoroughly botched or confused. Also **fubar'd**. Occasionally as *noun. Jocular.*

1944 *Yank* (Jan. 7) 8: The FUBAR Squadron.... FUBAR? It means "Fouled Up Beyond All Recognition." **1944** *Newsweek* (Feb. 7) 61: Recent additions to the ever-changing lexicon of the armed services: *Fubar*. Fouled up beyond all recognition. **1944** in R. L. Tobin *Invasion Journal* 48: The Italian campaign was SNAFU for so long.... SNAFU... means, Situation Normal All Fouled Up—with, of course, an unprintable variation in the most common use....To be FUBAR is much worse. It means Fouled Up Beyond All Recognition. **1952** L. Uris *Battle Cry* 114: Fubar on the nets and you can louse up an entire landing team. *Ibid.* 300: A full-scale fubar'd mess. **1957** A. Myrer *Big War* 119: What's to this yarn about you being a fubar character from the word advance? **1972** B. Davidson *Cut Off* 30 [refers to WWII]. An even stronger superlative was Fubar—Fucked Up Beyond All Recognition. **1982** *Daily Beacon* (univ. newspaper) (Feb. 3) 2: Move it, fubar! **1987** *Daily Beacon* (univ. newspaper) (Apr. 9) 4: I already have a name picked out for my license plate...."FUBAR." figure it out for yourself. [*Hint*]...beyond all repair. **1990** E. W. Rukuza *West Coast Turnaround* 196: And the situation? FUBAR.

2. thoroughly intoxicated.

1985 U.S. college student: *Fubar* means drunk. Like, "Man, I was fubar last night." **1990** J. Sanders *Cal Poly Slang* 4: *Fubar*—intoxicated beyond all recognition. [Example:] I was so *fubar* I couldn't find my date to take her home. **1991** C. Eble *Campus Slang* (Fall) 2: *Fubar*—very drunk. **1998** *Canberra Times* (Australia) (May 30) A2: Many terms [for drunkenness] are insults—"full as a tick" and the acronym FUBAR, "fouled up beyond all recognition."

fubar *verb*

to ruin; botch; SNAFU, *verb.*

1946 "J. MacDougal" in *Astounding Science Fiction* (Oct.) 55/1: Well, there are a lot of minor ones, which must have fubared things in all directions once Co-ordination accepted them. **1953** L. M. Uris *Battle Cry* 114: Fubar on the nets and you can louse up an entire landing team. **1995**

N. Stephenson *Diamond Age* 147: Financial transactions could no longer be monitored by governments, and the tax collection systems got fubared. **2001** O. West *Sharkman Six* xxii. 271: Nothing—not these fubared rules, this fubared country, or even the ambush—excuses Armstrong.

FUBB *adjective* [suggested by FUBAR]
Originally *Military*. *"fucked up beyond belief." Jocular.* [In 2000 quote, as *noun*.]

1952 *Time* (Aug. 18) 6: Snafu and cummfu are a bit old hat in Washington, along with tarfu ("things are really"), fubar ("beyond all realization"), fubb ("beyond belief"). **1979** J. Homer *Jargon* 162. **1984** K. Weaver *Texas Crude* 40: *F.U.B.B.*... Fucked Up Beyond Belief. **2000** P. Morgan *Parrot's Beak* 143: In Vietnam, we called it a FUBB, fucked up beyond belief.

FUBIO *interjection*
Military. *"fuck you, bub, it's over." Jocular.*

1946 *American Speech* (Feb.) 72: The final word came after V-J day, FUBIO. Its description of the post-war attitude...meant "F— You, Bub, It's Over."

FUBIS or **FYBIS** *interjection*
Army. *"fuck you, buddy, I'm shipping out (or short)."* Compare FIGMO.

1967 H. Wentworth & S. B. Flexner *Dictionary of American Slang* (supplement) 685: *Fubis*...Fuck you, buddy, I'm shipping (out). *Army use since c1960.* **2007** L. Bucher *Sea Stories* 331: My own simple design consisted only of large, fat letters: FYBIS (Fuck You, Buddy, I'm Short).

fuck *noun* [see etymology and note at the verb]
1. a. an act of copulation.

1663 R. Head *Hic et Ubique* I. vi. 18: I did creep in...and there I did see putting [*sic*] the great fuck upon my weef. **1676** *Lampoon* in G. Williams *Dict. Sexual Language & Imagery in Shakespearean & Stuart Literature* (1994) I. 563: Her wider cunt did gape/For a more substantial fuck.

1680 Lord Rochester *Poems* 37: Thus was I Rook'd of Twelve substantial Fucks. **1763** in J. Atkins *Sex in Literature* IV 154: Then just a few good fucks, and then we die. *a***1850** in H. N. Cary *Slang of Venery* I 91: Well mounted on a mettled steed,/Famed for his strength as well as speed,/Corinna and her favorite buck/Are please'd to have a flying f—k. **1865** "Philocomus" *Love Feast* vi. 59: Whoever thought 'twould be my luck/To get from my own sex a fuck. *ca***1866** *Romance of Lust* 35: I wished to quietly enjoy a fuck. **1867** in A. Doten *Journals* II 949 [in cipher]: Me & my love have had this far just one hundred good square fucks together. **1879** *Harlequin Prince Cherrytop* 28: Now we can do no better I'll be bound,/Than to celebrate our joy with fucks all round. **1879** *Pearl* 127: Oh! What a nice fuck! **1888** *Stag Party* 42: Adonis...gave her a most systematical fuck. **1899** *Memoirs of Dolly Morton* 249: Here goes for the fust fuck. **1923** *Poems, Ballads, & Parodies* 22: He was working like a son of a bitch/To get another fuck. **1928** in A. W. Read *Lexical Evidence from Folk Epigraphy* (1935) 55: Me and my wife had a fuck **1934** "J. M. Hall" *Anecdota Americana* (Second series) 26: Every time you threw a fuck into me I put a penny in the bank. **1934** H. Miller *Tropic of Cancer* 78: He has absolutely no ambition except to get a fuck every night. **1938** H. Miller *Tropic of Capricorn* 104: Into each...one...I throw an imaginary fuck. **1940** *Ramirez v. State* [of Arizona], in *Pacific Reporter, 2d Series* CIII 461: While she was in bed asleep the defendant entered her room, grabbed her by the throat... he stood at the head of her bed and when she awoke made this statement to her: "Gonna throw a fuck into you"; that he did not say, "I'm going to" but just "gonna"; that after telling her this he loosened his grip somewhat and kissed her. **1947** C. Willingham *End as a Man* 240: A fuck for a buck. **1956** J. Cheever in *Letters* (1988) 178: You've just talked yourself out of a fuck. **1971** *Go Ask Alice* 117: All I needed was a good fuck. **1987** K. Lette *Girls' Night Out* (1989) 99: There aren't many things that beat getting your best friend arrested. One is losing a limb down the food disposal unit. Another is remembering in the middle of a fuck that you've still got a tampon in. **1990** L.B. Rubin *Erotic Wars* 75: All she wanted was "a good clean fuck." **1997** *GQ* (Mar.) 166: Good cry, good hug, one last fuck for old times' sake. **2006** L. Douglas *Catastrophist* 263: "So why did you stop after only two fucks? Well?" "I don't know. It just seemed enough."

b. as a mass noun: copulation.

*ca***1675** in R. Thompson *Unfit for Modest Ears* 49: If guifted Men before now sweare and Rant/(Then surely I for Fuck may Cant). **1687** *Last Night's*

Ramble in G. Williams *Dict. Sexual Language & Imagery in Shakespearean & Stuart Literature* (1994) I. 563: Half Ten Guineas spent in wine and F—k. **1689** *Satire on Benting* in G. Williams *Dict. Sexual Language & Imagery in Shakespearean & Stuart Literature* (1994) I. 563: She wanted fuck in her old age. **a1720** in T. D'Urfey *Pills* VI 266: She'd dance and she'd caper as wild as a Buck,/And told *Tom* the *Tinker*, she would have some —. **1860** in M. E. Neely *Lincoln Encyclopedia* (1984) 155: When Douglas found his chances were scarcely worth a shuck/He bade his Delegates, go home, to take a little fu—. **1889** Capt. C. Devereaux *Venus in India* 37: He added his initials and "WTBF?" "What does it mean?" I asked. "'Will there be fuck?' of course." **1918** in M. B. Carey *Mlle. from Armentières* II (unpaged): The S.O.S. was sure out of luck,/They stayed behind and got all the —. **1938** H. Miller *Tropic of Capricorn* 104: The place is just plastered with cunt and fuck.

c. a person considered as a sexual partner. Chiefly with a modifying word.

1870 *Cythera's Hymnal* 75: A young woman got married at Chester,/ Her mother she kissed and she blessed her./Says she, "You're in luck,/ He's a stunning good fuck,/For I've had him myself down in Leicester." **1874** *Letter from Friend in Paris* II. 168: I had always held that dear momma was the best fuck in the family, and in every way a most desirable and splendid creature. **ca1890** *My Secret Life* II. iii. 57: Is she a good fuck? Where does she live? **ca1927** in P. Smith *Letters from Father* 141: What a fuck she was. **1934** "J.M. Hall" *Anecdota Americana* (Second series) 27: You are a much better fuck than your old mammy here. **1938** "Justinian" *Americana Sexualis* 23: She'd make a good fuck! **1963–64** K. Kesey *Sometimes a Great Notion* 193: A cigar is just a cigar, but a good woman is a fuck. **1969** M. Lynch *American Soldier* 163: She was a good fuck. She did everything I told her. **1972** B. Rodgers *Queens' Vernacular* 87: Was Tyrone a good fuck? **1977** N. Wexler *Saturday Night Fever* (film): If you're as good in bed as you are on the dance floor, I bet you're one lousy fuck. **1977** A. Patrick *Beyond Law* 57: One o' the nicest little gals and sweetest little fucks a man could ask for. **1979** O. Clark *Diary* (May 10) in H. Rous *Ossie Clark Diaries* (1998) 84: Angie stayed in Marianne's bed—she is a junkie who was in Jimi Hendrix's dressing room so long ago. "She's a wonderful fuck," said Marianne the following day. **1983** J. Groen & D. Groen *Huey* 122: She's sure a wild fuck. **1984**

"Pickles" *Queens* 34: Perhaps the commonest threat to success is the arrival of friends or former fucks. **1992** J. Eszterhas *Basic Instinct* (film script): I think she's the fuck of the century, don't you? **1993** B. Moore *Lexicon of Cadet Language* 151: *Fuck*...a girlfriend.... "Are you off with the fuck tonight?" **2000** E. L. Harris *Not a Day Goes By* 212: "He is the best fuck I've ever had." "You slept with him?" "There was no sleeping going on." **2008** A. Guthrie *Savage Night* 14: She was a great fuck, but she wasn't worth dying for.

2. a. the least bit; a damn.—usually used in phrases like *not give a fuck* or *not care a fuck*. [The *ca*1790 quotation, from a satirical poem ("The Discontented Student"), concerns a young man who cannot make love to his wife at night because he is preoccupied with his books, yet conversely cannot concentrate on his studies during the day. Sense seems to demand that the excised phrase in its final line be "a fuck"; no other word is correspondingly vulgar, and only *fuck* makes the pun work.]

*ca***1790** St. G. Tucker in *Poems* (1977) 144: Our scholar every night/ Thinks of his books; and of his bride by light.... /"My wife—a plague!— keeps running in my head/In ev'ry page I read[,] my raging fires/Portray her yielding to my fierce desires."/"G— d— your books!" the testy father said,/"I'd not give — for all you've read." **1879** *Harlequin Prince Cherrytop* 19: For all your threats I don't care a fuck./I'll never leave my princely darling duck. **1917** in E. Wilson *Prelude* 184: An English soldier on the boat: "I down't give a fuck if the bowt goes dahn, it doesn't belong to me!" **1926** F. Wray trans. H. Barbusse *Under Fire* 283: He doesn't care a f— for us. **1929** F. Manning *Middle Parts of Fortune* 48 [refers to WWI]: They don't care a fuck 'ow us'ns live. **1931** J. Dos Passos *Nineteen Nineteen* 200 [refers to 1919]: The bosun said it was the end of civilization and the cook said he didn't give a f—k. **1934** H. Miller *Tropic of Cancer* 22: Nobody gives a fuck about her except to use her. **1935** T. Wolfe *Death to Morning* 74 [refers to 1917]: I don't give a f— what ya t'ought. **1936** in P. Oliver *Blues Tradition* 246: When I first met you I thought I fell in good luck,/Now I know you ain't worth a —. **1946** in J. Jones *Reach* 61: It dont mean a *fuck* to me. **1960** G. Sire *Deathmakers* 44: They don't give a fuck about you. **1965** B. D. Reeves *Night Action* 86: It mattered not a fuck. **1969** N.Y.C. man, age *ca*30: Doesn't that pull on your heartstrings? Or don't you give a rusty fuck? **1969–71** R. Kahn *Boys of Summer* 107: Rocco's a helluva man, but that don't mean a fuck. **1974** R. Carter *16th Round* 53: What makes you think that I give a fuck about you—or the horse you came to town on? **1972–76** C. Durden *No Bugles, No Drums* 9: Nobody gives two fucks. **1977** Dowd *Slap Shot* (film): It don't make a fuck's bit of difference. **1979** D. Thoreau *City at Bay* 36: Who gives a rusty fuck about some wino? **1995** *New York Review of Books* (June 8) 48: Education nowadays isn't worth a tup-ney fuck. **1998** J. Lahr in *New Yorker* (Sept. 7) 80: The actor doesn't care a fuck about Shakespeare. The director doesn't care a fuck about Shakespeare. He never really encounters Shakespeare. **2005** A. Smith *Accidental* 26: Why should I care about him when he clearly doesn't give a fuck about me.

b. anything whatsoever.—used in negative.

1970 D. Crosby in *Rolling Stone* (July 23) 27/2: The Byrds would come there and be a mechanical windup doll. They didn't play fuck. **1971** *National Lampoon* (Dec.) 58: That croaker don't know fuck.

c. (used with *like, as,* or *than* as an emphatic standard of comparison).—also used with *a.*

1938 in G. Legman *Limerick* (1954) 393: The colloquial comparative, "hotter than a Persian fuck." **1969** T. Raworth *Serial Biography* 66: Burned like fuck he said. Had to smear ointment all over it. **1976** C.R. Anderson *Grunts* 61 [refers to 1969]: To them it was still hotter than fuck and rising. **1978** in T. O'Brien *Things They Carried* 171: I'm sure as fuck not *going* anywhere. **1980** S. Whalen *It Takes a Man to Cry* 272: "You in pain, man?"… "It stings like a fuck." **1983** M. Thickett *Outrageously Offensive Jokes* 60: It's raining like a fuck outside. **1980–86** in D. J. Steffensmeier *Fence* 5: You sure as fuck don't go around telling people: I'm a fence! **1988** "N.W.A." *Fuck tha Police* (rap song): I'm sneaky as fuck when it comes to crime. **1988** P. Duncan *84 Charlie MoPic* (film): He's gonna slow us down like *fuck*, man! *a***1989** in J. Kisseloff *You Must Remember This* 72: It was no good, that's all, and you suffer like a fuck. **1991** in *RapPages* (Feb. 1992) 67: Lawnge's production is dope as fuck. **1993** J. Watson & K. Dockery *Point Man* 105: Raining like a fuck out, ain't it? **1996** D. McCumber *Playing off Rail* 336: I sure as fuck hope so. **2002** J. Goad in *N.Y. Press* (Dec. 25) 28/1: I sure as fuck couldn't feel sorry for girls who earned in a five-hour shift what I made in a week.

d. a bit of difference.—used in negative.

1984 A. R. Sample *Racehoss* 198 [refers to 1950s]: It don't make a fuck who it is.

3. semen (*rare*); in phrase: ☞ **full of fuck,** full of sexual desire or (*broadly*) energy. Compare BULL FUCK.

1680 *School of Venus* in B. K. Mudge *When Flesh Becomes Word* (2004) 40: We were both of us so full of Fuck, that we did not let slip the least minute that was favorable to us; nay more; we sometimes did it in fear and had the ill luck to be disturbed and forced to give over our sport without spending, if it proved a false alarm we went at it again. *ca*1866 *Romance of Lust* 390: The cunt full of fuck only excited him the more. *a*1890–93 J. S. Farmer & W. E. Henley *Slang & Its Analogues* III 80: *Fuck,* subs.... The seminal fluid. *Ibid.* 85: *Like a straw-yard bull, full of fuck and half-starved....*A friendly retort to the question, "How goes it?" *i.e.,* "How are you?" **1916** H. N. Cary *Slang of Venery* I 98: *Full of fuck.*—Ready to work. **1938** "Justinian" *Americana Sexualis* 23: *Full of fuck,* amorously potent. **1966** A. Wainhouse & R. Seaver trans. de Sade *120 Days of Sodom* 494: She would raise her skirts, display her ass, and the libertine, all smiles, would spray his fuck upon it. [**1978** "F. Pulsing" *Whipped Cream* 16: The combination drew the fuck-load from Ed's shaking loins. He moaned and blasted. *Ibid.* 59: He gushed his fuck-load into the fink's writhing mouth.] **1993** *Farmer's Step-daughter,* on Usenet newsgroup alt.sex.stories: She had thought often about what it would be like to let [him] shoot a full load of his fuck into her face. *Ibid.*: She felt the warm fuck filling her mouth, coating her tongue and draining back toward her throat. **2003** J. Woodward *Mister Goodbye Easter Island* 42: I want my Redi-Serv Jesus with his eyes on fire, all fierce and full of fuck. **2006** P. May *Spring & His Summers* 39: They could have been having a huge orgy up there. They certainly looked like they were full of fuck and energy.

4. a despicable person, usually a man.

[**1788** S. Low *Politician Out-Witted* I ii: Do you call me a foutre, you rascal?] **1927** [J. Fliesler] *Anecdota Americana* 188: I won't sye nothin' nawsty, all I sye is my bloody arse 'ole to you, you bloomin' fuck. **1927** E. Wilson in *Twenties* 399: You oughtn'ta be a prizefighter, yuh fuck—yuh ought to be a bootblack! **1933** C. H. Ford & P. Tyler *Young & Evil* 40: Take that

75

fuck McAllen. **1934** H. Roth *Call It Sleep* 414 [refers to *ca*1910]: Yer an at'eist, yuh fuck, he hollers. **1942** in S. J. Perelman *Don't Tread on Me* 46: I was that superior fuck who smiled patronizingly and observed…"Recent statistics show that the French have the greatest land army in the world." **1946–50** J. Jones *From Here to Eternity* ch. xxxvi: I told you, you dumb fuck. **1958** T. Berger *Crazy in Berlin* 136: Go on, you fuck, or I'll take ya apart. **1964** H.S. Thompson *Letter* (Nov. 25) in *Proud Highway* (1997) 473: All these fucks who smile on the TV screen. **1967** J. Hersey *Algiers Motel Incident* 134: Them fucks took my tape recorder. **1968** J.P. Miller *The Race for Home* 294 [refers to 1930s]: "He said he don't, you dumb fuck," Dawg said. **1970** R. Byrne *Memories non-Jewish Childhood* 117: Come in off of there, you dumb fuck. **1972** B. Harrison *Hospital* 50: I swear I thought that fuck was going to offer me a bribe to save Tessa's life. **1973** A. Schiano & A. Burton *Solo* 80: He's the meanest fuck in town. **1973** P. Benchley *Jaws* 191: You lying fuck! **1987** Santiago *Undercover* 63: Don't bother with this fuck. **1991** "Who Am I?" in L.A. Stanley *Rap* 383: He was a big-ass fuck. **1997** W. Allen *Deconstructing Harry* (film): You fucked-up fuck!…Fuck you! **2006** R. Flanagan *Unknown Terrorist* 172: Standing there, throwing herself on the mercy of a miserable fuck like Moretti, she realised this was madness.

5. an evil turn of events; a cheat of fortune.

1972 W. Pelfrey *Big V* 9: "Regulars by God." Conscripts by fuck. *a***1984** in S. Terkel *"Good War"* 306: Know what they did? They made him a lieutenant colonel and me a captain. Ain't that a fuck? **1998** T. Gilliam in *New Yorker* (May 25) 74: To start pulling things off the soundtrack now is a fuck!

In phrases:

☞ **flying fuck**, see under FLYING.

☞ **for fuck's sake**, for heaven's sake.

1943 D. Brennan *Never so Young Again* xxiii. 206: They're coming up to starboard! Weave! For f— sake! **1961** J. Jones *Thin Red Line* 16 [refers to WWII]: Don't *talk* like that!…for fuck's sake. **1964** A. Davidson in *Worlds of Tomorrow* (Aug.) 11: You space-apes who haven't signed the Declaration, don't hang around picking your toes, for — sake, come on out and *sign* it! **1966** G.M. Williams *Camp* 94: What'll we call you then for fuck's sake? **1976** A. Schroeder *Shaking It Rough* 20: An inmate kicked irritably at an uncooperative piece of machinery and announced succinctly that "the fuckin fucker's fucked, fer fuck sakes!" **1964–78** J. Carroll *Basketball*

Diaries 26: Now he's on tour for fuck's sake. **1997** *Sick Puppy Comix* (Sydney, Australia) (No. 5) 17: The moral of this story is: for fuck's sake don't talk to strange little kids! **2008** L. Weisberger *Chasing Harry Winston* 129: Come here, for fuck's sake, and hug me again!

☞ **fuck knows,** Chiefly *British.* (used to indicate that something is unknown to the speaker); "God knows."

    1976 P. Callow *Story of my Desire* vi. 42: "When's your case come up?" David said. "Fuck knows." **1988** G. Patterson *Burning your Own* (1993) 245: I know what youse're thinking: "he must be mad." Well, if that was mad, then fuck knows what youse'll say when youse see the next knock-down bargain. **2001** C. Glazebrook *Madolescents* 302: Tell spaceboy to turn the volume down. I can't get through to him, fuck knows what he's on. **2007** I. Welsh *If You Liked School, You'll Love Work* 85: Fuck knows what they are, I ain't seen them anywhere else.

☞ **fuck of,** a notable example or quantity of; "hell of."

    1928 in A. W. Read *Lexical Evidence from Folk Epigraphy* (1935) 55: This is a fuck of a rain. **1942** H. Miller *Roofs of Paris* 121: It would be a fuck of a lot more interesting. **1970** T. Thackrey *Thief* 230: Oh, wow! What a fuck of a way for a couple hot-rocks like them to go out. **1973** J. Flaherty *Fogarty & Co.* 26: It was a fuck of a country that could scrimmage for souls. **1977** K. Bartlett *Finest Kind* 20: I'll have a fuckuva time getting back in. **1978** L. K. Truscott *Dress Gray* 219: It's gonna be one fuck of a long two months. **1982** C.R. Anderson *Other War* 171: Thanks a lot, Altizer. Thanks a fuck of a lot. **1985** D. Bodey *F.N.G.* 114: He's lost a fuckuva lot of blood. **1996** P.F. Hamilton *Reality Dysfunction* 983: The doctors wired your neural nanonics to your liver....It was one fuck of a lot smarter than your brain. **2002** W. Self *Dorian* 120: Finding out you're going to die a fuck of a lot sooner, rather than the hoped-for hell of a lot later. **2006** H. Shearer *Not Enough Indians* 147: Lobbyists...get paid a fuck of a lot better than G-15s at the Bureau of Indian Affairs.

☞ **holy fuck!** (used to express astonishment).

    1945 in T. Shibutani *Derelicts of Company K* 202: Holy fuck! We're gonna freeze our ass off. **1967** H. Wentworth & S. B. Flexner *Dictionary of American Slang* (supp.) 690. **1977** T. Jones *Incredible Voyage* 373: "Holy fuck!" I thought, "I've only got a mile of sea-room." **1983** W. D. Ehrhart *Vietnam to Perkasie* 138: "Holy fuck," he muttered. **1989** R. Zumbro & J. Walker *Jungletracks* 89: Holy fuck, Lieutenant, kill 'em quick! **1996** *Picture* (Sydney, Australia) (Dec. 4) 3: "Holy fuck!" whispered one. "Jeez!" murmured another. **1999** K. Smith *Dogma* (film script) 41: Holy fuck—all the fine, immoral bitches coming out of that place, and we gotta find the one Jesus freak! **2006** M. Pessl *Special Topics in Calamity Physics* 397: "Holy fuck," Milton said, staring down at the photograph. I turned it over, but there was nothing written on it, no date. "It's her isn't it?"

☞ **like fuck**, Chiefly *British*, absolutely not; "like hell." Compare definition 2c, above.

*a*1950 E. Partridge *Dictionary of Slang & Unconventional English* (ed. 3) 1054: *F*ck! like*...."...certainly not!": low: late C. 19-20. **1966** S. Hignett *Picture to Hang on the Wall* 237: "Don't worry too much, lad.""Thanks. Like fuck, I won't." **1980** J. P. Donleavy *Schultz* 292: "I will scratch your face." "Like fuck you will." **1990** H. Benedict *World Like This* 99: "I'm only telling you what they say, Larry." "Like fuck you are." **1995** N. Hornby *High Fidelity* 302: Like fuck you are. **1995** A. Enright *Wig my Father Wore* 134: "Game show one night, date show the next," says Marcus. "Same set?" "New set. Two new sets." "There's posh. And after that, twice as much for their money." "One and a half," he says. "Like fuck. We'll be going live in half the time," I say, "because I'm a fucking eejit." **1997** M. Evans *Glass Mountain* ii. 17: "What in the fuck are you?" I looked at Jimmy Barry, surprised. "I'm a punkette," I said. "You are like fuck." **2001** I. Sinclair *Landor's Tower* i. ix. 122: If Tunstall rewound the tape, he could enjoy once more his envelope of meditative calm.... Unknowing knowingness. Like fuck he could. In telling me, he confirmed the tale. **2005** L. Dean *This Human Season* xlvii. 280: There are some things you hear and you can't forget and they stay with you and you wish like fuck you'd never heard them or never seen them.

☞ **the fuck**

1. (used as an expletive); the hell.—also used with *in*. [The phrase *why* or *what the puck* in the 1864 and *a*1903 quotations is precisely synonymous with *why the devil*; the similarity of both the phonetics and the construction may have influenced the development of the present usage of *fuck*.]

[**1864** S. LeFanu in *Oxford English Dictionary* (ed. 2) under *puck, n.*: And why the puck don't you let her out?] [*a***1903** in *English Dialect Dictionary* under *puck, n.*: What the puck are you doing?] **1934** H. Roth *Call It Sleep* 23 [refers to *ca*1910]: An de nex' time watch out who de fuck yer chas—. **1936** M. Levin *Old Bunch* 122: Where the f— you think you're trying to horn in?...Who the f— wants to ride in your robber hacks anyway? **1942** H. Miller *Roofs of Paris* 23: I don't know what the fuck to say. **1943** R. Tregaskis *Invasion Diary* 45: You f—g eight balls get the f— off this God-damn hill before I rap this rifle-barrel around your neck! **1945** in T. Shibutani *Derelicts of Company K* 291: Where in the fuck's that truck? **1951** *American Journal of Sociology* XXXVII 138: But what the f—, that's his business *Ibid.* 140: Sure, they're a bunch of f—ng squares, but who the f— pays the bills? **1959** W. Burroughs *Naked Lunch* 33: How in the fuck should I know? **1962** G. Mandel *Wax Boom* 273: I might blow my top...if people don't start leaving me the fuck alone! **1963–64** K. Kesey *Sometimes a Great Notion* 6: He don't even the fuck know! **1968** J. Schell *Military Half* 185: Abruptly, someone called out, "Where the fuck are we?" **1971** L. Bangs in *Psychotic Reactions* (1987) 86: Why'n the fuck d'ya think? **1977** Illinois photographer, age *ca*35: What the flying fuck is he talking about? **1979** *National Lampoon* (Dec.) 59: I go to Medicine Hat, way the holy fuck up in fuckin' Alberta, Canada, man. **1966–80** J. McAleer & B. Dickson *Unit Pride* 128: "Did you ever see such a screwy bunch?"..."Guess the fuck I ain't." *a***1987** C. Bunch & A. Cole *Reckoning for Kings* 42: "Looks that way." "What the fuck, over." **1990** L. Bing *Do or Die* 218: What the fuck I want to change for? **1997** *New York Magazine* (June 16) 81: It's always those people who get harassed and picked on who flip the fuck out. **1997** A. Bourdain *Chef's Night Out* in K. Williamson *Rovers Return* (1998) 137: Save me from vegetarians and the lactose intolerant. Deliver me from the tyranny of the food critics, for they know not what the fuck they do. **1998** G. Ritchie *Lock, Stock & Two Smoking Barrels* 92: *Dog* (*seeing an unconscious man at his feet*): What the fuck did you do to Fauntleroy? *Plank* (*fumbling and panicking*): I didn't touch him, he just passed out. **1999** F. Renzulli *"Toodle-fucking-oo"* (television shooting script) in *Sopranos* (2nd Ser.) 6. I don't know Carm'. I yelled. What the fuck else could I do? **2004** J. Jameson & N. Strauss *How to Make Love Like Porn Star* i. xi. 82: What the fuck did you do with my meth?... The whole fucking bag is gone.

2. (used to introduce a response expressing emphatic disagreement); "the hell"; "like hell." Also: (used as an expletive); "what the fuck?", etc.

1965 S. Linakis *In Spring the War Ended* 50 [refers to WWII]: "They don't keep you locked up."... "The fuck they don't." **1966** F. L. Keefe *The Investigating Officer* 184: "This one I happen to remember very well." "The fuck you do." **1970–71** J. Rubinstein *City Police* 328: "You ain't [arresting] my mother." ..."The fuck I ain't." **1974** G. V. Higgins *Cogan's Trade* 4: The fuck you sell driving lessons to people. **1975** J. Sepe & L. Telano *Cop Team* 148: The fuck I am! **1983** P. Dexter *God's Pocket* 65: The fuck I have, you think I'm crazy? **1998** J. Cahill *Boca* in *Sopranos* ((television shooting script) 1st Ser. 2) 7: *Vin Makazian has just come in, blinded by the relative darkness. Tony goes to meet him.* Tony: The fuck you doing here? **1998** M. Burgess & R. Green *Isabella* in *Sopranos* ((television shooting script) 1st Ser. 1) 3: *Jimmy*: How many of these things you gotta go to, huh? Brendan Filone's mother at that kid's funeral: *The way she carried on. Junior*: The fuck? **2000** W. Monahan *Light House* xxvi. 145: "Give me another one." "No more drink." "The fuck you say."

3. daylights; hell; used in phrases of the sort **to — the fuck out of** to —— (a person or thing) to an excessive, violent, unpleasant, or powerful extent.

1957 N. Coward *Diary* (Feb. 17) (2000) 349: I am very old indeed and cannot understand why the younger generation, instead of knocking at the door, should bash the fuck out of it. **1960** N. Coward *Diary* (June 19) (2000) 442: There was a real blazing row in the course of which Peggy and I roared at him, banged the table and generally frightened the fuck out of him. **1970** G. Slick in *Rolling Stone* (Nov. 12) 28/1: When they busted me in Hawaii I even got another guy out of jail, a spade cat they'd busted the night before and beat fuck out of, and we just bailed him out. **1972** College student: There's only one thing left to do—beat the fuck out of you. **1974** B. Greene *Billion Dollar Baby* 87: I always wanted to beat the fuck out of somebody on stage. **1985** S. Braudy *What the Movies Made Me Do* 102: All I want is to act the fuck out of the best role I ever had in my life. **1987** B. E. Ellis *Rules of Attraction* 111: But thinking about it bores the fuck out of me so I just walk around the dorm for a while and then split. **1987** O. Hawkins *Scars & Memories* 140: It pains the fuck out of me sometimes, in a beautiful way, to think that I learned, figured out, studied a bunch of garbage, to become intellectually intelligent. **1989** *Life* (July) 27: "This s—, literally, scares the f— outta me."...girl, 15. **1999** L. Leblanc *Pretty in Punk* iv. 104: Hey, Tad, Cooper, we gotta beat the fuck out of Chris. **2003** M. McDonagh *Pillowman* 53: I'd've tortured the fuck out of them if I had them here, just like I'm gonna torture the fuck out of you now too. **2004** T. Lee & A. Bozza *Tommy Land* 102: Every night after our show, we'd party all night in whatever town we were in...then show up in a new town the next morning, rock the fuck out of it, fuck the fuck out of it, and move on again.

☞ **the fuck of it**, the fun of it; the hell of it.

1970 College student: I'd beat him up just for the fuck of it. **1976** S. Hayden *Voyage* 196: Take a look. Just for the fuck of it. **1985** D. Bodey *F.N.G.* 174: I wonder if he is doing it officially or just for the fuck of it. **1990** L. Bing *Do or Die* 123: Who's gonna die "for the fuck of it"? **1994** "Nine Inch Nails" *Big Man with a Gun* (rock song): Maybe I'll put a hole in your head you know, just for the fuck of it. **1995** T. Rebeck *Family of Mann* 44: I drove through Compton just for the fuck of it, and that scared me so bad I went back to Beverly Hills. **2000** W. T. Vollmann *Royal Family* 438: I wish we had more time to plan and shit. Just for the fuck of it we can...we can...oh, Henry, it's gonna be over so soon. **2006** D. Kalla *Rage Therapy* 113: "Why would I make it up?" Attention seeking? Manipulation? Just for the fuck of it? I kept the thoughts to myself.

☞ **to fuck**, very much, a great deal; "to hell."

1919 W.H. Downing *Digger Dialects* 12: *Blow to-fook*, shatter to fragments. **1970** H. S. Thompson *Letter* (Jan. 29) in *Fear & Loathing in Amer.* (2000) 277: I wish to fuck I could lay off some kind of healing wisdom— for either one of us. **1978** L. Kramer *Faggots* 135: He's medium height, reddish-blond, very handsome, and I wish to fuck he would hurry up. **1986** R. Hewitt *White Talk Black Talk* i. 27: But then I thought I'd be cut to fuck. I mean I'd be stabbed. I knew it. **1994** J. Kelman *How Late it Was* 17: Mind you he once telt it to a woman and it annoyed her to fuck, she thought it was a load of bullshit. **2002** *Time Out* (Jan. 2) 111/3: Because it's a soul album…modernised and styled to fuck, for sure, but simultaneously dignified, mellifluous, tough, funky and exquisitely, properly soulful. **2003** A. Swofford *Jarhead* 212: Word has it that two light-armored-vehicle crew members were blown to fuck yesterday by friendly fire—an A-10 Warthog dropped a bomb on them, by mistake, a big fucking devastating bomb, *by mistake.*

fuck *adjective*

describing, depicting, or involving copulation; pornographic; erotic.—used before a noun.

1941 W.C. Williams *Letter* (Jan. 6) in Witemeyer *Williams-Laughlin* (1989) 61: You've got to feed 'em the bunk—love and war and all the old fuck stuff. **1942–44** in *American Speech* (Feb. 1946) 33: *F—k Books, n.* Sexy pulp magazines. **1950** E. Hemingway in *Selected Letters* (1981) 694: They start writing those over-detailed fuck scenes. **1966** in G. L. Steinbrook *Allies & Mates* 70: A boy approached me and asked if I wanted to buy some "f--k pictures." **1966** Fry *Slang Transcript*: Will show fuck movies. **1967** N. Mailer *Why We Are in Vietnam* 27: Pretending to write a…fuck book in revenge. **1967** J. Rechy *Numbers* 105: I got some fuck-movies at home. **1969** in M.J. Estren *History of Underground Comics* (1974) 11: The State University will never contain any "fuck books." **1975** T. Berger *Sneaky People* 60: He's got a fuck-book there, too. **1975** C. Skinner *Carol's Curious Passion* 23: You mean, I might have a career with Bobby in fuck films? **1976** "N. Ross" *Policeman* 105: Phil liked to hear fuck stories on stakeouts. **1981** *National Lampoon* (Aug.) 68: Let's turn this solemn occasion into a real fuck party. **1984** J.R. Reeves *Mekong* 12: Bullshitting, kidding, telling fuck jokes. **1987** H. Zeybel *Gunship* 6: I'd watched the live fuck shows in the Angeles night clubs. **1994** M. Gilmore *Shot in the Heart* 166: If a girl went out with Gary… they knew it was a fuck date. That was his reputation. **1995** V. Chandra *Red Earth & Pouring Rain* 392: The thing was, I'd been negotiating for months with a major studio, which, with an already Oscared director, was trying to put together that elusive thing—a mainstream fuck film, you know, big budget, cast of thousands, maybe some real stars. **1998** *New Yorker* (Apr. 6) 89: A stack of fuck books on one side of the toilet. *a***2002** S.-L. Parks *Topdog/underdog* 49: I was over there looking for something the other week and theres like 100 fuck books under yr bed and theyre matted together like a bad fro, bro, cause you spunked in the pages and didnt wipe them off. **2002** I. Welsh *Porno* 42: They make their fuck films and show clips of them on the Net.

fuck *verb* [English form of a widespread Germanic word; compare Middle Dutch *fokken* 'to thrust, to beget children, copulate with'; Norwegian regional *fukka* 'to copulate'; dialectal Swedish *focka* 'to strike, push, copulate'; and *fock* 'penis'; and German *ficken* 'to copulate'; probably borrowed into English in the fifteenth century from Low German, Flemish, or Dutch; part of a group of words in Germanic languages having the basic meaning 'move back and forth', and the common figurative meaning 'to cheat'; see Introduction for a fuller discussion; the recent forms *fug, fugg* are printed euphemisms and do not represent pronunciation.]

1.a. *transitive.* to engage in heterosexual intercourse involving the penetration of the penis into the vagina with (a person). [The date of the initial citation, from a poem attacking the Carmelite Friars of Ely (a town in Cambridgeshire), may be as early as 1450–75. The poem is written in a garbled mixture of English and Latin, and several English words have pseudo-Latin endings. In the manuscript, the English words in this passage, from *fuccant* (the *-ant* is pseudo-Latin) to *heli* (i.e. Ely) are written in a cipher in which each letter is replaced with the one following it in the alphabet. The cipher suggests that the word was considered taboo even at that time (the word *swive*, a now-archaic vulgarity for sex, was also in cipher). It translates as "They [the monks] are not in heaven/because they fuck the wives of Ely." For asterisks in 1848 quotation, see note at FUCKING, *adjective*.]

*a***1500** *Flen, Flyys* (ms. Harl. 3362) f. 47, in T. Wright & J. O. Halliwell *Reliquae Antiquae* (1841) I. 91: Non sunt in cœli, quia gxddbov xxkxzt pg ifmk [= fuccant uuiuys of heli]. **1730** N. Bailey *Dictionary: To Fuck*…a term used of a goat; also *subagitare foeminam*. **1760** in I. McCormick *Secret Sexualities* 109: He asked me, if I never got any girls, or if I never f—ed 'em. **1775** J. Ash *New and Complete Dictionary: Fuck* (*v.t. a low vulgar word*) To perform the act of generation, to have to do with a woman. **1778** in Connor *Songbag* 24: He often times fuck't the old whore in the Night. **1785** F. Grose *Classical Dictionary of the Vulgar Tongue*: *To f—k.* To copulate. **1848** [G. Thompson] *House Breaker* 42: I was going to **** that same little *blowen*, in Boy Jack's *crib*. **1865** in M. Hodes *White Women, Black Men* 142: Did he say he fucked the young gal? **1865** Capt. E. Sellon *New Epicurean* 14: I don't see why I am not to be fucked as well as her! **1872** *Contested Election* 155: Mr. Miller said to him these words: "You cock-sucking son of a bitch, you have been fucking half of your congregation to-day, keeping two or three whores, and now come here to vote the Reform ticket." **1877** in P. Y. Stallard *Glittering Misery* (1978) 146: Didn't you — that girl yourself? **1879** *Harlequin Prince Cherrytop* 5: Flat on my back he stretched me in the sun,/Fucked me three times, and paid for every one! **1882** *Boudoir* 226: She f—d me as dry as a stick, last night. **1887** Stanislaus de Rhodes *Autobiography of a Flea* 141: "In fact, I want to fuck you, my darling." Bella saw the huge projection give a flip up. "How nasty you are!—What words you use." **1922** J. Joyce *Ulysses* III. 729: His wife is fucked yes and damn well fucked too. **1928** D. H. Lawrence *Lady Chatterley's Lover* iv. 44: Fellows with swaying waists fucking little jazz girls. **1939** H. Miller *Tropic of Capricorn* (1961) 256: I used to fuck her standing up in the vestibule. **1947** J. Kerouac *Letter* (Sept. 13) in *Selected Letters 1940–56* (1995) 127: I've met a lot of girls out here, and at least two of them are anxious for me to fuck them. **1964–66** R. Stone *Hall of Mirrors* 194: Is she fuckin' other people? **1966** R. Fariña *Been Down So Long* 105: I wasn't making love to her, I was *fucking* her. The difference is kind, not goddamned degree. **1967** J. Morrison *The End* (rock song, perf. "The Doors"): "Father?" "Yes, son." "I want to kill you. Mother? I want to fuck you." **1985** E. Leonard *Glitz* 88: Iris was fucking *some*body. **1993** L. Phair *Flower* (pop. song): Every time I see your face…I want to fuck you like a dog….I'll fuck you till your dick turns blue. **1996** T. McMillan *How Stella Got Her Groove Back* 145: "Well, I didn't like just *fuck* him." "Oh, don't tell me you guys *made love* and shit." "We did. That's exactly what we did." "You fucked him, Stella. Get real." **2001** S. MacGowan in S. MacGowan & V. M. Clarke *A Drink with Shane MacGowan* 76: Then I fucked her afterwards. And that was an amazing fuck cause she was going different colours while I was doing it. **2007** J. Hayes *Precious Blood* 272: "I think you've been incredibly brave." "Was that what you were thinking while you were fucking me?"

b. *intransitive.* to engage in heterosexual intercourse involving the penetration of the penis into the vagina.

ca1500 in W. Dunbar *Poems* 40: He clappit fast, he kist, he chukkit... Yit be his feiris he wald haif fukkit. **1535–36** in D. Lindsay *Works* I 103: Ay fukkand lyke ane furious Fornicatour. **ca1550** in D. Lindsay *Satyre* 88: Bischops ar blist howbeit that thay be waryit/For thay may fuck thair fill and be unmaryit. **a1568** in J. S. Farmer & W. E. Henley *Slang & Its Analogues* III 80: Allace! said sche, my awin sweit thing,/Your courtly fukking garis me fling. **1598** J. Florio *Worlde of Wordes* 137/1: *Fottere*...to iape, to sard, to fucke, to swive, to occupy. **ca1610** in E. J. Burford *Bawdy Verse* (1983) 63: She's a damn'd lascivious Bitch/And fucks for half-a-crown. **ca1650** in J. Wardroper *Love & Drollery* (1969) 187: Had ever maiden that good luck.../O 'twould invite a maid to —. **1683** in J. S. Farmer & W. E. Henley *Slang & Its Analogues* III 80: From St. James's to the Land of Thule,/There's not a whore who f—s so like a mule. **ca1800** in J. Holloway & J. Black *Later English Broadside Ballads* (1975) 223: Jenny cries nay, I won't F—k for a shilling. **1845** in A. Johnson *Papers* I 218: In other words...he was "Chewing drinking & *fucking* his way to the legislature." **1864** in G. C. Rable *Civil Wars* (1991) 161: Have you any sisters? If you have I should like to fuck them. That was my business before I came into the service, and now I am fucking for Uncle Sam. **1916** M. Cowley in P. Jay *Burke-Cowley Correspondence* 22: He drinks, fucks, swears,...is popular with girls. **1918** in M. B. Carey *Mlle. from Armentières* II (unpaged): Over the top with the best of luck,/The first over there is the first to —. **1938** J. O'Hara in *Selected Letters* 134: Oh, and Mrs. — — — —, who wanted everybody to get drunk and start fucking. **1940** in T. Williams *Letters* 11: I am taking free conga lessons...and fucking every night. **1965** L. Ferlinghetti *Situation in the West* in *Starting from San Francisco* (1967) 63: Let's repeat it together/To fuck is to love. **1968** *Harper's Mag.* (Apr.) 52: I like your looks. Come to my room tonight at seven o'clock, we'll fuck. **1973** E. Jong *Fear of Flying* 33: Silent Bennett was my healer. A physician for my head and a psychoanalyst for my cunt. He fucked and fucked in ear-splitting silence. **1982** R. M. Brown *Southern Discomfort* 195: Great ladies don't even admit fucking with their husbands. **a1990** E. Currie *Dope & Trouble* 205: You know, they fucked, and everything. **2006** "L. Burana" *Try* 165: "Heard you fuck like a bastard," she hollered over the music.

c. *transitive* and *intransitive*. to make a sexual thrust into; rub against in a sexual way; engage in intercourse other than heterosexual genital intercourse [with].

[**1680** *School of Venus* II. 99: An hour after, he Ferked my Arse again in the same manner.] **1698** *Account of the Proceedings against Capt. Edward Rigby for the Abominable Sin of Sodomy* verso: Then Rigby sitting on Mintons Lap, kist him several times, putting his Tongue into his Mouth, askt him, if he should F----- him, how can that be askt Minton, I'le show you answered Rigby. *ca*1710 in L. S. A. M. von Römer *Rochester's Sodom* (1905) IV. 39: Then arse they fuck and bugger one another. **1829** *New South Wales State Archives* (Oct. 5) (T 143), in *Gay Perspectives* 34: I slept in the middle and the Prisoner kept putting his arms & legs over me & he said on different occasions "Fox I should like to fuck you" and added "you may do the same to me whenever you like." **1846** *Reports of the Supreme Court of Missouri* IX. 768: The slanderous charge was carnal knowledge of a mare, and the word "fuck" was used to convey the imputation. **1879** *Pearl* 203: Can't you just fuck her in the bum? *ca*1890 *My Secret Life* XI. iv.: I had taken home from *** a fine dildo which squirted liquids, and which it amused her to be fucked with. Then I fucked her with it, licking her clitoris whilst I did it to her. **1908** *Way of a Man with a Maid* 139: She felt Connie's cunt against hers and the exciting friction again commencing. Connie was evidently very much worked up, and she confessed afterwards that the consciousness that she was fucking Molly's mother in Molly's presence sent her to fever heat. **1909** J. Joyce *Letter* (Dec. 6) in *Selected Letters* (1975) 184: I feel mad to…fuck between your two rosy-tipped bubbies. **1923** *Poems, Ballads & Parodies* 47: A bull dog fucked him in the ear. **1955–56** A. Ginsberg *Howl* I: Who let themselves be fucked in the ass by saintly motorcyclists, and screamed with joy. **1967** N. Mailer *Why are we in Vietnam?* ix. 163: Gutsy will fuck any orifice, nostril, ear…even cream between two fat tits. **1968** P. Roth *Portnoy's Complaint* 145: They have a whore in there, kid, who fucks the curtain with her bare twat. **1970** "Viva" *Superstar* 249: Want to get fucked with this? (she pulls out a plastic dildo). **1971** A. Andrews in A. M. Zwicky et al. *Studies out in Left Field* (1992) 37: Butch fucked the mannikin through the hole he drilled in its crotch. **1976** J. Vasco *Three-Hole Girl* 164: Stick your tongue in my pussy hole, Lisa, fuck my pussy with your mouth! **1994** "G. Indiana" *Rent Boy* 23: Back in his own country guys only get fucked when they're real little and when they grow up they're supposed to, you know, do the fucking, and it's considered unmanly for a guy in his twenties like Mohammed to get off on getting fucked. **1995** L. Garrett *Coming Plague* x. 263: Why do faggots have to fuck so fucking much? *ca2000* E. Chapman *Flaunting It* in "Trixi" *Faster Pussycats* (2001) 47: "Good boy. You're learning now. I want to see you get your face fucked... Go on. Take it." She pressed my head down so that my throat had no choice but to engulf the entire length of silicone.

d. (in various similes and proverbs). See also FOUR Fs.

ca1677 in Lord Rochester *Complete Poems* 137: My heart would never doubt,/...To wish those eyes fucked out. **1884** *Randiana* 28: He had thrown her down...and had fucked her heart out in a shorter space of time than it takes me to write it. **1916–22** H. N. Cary *Sexual Vocabulary* I under *copulation*: *Fucking like a mink.* To copulate frequently. [**1928** S. V. Benét *John Brown's Body* 99: The whole troop grumbled and wondered, aching/ For fighting, fleeing or fornicating/Or anything else except this bored waiting.] **1932** S. Longstreet *Nell Kimball* 15: He...never did anyone a favor, fucked like a mink. **1938** "Justinian" *Americana Sexualis* 23: Fuck a dead horse! **1941** R.P. Smith *So It Doesn't Whistle* 102: Dutch would say: "The —ing you get ain't worth the —ing you get." **1942** W.L. McAtee *Supplement to Grant Co.* 6 [refers to 1890s]: *Mink*, *"fuck like a*, phr., with the senses of enthusiastically, enduringly, intensively. **1947** J. Cheever in *Letters* (1988) 125: I want to write short stories like I want to fuck a chicken. **1952** in G. Legman *Dirty Joke* 284: I'm going to fuck you till your ears fly off. **1964** J. Peacock *To Drill & Die* 140: He'd fuck a snake if someone would hold its head. **1965** S. Linakis *In Spring the War Ended* 60: The fellow said the fraulein's name was Gertie and she fucked like a mink. **1970** W. C. Woods *Killing Zone* 112: I wish you were here too, so I could fuck your brains out. **1971** S. Stevens *Way Uptown* 241: And 'fore you could fuck a duck they were into the whole white-guilt thing. **1972** In *Penthouse* (Jan. 1973) 116: Emily is fucking like a minx. **1974** Univ. Tenn. student: I'd like to fuck her eyes out. **1974** G.V. Higgins *Cogan's Trade* 14: I would've fucked a snake, I could've got somebody [to] hold it for me. **1975** J. Wambaugh *Choirboys* 248: You don't look big enough to fight, fuck or run a footrace. **1976** Kalamazoo, Mich., man, age 29: My father used to say, "Now you're ready to fight, fuck, or run a footrace." It meant all ready to go. **1976** S. Hayden *Voyage* 663: Make or break. Fuck or fall back. **1976** M. Braly *False Starts* 204: I thought I should have been able to fuck a bear trap if someone had glued a little hair on it. **1978** T. Alibrandi *Killshot* 235: These kids today don't know whether to fuck, fight or hold the light. **1978** L. Kramer

Faggots 228: Good evening! I am so happy we are all now here!... I shall personally build flower boxes for us all...and I shall continue my experimentation into the tambourine and I shall fuck fuck fuck like a bunny! **1979** U.S. college student: He was mad enough to fuck a duck. **1980** in *Penthouse* (Jan. 1981) 26: By that time she was so hot that she would have fucked a rock pile if she thought there was a snake in it. **1980** J. DiFusco et al. *Tracers* 35: Sounds like...two skeletons fuckin' on a footlocker. **1982** West Virginia woman, age *ca*27: Well, fuck a snake! Look who's here! **1983** W. D. Ehrhart *Vietnam to Perkasie* 14: While every...hippie in Trenton fucked her eyeballs out. **1986** R. Chapman *New Dictionary of American Slang: Fuck like a bunny*...To copulate readily and vigorously. **1988** C. Roberts & C. Sasser *Walking Dead* 143: Everybody said you'd fuck a snake if somebody held its head. **1988** P. Duncan *84 Charlie MoPic* (film): Quick, like a bunny fucks! *Ibid.* You two make more noise than two skeletons fucking on a tin roof. **1998** H. Peach *Outlaw Girls* in P. Banting *Fresh Tracks* 199: They fucked like alleycats/and like rabbits and then like elk... they fucked like timber falling/out of the sky and like a tsunami and/like a particular frail moonrise/they fucked like a housefire/the flames screaming up/from the inside out.

2.a. to harm irreparably; finish; damage; spoil; botch; (chiefly in *passive*) to put into a difficult or hopeless situation; doom.

1776 *Frisky Songster* (new edition) 36: Hey ho! the wind did blow, down they fell,/Breeches and petticoat into the well./O, says the breeches, I shall be duck'd./Aye, says the petticoat I shall be f—d. /O, how my old grannum will grumble and grunt,/When she's got ne'er a petticoat to cover her c—t. **1906** *Southwestern Reporter* XCV. 1083/2: Accused testified that prior to the homicide his brother had informed him that the deceased had stated that he would whip accused and his brother and fuck the whole family, a charge on manslaughter was not insufficient because it did not charge the jury that insulting conduct towards the female relatives of accused constituted adequate cause, for the word "fuck" only conveyed the idea of ill will towards the brother of accused, and a purpose to bring on a difficulty with him, especially in view of affidavits on a motion for a new trial averring that the word used meant "to whip, or beat, or chastise." **1929** in F. S. Fitzgerald *Correspondence* 226: Now you make them read the word cooked (+ fucked would be as bad) *one dozen times*. **1929** E. Hemingway *Farewell to Arms* (U.S. ed.) xxix. 219: The wheels spun and we pushed and pushed [the car]. But it wasn't any use. "It's ——," I said.

1931 J. Dos Passos *Nineteen Nineteen* 7 [refers to *ca*1914]: I guess I'm f—d for fair then. **1934** H. Miller *Tropic of Cancer* 48: We'll take his lousy review and we'll fuck him good and proper....The magazine'll be finished. **1935** L. Zukofsky in G. Ahearn *Pound/Zukofsky* 160: Time fucks it. **1937** A. Binns *Laurels Are Cut Down* 200 [refers to 1920]: We did all their fighting. Now that we've quit, they're —ed. **1938–39** J. Dos Passos *Young Man* 257: Less said everything was the matter, American Miners was f—d to hell and back, the boys in Slade County was f—d and now here was this christbitten hellbound party line f—g them proper. **1941** E. Hemingway in *Selected Letters* (1981) 532: We are fucked in this war as of the first day. **1948** N. Mailer *Naked & Dead* 10: Even *they* can't fug me this time. **1967** N. Mailer *Why We Are in Vietnam* 111: He, Rusty, is fucked unless he gets that bear. **1970** M. Thomas *Total Beast* 137: He was fucking old Sunshine with that knife! **1970** R. Byrne *Memories non-Jewish Childhood* 90: The snowdrifts and slush made darting and dodging impossible. I was, in short, fucked. **1972** D. Jenkins *Semi-Tough* 159. We got too many ways to fuck 'em. **1984** M. Wallace & G. P. Gates *Close Encounters* 155 [refers to 1968]: I drew a breath and continued, man to man. "Vietnam fucked you, Mr. President, and so, I'm afraid, you fucked the country." **1984** K. Weaver *Texas Crude* 3: I got you faded, fucked, and laughed at. **1989** S. Lee *Do the Right Thing* (film): I oughta fuck you just for that. **1995** D. McLean *Bunker Man* 41: He didn't want to slip going round a corner and fuck his ankle. **2000** I. Welsh in N. Hornby *Speaking with Angel* 178: My heartbeat's racing and there's a pain in my chest. I'll have to take things easier, drinking heavily in this heat always fucks me. **2005** W. Henderson in A. St. John *Clapton's Guitar* xiv. 135: I don't get distracted.... If I got distracted, I'd be fucked.

b. to botch; bungle; FUCK UP, definition 1.—also used with *it*.

1969 L. Sanders *Anderson Tapes* 43: It might fuck the whole thing. **1973** W. Karlin et al. *Free Fire Zone* 108: Pellegrini, you fucked it again. *Ibid.* 110: Them niggers fucked the roof—built this house so *fast.* **1972–79** T. Wolfe *Right Stuff* 243: Oh, it was obvious...that Grissom had just *fucked it*...that was all.

3. a. to cheat; deceive; betray. Compare synonyms *screw* and FRIG. [At the 1866 quotation, there is a note by the notary public following "fucked" that reads: "Before putting down the word as used by the witness, I requested him to reflect upon the language he attributed to Mr Baker, and not to impute to him an outrage upon all that was decent. The witness reitterated [*sic*] it, and said that it was the word used by Mr Baker."]

1866 G. Washington *Affidavit* (Oct. 20) in I. Berlin et al. *Black Military Experience in Civil War* (1982) 791: Mr Baker replied that deponent would be *fucked* out of his money by Mr Brown. **1927** [J. Fliesler] *Anecdota Americana* 76: It looks like you've fucked yourself out of a seat. **1932** H. Miller in *Letters to Emil* (1989) 114: But they fucked me all right. Fucked me good and proper. **1934** H. Miller *Tropic of Cancer* 49: One by one I've fucked myself out of all these free meals which I had planned so carefully. **1935** E. E. Cummings in *Letters* 136: "Fuck" has been changed to "trick" in new [*New English Weekly*] today arriving with editor's comments. **1942** L. V. Berrey & M. Van den Bark *American Thesaurus of Slang* 312: Cheat; defraud...*fuck (out of)*. **1945** in D. Levin *From Battlefield* 56: He has been fucked again and again by the Corps. **1951** in *International Journal of Psycho-Analysis* XXV (1954) 39: To "get fucked" is to be made a "sucker." **1954** L. Yablonsky *Violent Gang* 75: Although I hang with them for protection, I fuck everybody. They try to burn me, I get my blade, I'll get 'em all but good. **1959** W. Burroughs *Naked Lunch* 179: You're trying to fuck me out of my commission! **1960** G. Sire *Deathmakers* 44: They're out to fuck you. The whole fucking world. So fuck them first. **1961** J. Baldwin *Another Country* 77: We been fucked for fair. **1965** in J. Mills *On Edge* 8: You thought you were going to get laid, and what you really got was fucked. **1969** L. H. Whittemore *Cop!* 27: So it's the Puerto Ricans that fuck the Puerto Ricans. They sell their own people the worst shit. **1972** D. Halberstam *Best & Brightest* 66 [refers to 1961]: Carl Kaysen... brought in the news that the Soviets had resumed atmospheric [nuclear] testing. The President's reaction was simple and basic and reflected due frustrations of that year. "Fucked again," he said. **1978** W. Strieber *Wolfen* 201: But he ain't gonna fuck me. He must think I'm some kind of schoolboy. **1979–82** L. Gwin *Going Overboard* 195: As Mick tried to teach me, "Top dog fucks the bottom dog. That's the law of the jungle." **1983–86** G.C. Wilson *Supercarrier* 67: "Being in the Russian military is like being in a chicken coop," Belenko would say in his lectures. "You know you're going to be fucked, you just don't know when." **1994** Q. Tarantino *Pulp Fiction* 32: *Brett.* I just want you to know how sorry we are about how fucked up things got between us and Mr. Wallace. When we entered into this thing, we only had the best intentions—... *Jules*. Does he look like a bitch?... Then why did you try to fuck 'im like a bitch?... Yes ya did Brett. Ya tried ta fuck 'im. **2004** P. Biskind *Down & Dirty Pictures* vi. 215: According to their bookkeeping, the film never made anything, even though it made so much money all over the world. I just got fucked out of everything.

b. (in variations implying especially cruel deception or brutalization).

1945 in T. Shibutani *Derelicts of Company K* 115: We'd get fucked out of Saturday afternoon though....In this place they always fuck you in the ass when they get a chance. **1965** in H.S. Thompson *Shark Hunt* 114: We read/a newspaper and saw where just about everybody/ had been fucked in the face/or some other orifice or opening.../by the time the Chronicle went to press. **1974** R. Carter *16th Round* 257: The cops knew that they were fucking me with a dry dick. **1977** E. Torres *Q & A* 75: You got ten big ones....We will fuck Reilly in the ass. **1978** R. Price *Ladies' Man* 106: Me? I went to [college]. I got fucked up the ass...I dropped out of school with six months to go. **1983** D. Mamet *Glengarry Glen Ross* 36: When they *build* your business...fuck them up the ass. **1991** "Ice Cube" *No Vaseline* (rap song): You're gettin' fucked out your green by a white boy, with no Vaseline. **1997** *New Yorker* (Sept. 8) 37: Gil didn't understand how much firepower Steve had....Steve is going to fuck Gil so hard his eardrums will pop. **2001** in L. Gottlieb & J. Jacobs *Inside the Cult of Kibu* 245: The company was doomed....They got fucked up the ass, hard, without lube.

4.a. (used as an imprecation or oath); God damn; to hell with; curse. See also *fuck it*, below, and *fuck you*, below.

1918 in E. Wilson *Prelude* 213: I've often seen a couple o' chaps bringin' back a wounded prisoner and they get tired of leadin'"im and one of 'em says: "Aw, fuck 'im, Jock! Let's do 'im in," and they shoot 'im and leave 'im there. **1914–21** J. Joyce *Ulysses* 603 [refers to 1904]: God fuck old Bennett. **1924** E. Hemingway in *Selected Letters* (1981) 113: I have lost the fine thrill enjoyed by Benj. Franklin when entering Philadelphia with a roll under each arm. Fuck Literature. **1926** F. Wray trans. H. Barbusse *Under Fire* 110: F— them. **1929** in E. O'Neill *Letters* 341: But I am forgetting our old watchword of the Revolution— F—k 'em all! **1934** H. Miller *Tropic of Cancer* 280: He was for eating a sandwich. "Fuck that!" I said. **1943** in M. Morriss & R. Day *South Pacific Diary* (1996) 72: So cheer up lads—fuck 'em all. **1948** N. Mailer *Naked & Dead* 169 [refers to WWII]: I'm fugged if I'm going to tote a box all the way back. **1949** V. Van Praag *Day Without End* 215: "Orders be fucked!" he muttered. **1952** S. Bellow *Adventures of Augie March* 397: Oh, fuck Oliver! **1958** I. Fleming *Dr. No* (1960) xvii. 154: Bond said out loud, viciously, "— them all," and turned sullenly back on his stomach. **1961** J. Peacock *Valhalla* 425 [refers to 1953]: Eat the apple and fuck the Corps in '54! **1965** S. Linakis *In Spring the War Ended* 206: "Are you?" "Fucked if I know." **1967** L. Yablonsky *Hippie Trip* 206: I said fuck this shit and moved over here. **1983** W. D. Ehrhart *Vietnam to Perkasie* 55 [refers to 1967]: Fuckin' ARVN got better equipment than we do. Eat the apple and fuck the Corps. **1995** *CA v. Simpson* (Court-TV) (Sept. 6): Fuck the rules. We'll make them up later. **1998** D. Shapiro *Slow Motion* viii. 201: *Alcoholics Anonymous,* she had scribbled, along with a few names of churches and times of meetings. Fuck her, I thought. What does she know? **2005** S. Horn *Restless Sleep* ii. 23: If the detectives really weren't doing their jobs and clearing these cases, fuck 'em.

b. (in stronger, more vivid, or more elaborate curses). See also *fuck you and the horse you rode in on,* below.

1940 J. Del Torto *Graffiti Transcript* (Kinsey Institute): Fuck you where you breathe. **1958** *Stack A Lee* 1: So fuck Billy the Lion in his motherfucking ass. **1962** G. Mandel *Wax Boom* 72 [refers to WWII]: I fuck you all where you breathe. **1967** J. Rechy *Numbers* 68: Fuck you in the ears, muscle-ladies. **1968** R. Gover *JC* 164: As for the board [of directors], fuck it with a sixpenny nail. **1969** N.Y.C. man, age *ca*45: When we were kids we'd say, "Fuck 'em all, big and small, right up to the nostrils!" **1970** J. Conaway *Big Easy* 94: "*Chinga su madre!*" "Fuck you in the heart," he rejoined. **1971** H. Selby *Room* 134: You're a rotten lousy son of a bitch and I fuck you where you eat, and your mother too. **1973** M. Scorsese & M. Martin *Mean Streets* (film): I fuck you where you breathe! I don't give two shits for you! **1975** S. P. Smith *American Boys* 309: Fuck you in your mouth, Red! **1977** E. Bunker *Animal Factory* 117: If she's been a jiveass bitch, fuck her in her ass. **1978** L. K. Truscott *Dress Gray* 370: Yeah? Well, fuck them and their marching orders. **1979** *National Lampoon* (Dec.) 17: Fuck you in the eye. **1980** H. Gould *Fort Apache* 51: Fuck them and the horse they rode in on....Fuck 'em all, big and small. **1979–82** L. Gwin *Going*

Overboard 185: Fuck you in the mouth, kiddo. This job is mine. **1983** S. Wright *Meditations* 297: Fuck you in the ear. **1984** W. J. Caunitz *One Police Plaza* 254: Fuck 'em where they breathe. **1984** A. R. Sample *Race-hoss* 217 [refers to *ca*1960]: Fuck all ya'll rat dead in the ass! **1987** N. Bell *Cold Sweat* 11: So fuck you both in the heart. **1993** G. Lee *Honor & Duty* 130: Fuck you in the ear. **1995** A. Ginsberg in *Nation* (Nov. 27) 669: Fuck you in the face. **1996** D. Gilbert in *Harper's* (July) 72: "Man, you're hopeless."..."Fuck your teeth." **1997** *Village Voice* (N.Y.C.) (Apr. 22) 53: Fuck my gums! **2007** A. Kentawy *Sunset Tales from New Iraq* 199: Fuck you in the goat ass you fucken piece of fucken Chinese crap.

c. to cease or abandon, especially suddenly; ditch. See also *fuck it*, below, and *fuck this shit*, below.

1925 *Englische Studien* LX 279 [refers to WWI]: *Fuck it*...meant much the same as *chuck it*, "put a sock in it"—stop talking; or even "clear out." **1965–70** J. Carroll in *Paris Review* (No. 50) 103: No solution is coming so I fuck it and start to yell. **1973** R. Roth *Sand in Wind* 150: I got the idea to fuck everything and head for California. **1979** J. Charyn *Seventh Babe* 174: Hell...Carl, why don't we fuck baseball camp and stay right here? **1980** L. Fleischer & C. Gore *Fame* 158: Coco's temper snapped. "Look, I'm not 'my dear,'" she exploded. "You can fuck 'my dear'!" **1984** W. Henderson *Elvis* 8: For two cents I'd fuck this job! Two goddamn cents —.

d. chiefly *British*. to be willing to make the required effort; to be bothered. Used in passive, in negative constructions.

1982 M. Amis *Money* 253: The Fiasco is still in custody. I keep meaning to go along and spring it from the pound. But I can't be fucked. **1987** in F. Vermorel *Sex Pistols* 78: Boogie expected me at the office early but I couldn't be fucked to hurry. **1995** D. McLean *Bunker Man* 154 Rob decided he couldn't be fucked rushing back to the school. **1997** J. Owen *Camden Girls* 52: I can't be fucked. It's so fuckin eighties and you know what, I think I'm all charitied out. **2000** J. Goodwin *Danny Boy* xi. 233: I left school aged sixteen with no qualifications; not because I'm thick, but cos I couldn't be bothered, couldn't be fucked. **2004** G. King *Three* 52: I also realise the putrefied contents of my downstairs bin have survived to fester and mutate another week as I can't be fucked throwing on clothes and rushing them to the curb. **2005** L. Dean *This Human Season*

100: Kathleen would go on wearing a bra, but she couldn't be fucked with doing the ironing anymore.

5. to trifle or interfere with; fool; lie to.

1989 S. Lee *Do the Right Thing* (film): Look, don't fuck me, awright? **1995** J. Sack *Co. C* 185: "You're *fuckin'* me, XO," Burns erupted. "You said it's a *T-55* and it's plainly a *Bradley!*...You're lying to *me!*"

In phrases:

☞ **fuck a duck**

1. get out! go to hell!—used with *go*.

[**1785** F. Grose *Classical Dictionary of the Vulgar Tongue*: Duck f-ck-r. The man who has the care of the poultry on board a ship of war.] **1931** H. Miller *Letter* (June 16) in *Letters to Emil* (1989) 133: Tell her to go fuck a duck! [**1932** *American Speech* VII (June) 332: *Go milk a duck*—"mind your own business."] **1946** W. L. Gresham *Nightmare Alley* 47: Go frig a rubber duck. **1953–55** MacK. Kantor *Andersonville* 183: Aw, go fuck a duck. [**1958** R. Chandler *Playback* 168: Why don't you go kiss a duck?] **1965** W. Beech *Make War in Madness* 67: Go fuck a duck, Otis. **1967–72** T. Weesner *Car Thief* 258: I don't give a shit, they can go fuck a duck. [**1972** G. Lukas et al. *American Graffiti* (film script) 50: Steve. Hey Kroot (*The teacher turns, surprised by the omission of the "Mr."*) Steve. (*cont.*) Why don't you go kiss a duck. (*Kroot's beady eyes widen and he comes back.*) Kroot. What? What did you say? Steve. I said go kiss a duck, marblehead.] **1973** *TULIPQ* (coll. B.K. Dumas): You mother, go fuck a duck. **1977** in E. Partridge *Dictionary of Catch Phrases* (ed. 2) 104: *Go fuck a duck!* "Get lost!" "Beat it!" Current, 1920s (in US), now virtually dead. *a***1990** D. Poyer *Gulf* 389: Bernard gave him a go-to-hell sneer....He could fuck a duck. **1992** J. L'Heureux *Shrine at Altamira* 81: When he asked for an advance against his paycheck, the boss had laughed and told him to go fuck a duck. **2005** M. Marnich in *Theatre Forum* (Winter/Spring) 72/2: *Peter*: You never miss a deadline. And you never swear. *Amy*: There's a first time for everything. Go fuck a duck.

2. to engage in indiscriminate sexual activity.—used with *will* or *would*.

*a***1930** in G. Legman *No Laughing Matter* (1975) 177: Fuckaduck film. **1951** R. Thacher *Captain* 40: Hambley, as the saying goes, would frake a drake. **1972** *National Lampoon* (Apr.) 34: You can get anything from an ugly chick....Really foul, but they'll fuck a duck. **2004** J. R. Lansdale *Sunset & Sawdust* 14: "Shit, I'd fuck a duck if it winked and bent over." "I don't think you'd care if it winked or not." **2008** S. Offit *Friends, Writers, & Other Countrymen* 90: I've always been quite candid about sex—I would fuck a duck—and have.

3. (used as an interjection to express anger or astonishment).

1934 H. Miller *Tropic of Cancer* 36: Well, fuck a duck! I congratulate him just the same. **1954–60** H. Wentworth & S. B. Flexner *Dictionary of American Slang.* **1972–76** C. Durden *No Bugles, No Drums* 234: I looked at Ski. He looked away. Lord fuck a duck. **1976** S. Hayden *Voyage* 420: Well, now, fuck a duck, whaddaya know about that? **1977** D. Bredes *Hard Feelings* 250: Operation Rollaway!...Fuck a duck! **1981** R. Meltzer *Belsen Is No Longer Gas* in *Whore Just Like Rest* (2000) 310: But fuck a duck Hitler was a vegetarian. **1986** I. Wedde *Symmes Hole* 117: There are men running in many directions...uniforms, mufti, pyjamas... "Fuck a duck!" the other running on. "...hey, you jokers, it's a breakout from Crawford!" **1990** P. Munro *Slang U.* 85: *Fuck a duck!*...Damn! **1993** G. F. Newman *Law & Order* 20: "I'm getting a lot of aggro from the filth on account of some videos I done a couple of weeks ago." "Fuck a duck!" Lynn said. **1996** M. Cheek *Sleeping Beauties* iv. 30: And Chloe, tweezers poised, said spontaneously, "Fuck a duck, that's *terrible*." **2002** M. Crichton *Prey* 226: "Hey, Charley...I think it's found a way." "Yeah, I see it. Fuck a duck."

4. (see 1971, 1979 quotations at definition 1c, above).

☞ **fucked [up] and far from home** and variants, chiefly *Military*, in a hopeless situation. See also *fed up, fucked up, and far from home* under FED UP.

1921–24 A. G. Pretty et al. *Glossary of Slang & Peculiar Terms Used in the A.I.F.: F.F.F.* Completely miserable; friged [*sic*], fucked, and far from home. **1936** E. Partridge *Dictionary of Slang & Unconventional English* 305: *F*cked and far from home*. In the depths of misery, physical and mental: a military [catch phrase]: 1915. **1950** E. Partridge *Dictionary of Slang & Unconventional English* (ed. 3) 1054: *F*cked-up and far from home*... dates from 1899. **1955** W. Gaddis *Recognitions* 937: The hell with them, anyway, they're all of them fucked and far from home, sitting over there right now pretending they're in New York pretending they're in Paris. **1972** R.A. Wilson *Playboy's Book of Forbidden Words* 117: When the IRS was through auditing my return, I was fucked and far from home. **1974** B. Broadfoot *Six War Years* 75: We used to have this expression in the [Canadian] army. A guy would say he was fucked and far from home. **1988** G. Swift *Out of this World* 170: Fucked-up and far from home. Or, as one hollow-faced Marine lieutenant, who was at the frivolous stage, put it: Dug-in, doped-up, demoralized or dead. **1995** T. Willocks *Bloodstained Kings* 207: You were well fucked and far from home.

☞ **fucked by the fickle finger of fate**, thwarted or victimized by bad fortune. *Jocular.*

   1944–46 in *American Speech* XXII 56: *Flucked by the flickle flinger of flate.* Doomed by Army snafu. **1957** E. Brown *Locust Fire* 93 [refers to 1944]: The fickle finger would foul you sure in the end. It would goose you over the edge. Fouled by the fickle finger of fate. **1968** D. Stahl *Hokey* 220: I was being totally and fatally fucked by the fickle finger of fate. **1972** R.A. Wilson *Playboy's Book of Forbidden Words* 104: *Fucked by the fuckle*[*sic*] *finger of fate,*(said by those whose plans are thwarted). **1976** in E. Partridge *Dictionary of Slang & Unconventional English* (ed. 8) 433: *Fucked by the fickle finger of fate*…Current in U.S. (student) circles at least several years earlier [than WWII]. **1983** A. Sillitoe *Lost Flying Boat* 92: "Fucked by the fickle finger of fate," said Bull. "Alliteration will do for you yet," said Rose. **1986** W. E. B. Griffin *Generals* 166: At that moment, Lieutenant Geoffrey Craig understood that he had been fucked by the fickle finger of fate. **1990** B. Graham *Bill Graham Presents* (2004) 41: He always played the role of the guy that was fucked by the fickle finger of fate. He was never totally a bad guy.

☞ **fuck 'em all but six [and save them for pallbearers]**, Especially *Military.* to hell with them all. Also in euphemistic variants.

   1916–17 in *Tennessee Folklore Society Bulletin* XXI (1955) 100 [bowd-lerized]: Cuss 'em all, cuss 'em all,/Cuss 'em all but six! [**1932** K. Nicholson & C. Robinson *Sailor Beware!* 22: "All but six." "And you can use them for pallbearers."] **1931–34** L. A. Adamic *Dynamite* 393 [refers to *ca*1925]: The motto in a factory where I once worked was: "To hell with 'em all but six; save them for pallbearers!" **1950** J. Stuart *Objector* 216: "Screw the Army, the whole God-damned Army." "All but six….They'll need pallbearers." **1952** L. Uris *Battle Cry* [refers to 1942]: "Fugg you guys and save six for pallbearers," Levin shouted. **1920–54** V. Randolph *Bawdy Elements* 120: Oh, fuck 'em all but six, and save them for pall-bearers. **1960** D. MacCuish *Do Not Go Gentle* 116 [refers to 1941]: Screw all but six and save them for pallbearers. **1972–76** C. Durden *No Bugles, No Drums* 7: Dumb bastards. Fuck 'em all but eight. Leave six for pallbearers and two to beat the drums. **1987** *National Lampoon* (June) 14: How about the famous Army saying "Fuck all of them but six and save *them* for pallbearers." **2000** J. Blackthorn *I, Che Guevara* 84: Fuck 'em all but six, and keep them for pallbearers.

☞ **fuck 'em if they can't take a joke** (used to dismiss or reject someone for being (esp. hypocritically) dismissive).

1973 E. Cray *Burden of Proof* 365: The ultimate condemnation, "Fuck 'Em If They Can't Take a Joke." **1978** A. Maupin *Tales of City* 42: "Fuck 'em, if they can't take a joke!" She laughed, hoping it would cover her embarrassment. **1985** J. Dillinger *Adrenaline* 102: He drew a few stares in his…Bermudas and…sport shirt. Fuck 'em if they couldn't take a joke. *a***1991** C. Heimel *If You Can't Live Without Me, Why Aren't You Dead Yet?* 221: It is your sacred duty to forge new ways, turn expectations asunder, and fuck 'em if they can't take a joke. **1994** *Esquire* (Feb.) 80: Fuck 'em if they can't take a joke. **2003** J. Smiley *Good Faith* 377: And now I'm late for dinner, but, hey, fuck 'em if they can't take a joke.

☞ **fuck it** (used to express dismissal, exasperation, resignation, or impetuousness).

1922 E.E. Cummings *Enormous Room*: F— it, I don't want it. **1925** *Englische Studien* LX 279 [refers to WWI]: *Fuck it*…meant much the same as *chuck it*, "put a sock in it"—stop talking; or even "clear out." **1926** F. Wray trans. H. Barbusse *Under Fire* 27: Ah, f— it! **1933** H. Miller in *Letters to Emil* (1989) 131: Fuck it! I'm starting off bad with my colors. **1934** J. O'Hara in *Selected Letters* 93: My message to the world is Fuck it! **1935** in P. Oliver *Blues Tradition* 231: Whee…tell 'em about me! Fuck it! **1959** J. Kerouac *Dr. Sax* 40: Ah fuckit, Zagg—helmets is helmets. **1968** H. Davies *Beatles* I thought, fuck it, fuck it, fuck it. That's really fucked everything. **1978** B. Seale *Lonely Rage* 81: If you don't want to forgive me—well, fuck it, I'm still sorry. **1985** R. B. Parker *Catskill Eagle* 356: Costigan looked back at me, "Fuck it," he said, "get it done." I shot him. A hole appeared in his forehead and the impact spun his swivel chair half around. **1990** L.B. Rubin *Erotic Wars* 180: Fuck it, why not? **1998** W. Lamb *I Know This Much is True* 547: Fuck it, man. Couldn't keep the Grim Reaper waiting. **2008** P. Carey *His Illegal Self* 53: Fuck it. She balled it in her fist and squeezed it. Wringing the water into her lap. Fuck it fuck it fuck it fuck it.

☞ **fuck me!** (used to express anger or astonishment); "I'll be damned!"—also in elaborated variants.

1929 F. Manning *Middle Parts of Fortune* 126 [refers to WWI]: "Well, you can fuck me!" exclaimed the astonished Martlow. **1943** G. Biddle *Journal* (July 31) in *Artist at War* (1944) 77: Teddy's run of literary allusions is a pleasant relief after the too concentrated diet of "fuck me's" and "fuck you's" of the G.I.'s. **1944** L. Glassop *We Were the Rats* 194: And — me if he doesn't get stook into it with grenades. **1944–57** L. Atwell *Private* 64 [refers to WWII]: F— me, I'm not hangin' around here! **1958** W. Talsman *Gaudy Image* 197: Well, fuck me double…if it isn't Aphrodite Schultz in person. **1957–62** D. Higginbotham *U.S. Marine Corps Folklore* 24: Fuck me dead! **1970** D. Wakefield *Going All the Way* 296: Fuck me in the teeth. What a fuckin piece of luck. **1973** B. Hirschfeld *Generation of Victors* 32: Fuck me blind! That hole ain't half done. **1977** D. Bredes *Hard Feelings* 293: I'm just trying to talk myself out of being scared shitless because, fuck me, I have to go down there. **1984** K. Weaver *Texas Crude* 28: Fuck me naked! Fuck me a-runnin'! **1985** D. Dye *Run Between the Raindrops* 315: Well, fuck me blind. OK, Lieutenant. Got the picture right here. **1988** D. Waters *Heathers* (film script) 8: *Veronica.* Why can't we talk to different kinds of people. *Heather Chandler.* Fuck me gently with a chainsaw. Do I look like Mother Theresa? If I did, I probably wouldn't mind talking to the Geek Squad. **1991** E. S. Raymond *New Hacker's Dictionary* 170: Aiigh-hh! Fuck me with a piledriver and 16 feet of curare-tipped wrought-iron fence *and no lubricants!* **1993** G. Lee *Honor & Duty* 330: Well, fuck me to tears!…It's really Joe Schmoe the ragman. **1995** J. Díaz in *New Yorker* (Jan. 19, 1996) 78: I hop the fence, feeling stupid when I sprawl on the…grass. Nice one, somebody calls out. Fuck me, I say. **1997** Student slang survey: If something goes wrong, you say, "Well, fuck me up the goat's ass." **2004** R. Pickett *Sideways* 184: Oh, fuck me with a hot poker. **2006** I. Welsh

Bedroom Secrets of Master Chefs 188: I see a familiar figure approaching the bar, and fuck me if it isn't my old mate Dessie Kinghorn.

☞ **fuck (someone's) mind,** to astonish, intimidate, or befuddle (someone). Compare MIND-FUCK, *noun & verb.*

> **1966** R. Goldstein *1 in 7* 113: Mind-fucking is taking advantage of a student who is high on pot—and thus susceptible to suggestion. For instance: "You tell someone who's inhaled pot for a while that he's been holding his breath for twenty minutes, and he's liable to believe you. It really fucks his mind!" **1968** R. Gover *JC* 137: Hey that sure would fuck some minds, huh. **1970** E. E. Landy *Underground Dictionary* 84: *Fuck someone's mind...v.* To persuade forcefully without regard for the feelings of those being persuaded. *a*1974 in *Adolescence* XIII (1978) 467: [Solitary confinement] fucks your mind, you keep saying you want to go home. **1994** R. Flanagan *Death of River Guide* 128: They want to fuck your mind, that's what she said. **1998** *New Times* (Los Angeles) (Oct. 29): You can fuck my body, baby, but please don't fuck my mind. **2001** D. Brenna *Altar of the Body* 238: She knows how to bust your buns, how to fuck your mind. Well, I say fuck her!

☞ **fuck the deck,** see under DECK.

☞ **fuck the dog,** see under DOG.

☞ **fuck the duck,** see under DUCK.

☞ **fuck this shit** (used to dismiss a situation); "to hell with this."

> **1968** L. Yablonsky *Hippie Trip* 206: I said fuck this shit and moved over here. **1973** J. P. Donleavy *Fairy Tale of N.Y.* 74: I said fuck this shit I'm getting out of here and going there. **1983** D. Mamet *Glengarry Glen Ross* 62: What the fuck am I wasting my time, fuck this shit. **1990** G. Lee *China Boy* 92: Le's fuck dis shit an leave da sucka be. **1995** C. Sorrentino *Sound on Sound* 131: Who cares, fuck this shit. **2006** C. Messud *Emperor's Children* 270: Fuck this shit, man. Fuck this shit.

☞ **fuck wise,** to act or speak like a know-it-all.

> **1979** D. Gram *Boulevard Nights* 49: "Don't fuck wise!" shot back Chuco.

☞ **fuck you,** (used to express hostility or contempt); "go to hell!" See also sense 4.b., above, *fuck you and the horse you rode in on,* and *fuck you very much,* below.

[**1905** *Independent* (Mar. 2) 486: "D—n you, Jack, I'm all right," is being gradually adopted by the lords of the forecastle and quarter deck alike in place of the old time motto of generous consideration that was world famous, "Remember Your Shipmates."] *ca***1915** in J. Brophy & Partridge *Long Trail* 229: Dieu et mon droit./F— you, Jack, I'm all right. **1916** A. Tiveychoc *Diary* (June 16) in B. Gammage *Broken Years* (1974) 126: Goodbye and — you! **1916–18** in *Notes & Queries* (Nov. 19, 1921) 417: — you, Jack, I'm in the lifeboat. **1931** J. Dos Passos *Nineteen Nineteen* 249 [refers to WWI]: Hey sojer your tunic's unbuttoned (f—k you buddy). **1934** H. Roth *Call It Sleep* 420 [refers to *ca*1910]: Yu crummy bastard….Fuck yiz! **1935** H. McCoy *They Shoot Horses* 37: "F— you," Gloria said. **1942** R. Tregaskis *Guadalcanal Diary* (Sept. 1): "F— you, Mac," he said, indulging in the marines' favorite word. **1951** J. D. Salinger *Catcher in the Rye* 201: Somebody'd written "Fuck you" on the wall. It drove me damn near crazy. I thought how Phoebe and all the other little kids would see it, and how they'd wonder what the hell it meant….I kept wanting to kill whoever'd written it. **1962** E. Albee *Who's Afraid of Virginia Woolf?* 13: *George…* Alright, love…whatever love wants. Isn't it nice the way some people have manners, though, even in this day and age? Isn't it nice that some people won't just come breaking into other people's houses even if they *do* hear some subhuman monster yowling at 'em from inside…? *Martha.* FUCK YOU! **1969** M. Puzo *Godfather* 187: "You can't fire me?" Nino said with drunken cunning. "No," Johnny said. "Then fuck you." **1978** L. K. Truscott *Dress Gray* 291: Fuck you and all you "know" about that war…. So fuck you and your uppity crap about me and West Point and the army and Vietnam. **1983** D. Mamet *Glengarry Glen Ross* 42: And fuck you. Fuck the lot of you. Fuck you all. **1976–84** A. M. Ettinger & A. C. Ettinger *Doughboy with Fighting 69th* 8 [refers to 1918]: Fuck you. If you got any sisters, fuck them too. **1990** in N. George *Buppies, B-Boys* 143: Robin made saying "Fuck you" an art form. **1997** A. Nersesian *Fuck-Up* 74: "Fuck you!" I shouted unconcerned that we were the center of attention in the place…"Well fuck you too!" she yelled back and vanished back into the masses. **2006** in L. McNeil & G. McCain *Please Kill Me* 418: I was like, "*Fuck you! Fuck you! Fuck you! Fuck you!* Oh, sorry, Mom." **2007** J. Hayes *Precious Blood* 273: Fuck you! Fuck you, you fucking *coward*!

☞ **fuck you and the horse you rode in on** (an elaborated and intensified form of) *fuck you*, above.

1967 A. Dubus *Lieutenant* 6: Use[d] disrespectful language to Corporal Bradley…to wit, "Fuck you and the horse you rode in on, Mac" or words to that effect. **1971** G. V. Higgins *Friends of Eddie Coyle* 92: Fuck you, lady,… *and* the horse you rode in on. **1972–76** C. Durden *No Bugles, No Drums* 78: Fuck you…'n' the horse you rode in on. **1992** M. Crichton *Rising Sun* 111: "Senator Rowe…I'm afraid I'll have to ask you to — " "Fuck you and the horse you rode in on." **2004** *New York Magazine* (Aug. 9) 44/2: In the elevator, a bunch of…attorneys rode down together. A message flashed on all their BlackBerries. It was from London: "Fuck [assistant district attorney] Moscow and the horse he rode in on." **2008** S. Paretsky *Bleeding Kansas* 391: "Beelzebub, Demon Alcohol, Demon Gluttony, in the Holy Name of Jesus I cast you out! Leave this woman and leave this place!" "Fuck you, and the horse you rode in on, too!" Elaine yelled.

☞ **fuck you very much** (used as a sarcastic or blatantly insincere expression of undeserved thanks).

*a*1976 T. McNally *Ritz & Other Plays* 159: Fuck you, ducky, fuck you very much. Nice place you got here. **1978** A. Maupin *Tales of the City* 70: Fuck you very much. **1981** J. Wambaugh *Glitter Dome* 41: Good luck to the first team and fuck you very much. **1985** T. Kidder *House* 256: We Sincerely Appreciate Your Criticism[/]Fuck You Very Much. **1991** D. Gates *Jernigan* 77: Absolutely nothing to lose at this point. "Well, fuck you very much," I said. **1991** M. Lackey *Jinx High* 143: "And fuck you very much, sir," she said mockingly to the handset as she put it down on the tray. **1998** E. J. Dickey *Milk in My Coffee* 42: "Kim, why—" "*Kimberly*. My damn name is *Kimberly*, fuck you very much." **2007** G. Kaplan *Evil, Inc.* lx. 164: "Sure," Ken said, pulling his arm away from the goon's grip, "fuck you very much."

☞ **get fucked!** (used to express hostility or contempt); go to hell!

*a*1950 E. Partridge *Dictionary of Slang & Unconventional English* (ed. 3) 1054: F*cked!, go and get.…mid C.19-20. **1966** E. Shepard *Doom Pussy* 151: We told him to go ahead and ask. And he did. And *we* say, "Get f—." **1968** L. J. Davis *Whence All Had Fled* 218: "Get fucked," he said. **1986** D. Dye & O. Stone *Platoon* 16: Tell that dipshit to get fucked. *a*1990 C. T. Westcott *Half a Klick from Home* 125: Tell him ta get fucked with a mule's dick, I don't care.

☞ **go fuck [yourself]** (used to express hostility or contempt); go to hell! get out! be damned! Also variants with other objects, especially **go fuck your mother**. [*Go fuck your mother* is generally perceived as the most offensive and provocative curse in English; cf. MOTHERFUCKER.]

[**1879** *Pearl* 210: He'd been told,/To bloody well bugger himself.] **1895** *Report of the Senate Committee on the Police Dept. of N.Y.* III. 3158: By Senator Bradley: Q. Repeat what he said to you? A. He said, "Go on, fuck yourself, you son-of-a-bitch; I will give you a hundred dollars"; he tried to punch me, and I went out. [**1905** W. S. Kelly *Lariats* 273: If yer don't like 'em, go and puke yourselfs.] **1920** in J. Dos Passos *14th Chronicle* 306: As for an intellectual class it can go f— itself. **1922** T. E. Lawrence *The Mint* (1955) 99: "Go and fuck rattlesnakes," retorted Garner. **1926** F. Wray trans. H. Barbusse *Under Fire* 243: Go and f— yourself. **1929** D. Marquis in G. Legman *No Laughing Matter* (1975) 149: Go fuck thy suffering self. **1931** J. Dos Passos *Nineteen Nineteen* 150 [refers to WWI]: Joe got sore and told him to go f— himself. **1932** E. Hemingway *Winner* 152: F— yourself. F— your mother. F— your sister. **1933** in H. Miller *Letters to Emil* (1989) 126: Tell her to go fuck herself. **1938** R. Chandler *Big Sleep* 60: Go — yourself. **1942** in D. Schwartz *Journals* 88: "Then go fuck yourself!" said May, hanging up, enraged. **1948** N. Mailer *Naked & Dead* 12: Go fug yourself. [**1951** *African Studies* X 32: "Copulate with your mother!" Normally no insult could be more frightful.] **1955** J. Sack *Here to Shimbashi* 92: Sometimes they toss cigarettes to the MP's on patrol, and sometimes they have been known to shout, "Hey, GI — your mother!" in English. **1959** New York City schoolboy, age 13: Aw, go fuck your mother in bed, you little prick! **1961** J. Baldwin *Another Country* 34: Drop dead, get lost, go fuck yourself. **1961** R. Granat *Important Thing* 80 [refers to WWII]: You just go f—. **1967** N. Mailer *Why We Are in Vietnam* 94: Go fuck, D.J.'s got his purchase on the big thing. **1969** in M. Girodias *New Olympia Reader* 68: She [was] screaming, "Go fuck your mother." [**1976** C. Amuzie in *Journal of Black Studies* VI 416: Among the Igbos, one could hear male and very old female adults cursing [in Igbo] as follows: "fuck your mother," "fuck your sister," "may a dog fuck your mother." These curses are perceived by the Igbos as among the worst.] **1976** J. Harrison *Farmer* 28: Oh go fuck yourself. **1973–77** J. Jones *Whistle* 320 [refers to WWII]: "Appreciate it." "Go fuck." **1977** *Maledicta* (Summer) 12: Go fuck yourself with a rubber weenie. **1980** E. Morgan *Surgeon* 195: "Leah," screamed the little girl. "Go fuck your cat, fuck your mother." [**1985** J.M.G. Brown *Rice Paddy Grunt* 122: The gook tells him, "*Du Mau, Du Mau*" (to fuck his mother, in Vietnamese).] **2004** *Washington Post* (June 25) A4: A chance meeting with Sen. Patrick J. Leahy (Vt.), the ranking Democrat on the Judiciary Committee, became an argument about Cheney's ties to Halliburton Co., an international energy services corporation, and President Bush's judicial nominees. The exchange ended when Cheney offered some crass advice. "Fuck yourself," said the man who is a heartbeat from the presidency.

☞ **I wouldn't fuck her with your dick** and variants, (used to describe a sexually unappealing woman).

1968 G. Legman *Rationale of Dirty Joke* 367: Compare the folk-phrase, "I wouldn't fuck her with *your* prick." **1979** L. Gonzales *Jambeaux* 15: "I wouldn't fuck her with *your* dick," Link said. "You'd fuck anything that's warm." Page laughed. **1996** E. Leonard *Out of Sight* 219: Man, I wouldn't fuck her with your dick. **1998** J. Collins *Power* 63: "You *gotta* be kidding? I wouldn't fuck her with somebody else's dick." Trust Max to say exactly what everyone else was thinking. Angela looked like a heroin addict on the run. **2001** "L. Burana" *Strip City* 132: A man is loudly mocking a dancer.... "I wouldn't fuck her with somebody else's dick!" he howls to his friends. **2003** W. Heffernan *Time Gone By* 198: The broad's a lush. I wouldn't fuck her with *your* dick.

☞ **who do I (or you) have to fuck?** [in allusion to the alleged requirement of actresses to sleep with directors to get film roles] "what unpleasant thing do I have to do?"

1968 M. Crowley *Boys in the Band* 48: Who do you have to fuck to get a drink around here? **1971** T. Southern *Blue Movie* 13: Listen, who do I have to fuck to get *off* this picture? **1979** L. Gonzales *Jambeaux* 14: Who do you have to fuck to get a transfer outta this chickenshit outfit? **1986** T. McNally *It's Only a Play* 34: Who do you have to fuck to get something to eat around here? **1993** S. Corbin *Fragments that Remain* 264: Now I got plenty of cash money, and it's all about, Who do I have to fuck to spend my money with them? **2004** N. Munk *Fools Rush In* v. 99: I leave a message that says, "Who do I have to fuck to get you people to do your job?"

fuck *interjection*

1. (used as an interjection to express dismay, disbelief, resignation, surprise, etc.); "shit"; "hell." Compare FUCK, *verb*, definition 4.a.

1929 F. Manning *Middle Parts of Fortune* II. 161 [refers to WWI]: A man...uttered under his breath a monosyllabic curse. "Fuck." **1934** "J.M. Hall" *Anecdota Americana* (Second series) 146: "Oh, fuck!" he cried in disgust. **1943** in M. Morriss & R. Day *South Pacific Diary* (1996) 196: I welcome the day when people say "fuck!" in polite and mixed company. **1945** in T. Shibutani *Derelicts of Company K* 301: Fuck, we're gonna be in the army for another year anyway. **1958** I. Fleming *Dr. No* (1960) xx. 148: "—," said Bond, once. He got painfully out on to the side of the track. **1962** in B. Jackson *In the Life* 157: I'm no gambler because if I tried to gamble, fuck, I'd lose my goddamned drawers. **1964–66** R. Stone *Hall of Mirrors* 51: Fuck no, I ain't stoppin' you. **1973** P. Benchley *Jaws* 194: "Fuck!" he said, and he threw the full can into the wastebasket. **1981** J. H. Stiehm *Bring Men & Women* 263: One woman officer...told of stopping an activity because a frustrated woman had said, "Oh, fuck." **1985** E. Leonard *Glitz* 207: I thought, fuck, the guy's a natural. **1987** P. D. Chinnery *Life on the Line* 208: Brian...said, "Oh, f***." Then he died. **1998** M. Waites *Little Triggers* iii. 23: She lit her cigarette and pulled a deep drag.... After holding on for a few seconds she let go. Her tension ebbed along with the smoke. "Fuck, I needed that." **2002** M. Crichton *Prey* 144: "I'm not sure we can just deny—" "Fuck yes, deny."

2. [reduction of *fucked*, past participle of FUCK, *verb*, definition 4] damned [if].

1967 N. Mailer *Why Are We In Vietnam?* x. 178: "Well, you ain't no I.Q. competitor." "Fuck, I ain't. I compete you in anything." **1978** A. Maupin *Tales of the City* 18: Fuck if I know. **1983** W. D. Ehrhart *Vietnam to Perkasie* 143: Fuck if I'm stickin' around. **1984** W. D. Ehrhart *Marking Time* 123: Fuck if I know. **1998** *Daily Variety* (Apr. 23) A45: When was the moment we broke out? Fuck if I know, even I have a hard time dissecting that one. **2003** D. Lehane *Shutter Island* iii. 50: "Fuck if I know."... "Quite similar to our clinical conclusion."

3. = *the fuck*, definition 2, under FUCK, *noun*. Also: (elliptical for) "what the fuck," "who the fuck," etc.

1983 S. King *Christine* 147: "Turn out your pockets, Buddy."…"Fuck I will." **1989** B. M. Cooper & T. L. Wright *New Jack City* (film script) 30: Fuck is wrong with you? **1996** D. McCumber *Playing off Rail* 272: "I don't do that to you." "Fuck you don't." **1999** J. Williams *Five Pubs, Two Bars & Nightclub* 156: "Who you been talking to, Tone?" he asked now. "Kenny." "Fuck you talking to Kenny for?" **2003** J. Lethem *Fortress of Solitude* i. iv. 60: Fuck you know about it, anyway?

fuckability *noun*

ability to be copulated with; (*specifically*) sexual attractiveness.

1969 *Screw* (Sept. 1) 6/3: The SCREW sex laboratory must find the vibrating dildo limited in functionality and fuckability. **1992** M. Leyner *Et Tu, Babe* v. 126: I don't think that those folks wrote to enhance their fuckability. **1999** *Empire* (Nov.) 150/3: But the book is at its best when Figgis coaxes anecdotal material to back up the theories:…Ally Sheedy revealing she was told to "up her fuckability quotient" if she wanted to work. **2005** J. MacGregor *Sunday Money* iv. 118: For Cup drivers with talent and a good work ethic but a low mojo quotient ("deficient fuckability," per Hollywood), there is applause but no hysteria.

fuckable *adjective*

1. sexually desirable.

1889 Capt. C. Devereaux *Venus in India* 110: The poor man had at last outwitted his careful wife and obtained the much-longed-for fuckable cunt. *a*1890–93 J. S. Farmer & W. E. Henley *Slang & Its Analogues* III 80: *Fuckable*…Desirable. **1938** "Justinian" *Americana Sexualis* 23: *Fuckable*, sexually desirable (of a female). **1971** J. F. Hunter *Gay Insider* xvii. 217: Youth is the *sine qua non* of desirability: males under twenty-five, butch and fuckable. **1974** J. Lahr *Hot to Trot* 15: "I'd like to dip my wick into that." "Fuckable." **1973–77** J. Jones *Whistle* 233: She was…eminently fuckable. **1978** L. Kramer *Faggots* 28: If clothes make the man, what were they making?… And why was the same guy Hot and fuckable in a Pendleton and not in a Polo? **1986** R. Campbell *In La-La Land* 3: Showing how brave, how manly, how fuckable he was. **1997** *GQ* (Sept.) 258: Anne-Marie…is a blow-up doll—highly fuckable for her lack of will and personality. **2001** C. Whitehead *John Henry Days* iv. 323: They were all there, from the eminently fuckable to the differently attractive, the not conventionally handsome and the walking airbrushed in complimentary [*sic*] pairs. **2004** H. Walsh *Brass* i. 21: A simple course of lazer treatment would kill the problem forever and thus transform her from an unfuckable attractive lady to a fuckable stunner.

2. sexually available.

1889 Capt. C. Devereaux *Venus in India* 142: I should never at any time object to so great a pleasure as having my prick and my balls handled by a very pretty girl, whom I knew to be fuckable. **1972** B. Rodgers *Queens' Vernacular* 25: *Available* open for sexual consideration.... Syn[onyms]: *catchable; fuckable;* [etc.]. **1977** College student: What you do is, you just come right out and ask her, "How fuckable are you?" **1994** *Guardian* (Sept. 17) (Weekend Suppl.) 5/3: Where are all the fuckable younger men for the older woman? **1995** *Independent* (Jan. 28) 27/2: Because there is only one reason for women to exist in Updike's world: to be fucked, or at least fuckable. **2004** S. Kandel *I Dreamed I Married Perry Mason* xxvi. 184: Thick wool legs at cocktail hour! What an affront!... Silk stockings mean you're fuckable.

fuck-a-doodle-doo *interjection*
(used to express ironic delight); "oh, wonderful"; "big deal."

1976 J. F. Daly (book title): Fuck-a-doodle-doo. **1980** C. Garrison *Snakedoctor* 186: Well, fuck-a-doodle-doo! **1990** N. Simon *Rumors* 86: ERNIE....(*Covering the phone.*) It's a woman. For Glenn. CLAIRE. So? ERNIE. It sounds like Myrna. COOKIE. Oh, fuck-a-doodle-doo. **1994** *Four Weddings & a Funeral* (film): Fuck-a-doodle-doo. **2004** *Shaun of the Dead* (film): "I like having him around, he's a laugh." "Because he can impersonate an orangutan? Fuck-a-doodle-doo."

fuckaholic *noun* [FUCK, *verb*, definition 1a + -*aholic*]
a person who compulsively engages in promiscuous sexual intercourse. *Jocular.*

1981 D. Jenkins *Baja Oklahoma* 246: He's just a fuckaholic, is all he is. **1989** S. Chapple & D. Talbot *Burning Desires* 294: Both were serious fuckaholics. **1997** N. Kotker *Billy in Love* 50: Every Tuesday morning. We had a regular date. Plus Marie twice a week. Plus Alice, whenever. That's what I mean fuckaholic. I needed to have it. **2002** F. C. Wilson *Jaded Rose* v. 30: I'm still a fuckaholic and I enjoy it! Why the damn tears? More sex, more better, I always say.

fuck all *noun*

1. absolutely nothing; FUCK, *noun*, definitions 2a & b; (in negative constructions) anything at all; the least thing.—also as *adjective*.

1916 *Record of the Trial of H. Farr* (Public Record Office: WO 71/509) f. 4: He then said, "You are a fucking coward & you will go to the trenches— I give fuck all for my life & I give fuck all for yours & I'll get you fucking well shot." **1918** Noyes *Slang Manuscript* (unpaged): *Fuck-all.*—(1) nothing. "There's not a fuck-all to do this afternoon." **1919** *Athenaeum* (Aug. 1) 695: There is a very queer phrase denoting "nothing"—"— all!" No record of war slang is complete without it. **1929** F. Manning *Middle Parts of Fortune* 130 [refers to 1916]: We all go over the top knowing sweet fuck-all of what we are supposed to be doing. **1939** A. C. Bessie *Men in Battle* 133: Nobody's seen fuck-all of 'em. **1941** in G. Legman *Limerick* (1954) 35: The cube of its weight…/Was four fifths of five eighths of fuck-all. *ca*1944 in A. Hopkins *Front & Rear* 54: The officers they know fuck all. *ca*1950 in E. Cray *Erotic Muse* 116: There was fuck-all else to do. **1965** S. Linakis *In Spring the War Ended* 74: Didn't mean fuck-all to the ones that busted you. **1967** J. Kornbluth *Notes from the New Underground* 91: The *Daily Mirror* carried thirteen thousand inches of advertising—and fuck-all to read. **1976** P. Atlee *Last Domino Contract* 160: They would have fuckall chance against us. **1978** L. K. Truscott *Dress Gray* 45: Said the supe…didn't know fuckall. **1979** L. Bangs in *Psychotic Reactions* (1987) 283: What have we got! Fuckall! **1984** J. Hughes *Breakfast Club* (final draft screenplay) 139: Brian, *apprehensive* What if he calls my mother? *A satisfied, fuck-all grin spreads across his face.* I'll trash the bitch. **1994** *Loaded* (Sept.) 41/2: My ambition is to go on the *Antiques Roadshow* and say to some old bag, "You're thinking this old wardrobe is worth a million quid but it's worth fuck all." **1994** J. Kelman *How Late it Was* 99: Sammy sniffed. There was fuck all to say. He wasnay even angry any longer. **1995** R. Williamson, folk singer, in concert in N.Y.C.: Shut up, Dad, you don't know fuck-all! **1997** *Harper's* (Feb.) 68: I taught you nothing. I taught you fuck-all. **1997** A. Proulx in

New Yorker (Oct. 13) 83: But fuck-all has worked the way I wanted. **2002** E. Hartmann *Truth About Fire* vi. 52: The local police aren't doing fuck-all about the investigation. Another dead Injun, what's the big deal. **2006** G. Malkani *Londonstani* ix. 100: There were other people with fuck all to do with the fight out by the track that afternoon.

2. hell (as an expletive).

1938 E. Hemingway in *Selected Letters* (1981) 466: It's been a fuckall of a six weeks. Nobody's got any social standing at all now who hasn't swum the Ebro at least once. **1958** L. F. Cooley *Run for Home* 138 [refers to 1920s]: Who the fuck-all does he think he is?

3. a damn; a fuck.

1958 L. F. Cooley *Run for Home* 20 [refers to 1920s]: I don't give a fuck-all what you think! **1998** P. Biskind *Easy Riders, Raging Bulls* 177: We didn't give a fuck-all; we'd let anybody have a screening. **2007** L. Kleypas *Sugar Daddy* 400: Honey, I don't give a fuck-all if you believe me or not.

fuck-all *adverb*

utterly; at all; absolutely.

1961 G. Forbes *Goodbye to Some* 169 [refers to WWII]: Nothin'. Absolutely fuckall nothin'. **1961** E. Hemingway *Islands in the Stream* 336: I feel fuck-all discouraged about things sometimes. **1961** E. Hemingway *Islands in the Stream* 400: But I am not going to put Willie and Ara and Henry into one of those burp-gun massacres in the mangroves for fuck-all nothing. **1975** N. Dickens *Jack Nicholson* 122: She was a guest of the company and we didn't have to do fuck-all anything for her. **1991** O. Stone & Z. Sklar *JFK* (film): Don't matter fuck-all. **1992** J. Wolcott in *Vanity Fair* (Sept.) 301: The flatulent influence of Foucault on sex, about which Foucault...knew fuck-all nothing. **1997** *Esquire* May 64/1: Darrell Miers, big as a Buick with loose steering, possesses the fuck-all equanimity of a bail bondsman. **2005** J. Walter *Citizen Vince* 177: You think the job is a certain thing and you can just go along, fuck-all blind.

fuck-all *interjection*

= FUCK, *interjection*, definition 1.

1918 Noyes *Slang Manuscript* (unpaged): *Fuck-all*...(2) Also used as an expression of disgust. "Oh fuck-all!" **1963** H. S. Thompson *Letter* (Nov. 22) in *Proud Highway* (1997) 418: It hardly matters what you believe as long as you're on top, and laughing. Fuck all. **1966** F. Reynolds & M. McClure *Freewheelin Frank* 29: FUCK ALL! I GOT THE CLAP. **1993** G. F. Newman *Law & Order* 2: I mean, what can you do about it anyway?... I mean, fuckall, they come back and nick you, can you? You can get up in court and scream about them fitting you.... But you're up the steps before a wrong sort of judge, you see what good it does you. **2000–01** *Ploughshares* (Winter) 174: Her voice is so slight, so worried-like, that, well, fuckall, I feel leaky, wrinkled, like an old birthday balloon.

fuck almighty *interjection*

(used to express extreme pleasure, distress, disbelief, etc.; FUCK *interjection*).

1977 M. Scott *Threeway Team* 101: Fuck...shit, I'm coming! I'm coming, Don! Oh holy fuck almighty! **1985** S. Saladino *Erebus* 7: "Fuck almighty," Jay yelled, eyes bulging, a grin across his face. **1993** T. King *One on One* 134: Two bodies flow and change and rise to meet each other, harder here, softer there, opening up and enclosing, tightening and releasing. So close. So close. Almost there. Oh Fuck Almighty. **2006** I. Welsh *Bedroom Secrets of Master Chefs* 289: Jesus fuck almighty...I get a big shock as a stunningly beautiful girl of about nineteen, twenty, appears before me.

fuckaround *noun*

contemptuous treatment; a disappointing situation. Also: a worthless person.

1965 H.S. Thompson *Letter* (Apr. 18) in *Proud Highway* (1997) 509: My good time badass fuckaround is going out of style. **1970** in H.S. Thompson *Great Shark Hunt* 101: Well, to hell with it. You don't need publicity and I sure as hell don't need this kind of fuckaround. **1972** in H.S. Thompson *Great Shark Hunt* 123: A gig that was a... fuckaround from start to finish. **1980** P. Conroy *Lords of Discipline* 394: This is the last night we're going to play fuck-around with that bunch. **1987** J. Ferrandino *Firefight* 39: I'll teach you to play fuck around with me. **1996** D. McCumber *Playing off Rail* 245: Just another fuckaround, waiting all night for no action. **1999** T. Corcoran *Gumbo Limbo* 213: All these years, Rutledge has been a straight dealer, never a player, never a fuck-around.

fuck around or (*Brit.*) **fuck about** *verb*

1. to engage in promiscuous sexual intercourse.

*ca*1890 *My Secret Life* VIIII. ix.: Liz had learned to like the red knobbed flesh stick far better than another woman's cunt, and I dare say is merrily fucking about somewhere now, and I hope is happy. **1931** H. Miller *Letter* (Feb. 16) in *Letters to Emil* (1989) 76: I fucked around with this one and that. **1942** H. Miller *Roofs of Paris* 201: Does she know that you've been fucking around with her father? **1951** *American Journal of Sociology* XXXVII 138: Eddie f—s around too much; he's gonna kill himself or else get killed by some broad. And he's got a nice wife too. **1969** J. Crumley *One to Count Cadence* 100: Yes, I know my wife is fucking around. **1978** P. Schrader *Hardcore* 39: Your daughter was an absolutely clean girl, she never had rebellious or impure thoughts, she didn't fuck around. **1987** C. Fischer *Postcards from the Edge* 127: Sometimes I think I should marry one of them and just fuck around. **1989** A. Sorkin *A Few Good Men* 36: Don't fuck around with this one, Danny. **1991** N. Friday *Women on Top* 343: I'd do anything to have a chance to fuck around with a girl. **1997** C. Rock *Rock This!* 137: Some guys don't fuck around because they just don't. Other guys know they won't be able to see their kids.... For most of us it's much simpler: who's got the time to fuck around? **2007** J. Díaz *Brief Wondrous Life of Oscar Wao* 168: At college you're not supposed to care about anything—you're just supposed to fuck around—but believe it or not, I cared about Lola. **2008** "J. Jameson" *Something Blue* 37: You fucked around with a woman? When?

2. to play or fool around; trifle; mess. Compare FRIG, *verb*, definition 3.

1922 T. E. Lawrence *The Mint* (1955) 49: I wasn't going to fuck about for those toffee-nosed buggers. **1929** F. Manning *Middle Parts of Fortune* 17 [refers to WWI]: They kept 'em fuckin' about the camp, while they sent us over the bloody top. *ca*1933 in E. Sevareid *Wild Dream* 39: What's the difference between a mountain goat and a soda jerk?...The soda jerk mucks around the fountain. **1935** T. Wolfe *Death to Morning* 73 [refers to

1917]: What are ya doin' here ya f— little bastards!—who told ya t'come f— round duh hangah? *Ibid.* 74: Don't f— aroun' wit' me, ya little p—. **1936** J. Dos Passos *Big Money* 313: If you f—k around it'll cost you more. **1942** H. Miller *Roofs of Paris* 260: And here I am fucking around trying to get her to buy a camera. *ca***1944** in A. Hopkins *Front & Rear* 55: They fuck around but they never work. **1948** N. Mailer *Naked & Dead* 539: We're gonna move out in half an hour, so don't be fuggin' around. **1950** G. Legman in *Neurotica* (Autumn) 13: I could stop fugging around writing pulp. **1952** J. Kerouac *Visions of Cody* 220: I stayed out all night and fucked around. **1954** J. A. Weingarten *American Dictionary of Slang* 141: *Stop f—g around.* Common in the street language. **1955** L. Yablonsky *Violent Gang* 48: We don't fuck around—man, when you want to whip one on, just call....Our boys are always ready. **1971** J. Torres *Sting like a Bee* 34: He's just fucking around....He'll be O.K. **1978** *N.Y. Post* (Dec 9) 13: I won't shoot to kill, but I'll shoot them so they know not to fuck around with me no more. **1981** T.C. Boyle *Water Music* 67: A sandstorm is nothin' to fuck around with. **1984** J. Kelman *Busconductor Hines* (1992) iv. 167: What's the point of fucking about. You leave half of the second pint and get off your mark. **1994** I. Welsh *Shooter* in *Acid House* 4: That's my man, Gary slapped my back.—Always knew you had the bottle, Jock. All you fucking Jocks, all fucking crazy! We'll show that cunt Whitworth just who he's fucking abaht wiff here. **1995** W. Monahan in *N.Y. Press* (Apr. 26) 18: Brompton Cocktail[:] Heroin, Morphine, Cocaine, Gin.... There's definitely no fucking around with a Brompton Cocktail. **1999** T. Parker et al. *South Park* (film script) 53: *Canadian Prime Minister* We're not fucking around. This is not aboot deals. This aboot [*sic*] dignity. This is aboot freedom. **2005** K. Alley *How to Lose Your Ass* 167: That's the best fudge recipe in the world. Why candy companies fuck around and try to improve it, I'll never know.

3. to cheat or treat with contempt; make trouble for.

[*a***1900** in *English Dialect Dictionary* under *frig:* They are not going to frig me about.] **1944** L. Glassop *We Were the Rats* 69: "It's the way they — you around ....They — you around."..."You're in the army, aren't you? You're being — around by experts." **1960** F. Pollini *Night* 29: Why you fucking me around? **1970** A. Young *Snakes* 144: Big a juicehead as he is, he gon fuck me round over some gauge. **1970** E. Thompson *Garden of Sand* 328: Don't try to fuck me around, old man. **1970** T. Wolfe *Radical Chic* 125: They ripped off the white man and blew his mind and fucked him around like nobody has *ever* done it. **1973** W. Crawford *Stryker* 68: Don't try fucking me around. **1975** T. Cook *Vagrant Alcoholics* vii. 128: Some of the geezers fucked her about and then she began to change. **1977** E. Bunker *Animal Factory* 105: "Would he kill somebody over that?" "Oh yeah...quick if he thought the guy was deliberately fuckin' him around." **1991** M. S. Power *Come the Executioner* xiv. 143: "Your contact in Dublin— who is he?" Parr hesitated. "Don't fuck me about," Harwood told him. "A Mr Clancy." **1992** A. McGahan *Praise* 72: I don't think you'd fuck me around or anything, or have other women. **2002** T. Geoghegan *In America's Court* i. xxix. 131: These types of guys in the 1960s would get "fucked around" by us. By us, who went to the real college.

4. to astonish; bring up short.

1978 W. Brown *Tragic Magic* 139: *Sands of Iwo Jima*. That's the one that really fucked me around.

fuckass *noun*

a despicable or contemptible person.

*a***1960** E. Partridge *Dictionary of Slang & Unconventional English* (ed. 5) 1099: *F*ck-arse*. A low term of contempt: C.20. **1968** G. Cuomo *Among Thieves* 219: LaSala was really a slob, old fuck-ass everybody called him. **1969** R. Hugo *Good Luck* 40 [refers to WWII]: Fuckass...shithead...cunteyed bastard. **1978** E. Morris *Straightjacket* 108: "Fuck-ass," I told her behind my face. "Shit-fart." **1989** V. Eaton *Self-Portrait of Someone Else* 234: You're going to need it, fuckass. **2002** G. Easterbrook *Here & Now* 133: Don't touch me, you fuckass, I'll kill you with my bare hands. **2008** D. Glib *Flowers* 221: Don't yell at my mom, fuckass!

fuckass *adjective*

contemptible.—used before a noun.

1961 J. Jones *Thin Red Line* 30 [refers to WWII]: Any man'd leave it layin around's a fuckass soldier anyway. **1968** R. Sukenick *Up* 106: It strikes me...that you have a very fuck-ass attitude toward witch burning. **1975** D. Curzon *Misadventures of Tim McPicks* (1980) 230: Get the fuck-ass white folk! **1986** N. Freeling *Cold Iron* 194: Tying us up or something tricky out of some fuckass movie even if he doesn't think it funnier still to blow our heads off and bury us in the sand. **1993** J. Womack *Random Acts of Senseless Violence* 141: We gonna halfway house fuckass white girls now? **2000** P. Cadigan *Dervish is Digital* 208: They're sure not ready for what happens to them, and the fuck-ass company that supplies them don't care. **2006** J. Solow *Booster* 285: I ain't talking to none of you people. Fuckass shitwads.

fuckathon *noun* [FUCK + mar*athon*]

a prolonged period of orgiastic sexual activity. *Jocular.*

1968 M. Bloomfield in *Rolling Stone* (Apr. 6) 13/4: If you were at a fuck a thon, you'd have to know when a good fuck went down to know what's happening. **1970** D. Wakefield *Going All the Way* 97: Gunnar had gone over the apartment…to remove any traces of evidence of what he called the "fuckathon" of Saturday night. **1972** *Anthropological Linguistics* (Mar.) 102: *Fuckathon* (*n.*): Refers to an extended period of sexual activity in which a large number of persons participate. **1973** *Ribald* (Sydney, Australia) (May 18) 7: We are giving our services free for the night.…She's calling it a fuckathon. **1982** J. M. Del Vecchio *13th Valley* 336: How could he confess to him that he'd been on a fuckathon? **1988** R. M. Brown *Bingo* 272: It sounded as though the guy went on one big fuckathon. **1991** D. Jenkins *Gotta Play Hurt* 295: We'll have an old fashioned fuck-a-thon. **1998** J. Collins *Thrill!* 173: His supply of females had accelerated, a new one arriving every other day. Roxy commented he was having a fuckathon. **2003** "J. Le Carré" *Absolute Friends* 139: You remember how you called it our fuckathon? Well, let's have another, and take life from there.

fuck away *verb*

to squander or idle away; "piss away."

[**1948** in G. Legman *Limerick* (1954) 308: On his honeymoon sailing the ocean/A tightwad displayed much emotion/When he learned, one fine day,/He'd been fucking away/What could have been bottled as lotion.] **1965** J. Cremer *I, Jan Cremer* 209: To keep him from fucking away the entire family fortune. **1971** M. Schulman *Potatoes are*

Cheaper 64: I ain't gonna provide the vehicle for you to fuck away the Zimmerman millions. **1975** S.P. Smith *American Boys* 171: The others... fucked their bread away on booze. **1979** C. Keller *Subway Orgy* 158: The money he would receive from the kidnapping would be gone soon. He would spend it on broads, booze, and just fuck it away in general. **1989** E. L. Doctorow *Billy Bathgate* 208: While the Feds have been fucking away the summer on the beach we been up here sowing our oats. **1999** P. Caputo *Voyage* 258: Hey, mon, you got to *work* to drink up and fuck away four t'ousand dollars. **2004** S. Bishop-Stall *Down to This* 374: I mean, they're really fucking away any burgeoning sense of community down here. The dealers are going to grab it all.

fuckbag *noun*

a disgusting person; "asshole"; etc.

> **1969** J. Nuttall *Pig* 50: Silly old fuckbag.... Completely off her head. **1970** W. J. Craddock *Be Not Content* 75: What sort of a ruined mind would want to be a fuckbag cop? **1984** M. Amis *Money* 76: Apparently I called her a whore, cursed her for a gold-digging fuckbag, and kicked her out. **1989** R. McL. Wilson *Ripley Bogle* (1998) 8: They were, undoubtedly, rancid Welsh fuckbags like himself. **1993** I. Welsh *Trainspotting* (2002) 255: She discovered that the rapist fuckbag was HIV. Then she discovered that she was. **1998** *Re: Wrestling*, on Usenet newsgroup rec.sport. pro-wrestling (Nov. 3): What a fuckbag. If this guy was my dad, I'd open my wrists with a rusty can opener. **2007** D. Matthews *Ace of Spades* 174: I have never been able to process...humans and their true meanings. If someone were to walk by me and say *top of the morning, fuck-bag!* I would be halfway through my *why...hello* before the insult registered.

fuckbar *noun*

Homosexuals. a bar in which one can engage in sexual activity, esp. one having a back room for such a purpose.

> **1977** M. Christofer *Shadow Box* II. 69: I go inside the bar and *he* goes inside the bar. A real "fuck bar."...People are humping on the tables. **1981** *Gay Community News* (Nov. 28) 8: After hours, there are several possibilities for the gay male on Oxford Street. There are three fuck bars.... There

are the 253 Baths, one of four baths in the city, and a porn bookshop-cum-movie-house-cum-fuckbar called Numbers. **1996** G. W. Dowsett *Practicing Desire* 158: A good example is Ralph's first visit to a backroom fuck bar. **1998** B. Rumph trans. G. Dustan *In My Room* 50: I said to Stéphane I want to fuck you in a sling in a fuck bar. **2001** P. Gilovich et al. *Stranger Guide to Seattle* 7: The city's most down-and-dirty faggot fuck bar is also the only gay bar where DJs play rock.

fuck beggar *noun*

an old man with whom only a female beggar is willing to copulate.

1785 F. Grose *Classical Dictionary of the Vulgar Tongue*: F—k Beggar... An old superannuated fumbler, whom none but beggars will suffer to kiss them.

fuck book *noun*

see under FUCK, *adjective*.

fuck box *noun*

the vagina or vulva.

1976 J. Vasco *Three-Hole Girl* 158: She felt it building in her fuck box as she watched Tad's swollen purple dong head. **1998** *A Swinger's Story*, on Usenet newsgroup alt.sex.swingers (Oct. 24): Peggy reached down and grabbed her fuck box with one hand and her breast with the other. *a***2002** *Letters to Penthouse XV* 60: He unloaded his sperm inside her sloppy fuck-box.

fuckboy *noun*

a catamite; (*hence*) a man who is victimized.

[**1954** F.I. Gwaltney *Heaven & Hell* 233 [refers to WWII]: Grimes loves the army and the army's using him for a screw-boy.] **1971** J. Blake *Joint* 67 [refers to 1954]: They were known as pussyboys, galboys, fuckboys, and all had taken girls' names like Betty, Fifi, Dotty, etc., and were universally referred to as "she" and "her." **1974** R. Carter *16th Round* 76: A goddamned faggot, a fuckboy. **1973–76** J. Allen *Assault* 124: One or two slip through who aren't so obvious. There's a lot of them we call undercover fuck boys. **1980** G. G. Liddy *Will* (1996) 393: [In prison] A "fuck boy" or "punk" for homosexual gratification. **1994** in *Esquire* (Jan. 1995) 91: [In prison] Once you've become somebody's fuck-boy, you stay a fuck-boy, and your new "man" will use you any way he wants. **1996** T. Parker *Violence of our Lives* i. 44: He looked me in the eye and he said "Do you mind that idea son, do you want to be somebody's fuckboy?" **2007** C. Eshleman in *American Poetry Review* (Mar./Apr.) 26/1: The "Victorious Cupid," a naked fuck-boy with wings, offering himself joyously to the viewer. **2008** "50 Cent" & D. R. Pledger *Diamond District* 148: You ain't nothing but that white cop's little fuck boy! Whose side are you on, nigga?

fuckbrain *noun*

= FUCKHEAD. Hence **fuckbrained**, *adjective*.

1970 T. Whitmore *Memphis-Nam-Sweden* 35: Not at all like the lazy fuckbrain before him. *a***1981** R. Spears *Slang & Euphemism* 149: *Fuck-brained.* stupid. **1986** N. Jimenez *River's Edge* (film): You pothead fuckbrain! **1987** J. Kellerman *Over the Edge* 373: I asked you a question, fuckbrain. **1991** J. Keenan *Putting on Ritz* xx. 215: Well, go ahead, fuck-brain! See if I care! **1994** *New Statesman* (Dec. 16) S1: You fuckbrained little parasite. **2000** J. Klein *Running Mate* 79: If those fuckbrained college kids can march in the streets and get what they want, think of the leverage we'd have. **2006** *New York Magazine* (Apr. 3) 20/1: Magazine editors gripe about the rings they have to jump through to book the hottest possible celebrities ("The PR people," one complained to me, "are really such fucking fuckbrains").

fuckbreak *noun*

an interruption in an activity taken in order to engage in sexual intercourse.

1973 W. Rostler *Contemporary Erotic Cinema* 158: There was Jim, who screwed for money all day, took a fuck break during the shooting when he was off camera, and balled this chick. **1994** *Personal letter to editor*: You know the term *fuckbreak*? It's when you take time away from work to try to get pregnant. **2001** C. Miéville *Perdido Street Station* 134: Your mates are very understanding about you just up and taking a fuck-break, aren't they? **2008** M. Henry *Happy Hour of the Damned* 234: The swing shift crew only had another ninety-seven hours until half-shift fuckbreak.

fuck-buddy *noun*

Especially *Homosexuals.* a sexual partner; (*specifically*) a friend with whom one engages in casual sex.

[**1972** B. Rodgers *Queens' Vernacular* 184: *Fucking buddies* two who are not lovers cruising together for threesomes, *etc.*] **1973** A. S. Jackson *Gentleman Pimp* 71: We ran into an old fuck buddy of mine. **1983** in E. White *Burning Library* 150: Even the word *lover* is too rude for all the gradations of commitment and intimacy; one friend uses an ascending scale of Trick, Number, Fuck Buddy, Lover, and Husband. **1992** in *Gay Perspectives* 161: Andrew has a few friends with whom he has sex, but this is no "fuck buddy" circle. **1995** "Pansy Division" *Fuck Buddy* [rock song]: Fuck buddy..../Someday I'll find a guy/Who means something more/But that's not what/This relationship is for. **1995** R. Athey in *Village Voice* (N.Y.C.) (Feb. 14) 32: I try role-playing and maintaining a fuck-buddy relationship with my butch stud Cuban daddy. **1996** *Guardian* (London) (Mar. 26) T6: Young lesbians…know themselves and they will announce that they are father, mother, butch, femme, fuck-buddy, boy, girl, top, bottom or any mixture that they choose. **1996** *SF Weekly* (Nov. 13): Paul Ramana Das Silbet, not his wife/fuck-buddy Marilena, seems to be the real brains… behind this operation. **1997** *Village Voice* (N.Y.C.) (Apr. 22) 123: Fuck buddies—friends who fuck—usually don't date prior to becoming fuck buddies. **2000** M. Albo *Hornito* 224: We are simply "fuck buddies" to each other. Casual casual casual. **2005** E. Morrison *Last Book You Read* 125: He doesnae need a girlfriend. I canna go through this again with anyone. We're fuck buddies—that's all.

fuck button *noun*

the clitoris.

[**1968** R. H. Rimmer *Proposition Thirty-One* 220: Or were we both just mechanical robots on whom someone had pushed the fuck button?] **1969** "Joey V." *Portrait of Joey: Case Study of a Super Stud* 85: There were times when I could make her come just from the feel of my lips tugging on that little fuck-button of hers. **1994** *Strawberry Blonde ff teen* on Usenet newsgroup alt.sex.stories (Apr. 25): My finger was grinding down against her fuck button and the heat was rising down between her legs as her slot began to moisten. **2007** R. L. Duncan *Lost in Venice* 267: "I just touched your little fuck button." "Oh Johnny it felt so good."

fucked *adjective*

1. Chiefly *British*. completely exhausted.

1949 E. Partridge *Dictionary of Slang & Unconventional English* (ed. 3) (Addenda) 1054/2: *F*cked*, adj. Extremely weary; (utterly) exhausted; late C. 19-20. **1977** H. Garner *Monkey Grip* 216: I only want to crash, right now. I'm absolutely fucked. **1987** G. Matthews *Little Red Rooster* xiii. 201: It's...time for sleep.... I'm totally fucked. **1996** C. J. Stone *Fierce Dancing* ix. 132: We've hitched from the West Country. We've just walked about twenty miles and we're fucked. Can you come and pick us up? **2005** *Independent on Sunday* (Nexis) (Aug. 28), We were all completely fucked, we'd been out in Liverpool the night before.

2. exceedingly bad or offensive; rotten; awful; ruined; FUCKED UP, *adjective*, definition 1; (also) doomed, in a difficult situation.

1949 W. S. Graham *Letter* (Mar. 7) in *Nightfisherman* (1999) 87: My nose fucked, my jersey steeping in its navyblue water, the fire a ruin of paling embers. **1960** P. Larkin *Letter* (Aug. 8) in A. Thwaite *Selected Letters* (1992) 318: On getting back to Hessle he found the shutter had been set at Time exposure which means that the whole lot were fucked. **1971** L. Bangs in *Psychotic Reactions* (1987) 86: Some cat... made a really fucked album. **1975** S.P. Smith *American Boys* 58: Morgan [was] yelling at the top of his lungs about how fucked everything was while Padgett...egged him on. **1976** A. Schroeder *Shaking It Rough* 121: I mean, like, the last stanza's completely fucked, man! **1978** A. Maupin *Tales of the City* 92: Your karma is *really* fucked! **1980** P. Conroy *Lords of Discipline* 311: We're living in fucked times. **1985** J. Dillinger *Adrenaline* 115: "Want to know something fucked?"... "How fucked?" "We're outa gas." **1985** O'Bannon *Return of Living Dead* (film): first, I got a really fucked headache; then my stomach started cramping up. **1990** P. Munro *Slang U.* 85: *Fucked...* unfair. **1991** J. Barth *Last*

Voyage of Somebody the Sailor 144: The page whispered. "We're fucked."
1986–91 B. Hamper *Rivethead* 161: Squeezing rivets is fucked! **1997**
Nunez *Ulee's Gold* (film): Everyone's life you've ever touched is fucked.
You know that, Ulee? **2007** *Poets & Writers* (Mar./Apr.) 48: When I found
out I didn't get the job, I thought, "I am so fucked!" I had no clue what
I was going to do.

3. intoxicated by alcohol or drugs; = FUCKED UP, definition 2a.

 1970 E. E. Landy *Underground Dictionary* 84: *Fucked*...under the influence of a drug. **1972** D. E. Smith & G. R. Gay *Don't Try It* 202: *Fucked
up*. High on heroin (sometimes other drugs): "He was so fucked up he
couldn't even drive a car."...Also *fucked around, fucked over,* and just plain
fucked. *a***1973** in D. W. Maurer *Language of the Underworld* 301: *Fucked* or
fucked up. Stoned. **1976** L. Bangs in *Psychotic Reactions* (1987) 195: When
you first arise you're probably so fucked (i.e. still drunk) that it doesn't
even really hurt yet. **1990** P. Munro *Slang U.* 85: *Fucked*...drunk...under
the influence of drugs. **2000** G. Marinovich & J. Silva *Bang-Bang Club*
(2001) xii. 191: My heart sank, thinking Kev must be fucked on buttons,
and I mentally ran through a list of possible excuses. **2005** N. Barham
Dis/Connected 137: At Homelands I got fucked and I came up and it was
just fantastic and Sam was like, "I'll just have a tiny bit," and I was like, yes,
sure; a tiny bit of these pills will still knock your head off.

4. lacking in sanity or good sense; crazy. Also **fucked in the head**.

 1970 E. E. Landy *Underground Dictionary* 84: *Fucked*... messed up;
confused. **1971** P. Theroux in *Atlantic* (Nov.) 45/1: I used to think you
Asians knew where it was at...and now I been all over Asia and, like, now
I can see you're all fucked in the head. **1975** L. Bangs in *Psychotic Reactions* (1987) 180: You're allll [*sic*] fucked....I can do anything I want. **1978**
B. Johnson *What's Happenin'* 64: "He don't care what he says as long as
people notice him." "He's fucked, man," *Ibid.* 167: You guys are fucked.
You don't even know what you talkin' about. **1981** C. Nelson *Picked Bullets
Up* 31: Babich looked at me through jaundiced eyes. "Kurt, you're fucked."
1985 B.E. Ellis *Less than Zero* 100: Girls are fucked. Especially this girl.
1990 *National Lampoon* (Apr.) 97: They're fucked in the head. **1995**
R. Lurie *Once Upon a Time in Hollywood* 77: "Are you fucked!" she
screamed at Aubrey over the phone. "How could you give up that much

money to anybody without a contract?" **2003** A. Swofford *Jarhead* 39: He was not a crazed, fucked-in-the-head grunt.

fucked duck *noun*

Military. a person doomed to die; "dead duck."

1939 A. C. Bessie *Men in Battle* 133: If France don't come in now, we're fucked ducks. *Mucho malo.... Mucho* fuckin' *malo*. **1968** J. P. Spradley *Owe Yourself a Drunk* 30: I had twenty-three bucks when booked. Now they tell me I've got $3.30. I guess I'm a fucked duck—I've got twenty days hanging. **1999** A. W. Newton & W. Eldridge *Better than Good: Black Sailor's War 1943–1945* 106: If one of those guys, especially the big boatswain, took a swing at me, I would be a fucked duck before Packard could get back. **2006** P. Jennings *Nam-A-Rama* 154: You saved our ass on this one. We'd a been a fucked duck if you hadn't stayed on that horn all day.

fucked off *adjective*

angry; irritated; "pissed off." [The sense in the 1923 quotation, from a French–English dictionary of slang, is not clear.]

1923 J. Manchon *Le Slang* 131: Fucked off, *foutu(e)*. **1940–45** in M. Page *Kiss Me Goodnight* (1975) 80: Because I'm fucked off, fucked off, fucked off as can be.... Fucked off lads are we. **1971** H. Dahlskog *Dictionary of Contemporary & Colloquial Usage* 25: *Fucked off...*Angry; irritated; tee'd off. **1973** N.Y. college student: *Fucked off* means the same as *pissed off*. **1974** Social worker, age 26: I've heard a few people say, "He was really fucked off," when they meant "pissed off." This was in the past couple of years. **1997** *Scotland on Sunday* (Apr. 6) 7: Paul is deeply fucked-off with a certain type of Welsh nationalist...attitude. **1998** *SF Weekly* (Jan. 7): Hatred, revenge, and violation are...strangely heartbreaking and entirely convincing. Clearly, Reid Paley has every right to be fucked off with the world. **2003** R. Herring *Talking Cock* 126: An ex-girlfriend walked in—she was a bit fucked off as we hadn't had sex in a while and took it as a sign that I was losing interest in her.

fucked out *adjective*

exhausted from excessive copulation; (*hence*) utterly exhausted; worn out.

1862 O. A. Hammer *Letter* (Dec.) in T. P. Lowry *Story Soldiers Wouldn't Tell* (1994) iii. 37: I together with several other officers went over to Petersburg, got drunk and f—ked out. We staid two days and nights, you ought to have seen me going to bed with a gal. **1865** "Philocomus" *Love Feast* iv. 29: However tired and jaded,/Fucked out, used up, fatigued and faded,/ He still would find a spur should stir/My lusts as nimbly as before. *ca***1866** *Romance of Lust* 443: Poor Mr. Nixon was evidently fucked out. **1879** *Harlequin Prince Cherrytop* 29: Changed from the gorgeous king to a buffoon,/Be weak-kneed, cunt-struck, fucked-out Pantaloon. **1884** *Randiana* 71: The inward and spiritual grace so necessary to please the ladies is now almost dormant in my fucked-out nature. **1934** H. Miller *Tropic of Cancer* 225: It is…the dry, fucked-out aspect of things which makes this crazy civilization look like a crater. **1942** H. Miller *Roofs of Paris* 259: She's as drunk as we're fucked out. **1945** E. Hemingway in *Selected Letters* (1981) 605: Suffer like a bastard when don't write, or just before, and feel empty and fucked out afterwards. **1950** in A. C. Inman *Diary* 1480: I guess…Billy was just plain fucked out, the way he looked. **1966** J. Susann *Valley of Dolls* 121: And what should an ingenue look like? A fucked-out redhead with big tits. **1969** M. Girodias *New Olympia Reader* 91: By Christ, you tired old bag, you're asleep. Fucked out. **1973** R. Roth *Sand in Wind* 239: The ones he had seen didn't have the fucked-out eyes of American prostitutes, and so many other American women. **1975** R.P. Davis *Pilot* 144: They called her the "fucked-out, boozy bitch" or the "FOBB." **1977** J. Sayles *Union Dues* 144: It's a Monday, they're all fucked-out from the weekend. **1978** *National Lampoon* (Oct.) 26: Gertrude was so fucked out that she never wanted to do it with anyone again. **1981** W. T. Hathaway *World of Hurt* 162: Must've got so fucked out in two days, you had to come back to rest up. **1994** "Gary Indiana" *Rent Boy* 25: A great-looking dude who's so fucked out he needs a half-hour blow job just to get semi-hard. **1995** M. Amis *Information* 466: And he spent the night in the master bedroom, and might even have made love to her, tenderly, tearfully, absolvingly, if he hadn't been feeling so fucked out—and worried about getting her pregnant. **2003** B. Trapido *Frankie & Stankie* x. 241: She's got a big untidy mouth and she walks, unselfconsciously, with a slightly knock-kneed gait. This, together with her hint of hollow thighs, has given Maddie a sexy, fucked-out look which, oddly enough, she manages to combine with the manner of the girl-next-door.

fucked over *adjective*

1. messed up, broken, ruined, victimized; = FUCKED, definition 4.

1969 *Progressive Labor* (Aug.) 28/2: Never really trying to reach the people, building coffeehouse after coffeehouse, striking pose after pose, the struggle becomes an attempt to blow up a balloon of our own new world. The balloon is to grow and grow as more take on our groovy life styles and strike our pose and finally the whole fucked-over goddamn dumb society will shrivel beside it and die. **1978** W. Wharton *Birdy* 197: You know,... this is really a fucked-over situation. **1983** S. King *Christine* 257: You look like a sleepwalker. You look absolutely fucked over. **1995** G. Burn *Fullalove* (2004) vii. 175: The toe-rags; the twisters; the fucked-up; the fucked-over; the shat-upon; the shitters; the benefit-dependent; the multiply-deprived. **2000** W. Self *How Dead Live* viii. 196: But at the time I'd forgotten all the weary weepfests of Families Anonymous I'd attended—along with other fucked-up mums and fucked-over spouses—to try and get a handle on Natasha's limitless capacity for destroying herself and others.

2. extremely intoxicated by drugs or alcohol; = FUCKED UP, definition 2a.

1972 D. E. Smith & G. R. Gay *Don't Try It* 202: *Fucked up*. High on heroin (sometimes other drugs): "He was so fucked up he couldn't even drive a car."...Also *fucked around, fucked over*, and just plain *fucked*. **1973** College student: *Fucked over* can mean very, very drunk. Like I've heard guys say, "I was *fucked over* last night. Man, I wasn't worth a dime." **1979** College student paper: [Drunk:] queezy, fucked over, stewed, zonked.

fucked up *adjective*

1. Especially *Military*. ruined or spoiled, especially through incompetence or stupidity; botched; chaotic; in difficulty; (*broadly*) messed up. Also (especially *Military*) in fanciful similes.

1863 *Record of the General Courts Martial & Courts of Inquiry of the U.S. Navy* (U.S. National Archives) CVI. (Case 3401, Nov. 18) 3: He stepped to the front of his tent..., and in a loud voice said, "What the bloody hell is wanted now, this is a fucked up Company anyhow, and always has been since the Guard came on shore." **1939** A. C. Bessie *Men in Battle* 133: The detail's all fucked-up. **1942** in M. Morriss & R. Day *South Pacific Diary* (1996) 44: The trouble with the Army is it isn't fucked up enough—somebody is always trying to go 'em one better. **1943** in

H. Samuelson *Love, War* 200: You've never seen such a fucked-up mess in your life. **1954–60** H. Wentworth & S. B. Flexner *Dictionary of American Slang: Fucked-up*...in trouble. **1961** G. Forbes *Goodbye to Some* 173: Their balance is all fucked up too....They can't stay right side up. **1962** G. Ross *Last Campaign* 36: I never heard of such a fucked-up mess. *Ibid.* 293: The boxes are busted open, see. And the [machine gun] belts are all fucked up with snow. **1963** T. Doulis *Path for our Valor* 108: Man, there ain't *ever* been such a fucked-up operation! **1964** H. Rhodes *Chosen Few* 118 [refers to *ca*1950]: It don't make sense t'get fucked up on a humble. **1972** D. Pearce *Pier Head Jump* 49: They're as fucked up as a Mongolian fire and lifeboat drill. **1972–76** C. Durden *No Bugles, No Drums* 1: Right off I knew things were gonna be fucked up as a picnic in a free-fire zone. **1976** P. Atlee *Last Domino Contract* 53: My company has a reputation for quality, but we've been fucked up here like Hogan's goat. **1987** Kent *Phrase Book* 156: As fucked up as a Chinese fire drill. **1997** U.S. student slang survey: *More fucked up than a soup sandwich in a rainstorm*...extremely unusual. **2003** "S. Pax" *Weblog Diary* (May 22) in *Baghdad Blog* 178: The exchange rate is totally fucked up and the property market is getting bizarre.

2.a. intoxicated by liquor or drugs.

*a***1944** in A. Hopkins *Songs from Front & Rear* (1979) 179: There was old Uncle Ned, he was fair fucked up. **1965** in H.S. Thompson *Hell's Angels* 236: We'll smoke up some weed, get all fucked up, feel no fuckin pain. *ca***1969** D. Rabe *Basic Training of Pavlo Hummel* 44: Ohhh, you know how much beer I hadda drink to get fucked up on three-two beer? **1970** A. Young *Snakes* 40: Man, I was fuhhhhhked-up! **1973** *Oui* (Apr.) 108: God, but I'd love some cocaine....I got so gloriously fucked up the other night. **1973** R. Roth *Sand in Wind* 148: I was timing myself on every glass. I was getting fucked up but not as fucked up as I wanted to be. **1977** A. Patrick *Beyond Law* 144: Either you can sit around here gettin' fucked up and feelin' sorry for yourself, or you can straighten up and solve this God damn case. **1978** P. Fisher & M. Rubin *Special Teachers/Special Boys* 31: He was fucked up on weed. **1979** C. Hiler *Monkey Mountain* 109: "Eddy!... You fucked up?"..."No, he's not fucked up....He's just crazy." **1967–80** E. Folb *Runnin' down Some Lines* 238: *Fucked up.* Excessively *high.* **1985** D. Steel *Secrets* 48: Sandy's not fucked up again, is she? **1997** G. Sykes *8 Ball Chicks* 87: Janet's always so fucked up on sherm [PCP]. **1997** D. Simon & E. Burns *Corner* 509 He's taking in the boom and beat from the half-assed stereo, with Dre and Snoop and the rest of the Death Row crew telling all them other niggas to make their shit the chronic, 'cause they gots to get fucked-up. **2002** B. L. Thomas *Threesome* 146: I could tell he was fucked up. He'd been smoking blunts and doing shots of Grand Marnier all night.

b. thoroughly confused; mentally or emotionally ill; crazy. Also (especially *Military*) in fanciful similes.

1945 in A. Dundes & C. Pagter *Urban Folklore from Paperwork Empire* (1975) 109: The returning soldier is apt to find his opinion different from those of his civilian associates. One should call upon his reserve of etiquette and correct his acquaintances with such remarks as "I believe you have made a mistake" or "I am afraid you are in error on that." Do NOT say "Brother, you're really f—d up!" **1945** J. Bassett *War Journal* 7: It's no good to keep going, it's all fucked up, it's crazy. **1946–50** J. Jones *From Here to Eternity* 537: I've even seen a couple of them that clean lost their head and had to actually be carried out finally they got so fucked up. **1961** J. Peacock *Valhalla* 385: If he didn't see Chebe-san he would be more fucked up than Hogan's goat. **1965** S. Linakis *In Spring the War Ended* 214: I would even go so far as to say that you're all fucked up from the war, as they do say. **1967** J. Rechy *Numbers* 138: It happened long ago, when I was fucked up! **1968** H. Ellison *Deadly Streets* 103: He wasn't a bad kid, just fucked-up. **1970** in M. J. Estren *Underground of Underground Comics* (1974) 155: Wow, man, what kind of fucked up trip are *you* on? **1973** G.C. Scott in *Penthouse* (May) 61: Fucked-up kids live in fantasy worlds anyway. **1972–76** C. Durden *No Bugles, No Drums* 31: You're fucked up like a Filipino fire drill. **1976** A. Walker *Meridian* 178: I know white folks are evil and fucked up. **1978** in H. Fierstein *Torch Song Trilogy* 52: And here you are, more fucked up than ever. **1984** J. McCorkle *Cheer Leader* 162: You're crazy, Jo, fucked up. **1989** "Capt. X" & Dodson *Unfriendly Skies* 115: "Aw, hell" said one of the pilots, "now I'm all fucked up here." **1992** in *Harper's* (Jan. 1993) 23 [cartoon]: You're too fucked up—Next patient, please. **2001** J. Gough *Juno & Juliet* i. ix. 23: Fucked-up people are paying someone money to listen to them talk about how amazingly fucked-up they are. **2008** A. Valdes-Rodriguez *Dirty Girls on Top* 130: I almost wish I didn't know how fucked up I was, because then I could just go around feeling okay and still being fucked up.

c. deeply troubled or upset; distraught.

1948 E. Hemingway in *Selected Letters* (1981) 648: I was all fucked up when I wrote it and threw away about 100,000 words which was better than most of what I left in. **1951** *American Journal of Sociology* LI 421 [refers to WWII]: We learn of soldier attitudes to authority by noting the sympathy for those who are not successful in adjusting but are "f—ed up."...It may connote inability or inefficiency. **1962** V. Riccio & B. Slocum *All the Way Down* 68: I ain't hooked. I only use it when I feel all fucked up. **1970–71** J. Rubinstein *City Police* 404: He's so fucked up about it he's thinkin' of quittin'. **1966–80** J. McAleer & B. Dickson *Unit Pride* 115: I was gonna change it myself but I was too fucked up at the time. **1983** P. Dexter *God's Pocket* 158: I got to have this funeral on time....Jeanie's all fucked up over this. **1998** Phila. drug addict, on *All Things Considered* (National Public Radio) (Mar. 4): I felt real fucked up because I didn't want to hit [i.e., inject] her. **2004** B. Shoup *Wish You Were Here* (2008) 25: And I am fucked up. I am clearly fucked up. Even I know I ought to be over the divorce after all this time. **2007** G. Kaplan *Evil, Inc.* 203: If *I'm* still fucked up about losing Sandy and Sara the way we did, can you even begin to imagine how fucked up *you* must be?... Of course, you can't imagine because you're still so fucked up with your grief and mourning and all that.

3. contemptible; worthless; miserable; (*hence*) damned; FUCKING.

1945 in T. Shibutani *Derelicts of Company K* 124: I never been in such a fucked up place in my life. *ca*1960 in R. D. Abrahams *Deep Down in Jungle* 130: He throwed me a stale glass of water and flung me a fucked-up piece of meat. **1963** J. Ross *Dead Are Mine* 269: And you won't worry about Felix and all the other Felixes in the whole fucked-up Army. **1970** *Playboy* (Sept.) 278: I've met a lot of politicians, and politicians are fucked up everywhere, and they fuck us up because we allow them to. **1970** S. Terkel *Hard Times* 136: It's the textbooks that are fucked up. **1974** V.E. Smith *Jones Men* 103: Shit!...This is fucked up. **1982** D.A. Harper *Good Company* 76: A half gallon of that old fucked-up wine. **1980–89** J. E. Cheshire *Home Boy* 105: They'd go for your ankles and sink their fucked-up teeth right into you. **1990** "Ice Cube" *Who's the Mack?* (rap song): Rolling in a fucked-up Lincoln...[with a] leopard interior. **1994** in C. Long *Love Awaits* 95: That good-look'n, clean-look'n girl can have some good look'n, fucked up shit [*sc.* venereal disease]. **2005** C. Klosterman *Killing Yourself* *to Live* 26: I'll make this fucked-up decision to satisfy the statute of limitations on your fucked-up ultimatum.

4. utterly fatigued; FUCKED, definition 1.

1979 D. Gram *Boulevard Nights* 93: I'm tired man. Fuckin' fucked up. **1998** Poker player in N.Y.C.: I've gotta go home, I'm so tired....I'm too fucked up to play any more.

fuckee[1] or **fucky** *noun*

(used in pidgin English, or the imitation thereof, in various constructions referring to sexual intercourse). Often as **fuckee fuckee**. In **fuckee-suckee**, a combination of oral and vaginal intercourse.

*a***1866** E. Sellon *Ups & Downs of Life* (1987) ii. 43: For make fuckee business, sahib, that girl who is splashing the other one would be too much good. **1946** V. Sheean *This House against This House* 118: The only Arab women I ever saw to speak to always said to me, "Fuckee, Fuckee, fitty cents." **1960** H. Miller *Nexus* (1965) viii. 171: No tickee no fuckee, buy me, take me, squeeze me. **1975** *Ribald* (Sydney, Australia) (Nov. 13) 7: Newcomers visiting *Ribald's* offices often get all bug-eyed about the fuckee-suckee pix lying around the place. **1987** S. Kubrick et al. *Full Metal Jacket* (film): Do you want number one fuckee? **1998** J. Stewart *Naked Pictures of Famous People*: Their father [was]...shacked up in some Backwater Indonesian Fuckee Suckee bar. **2003** A. Martinez *I'll be Damned if I Die in Oakland* 147: One bored fat lady reclined under a large sign that read, Fuckee Fuckee.

fuckee[2] *noun*

1. a person who plays the recipient role in copulation. *Jocular*.

1881 *Amatory Experiences Surgeon* i. 11: My double position of fucker and fuckee soon drove me almost mad with delight. *ca***1890** *My Secret Life* VI. xv. 312: She was altogether a choice morsel for those who like a woman full sized.... She was a most voluptuous fuckee. *ca***1938** in C. Barkley *Sex Cartoons* 118: The fuckee does a handstand while the fucker simply drops it in. **1979** D. Riepe *Owl Flies by Day* ii. 29: The attractive assistants were looking into the face of the lady receiving the male offering. Both arms of the fuckee were gracefully stretched out. **1995** *Village*

Voice (N.Y.C.) (Feb. 14) 38: Early flashes of fiery pain in the fuckee as well as surprise soft bendings of the fucker make ass-fucking in any position a [complex] negotiation. **1995** *Village Voice* (N.Y.C.) (Nov. 28) 73: Vidal also wants to make quite sure we understand that in his many sexual exploits he's always been the fucker, never the fuckee. **2007** J. Sandford *Dark of the Moon* 167: When he was a teenager, there were locker-room fantasy stories…of guys getting the farmer's daughter up in the hayloft… In what Virgil assumed was nothing more than an effort at verisimilitude, the alleged fuckee warned Virgil against hay cuts, or hay rash.

2. the victim of malicious treatment. *Jocular.*

1971 S/Sgt., U.S. Army, Fort Campbell, Kentucky: I am one big ugly fucker and I am always on the lookout for fuckees! You *don't* want to be one of them! **1973** T. Pynchon *Gravity's Rainbow* 559: Fuck not with the Kid, lest instead of fuckei thou become fuckee. **1980** W. Sherman *Times Square* 23: You're either the fuckee, the fucker, or you're not in any kind of business. **1983** W. N. Rowe *Clapp's Rock* 105: He considers Newfoundland to have gone from eldest ugly step-daughter of the British Empire to youngest fuckee of the Canadian Federation, without getting so much as a kiss during the transition. **1986** R. B. Merkin *Zombie Jamboree* 44: They'd rather be fuckers than fuckees. **1991** *Inside Media* (Dec. 18) 1: Lee Wolfman, in speaking of back-end cash blending, often referred to BMC [a marketing company] as the "fucker" and to its clients as the "fuckees." **1996** *N.Y. Observer* (Jan. 8) 4: Behold the…smug shifting the blame from society's fuckers to its fuckees. **1996** *Village Voice* (N.Y.C.) (May 14) ("Choices") 1: Belzer's politics rise off his don't-fuck-with-me stand. Most of the time, identifying with potential fuckees, he sprays a democratic vitriol that's bracing in stand-up. **2006** S. Kinzer *Overthrow* 187: Kennecott and Anaconda were not awarded a cent. "We used to be the fucker," one of Anaconda's lawyers lamented. "Now we're the fuckee."

fuckee or **fucky** *verb*

(used in pidgin English, or the imitation thereof, in various constructions referring to sexual intercourse).

*ca***1890** *My Secret Life* X. xiv. 331: The women had learnt a few English words explanatory of copulation—"Me fuckee prick" said one. **1963** H.S. Thompson *Letter* (Apr. 29) in *Proud Highway* (1997) 379: The filthy whore in the laundry said we can go out to the *"campo"* (country) and fuckee-fuckee. If I ever hear that phrase again I am going to break teeth. **1982** N. L. M. Petesch *Duncan's Colony* 167: Take me, joe. Fuckee plenny backside. **1996** S. Zeeland *Muscular Marine* 66: Mama-san give you money back if you not wanna go fuckie. **2003** M. Gruber *Tropic of Night* 84: When you start fuckee?... You likee orgasms? You let boy touch-em titties?

fuck-else *noun*

nothing else.

1978 W. Groom *Better Times Than These* 33: You mean you got fuck-else to worry about than something happened sixty years ago? **1988** D. Caute *Fatima's Scarf* 259: Call Hikmat.... There's fuck-else to do in this dump. *a***1990** in J. F. Tuso *Singing the Vietnam Blues* 140: Though my chances were nil there was fuck else to do,/But head for the Black with our whole fuckin's crew!

fucker *noun*

1. a person, usually a man, who copulates, especially promiscuously.

1598 J. Florio *Worlde of Wordes* 137/1: *Fottitore*, a iaper, a sarder, a swiver, a fucker, an occupier. **1598** J. Florio *Worlde of Wordes* 137/1: *Fottitrice*, a woman fucker, swiver, sarder, or iaper. **1866** *Romance of Lust* 275: She grew madly lewd, called me her own dear delightful fucker. **1882** *Boudoir* 239: Such a prince of f—kers as he is. **1889** Capt. C. Devereaux *Venus in India* 124: I have known so many instances of girls marrying against their wills...yet become quite happy women simply and solely because their husbands turned out to be first-class fuckers. **1928** D. H. Lawrence *Lady Chatterley's Lover* xviii. 334: I'm not just my lady's fucker, after all. **1963** C. Bukowski *Letter* (Dec. 7) in *Screams from Balcony: Selected Letters* (1998) 96: I got the idea that Henry Miller the ALL-KNOWING didn't know much more about fucking than to talk about it, and that's the way most non-fuckers are. **1978** L. Kramer *Faggots* 117: He...quietly... exited through the hall and living room and foyer..., past the islands and inlets and peninsulas of fuckers and suckers and kissers and talkers. **1994** E. McNamee *Resurrection Man* (1998) i. 12: At the start it was all Jesus, Victor, I could eat you with salt. Her big slow voice. Come on, you big

fucker. I'm dying for a fuck. Take you home and fuck you bendy. **1998**
M. Merlis *Arrow's Flight* 292: That rhythm: it used to mean they were one
body, Philoctetes and some anonymous fucker on top of him, pulsing together with one life. **2005** L. McNeil & J. Osborne *Other Hollywood* 191:
Harry wasn't a good actor. If he was, they would've given him a piece of
the pornos. But he couldn't carry them. Harry wasn't a great actor—but he
was a great fucker.

2. a person, especially a man, who is despicable, wretched, formidable, etc.; bastard; (*broadly*) a person; fellow.

*a***1890–93** J. S. Farmer & W. E. Henley *Slang & Its Analogues* III 80:
Fucker...a term of endearment, admiration, derision, etc. **1918** in *Englische Studien* LX (1926) 277: We had a sergeant-major/Who never saw
a Hun,/And when the Huno came over/You could see the fucker run.
1914–21 J. Joyce *Ulysses* 600 [refers to 1904]. I'll wring the bastard fucker's
bleeding blasted fucking windpipe! **1926** *Englische Studien* LX 279 [re-
fers to WWI]: The noun *fucker*...the very old term of derision, as well
as pity (cp. "that poor blighter!")...was used in the sense of "bloke," "rotter," "blighter," or "bastard," a word which decorated the speech of over
seas men and Americans. **1927** *Immortalia* 159: The dirty old fucker. **1929**
F. Manning *Middle Parts of Fortune* 146 [refers to WWI]: Laugh, you silly
fuckers! *Ibid.* 150: I'd rather kill some other fucker first. *Ibid.* 208: If any
o' us poor fuckers did it, we'd be for th' electric chair. **1945** in T. Shibutani
Derelicts of Company K 197: Them fuckers piss me off. **1945** in D. Levin
From Battlefield 52: Hey, you old fucker!...How long you been out here?
1949 V. Van Praag *Day Without End* 168: Make your shots count!...Kill
the lousy stinking fuckers! **1959** G. Morrill *Dark Sea Running* 11: We carry
high-octane gas that burns. If I catch any of you fuckers smoking forward
of the messroom doors, I'll crack your nobs. **1960** G. Sire *Deathmakers* 43:
You're a mean fucker, Chico. **1961** L. McMurtry *Horseman, Pass By* 142:
"I used to ride them bulls when I was a young fucker," he said. **1961–64**
D. Barthelme *Come Back, Dr. Caligari* 43: Oh that poor fucker Eric.
1965–70 J. Carroll in *Paris Review* (No. 50) 107: Her mother [was a]
dumb, New Jersey, housewife fucker. **1969–71** R. Kahn *Boys of Summer* 96: Gonna get them fuckers....Teach them fuckers to mess with
me. **1972** B. Hannah *Geronimo Rex* 96: Monroe, you dopey fucker. **1975**
S. Brownmiller *Against Our Will* 364: I hate that fucker more today
than I did when it happened to me. **1981** A. A. Gilliland *Revolution*

from Rosinante 117: The fucker is going to set himself up as *king.* **1989** M. Norman *These Good Men* 115: I love my son; I love that little fucker. **1992** G. Wolff *Day at Beach* 127: Only thing to keep the fuckers out. **2003** A. Swofford *Jarhead* 175: The Vietnam War was not an official war either, but a perpetually escalating conflict with many poor, dead, sad fuckers.

3. an annoying or hateful thing, task, situation, etc.; (*broadly*) a thing, esp. if striking or remarkable.

1945 in T. Shibutani *Derelicts of Company K* 155: I don't think I could walk a mile with this fucker on. **1948** N. Mailer *Naked & Dead* 10 [refers to WWII]: Let's stop shuffling the fuggers and start playing. **1958** T. Berger *Crazy in Berlin* 186: If you are that close to the end, you can put the fucker aside for fifteen minutes and write me a letter to the wife. **1961** C. Bukowski *Letter* (June 22) in C. Bukowski & S. Martinelli *Beerspit Night & Cursing: Letters* (2001) 245: For a short letter this has turned out to be a fucker. **1968** A. Myrer *Eagle* 695: And the fucker better work, I'm telling you! **1973** *Penthouse* (May) 62: Oh my God, I've got to come back tomorrow and do this fucker again. **1976** in S. Mack *Stan Mack's Real Life Funnies* (unpaged): Sixteen out of 178 of us got in! It's a *fucker* isn't it! **1980** W. Kotzwinkle *Jack in the Box* 156: She'll burn up the competition....It's one fucker of an engine. **1980** in *Penthouse* (Jan. 1981) 173: He wanted me to wear this schoolgirl rig and shoes—and shine the fuckers first. **1981–85** S. King *It* 30: Just give me the fucker. **1987** W. D. Blankenship *Blood Stripe* 68: Took me five years to earn that fucker. **1992** G. Wolff *Day at Beach* 180: You fucking get the fucker up, Dad. **2000** D. Eggers *Heartbreaking Work of Staggering Genius* 435: You slash away with that fucker [*sc.* a frisbee], it's such a violent act, throwing that white thing, you're first cradling it to your breast and then then you whip that fucker as hard as you possibly can while keeping it level, keeping it straight. **2008** A. Davies *Mine All Mine* 149: "It's just the brass. It ejected funny." "Brass?" "The shell." "Fucker is hot."

fuckerware party *noun* [FUCK + (*Tupp*)*erware party*]
Especially *Homosexuals.* a gathering of women for the group use or purchase of sexual toys.

1983 G. Davis *Romance* 63: The nicest women on the Peninsula get together for what they themselves have labelled Fuckerware parties, where a representative comes equipped with Benoit balls, edible underwear, all manner of lubricious devices for sale. **1985** *Hustler* (Nov.): She joins Erica Boyer, Beverly Bliss and Barbie Dahl in a "fuckerware" party. As the girls try on lingerie and sample lotions, body paints and sex toys, the party breaks out in a rash of dueling dildos. **1986** *Playboy* (Nov.) 25: The authors attend a fundamentalist sex seminar..., a fuckerware party and other events. **1990** S. Bright *Susie Sexpert's Lesbian Sex World* 47: How many of you have attended a home sex toy presentation with a group of friends? They're called fuckerware parties in the business. **1998** T. Dalzell *Slang of Sin* 177: *Fuckerware party...*a women's party where sex toys are displayed and sold.

fuckery *noun* [FUCKER + *-y*; or FUCK + treach*ery*]

1. a brothel.

1903 J. S. Farmer & W. E. Henley *Dictionary of Slang & Its Analogues* V. 12/2: *Nanny-shop...*a brothel... *English synonyms...*fuckery. **1966** B. Miller (book title) *Devotions Written in a Fuckery.* a1973 in R. S. Silverberg *New Dimensions* III. 138: Well, OK: one time in a regular seaport fuckery, Marseilles I think, I got a deaf-mute ginch. It was—restful, sort of; you don't have to talk. **1978** H. Mathews trans. J. Cordelier *The Life: Memoirs of a French Hooker* 163: You're sure you haven't come to the wrong fuckery? **1994** U. K. LeGuin *Matter of Seggri* in *Birthday of the World & Other Stories* (2002) 51: Chochi had a favorite man at their local fuckery to whom she went now and then for pleasure. **2008** H. Kureishi *Something to Tell You* 107: But inside the fuckery it was warm and friendly. Everyone said hello.... "There were people on dog's leads, and lying in baths to be urinated on, others facedown in a sling."

2. sexual activity; FUCKing.

1961 J. Ashmead *Mountain & the Feather* 132: By definition, homosexuals did not speak endlessly and monotonously of the drab arts of fuckery. **1966** A. Wainhouse trans. Marquis de Sade *120 Days of Sodom* 405: As always partisan to thigh-fuckery, the Duc, obliged as he was to abstain from the capital practice, impaled Zelmire in this style. **1974** *New Society* XXIX. 170: Although she assesses herself a unique phoenix of fuckery, Ms Lovelace does only what any accomplished whore is expected to do in a society where the profession of prostitution demands specific sexual virtuosities. **1978** A. Carter *Sadeian Woman* 62: A tragic resonance to illicit fuckery is as silly as a straightforward denial that it exists. **1982** J. A. Atkins *Sex in Literature* IV. 310: He enjoys old-fashioned cunt-fuckery more than anything else and describes it with immense gusto. **1982** J. Machlis *Lisa's Boy* 201: They came together for what his friend Sidney called pure fuckery, and that goal seemed best served by their not becoming too deeply involved with each other. **2004** J. H. Kunstler *Maggie Darling* 48: An upward-reaching fugue of fuckery that culminated with Maggie bowed backward in a near headstand and Kenneth yogically arched above, as though he were copulating with a wheelbarrow, and then they collapsed in a heap on the floor.

3. despicable behavior; (*also*) treachery.

1978 S. King *Stand* 461: That was an act of pure human fuckery. **1993** T. Olson *At Sea* 70: No vigilante, high seas pirate fuckery is going down while I'm around here! **1994** *Village Voice* (Nov. 1) 69: Taking on the genre's most seismic vocalist was arrogant fuckery to begin with. **1998** C. Channer *Waiting in Vain* vii. 184: He'd even asked her to marry him... and she'd said no. Said some fuckery like, Only if we're allowed to see other people. **2006** A. Winehouse *Me & Mr. Jones* (pop. song): What kind of fuckery is this? **2007** D. Moskowitz *Words & Music of Bob Marley* 122: The omitted word could have been "fuckery," which was Jamaican patois for wrong or unfair actions.

fuckface *noun*

an ugly or contemptible person.—usually used abusively in direct address.

1945 in *Verbatim* (Autumn, 1989) 6: Fxxxface...1. A fool, a joker, one not held in high regard or likable....2. Greeting, form of address, semi-humorously or strongly contemptuous. **1961** J. Jones *Thin Red Line* 39 [refers to WWII]: All right, fuckface! Where's that fucking platoon roster...? **1967** W. Crawford *Gresham's War* 139: Hey, frickface. **1968** J.P. Miller *Race for Home* 294 [refers to 1930s]: "Tell what happened to 'im, fuckface," Dawg said. **1968** W. Mares *Marine Machine* 5: You come down here with this blade to cut me, fuckface? *Try it!* **1971** T. Mayer *Weary Falcon* 126: I tried giving it to the fuck faces whole, but then they sell it. **1983** W. Walker *Dime to Dance* 55: Why don't you mind your own business, fuckface? **1985** R. Meltzer *Rock-Crit Blood 'n' Guts (Part 1)* in *Whore Just Like Rest* (2000) 9: The first thing he says is "Get me some tea." Get your own tea, fuckface! **1991** N. Baker *U & I* vii. 120: That dirty little fuckface! **1993** S. Turow *Pleading Guilty* IV. xiv. 217: Who am I looking for, fuckface? **1999** T. Parker et al. *South Park* (film script) 27: *Phillip*. I did, Terrance, I learned that you are a boner biting dick fart fuck face! **2004** J. Meno *Hairstyles of Damned* 142: "Do I look like a dude to you, you fuckface?" she asked. *Fuckface?* I thought to myself. Who even uses the word "fuckface"?

fuckfaced *adjective*

1. having an ugly or miserable face; despicable. [The 1940 quotation is euphemistic.]

1940 E. Hemingway *For Whom the Bell Tolls* 369: Muck my grandfather and muck this whole treacherous muck-faced mucking country. **1973** W. Crawford *Gunship Commander* 24: You fuckfaced animal. Either do something with that or put it away. **1991** M. Olden *Kisaeng* 265: He... held the cigarette lighter to the guard's nose. "You fuckfaced twerp. Go feebleminded with me and I'll roast you." **1995** L. Uris *Redemption* 15: What would you give for another stupid paddy like me to come off the ship and bail you out, you fuck-faced monster? **2001** B. Denton *Dealing* vi. 155: He wrote a letter to his cell mate's girlfriend in Fairlea calling Marcia a "fuck-faced dog who gave me up."

2. Tired; bleary-eyed; (also) appearing like someone who has recently engaged in copulation.

1976 R. Price *Bloodbrothers* 59: At seven the sound of cartoons and the shifting silver reflection of the TV screen had Stony sitting up in bed dazed blind and fuckfaced. **1978** *Penthouse* (Apr.) 130: Gradually people file down for breakfast. Totally bleary-eyed and fuck-faced. **2004** H. Walsh *Brass* i. 4: She props herself up, fuck-faced and shining with the stench of her latest trick and stares into me.

3. Drunk; "shit-faced."

1993 T. Hawkins *Pepper* iv. 85: Go screw yourself. Waste your own life watching videos, I'm going out to get fuck-faced. **2004** P. J. O'Rourke in *National Lampoon's Big Book of Love* 54/1: They won't let me drive drunk...

They must think I'm crazy. That stuff scares me. I have to get completely fuck-faced to even think about driving fast.

fuckfest *noun*

an occasion, period, or portrayal of unrestrained or orgiastic sexual activity.

1932 H. Miller *Letter* (July 30) in G. Stuhlmann *Literate Passion* (1989) 82: When you return I am going to give you one literary fuckfest—that means fucking and talking and talking and fucking—and a bottle of Anjou in between—or a Vermouth Cassis. **1967** J. W. Corrington *Upper Hand* II. vii. 292: I know what money is. I know who pays five bucks to see a fuck-fest. **1976** J. Lee *Ninth Man* 183: They had simply engineered themselves a good old-fashioned fuckfest. **1992** Rudner & Bergman *Peter's Friends* (film): I hardly think my three-year-old marriage is the same as your two-week-old fuckfest. **1996** *Village Voice* (N.Y.C.) (Apr. 30): Mom was speaking of childhood slumber parties, not all-night saffron-scented fuckfests. **1997** *SF Weekly* (Apr. 2): The black-and-white existential fuckfest *Sex Garage* (1972), which brilliantly evokes both Kenneth Anger's bike fetish and the car-sex crazies of *Crash* in a sequence where a bored biker graphically attacks the exhaust pipe of his Harley. **1998** *Playboy* (Apr.) 66: In the Seventies, life was a real fuckfest for me. I worked at a bar…and women in their early 20s used to wait around to see who I would go home with. **2005** *FHM* (Jan.) 131/3: There's barely any skin-flicks for chicks: books are more our bag—and a well-penned fuck-fest gets us *seriously* hot.

fuckfriend *noun*

= FUCK-BUDDY.

1994 P. Manso *Brando*: He went out of his way to apologize to Valerie Fudd, too, for having described her as one of his "fuck friends." **1998** C. Preston *Jackie by Josie* 147: Was Terry Grif's girlfriend? The word seems too innocent for the activities of those two. Leslie called her his fuckfriend. **2005** *Toronto Star* (Jan. 8) L3/2: Booty call, CSBF (casual sex between friends), (f--- friends)… There has always been a euphemism for friends crossing the line into the grey area of sex. For some teens, what they call "friends with benefits" is replacing monogamous relationships.

2007 J. H. Kessler *Hell's Belles* 137: This was Daun. My bed buddy, my fuck friend.

fuckhead *noun*

a stupid or contemptible person.

1945 in *Verbatim* (Autumn, 1989) 6: *Fxxxhead*...A cheese head, an easily confused or misled individual. **1946** L. Bergman *I Cannot See Their Faces & Keep Silent* 35: He swore at me,/"Get over there, you dumb bastard,/Keep in step, you fuckhead,/Hold that rifle up, you turd." **1962** in B. Rosset *Evergreen Reader* 467: Manager merchant banker professional professional [*sic*] fuckhead. **1964** in L. Bruce *Essential Lenny* 97: I mean, it's the fault of the motion pictures, that have made the Southerner "a shit kickuh, a dumb fuckhead." **1965** S. Linakis *In Spring the War Ended* 348 [refers to WWII]: Go ahead fuck head. You'll do me a favor. **1964–66** R. Stone *Hall of Mirrors* 116: You simple-minded fuckhead. **1969** R. Jessup *Sailor* 389: You're nothing but a dumb fuckhead sailor. **1980** W. Kotzwinkle *Jack in the Box* 56: How ya doin', fuckhead. **1987** S. MacLaine *It's All in Playing* viii. 98: Melissa doesn't think I'm cute. She thinks I'm a fuck-head. **1990** H. G. Bissinger *Friday Night Lights* x. 200: Playing to him is not what it's all about.... Fuckheads can just play. He wants to be number one. **1996** *Picture* (Sydney, Australia) (Dec. 4) 59: I'd say your brother is indeed a fuckhead. **2002** J. S. Foer *Everything is Illuminated* 127: I'm sorry. You're not a fuckhead. I'm very sorry. **2007** J. Collins *Drop Dead Beautiful* 264: Good riddance to a misogynous murderous fuckhead.

fuckheaded *adjective*

stupid.

1968 R. Linney *Broofer* (1981) 20: Look, what kind of a fuck-headed situation—. **1971** T. Mayer *Weary Falcon* 121: Shut up, you fuckheaded slope. **1975** W. Kennedy *Legs* 148: Charlie, give me a hundred, you fuckheaded fuck! **2005** S. Monette *Melusine* 125: I knew she hadn't turned me in...even though I'd been fuckheaded enough to tell her my real name.

fuckhole *noun*

1.a. the vagina as an object of sexual penetration.

*ca*1890–93 J. S. Farmer & W. E. Henley *Slang & Its Analogues* III 80: *Fuck-hole…*The female *pudendum.* 1916 H. N. Cary *Slang of Venery* I 97: *Fuck hole*—The vagina. 1934 "J.M. Hall" *Anecdota Americana* (Second series) 14: First you much [*sic*] up me fuck hole and now you wants to fuck up me muck hole. 1959 in E. Cray *Erotic Muse* 73: At the fuck-hole of Kathusalem. 1975 *Ribald* (Sydney, Australia) (May 29) 15: Her gaping, hot fuck-hole readying itself for the prick. 1976 J. Vasco *Three-Hole Girl* 152: Cherry's fuck hole opened to her probing tongue. 1991 B. E. Ellis *American Psycho* 177: I find myself…trying to remember if I switched the tapes in my VCR, and suddenly I'm worried that I might be taping *thirtysomething* over *Pamela's Tight Fuckhole.* 1994 A. Sheehan *Jack Kerouac is Pregnant* 21: He grabbed between her legs and hissed, "Your fuckhole is too loose, whore." 2004 T. Taormino in *Village Voice* (Dec. 1) 125/1: Men will love "I ♥ My Pussy" (or "I ♥ My Fuckhole") tank tops.

b. Especially in homosexual use: the anus or mouth as an object of sexual penetration.

1971 B. Cochran *Crotch Bait* 35: Then he felt the big broad head of his cock slipping into the tightest little fuck hole he had ever felt. 1981 M. Ward *Randy Pants* 89: The tip of my tongue touched his tiny fuck hole, and my mouth was filled with the spicy taste of male ass. 1994 N. Baker *Fermata* xiv. 224: "Fill my fucking fanny!" Sylvie shouted, looking in Marian's eyes and then down at her toy-filled fuckholes. 1998 in L. Antoniou *Leatherwomen* 69: Some pathetic straight guy being forcibly fucked by a gang of studs until he's nothing but a pair of fuck-holes dribbling cum and spit. 2006 C. Varrin *Female Submission* 169: My face was still being used as a fuck-hole while I thought this. Niles's cock was delicious to taste.

c. a person regarded as a sexual object.

1990 J. Hynes *Wild Colonial Boy* 67: She had raged at him, hitting him again and again, shouting, "I'm not your fuckhole!" until he backed away. 1996 J. W. Bean *Leathersex Q & A* 61: I'm sure I'm not alone in my fantasies: Being used as a fuck-hole, urinal, ass-lick, even an ashtray by a lot of men one after another, or even all at once. 1998 *Weekly's Literary Supplement* (Stern Publishing) (May 8) 22: The females in Miller's *Tropics* weren't mostly depersonalized fuckholes. 2002 L. Breedlove *Godspeed* 230: They are surprised by a girl whom they expected to run, just a fuckhole, doubled over all soft. **2003** M. Hemmingson *Amateurs* 80: They fucked for a while and again they were loud and he called her a slutty fuckhole which she liked, she liked the dirty talk. *a***2006** P. Munson *Fairgrounds* in S. Bright *Best American Erotica 2006* 70: You're Daddy's slut, his whore, his prostitute, his fuck-hole.

2. a despicable person; an asshole.

1978 in *North Eastern Reporter* (2nd Series) (1980) (vol. 401) 595: She used profane language to the other children. She would say "God damn you, you bitch, you fuck hole, and you ass hole." *a***1981** in S. King *Bachman* 621: Goddam...fuckhole! **1985** J. Dillinger *Adrenaline* 54: Unlock my cuffs, fuckhole. *Ibid.* 215: Hey, fuckhole. **1996** *Rivera Live* (CNBC) (Jan. 30) (transcript): Steps towards him kind of spits at him and calls him a "fuck hole." **1999** S. Turow *Personal Injuries* 235: When you get down through the layers, Brendan is an absolute fuck-hole of a human being. **2003** "DBC Pierre" *Vernon God Little* 70: What a fuckhole, I swear. I should jam a table-leg through his fucken eye.

3. a disgusting location; "shithole."

1980 *High Performance* (Summer) 26/2: The architecture of Rome is evil. The Colosseum is an evil fuck-hole. **1990** A. W. Gray *In Defense of Judges* 234: His body they found six weeks ago in his fuckhole of an apartment. **1995** C. Foster *Sleep on, Beloved* 242: I got the best stuff in this fuckhole place. **2000** S. King *On Writing* 58: I didn't want it—the work was hard and boring, the mill itself a dingy fuckhole overhanging the polluted Androscoggin River. **2004** L. Love *You Ain't Got no Easter Clothes* 70: My mother told us she was "tired of living in this fuckhole where niggers acted like savages and the honkies that made them that way didn't give half a shit." **2005** J. Castro *Truth Book* 154: If you ever want help getting out of that fuck-hole, let me know.

fuck-in *noun*

(esp. among hippies) a love-in that includes public copulation; an orgy. Usually *jocular.*

1965 E. Sanders *Fuck You* (June): A Fuck-in for Peace. **1967–68** N. von Hoffman *We Are the People Our Parents Warned Us Against* 211: That was when we had a fuck-in at the White House. **1968** in M. J. Estren

History of Underground Comics (1974) 17: Grand Opening of the Great International Fuck-In and Orgy-Riot. **1971** U. K. Le Guin *Lathe of Heaven* 69: And there were the riots, and the fuck-ins, and the Doomsday Band and the Vigilantes. **1971** *Playboy* (Apr.) 184: If you want to get rid of dormitory rules, you have a fuck-in. **1975** M. Amis *Dead Babies* (1991) 122: And I don't just mean the sex conventions and the fuck-ins. **1980** F. Rush *Best Kept Secret* 191: But when these young radicals approached thirty, they discovered that their love-ins and fuck-ins neither freed the poor, the parks nor liberated Washington. **2002** R. Coover *Adventures of Lucky Pierre* 268: His massive fuck-ins have closed down movie houses, clogged traffic, collapsed bridges, paralyzed City Hall!

fucking *noun*

1. sexual intercourse.

1568 A. Scott *Poems* (1896) iv. 55: Thir foure, the suth to sane, Enforsis thame to fucking. **1571** in J. Cranstoun *Satirical Poems Reformation* (1891) I. 202: For quha wald not lauche...To se forett þe holy frere his fukking so deploire? **1708** *School of Love* in *Indictment* (Public Records Office: KB 28/24) m. 9: My lovely Phil. is...as well vers'd in the various manners of ffucking and ffrigging, as the Captain of the virtuosa's. **1766** in N. E. Eliason *Tarheel Talk* (1956) 185: As to the flesh tho', I cannot say I have occasion for any violent longings, as I have reduced F—n almost to a regular matrimonial system. **1849** A. Doten *Journals* I 40: There are plenty of girls in Talcahuano and the principal business carried on is— F—ing. **1854** in *American Speech* IX (1934) 271: [According to the actor David Garrick,] when it was asked what was the greatest pleasure, Johnson answered *******. **1865** "Philocomus" *Love Feast* ii. 14: The fucking, tickling and the sight/Drove me half frantic with delight. **1867** in A. Doten *Journals* II 949 [in cipher]: Me and my love had thus far one hundred good square fucks—the best fucking on the face of the earth. **1888** *Stag Party* 219: Sodom...was the worst place for wild fucking of all descriptions...(barring Chicago). **1932** H. Miller *Letter* (July 30) in G. Stuhlmann *Literate Passion* (1989) 82: When you return I am going to give you one literary fuck-fest—that means fucking and talking and talking and fucking— and a bottle of Anjou in between—or a Vermouth Cassis. **1964** S. Bellow *Herzog* 214: But if the fucking is at home and the child exposed to it, the judicial attitude is different. **1988** F. Busch *Ralph Duck* in M. Atwood

Best American Short Stories 1989 (1989) 78: I wrote him a paper about the mechanics of corpse fucking. **1993** S. Brown *Where There's Smoke* 373: Some of the best fucking I ever did. **1995** H. Korine *Kids* 150: Fucking is what I love. Take that away from me, and I really got nothin. **2002** M. Faber *Crimson Petal and the White* 818: Fuck the girl and have done with it! Fuck all the females in the world while the fucking is good!

2. fooling around; wasting time. Used with (chiefly *U.S.*) *around* or (chiefly *Brit.*) *about*.

1931 H. Miller in *Letters to Emil* (1989) 76: "My dear," she says. "I just couldn't stay away from you. I'm sick of all this fucking around." **1964** K. Amis *Letter* in Z. Leader *Letters of Kingsley Amis* (2000) 658: I ought to have told you earlier, but general fucking about, including Xmas, and disinclination...to do anything whatever. **1984** J. Kelman *Busconductor Hines* (1992) iv, 167: What's the point of fucking about. You leave half of the second pint and get off your mark. **2000** *Village Voice* (Dec. 5) 138: His greatest ire is reserved for a snooty critic who refuses to concede that all the hyperbolic, blood-spattered fucking about might be worth a second look.

3. a defeat, a drubbing; an instance of exploitation or victimization.

1945 in *Verbatim* (1989) (Autumn) 5/2 *Fxxxing*..., a crushing (humiliating) defeat, a drubbing, a fleecing, a loss... We took a right regular fxxxing at Tobruk. **1958** in R. Schwitzgebel *Streetcorner Research* 50: If a kid went and fucked up, you just don't go out and give him a fuckin'. **1967** H. S. Thompson *Letter* (Mar. 21) in *Proud Highway* (1997) 605: Every time he says, "Don't look back," I focus more intensely to the rear, the past, and the indefensible fucking I got on the Hell's Angels contract. **1969** *Black Panther* (May 4) in P. S. Foner *Black Panthers Speak* (1970) 251: It's made that way by the royal fucking that the working class gets in this country. **1997** *Black Renaissance* (Oct. 31): A person like Miles [Davis] never realized that he was giving almost everyone else a royal fucking (but if he had realized it he still wouldn't have cared).

fucking *adjective*

1. that engages or is engaged in sexual intercourse. Also: used during sexual activity or for sexual gratification; relating to or describing sexual activity.

1528 *MS Brasenose College, Oxford VII* (marginal note) in *Notes & Queries* (1993) (Mar.) 29/2: O d [*perhaps* = damned] fuckin Abbot. **1571** in J. Cranstoun *Satirical Poems Reformation* (1891) I. 202: Than lat ws sing, O fukand flok! yor deid is not lyk yor say. **1680** Lord Rochester *Poems* 30: Through all the Town, the common Fucking Post,/On whom each Whore, relieves her tingling Cunt. **1880** *Pearl* (June) 427: The last improvement in dildoes—the new patent Fucking Machine. **1882** *Boudoir* 160: Hurray, hurray, she's a maid no more,/But a f—g wife for evermore! *ca***1890** *My Secret Life* VIII. ix. 307 She was...a magnificent bit of fucking flesh, but nothing more. **1917–20** T. Dreiser *Newspaper Days* 233 [refers to 1893]: A large, Irish policeman...[said] "She's a Goddamned drunken, fucking old whore, that's what she is." *Ibid.* 276: I'm living...with a Goddamned fucking whore. **1939** D. Thomas *Letter* (Sept. 11) in P. Ferris *Collected Letters of Dylan Thomas* (1987) 408: He's always got the same cracks to grind, but, after all, good fucking books are few & far, & if you look at *Tropic of Cancer* as the best modern fucking book...then I know you must enjoy & admire it enormously. *ca***1942** ? H. Miller *Opus Pistorum* (typescript, Library of Congress) II. iii. 55: I am going to America and I am going to buy or make or have made a good mechanical cunt, a fucking machine, which runs by electricity. **1990** R. M. Polhemus *Erotic Faith* xi. 306: Just the sort of subjective, pompous, silly eloquence and wisdom that might be popping in the mind of some happily fucking human being. **2001** K. Rexroth in D. Meltzer *San Francisco Beat* 237: Did you ever take a chick into a motel in Southern California? It has a fucking machine in it. The bed fucks. You don't have to do any work.

2. contemptible or despicable; goddamned; (often used with reduced force for emphasis). [Perhaps originally taken from opprobrious literal phrases such as *fucking whore* or *fucking bitch* (cf. sense 1, above). *Fucking* is probably the word intended in the 1857 quotation: the number of asterisks is correct for the length of the word, and any word less vulgar would only be partly omitted (compare representation of *bitch* in the same quotation); compare the identical use of asterisks in clearer contexts from the same era in the 1848 and 1854 quotations at FUCK, *verb*, definition 1a.]

1857 *Suppressed Book about Slavery* 211: The Dr... applied the lash. The Woman writhed under each stroke, and cried, "O Lord!"...The Doctor...

thus addressed her (the congregation must pardon me for repeating his words). "Hush, you ******* b—h, will you take the name of the Lord in Vain on the Sabbath day?" **1888** *Stag Party* [unpaged]: Now this gives us another fucking scene, leastways it is not exactly a fucking scene, though it came near being one. It shows you Joseph and Potiphar's wife. *a***1890– 93** J. S. Farmer & W. E. Henley *Slang & Its Analogues* III 80: *Fucking... Adj.* (common).—A qualification of extreme contumely. **1915** E. Pound in Materer *Pound/Lewis* 18: God damn the fucking lot of 'em. **1915** in P. Adam-Smith *ANZACS* 168: You fucking xt I've only just got the f...g thing off the other f...g table you b..t..d. **1918** in [H. V. O'Brien] *Wine, Women & War* 205 [diary entry for Sept. 26]: Hi, Tommy,'ere's one o' yer fuckin' English hofficers wants t' be saluted. **1914–21** J. Joyce *Ulysses* 595: I'll wring the neck of any bugger says a word against my fucking king. *Ibid.* 600: I'll do him in, so help me fucking Christ! **1921** *Notes & Queries* (Nov. 19) 415 [refers to WW1]: [*Fucking*] was used adjectively to qualify almost every noun in the soldier's vocabulary. **1923** R. McAlmon *Companion Volume* 51: What in fucking hell do youse think this is, a sunday school picnic, or a tea party? **1927** *Immortalia* 124: He's a fucking son-of-a-bitch. **1928** in A. W. Read *Lexical Evidence from Folk Epigraphy* (1935) 54: You god Dam fucken fool. **1929–30** J. Dos Passos *42nd Parallel* 77: Jack, it was a fucking shame. **1934** H. Roth *Call It Sleep* 231 [refers to *ca*1910]: Didja ever see dat new tawch boinin' troo a goider er a flange er any fuck'n hunka iron? **1935** T. Wolfe *Of Time & the River* 598: I'll kick duh f—kin' s—t outa duh f—kin' lot of yuh, yuh f—kin' bastards, you. **1937** E. Hemingway *To Have & Have Not* 225: A man alone ain't got no bloody fucking chance. **1938** in P. Oliver *Blues Tradition* 170: I...don't deny my fuckin' name. **1939** T. Sturgeon *Ether Breather* in D. Knight *First Flight* (1963) 88: He took his lips from hers, buried his face in her hair and said clearly: "I hate your — guts." And that "—" was the most perfectly enunciated present participle of a four-letter verb I have ever heard. **1942** N. Algren *Never Come Morning* 39: Dey ain't a book in da f— place. **1943** F. Wakeman *Shore Leave* 184: "The f—ing island," Crewson corrected. **1948** J. G. Cozzens *Guard of Honor* 561: Said why the f— holy hell didn't they get a boat from Lake Armstrong. **1951** D. R. Morris *China Station* 129: You're a fucking liar. **1953–55** MacK. Kantor *Andersonville* 224: What?—with this fucking pistol of yours? **1955** J. O'Hara *Ten North Frederick* 365: I think you're a fucking hypocrite. **1960** in A. Sexton *Letters* 97: My (fucking) book comes out March 1st in case you've forgotten. **1964** I. Faust *Steagle* 105: I can't ever get a fuckin break. **1972** Captain John W. Young on lunar surface in

Newsweek (May 1) 24: "I haven't eaten this much citrus fruit in twenty years," he snorted. "And I'll tell you one thing: in another twelve f— days, I ain't ever eating any more." **1987** T. Wolfe *Bonfire of Vanities* 59: I said please pick up the fucking phone! I mean holy shit! **1992** *Newsweek* (Nov. 23) 32: We're going to blow up your f— building. **1995** *New Yorker* (July 17) 50: I'm not your fucking scribe! I write what's meaningful to me! **1999** *New Yorker* (Aug. 23) 124/1: Keep you fokkin' head down! **2004** J. Meno *Hairstyles of Damned* 113: But Bobby is a fucking asshole. **2007** M. Wall *W.A.R.: Unauthorized Biography of W. Axl Rose* 267: You can't even hold a fucking candle to that fucking guy.

fucking *adverb*
exceedingly; damned; (often used with reduced force for emphasis).

*a***1890–93** J. S. Farmer & W. E. Henley *Slang & Its Analogues* III 80: *Fucking... Adv.* (common) Intensive and expletive; a more violent form of *bloody.* **1918** in E. Wilson *Prelude* 210: The situation is fucking serious! **1918** E. Pound in J. Joyce *Letters* II 424: The world is too fucking with us. **1929** F. Manning *Middle Parts of Fortune* 6 [refers to WWI]: They can say what they bloody well like....but we're a fuckin' fine mob. **1933** C. H. Ford & P. Tyler *Young & Evil* 31: It's too fucking cold to be running around trying to raise fifty dollars. **1934** H. Miller in *Letters to Emil* (1989) 153: I'm getting fucking critical of people. *Ibid.* 156: Maybe I'll get...fucking famous one day. **1942** H. Miller *Roofs of Paris* 250: I'm so fucking mad now that I don't care what she does. **1948** N. Mailer *Naked & Dead* 10: Pretty fuggin funny. **1956** T. T. Chamales *Never So Few* 510: You're asking too fucking much of me. **1963** S. Hayden *Wanderer* 126: You're pretty fucking dumb, kid, you know that. **1964** A. Sexton in *Letters* 254: It's too fucking hard to write. **1969–71** R. Kahn *Boys of Summer* 312: "Well, how did you get to play it like that?" "I worked, that's fucking how." **1973** R. Roth *Sand in Wind* 83: STOP! FUCKING STOP! **1977** R. Caron *Go-Boy* 152: I'll be fucking seeing you later. **1979** B. Gutcheon *New Girls* 12: "You're very fucking rude, Lisa," said Jenny. **1987** T. Wolfe *Bonfire of Vanities* 47: Why did you just fucking stand there, doing nothing? **1993** *New Yorker* (Jan. 11) 78: I'm getting out of here, you fucking crazy. **1998** B. Elton *Blast from Past* ii. 15: You can't just fucking use me—talk to me at the office and refuse to speak when I call. **2004** J. Meno *Hairstyles of*

Damned 113: I mean, he fucking told that girl Laura that she is his "ideal woman." Can you even believe that shit?

-fucking- *infix*

(used for emphasis in the middle of a word or set phrase). See also ABSOFUCKINGLUTELY, FAN-FUCKING-TASTIC, GUARANFUCKINGTEE.

1921 *Notes & Queries* (Nov. 19) 415 [refers to WWI]: Words were split up to admit [*fucking*]: "absolutely" became "abso—lutely," and Armentières became Armen— teers." "Bloody"...quite lapsed as being too polite and inexpressive. **1939** (quotation at FUCKED DUCK). **1945** in *Verbatim* (Autumn, 1989) 5: Twenty-fxxxing-four faces to feed. Blame it on your anti-fxxx'n-aircraft units, mate. **1952** in M. Russ *Last Parallel* 13: Reveille goes tomorrow at four o'fuckin' clock. **1957** J. Kerouac *Letter* (Oct. 1) in *Selected Letters 1957–69* (1999) 66: Bottles of Old Granddad, big articles in Sat. Review, in World Telly, everyfuckingwhere, everybody mad, Brooklyn College wanted me to lecture to eager students and big geek questions to answer. **1962** E. Sagarin *Anatomy of Dirty Words* 148: Irrefuckinsponsible, imfuckinpossible, unfuckinconscious,... unfuckinsociable. **1965** C. Brown *Manchild in the Promised Land* 86: I wondered if he thought he was Jesus or some fucking body like that. **1966** R. Fariña *Been Down So Long* 84: He gets himself infuckingvolved. **1968** W. Marcs *Marine Machine* xii: Outfucking-standing, Private Smith! **1968** R. Gover *JC* 158: That's the ee-fuckin-*end* of it. **1971** *Playboy* (Mar.) 189: Unfucking-believable! **1971** W. Sonzski *Punch Goes the Judy* 19: Tele-*fucking*-phone for you. **1972** D. Pearce *Pier Head Jump* 6: It's un-fuckin-believable sometimes. *Ibid.* 156: Six o'fuckin' clock. **1973** McA. Layne *How Audie Murphy Died in Vietnam* (unpaged): Do me one more favor, Private. Dis-a-fuckin-pear! **1975** C.W. Smith *Country Music* 230: How po-fucking-etic! **1978** R. Price *Ladies' Man* 128: Go away. Go afuckin'way. **1985** in *Maledicta* 8 (1984–85) 244: Of all the cocksucking, cuntlicking, asshole ideas I've ever heard of, this is the most unfuckingbelievable. **1998** T. Junod in *Esquire* (Nov.) 136: Holy shit! It's Mister Fucking Rodgers! **2002** B. James *Middleman* i. 11: If ever Corbett incorporated himself he would call the company No Man's Fucking Land. **2004** D. Barry in J. Williams *Wales, Half Welsh* 200: Very calmly, she said, "Where is she, then? If you know." "I don't know.... She's still back home. or in Timbuc-fucking-too, as far as I care." **2008** A. Davies

Mine All Mine 111: You're such a clownus. They don't speak Flemish in Netherfuckingland.

fucking A *noun*
the least bit.

1966 S. Stevens *Go Down Dead* 203: Youth workers. Shit on them. They don't know fucking A about us.

fucking-A *adverb, adjective, interjection,* & *infix* [FUCKING + *a* (origin unknown; perhaps taken from a phrase such as *"you're fucking A-number-one right!"*)]

1.a. Especially *Military.* yes, indeed; absolutely (correct); especially in phrase: ☞ **[you're] fucking-A**, occasionally with elaborations, especially **fucking-A [well] told.**

1948 N. Mailer *Naked & Dead* 21 [refers to WWII]: "You're fuggin ay," Gallegher snorted. **1961** J. Jones *Thin Red Line* 137 [refers to WWII]: "No, I never." "You fucking A you never." **1961** J. Peacock *Valhalla* 181 [refers to 1953]: Fucking A. **1967** M. Crowley *Boys in the Band* 827: Fuckin' A, Mac. **1967** D. Brelis *Face of South Vietnam* 29: "It can't be the same kid." "You're fuckin' A, it's the same fuckin' kid." **1969** J. Briley *Traitors* 273: You're fucking A I had to work. **1969** G. Sidney *For the Love of Dying* 146: Fuckingeigh. **1970** D. Wakefield *Going All the Way* 42 [refers to *ca*1950s]: Fuckin-A John Do. **1970** J. Bouton *Ball Four* vii. 389: We also talked about the expressions we used in high school.... If somebody said, "Are you taking Louise to the dance," you had to say, "Fuckin' ay I am." **1970** D. Ponicsan *Last Detail* 171: Fucking-ay-John Ditty-Bag-well-told I don't. **1970** W. C. Woods *Killing Zone* 143: Fuckin-A-well-told. *Ibid.* Fuckin-A-number-one-well-told. **1975** M. Larsen *Runner* 38: Your fucking A told he is. *Ibid.* "Fucking A told," Antonino agreed. **1982** H. Berry *Semper Fi, Mac* 192 [refers to WWII]: "Hey, Bull, you going on liberty?" "Fuckin' A doodle de doo." **1985** J. Dillinger *Adrenaline* 199: "You were traumatized." "You're fuckin' A we were traumatized." **1978** W. B. McCloskey Jr. *Highliners* (1980) Epilog 385: "You'd take me back?" "You're fuckin' A!... Need airfare?" **1985** N. Kazan *At Close Range* (film): "Looks like a nice gun." "Fucking-A-plus it's a nice gun." **1988** S. Rushdie *Satanic Verses* (1998) 245: Her sister nodded assent: "Crucial. Fucking A."

b. (used to express astonishment, dismay, or recognition).

1979 C. Hiler *Monkey Mountain* [refers to 1972] 103: "Three pair and…the deuce of spades."…"Fuckin' A!" **1980** J. Carroll *Land of Laughs* 168: Fuck-ing *A*!…The guy who walked around the world! **1988** C. Eble *Campus Slang* 4: *Fuckin' A*—exclamation, either positive or negative. "What? A Quiz today?…Fuckin' A!" **1992** *Vanity Fair* (July) 130: Fookin' A, she looks good. **1997** *New Yorker* (Aug. 18) 51: I jumped out of my chair. Fucking A! I love football! **1997** L. Yablonsky *Story of Junk* 253: Mary's no junkie, just a mule, and now she's stoned. Fucking A. **2001** S. King *Dreamcatcher* ii. 85: He lost his rifle, too. A brand-new Remington .30-.30, fuckin A, you won't never see that again.

c. splendid.

1986 J. C. Stinson & J. Carabatsos *Heartbreak Ridge* 29: The night had gone from fucking-A to all-fucked-up in record time. **1986** R. Chapman *New Dictionary of American Slang*: We won? Fucking a! **1987** W. Pelfrey & J. Carabatsos *Hamburger Hill* 51 [refers to Vietnam War]: The ham's fucking A, Ma.

2.a. Especially *Military*. (used as an intensifier); = FUCKING; goddamned. [The 1955 quotation is euphemistic.]

1955 J. Sack *Here to Shimbashi* 18: "That was a mighty freaking-A loud sneeze," declared the sergeant major. **1968** E. Bullins *In the Wine Time* 389: That's right…that's fucken "A" right. **1986** L. Heinemann *Paco's Story* 20: Guys with their chests squashed flat from fuckin'-A booby-trapped bombs. **1987** B. Raskin *Hot Flashes* 87: "That was too-fucking-A-much," Joanne says tersely. **1998** *Schizo* (#3) [inside front cover]: I can see you cum and cum…and finally DIE, all at the same fuckin-A time! **2003** *N.Y. Magazine* (May 5) 32/2: "We're the fucking-A greatest," he told employees, and then, shirtless, rolled onto his desk and did twenty push-ups. **2003** M. Lewis *Moneyball* ix. 193: This is the time to make a fucking A trade.

b. FUCKING WELL; very well; very; absolutely.

1960 G. Sire *Deathmakers* 211 [refers to WWII]: You can fucking-aye say that again. *Ibid.* 262: You fucking-aye have spoken, Captain. **1968** N. C. Heard *Howard Street* 72: You fuckin'-A-right! **1970** *Evergreen Review* (Apr.) 66: You know fucking-A I deserve it, Krim, now where is it going to be published? **1970** P. Appleman *In the Twelfth Year of the War* 89: You hear, I do not fuckin'-aye *intend* it! **1972** D. Ponicsan *Cinderella Liberty* 8: No one knew who first got carried away...and wound up with the melodious inventive "Fuckin' aye John Ditty Bag," but since then any number of sailors have gilded the lily and produced things like, "Fuckin' well told aye John Ditty Bag I be go to hell on a forklift!" **1973** B. Hirschfeld *Generation of Victors* 38: Now that is fucking-A important. **1973** "J. Godey" *Pelham* 151: He fucking-aye-right *better* be. **1976** C. R. Anderson *Grunts* 78 [refers to 1969]: You know fucking A well you can't ask the man no dumbass question like that. **1978** L. K. Truscott *Dress Gray* 443: You could fuckin'-A say that again. **1981** W. T. Hathaway *World of Hurt* 209: You're my fuckin'-A favorite ridge-runner. *a***1982** H. Berry *Semper Fi, Mac* 192: *Fuckin' A told* or *Fuckin' A right* were everyday expressions [in the Marine Corps during WWII]. **1985** R. Frede *Nurses* 237: I am fucking-A *ripped!* **1985** D. Bodey *F.N.G.* 4: Marines. Fuckin'-A filthy. **1998** R. B. Parker *Trouble in Paradise* 80: We're just going to fucking-A find that out, aren't we, my little chickadee? *a***1999** D. F. Wallace *Signifying Nothing* in *Brief Interviews with Hideous Men* (1999) 78: I know, for fucking-"A" sure, my father was not going to say anything to her about it.

fucking Able [FUCKING + former military communications alphabet *Able* 'A']

Military. = FUCKING-A.

 1966 R. Newhafer *No More Bugles in the Sky* 176: That certainly is tough shit, Danang. You are fucking able right I violated air space.

fucking-A well *adverb*

= FUCKING WELL.

 1976 H. Crews *Feast of Snakes* 83: He fucking-A-well had the words right.

fuckingly *adverb*

extremely; incredibly.

 [*ca***1890** *My Secret Life* IX. xii.: The cunt slightly open and fuckingly aromatic, smelling like the cunt of a woman.] **1927** E. Hemingway in

Selected Letters (1981) 261: Got a sheet to fill out from Who's Who and my life has been so fuckingly complicated that I was only able to answer two of the questions. **1930** J. C. Powys in *Diary* (1987) 191: Had Devilish & fuckingly sharp discomfort in my ulcer. *a***1932** A. Nin in *Henry & June* (1986) 181: Henry loves me, but not fuckingly, not fuckingly. **1952** in G. Legman *Limerick* (1954) 47: The skater, Barbara Ann Scott/ Is so fuckingly "winsome" a snot. **1952** M. Horwitz *Letter* (Aug. 9) in *We Will not be Strangers: Korean War Letters* (1997) 54: Fuckingly well done. **1971** P. Zindel *And Miss Reardon Drinks a Little* 10: That whole pack of academically defunct eternally matriculated and fuckingly overpaid nuts and what are they saying? **2002** N. Vida *End of Marriage* 215: I have this connection in New York, he gets the most fuckingly beautiful Stickley pieces.

fucking well *adverb*

very well; absolutely; (often used for emphasis). Compare similar use of *bloody well*.

1922 T. E. Lawrence *The Mint* (1955) 80: She'll stay as she fuckin' well is. **1931** J. Brophy & E. Partridge *Songs & Slang of the British Soldier* (ed. 3) 17 [refers to WWI]: By adding -ing and -ingwell [to *fuck*] an adjective and adverb were formed and thrown into every sentence. **1939** A. C. Bessie *Men in Battle* 177: God send the—day when we'll—fuckin' well march no more! **1939** in *Southern Folklore Quarterly* XL. 104: Look at the people, furkin' well cryin';/Isn't it nice to be furkin' well dead. **1945** E. Hemingway in *Selected Letters* (1981) 590: If he doesn't take care of you he better never fucking well run into me. **1948** R. Lowry *Find Me in Fire* 143: You're fucking well right he had his pension—and they had his leg. Did he have to keep reminding them of the bargain? Or did they feel they were being cheated? He could fucking well assure them they hadn't been. **1952** J. Kerouac *Visions of Cody* 201: You got the whole thing fuckingwell summed up. **1952** in M. Russ *Last Parallel* 13: I was behind the wheel of a fuckin' Diesel truck before you ever learned to fuckin' well drive.... **1965** S. Friedman *Totempole* 267: You better fucking-well believe it! **1971** H. Selby *Room* 42: You're fucking well right he did. **1973** P. Maas *Serpico* 200: Get this fucking-well straight. **1974–77** A. Hoffman *Property Of* 166: I fucking well do not know, all right? **1986** W. Gibson *Count Zero* 148: So you can fucking well buy me some clothes, okay? **1993** I. Welsh *Trainspotting* (1994) 110:

Whair ur ye fuckin well gaun?—That's fir me tae ken n you tae find oot. What ye dinnae fuckin well ken they cannae fuckin beat oot ay ye, ah sais. **1999** H. Fielding *Bridget Jones: Edge of Reason* 57: Cannot believe he still hasn't fucking, fucking, fucking well rung. **2000** M. Atwood *Blind Assassin* 346: Do whatever you fucking well feel like doing. **2006** M. Amis *House of Meetings* 103: Violence and escalation. You know fucking well what's going to happen.

fuckish *adjective*

eager for copulation.

*a***1890–93** J. S. Farmer & W. E. Henley *Slang & Its Analogues* III 81: *Fuckish*...wanton;...inclined for coition. **1969** "Iceberg Slim" *Mama Black Widow* 246: Dorcas is fuckish as hell. **1992** W. Kennedy *Very Old Bones* 172: Does your stripper make you feel fuckish? **1992** K. Amis in *Independent* (London) (Apr. 12) ("Review page") 37: If you wanna make me fuckish/get your ass into some lingerie & smell good. **1999** J. L'Heureux *Having Everything* 84: And so he was on Route 93 to Boston, dressed for the occasion, feeling fit and fuckish. And why not? He was a young man in his prime.

fuck job *noun*

an act of victimization; victimization.

1973 U.S. Air Force Sgt.: Someone's always tryin' to do the old fuck job on me. **1988** Southern attorney, age 36: I tell you, the fuck job never stops. **2003** J. Heywood *Chasing Blond Moon* 253: "This is a fuck job," Tavolacci said. "One more word and you are in contempt, Mister Tavolacci." **2006** J. Maberry *Ghost Road Blues* 306: You know, when I got up this morning I had no idea how much of a total fuck job this whole day was going to turn out to be. My team gets shot up, we get chased by the cops, crash our car, [etc.].

fuck-juice *noun*

semen or vaginal fluid.

1973 "D. H. Love" *Dial-a-Dick* 33: He ground his ass around to feel every spurt of fuck juice from Ken's weapon. **1975** *Ribald* (Sydney, Australia) (May 29) 15: My wife began to suck him madley [*sic*], licking all of Brad's and Trudy's mingled fuck juices. **1976** J. Vasco *Three-Hole Girl* 10: Clear fuckjuice oozed from the slit at the tip of the huge member. **1988** N. Zedd in B. Stosuy *Up is Up, But So is Down* (1996) 297/1: I slurped away at her quivering clit, oozing fuckjuice and sweat. **1989** *First Hand* (May) 103/1: I let out a huge load of thick, creamy fuck juice, all the while pumping his ass good. **1998** *A Fivesome Story*, on Usenet newsgroup alt.sex.stories (July 2): Her fuck-juice covered my face and hands and I smeared it all over her ass. **1999** J. Fletcher trans. A. P. de Mandiargues *Portrait of an Englishman in his Chateau* 113: I bit her pubes which were smeared with female fuck juice and alcohol. *a***2000** P. Califia *No Mercy* 71: She pulled away from Mack, curled up on her side, and was asleep in half a second, her thighs glued together with overworked lube and fuck juice.

fuck-knuckle *noun*
Chiefly *Australian*. a stupid or offensive person.

1981 A. Loukakis *For the Patriarch* 155: You stay outa this fucknuckle! **1994** in *Macquarie Dictionary* files: Don't worry about him, he's a fuck knuckle. **1997** *Sick Puppy Comix* (Sydney, Australia) (No. 6) 5: It's been such a long time since I've been to the beach, I've forgotten what an oily, muscle-headed, fuck-knuckle looks like. **2001** T. O'Farrell *Behind Enemy Lines: Australian SAS Soldier in Vietnam* 12: Right fuck-knuckle, get into those dixies over there. **2007** A. Theroux *Laura Warholic* xlvi. 740: What is it with these fuck-knuckles in rock that girls seem to like so much?

fuckless *adjective*
lacking in sexual activity.

1955 J. P. Donleavy *Ginger Man* 41: I'm hounded fuckless through the streets, beaten to the wall, scratching up pennies. **1967** N. Mailer *Why are we in Vietnam?* (1988) i. 19: Don' ask if it's Navaho, Apache, or any of those Jew shit questions, you anthropologist manqué, you fuckless wonder listening to the sex'l habits of all us mule-ass Texans. **1970** L. Gould *Such Good Friends* 8: It was the most beautiful solution a man could devise for keeping a fuckless marriage intact. **1974** U. K. Le Guin *Dispossessed* vi.145: As far as the eye can see the infertile desert lies in the pitiless glare of the merciless sun, a lifeless, trackless, feckless, fuckless, waste strewn with the bones of luckless wayfarers. **1982** S. Hite *Hite Report on Male Sexuality* 353: All those fuckless nights in college. **1995** W. H. Gass *Tunnel* 51: In a future which is to be fuckless between us as furniture. **2004** M. Barrowcliffe *Lucky Dog* 151: Health and fitness are the concerns of the fuckless.

fuckload *noun*

a large number or amount of; "shitload."

[**1978** "F. Pulsing" *Whipped Cream* 16: The combination drew the fuckload from Ed's shaking loins. He moaned and blasted. *Ibid.* 59: He gushed his fuck-load into the fink's writhing mouth.] **1984** R. Meltzer in *Whore Just Like Rest* (2000) 324: I was struck by the fuckload of inner capacities the guy was perceptibly calling on. **1988** J. Ellroy *Big Nowhere* vii. 92 Him and Marty pulled a righteous fuckin' fuckload of burglaries together. **1996** "Sublime" *Caress Me Down* (pop. song): I'm a star (with a fuckload of money 'cause you know I'm a star). **1999** W. Gibson *All Tomorrow's Parties* 325: Those motherfucker bulklifters come drop a fuckload of water on it, got about a hundred firetrucks and everything here. **2006** G. Malkani *Londonstani* xxiii. 285: She was my girlfriend, we'd both landed in a fuckload a trouble.

fuck machine *noun*

an extremely vigorous sexual partner. Compare *fucking machine* at FUCKING *adjective* sense 1.

1972 C. Bukowski *Erections, Ejaculations, & General Tales of Ordinary Madness* 35 (story title): The Fuck Machine. **1979** S. Spencer *Endless Love* 346: "They all know, everyone does." "Know what?" "That you're you, who you are. Mr. Fuck-Machine." **1981** H. Robbins *Goodbye, Janette* 244: He was nothing but a fuck machine. Her loins and anus felt swollen and aching. **1992** Q. Tarantino *Reservoir Dogs* (film): The pain is reminding the fuck machine what it was like to be a virgin. **1999** C. D. Wright *Floating Lady Retablo #1* in *Steal Away* (2002) 45: I was your/Personal all purpose all weather fuck machine. **2000** G. Duncan *Love Remains* ii. 120: I just can't face that lot tonight. Bloody Anthony with some nineteen-year-old fuck-machine. You don't mind, do you? **2006** K. Lobe *Paris Hangover* 90: It's a personal best on the pleasure meter. To be crass—no, very crass—Nico is a fuck machine.

fuck-me *noun*

in *plural* = FUCK-ME shoes.

[**1972** B. Rodgers *Queens' Vernacular* 53: *Come fuck-me's*...overly tight pants.] **1974** J. Mitzel & S. Abbott *Myra & Gore* 13: Shod in a pair of fabulous 1940's-Joan-Crawford-fuck-mes. **1993** A. Adams & W. Stadiem *Madam* 125: In her garter belt and silk stockings and Blahnik fuck-mes. **2005** A. Miles *Janet & John* 152: I fastened stockings and slipped on a new pair of *fuck-mes* that I had recently invested in.

fuck-me *adjective*

(especially of an article of clothing, typically footwear) intended to invite sexual advances; seductive, vampish, sexy. Compare CFM.

1972 C. Ludlam *Bluebeard* in M. Smith *More Plays from Off-Off Broadway* III. ix. 406: She is completely nude except for her fuck-me pumps. **1974** D. Bowie *We Are the Dead* (pop. song): I love you in your fuck-me pumps / And your nimble dress that trails. **1989** P. Munro *U.C.L.A. Slang* 41: *Fuck-me boots*...mid-calf or higher boots worn under a miniskirt. **1990** P. Munro *Slang U.* 86: *Fuck-me eyes*...flirtatious stares or glances / I'm feeling some serious fuck-me eyes from that guy in the corner. **1992** *Letters to Penthouse* III 63: Her legs ended in a pair of "fuck-me" stilettos. **1997** G. Williams *Diamond Geezers* ii. 15: Cindy C wearing nothing but a pink fuck-me swimsuit, still wet from the ocean, her hair slicked back and dripping. **1998** N.Y.C. writer, age 70: I remember clearly in the 1960s when the niece of the then-editor of *Vogue*, Diana Vreeland, startled me by referring to her "fuck-me boots." I am prepared to sign an affidavit that this happened in the '60s. High boots were just beginning to be the style. **1999** *Pi Mag.* (Univ. Coll. London Union) Feb. 17/2: They look the part—all spiky hair and fuck-me swagger—and they talk the talk—all big ideas and glammed-up dreams. **2002** I. Knight *Don't You Want Me?* xiv. 191: "And you've grown, I see," says Frank, still staring, looking down at my fuck-me footwear, a narrow, black suede pair of pointy boots with killer stiletto heels. **2006** G. Malkani *Londonstani* v. 47: They were upper sixth-formers, meanin they'd binned their dark green school uniforms a couple a years back an were now struttin around in their best casual garms. Good desi girls, though, so no fuck-me clothes.

fuck muscle *noun*

Esp. *Homosexuals.* the penis.

1977 F. Danton *Fist Club* 6: It was a big, thick, long thing that never quit, thirteen heavy inches of fuck muscle that any stud would be lucky to suck or take manfully up the ass. **1994** L. Eighner *American Prelude* 39: His muscles bulged—especially the fuck muscle in the middle of his slender belly. **2002** B. Vickery *Cocksure* 106: I'd love to fuck your ass right now. That is, if you think you can handle my throbbing gargantuan fuck muscle.

fucknob *noun* [probably from *nob* 'head'; compare FUCKHEAD]

a stupid or contemptible person.

1995 *New Yorker* (May 8) 76: Look who's talking, fucknob....Your whole life is fucked up. **1998** *Re: Crows & Umpiring*, message on Usenet newsgroup aus.sport.aussie-rules (Aug. 9): It's not considered polite to call someone a "fucknob."

fucknut *noun*

a stupid or contemptible person. Also **fucknuts**.

1986 S. King *It* 199: "Why did you do that?" "Because I *felt* like it, fucknuts!" Henry roared back. **1992** *Language in Society* XXI. 283: Ugly male...dick, dof, drip, dwax, dweep, dweet, dwors, fucknut, fuckup, [etc.]. **1997** M. T. Sullivan *Purification Ceremony* 267: You fucknut, I should bust your ass right here, right now. **2002** A. Davies *Frog King* 188: I think you're acting like a fucknut.... Say, "Evie, I'm sorry. Evie, I love you." OK? **2004** *Esquire* (Sept.) 126/1: I don't know anyone like the people on [TV family shows.].... I can't relate to any of them. These people are all fucknuts.

fuck-nutty *adjective*

obsessed with thoughts of copulation.

1942 H. Miller *Roofs of Paris* 32: Those fuck-nutty kids.

fucko *noun* [probably influenced by *bucko*]

= FUCKER, definition 2.

1969 R. Thorp *Dionysus* 93: Well, fucko, I see you've made yourself right to home. **1973** A. Schiano & A. Burton *Solo* 76: Hey, fucko, what're you following me for? **1974** S. Terkel *Working* 582: Hey, fucko, come over here....You fucker. **1976** R. Price *Bloodbrothers* 247: No sweat, fucko. **1988** G. Gallo *Midnight Run* (film): My name's *Carmine*, fucko! **1996** J. Díaz *Edison, New Jersey* in *Drown* 129: The boss wasn't having it. You fuckos, he said. You butthogs. He tore us for a good two minutes and then *dismissed* us. **2003** A. Swofford *Jarhead* 50: I entered the room.... Someone said, "Fucko is here."

fuck-off *noun*
Originally *Military.* a person who shirks duties or responsibilities; loafer or shirker; an incompetent.

   1948 N. Mailer *Naked & Dead* 229 [refers to WWII]: You think I'm just a fug-off, don't you? **1953** W. Eyster *Far from Customary Skies* 141 [refers to WWII]: How come you fuckoffs waited to now to start this fussing? How come you didn't pray none in calm water? **1961** E. Hemingway *Islands in the Stream* 356: Where you two fuck-offs been? **1964** H.S. Thompson *Letter* (Jan. 29) in *Proud Highway* (1997) 436: I have turned into a fuck-off as far as this journalism is concerned—one of those woodsy types who talks a good article but never writes it. **1968** "J. Hudson" *Case of Need* 271: The radiologist for the night is Harrison. He's a fuck-off. **1969** P. Spector in *Rolling Stone* (Nov. 1) 29/3: It's a lot different today. I tell you the whole world is a drop-out. I mean, everybody's a fuck-off. **1978** W. Wharton *Birdy* 176: I hate to think of going into combat with fuck-offs like these. **1984** J.R. Reeves *Mekong* 76: You fuckoff! **1996** M. Arax *In My Father's Name* 142: You know your Dad was a fuck off. Then he got married and almost overnight he got serious. **2003** *Prospect* (Sept.) 45/3: Around me, sipping coffees, seven or eight faces were familiar, even though the eagerness in some eyes had dimmed. "The fuck-offs are worse," said one teacher I remembered. "The lippiness. The low-level misbehaviour is worse," said another.

fuck-off *adjective*
1. Chiefly *British.* dismissive; hostile; threatening; (*hence*) impressive; huge.

1962 T. J. Scheff in *Administrative Science Quarterly* (vol. 7) 216: If there was shared role imagery on these wards, it was that of the cunning "goldbrick" who built what were called "fuck-off" kingdoms in the hospital. Within such kingdoms, treatment goals usually received lip service at the very most. **1993** R. Lowe & W. Shaw *Travellers* 12: Farmers'll come up and say, "Why haven't you introduced yourself round the village?"... That freaks us. We're more used to fuck-off looks from people. **1996** *Loaded* (Sept.) 158/2: We had some fancy idea about making a few records, receiving a big cheque and all going off to live in a fuck-off mansion. **1997** "Q" *Deadmeat* 205: Goldie, a young man who had definitely put some of his money where his mouth was by coating his teeth in gold, pulled up in a devious black Mercedes with fuck off fat chrome wheels. **1999** J. Poller *Reach* iii. 8: Fuck fairies... Kids want sex, drugs, violence. Big fuck-off guns. **2001** K. Sampson *Outlaws* 7: He looked like one of them stereotype American tourists—big mad camera and that, all sorts of fuck-off lenses and fucking secret tricky bits built in. **2004** L. Sutherland *Venus as Boy* 36: I liked art. Double period last thing on a Friday. Mostly, it was still-life and handicrafts, but every once in a while they'd give you free rein to draw big fuck-off pictures of the sea and stars.

2. lazy; shiftless; idle.

1970 L. Bangs in *Psychotic Reactions* (1987) 47: Eventually I apprehended that the music on *Fun House* is neither sloppy (in the sense that a fuckoff group like Deep Purple is sloppy...) nor inept. **1975** W. Harrington *Scorpio 5* 38: Whoever managed to steal fifty feet of mag tape off a reel and carry it out through Alpha Gemini plant security was somebody too smart for any fuckoff small-town cop to ever catch. *a***1996** R. Aman in *Maledicta* (vol. XII) 47: The University of Wisconsin...shamelessly protected an incompetent fuckoff professor who was more interested in peddling real estate than in teaching and thus cheated hard-working undergraduate and graduate students out of a decent education.

fuck off *verb*

1.a. to run away; get away; make off. [Comparatively rare in North American English.]

1929 F. Manning *Middle Parts of Fortune* I. iii. 37 [refers to WWI]: As soon as a bit o' shrapnel comes their way, [they] fuck off 'ome jildy, toot sweet. **1939** A. C. Bessie *Men in Battle* 89: No one ever saw him again. He "fucked off" over the border, as the men expressed it. **1943** in *American Speech* (Apr. 1944) 108: You would say of a man who has absented himself at the approach of some unpleasant job of work, "Oh, he *fucked off*." **1948** E. Hemingway in *Selected Letters* 640: The opposing characters will fuck off once the column shows. **1953** K. Amis *Letter* in Z. Leader *Letters of Kingsley Amis* (2000) 302: They all thought it must be appendicitis…, but the medico was summoned, but he said it wasn't. He gave me some filthy medicine…and fucked off. **1961** L. McMurtry *Horseman, Pass By* 58: "Fuck off," he said. "You ain't got no private milkin' rights." **1967** C. Aaron *About Us* 183: That wasn't brave. I knew they'd fuck off. **1985** A. Sillitoe *Life Goes On* 171: I told him to…fuck off to Scotland, but he wouldn't budge. **1999** *The Score* in M. Hunt *Junk Yard* 103: Me chips are done, so he sticks them in the bag and pours on plenty of salt and vinegar, just the way I like them. I give him eighty pence and fuck off. **2003** "DBC Pierre" *Vernon God Little* xvi. 170: Me, I snatch up my pack and fuck off.

b. *imperative.* "go away"; "go to hell." Also (emphatically) **fuck off and die**.

1939 A. C. Bessie *Men in Battle* 91: "You're talking through your hat." "Fuck off." **1944** in B. C. Bowker *Out of Uniform* 119: Another… use, exclusively intransitive, exists in combination with the preposition "off." In this case, the meaning is "to leave hurriedly." The most frequent usage occurs in connection with a request to stop annoying the speaker. Often it is followed by the words, "—will ya!" added for emphasis. **1948** E. Hemingway in *Selected Letters* (1981) 647: There is no substitute in English for the phrase "Fuck off, Jack," if you mean it and will make it good. **1966** W. Manus *Mott the Hoople* 23: Fuck off, and quick. **1971** M. J. Harrison *Committed Men* 24: Oh, fuck off. **1981** "Dead Kennedys" *Nazi Punks Fuck Off* (rock song title). **1984** *Maximum Rocknroll* (Dec.), My reply is "fuck off and die!" Why don't you do something original for a change? **1987** B. E. Ellis *Rules of Attraction* 224: Rip the pen that's hanging off her door from the string it's connected to and also a piece of paper and write "Fuck Off and Die" in big black letters. **1988** J. Cleese *A Fish Called Wanda* (film): Tell those pigs to fuck off. **1986–91** B. Hamper *Rivethead* 21: I…told everyone to fuck off. **1995** P. Roth in *New Yorker* (June 26) 117: He could have told her to fuck off, of course.

1999 S. Rushdie *Ground Beneath Her Feet* 463: You're nothing in my life, Rai, you mean even less than this punk, so do me a favor, fuck off and die. **2006** K. Slaughter *Triptych* 81: "Fuck off, asshole!" the hooker screamed, slamming her hands into Ray-Ray's chest.

2.a. to loaf; to evade work, shirk.

1945 in T. Shibutani *Derelicts of Company K* 275: What's the use of being on the ball....May as well fuck off. **1945** in D. Levin *From Battlefield* 55: They...fuckoff [*sic*],...quarrel, bellyache, beat their gums. **1946** *American Journal of Sociology* LI 42 [refers to WWII]: There is little stigma to the expression "f— off" applied to...acts, such as when a man gets away with something against the Army by evading a detail...or in some other way avoids an Army requirement. **1947** N. Cassady *Letter* (Apr. 15) in *Collected Letters* (2005) 39: I presume you'll work up there in his hotel.... It is really unimportant what you do, for, really, all anyone does there is drink, bang & fuck off in general. **1955** J. Klaas *Maybe I'm Dead* 327 [refers to WWII]: Vat are you furkin' off for? **1964** H. Rhodes *Chosen Few* 65: You missed formation. You fucked off and we don't tolerate fuckoffs. **1968** H. Maule *Rub-a-Dub-Dub* 127: And I personal am gonna see you get logged if you fuck off. **1970** S. Terkel *Hard Times* 136: If he didn't fuck off those four years in the steel mills, he could've gotten ahead. **1977** J. Sayles *Union Dues* 57: You let me know he stots fuckin off, right? **1980** U.S. college professor, age *ca*58: I first heard *fuck off* in 1939 when I was working in the railroad yards [in N.Y. state]. "Quit fuckin' off," they'd say. **1985** B.E. Ellis *Less Than Zero* 33: Don't fuck off. Don't be a bum. **1987** H. Zeybel *Gunship* 10: I fucked off in Bangkok a few days. **1989** D. F. Wallace *Girl with Curious Hair* 246: To accept prime wages for doing the bare minimal and spending the rest of his time fucking off. **1997** M. Huxley *Nine Inch Nails* 100: Hey, I'm not fucking off in there. It just takes a long time. **2005** J. C. Hartley *Just Another Soldier* 104: I wouldn't get anything done. I would totally squander my time fucking off all day at my ridiculous palace.

b. to make a mistake; fail through inattention. Also: to ruin (something) by ineptitude.

1954–60 H. Wentworth & S. B. Flexner *Dictionary of American Slang* 204: *Fuck off...* to make a blunder or mistake. **1964** H. Rhodes *Chosen Few* 225: You were on yo way t'breakin' some kinda record, son, bu'cha fucked off on th' five hundred. **1972** E. Bunker *No Beast* 158: It's too late. We fucked off a score because you weren't here. **1996** S. Jackson *Caught Up in the Rapture* 102: I can't go out like no sucka. Not now. Not after I done fucked off my relationships with everybody.

3. to disregard; brush aside; put off.

1962 G. Ross *Last Campaign* 431 [refers to 1951]: They been trying to retire him for months...but he keeps fucking them off and turning down his retirement and refusing to leave the division.

4. to idle away.

1966 M. Braly *On the Yard* 14: The big yard's a cold place to fuck off your life. **1969** *Playboy* (Dec.) 301: You're going to get tired of running around in a pair of dirty Levis, fucking off your time with those other young cats. **1972** In *Journal of American Folklore* LXXXVI (1973) ???: Do you know what an old whore does on her vacation?—She just fucks it off. *a***1979** A. Pepper & L. Pepper *Straight Life* 332: I used to get on his case all the time behind his talent, fuckin' off that talent in the pen. **1999** D. A. Levy *Buddhist Third Class Junk Mail Oracle* 12: Graduated from high school/& fucked off a summer/before joining the navy.

5. Chiefly *British.* to anger; upset; "piss off." Compare earlier FUCKED OFF.

1977 *Sniffin' Glue* (Jan.) 3/1: I was fucked off by that. **1995** N. Hornby *High Fidelity* 297: "I'm glad you're back to sort him out."...This really fucks me off. **1998** *Gay Times* (Aug.) 54/2: How can I put this without completely fucking him off...? He is a fantastic mixture of huge charm with a piranha's instinct. **2002** S. Orr *Attempts to Draw Jesus* 180: People like you fuck me off no end.

fuck-off money *noun*

= FUCK-YOU MONEY.

1993 "Bono" in *Rolling Stone* (Mar. 4) 42: Because we had been spoiled by success financially, we had what Groucho Marx called "fuck-off money." **1999** T. Clayton-Lea *Elvis Costello: Biography* 194: You should always have your fuck-off money, as they say. **2000** H. Robbins *Secret* 246: She was his fuck-off money. He could walk away from his law firm or walk away from me. With Vicky he had a comfortable living available to him. **2007** *New York Magazine* (June 18) 40: She received a $1 million settlement of her Talk contract. "… I got my fuck-off money," she [*sc.* Tina Brown] says, snickering.

fuckola

(used as an intensified form of FUCK in various senses).

1970 D. Rubin *Enough of this Lovemaking* 146: Right now killing is on top and the war has replaced the usual Hollywood fuckola as the national entertainment. **1979** L. Gonzales *Jambeaux* 194: "Fuckola," Page said, entering the dressing room. **1988** T. Harris *Silence of the Lambs* 105: *Fuckola*, Starling thought. "Nuts," she said aloud. **1990** C. Harrison *Break & Enter* 119: We got a call from the Mayor's office saying they wanted this done by the book…. That means he wants no fuckola bullshit screwups. **1998** E. Coen & J. Coen *Big Lebowski* (film): Fuck me! Fuckola, man. **2004** C. Naylor & M. Hare *Second Assistant* 213: "Holy fuckola!" Scott suddenly leaped up in his chair and high-fived me.

fuck out *verb*

1. of a thing: to fail, to break down; of a person: to back out; renege.

1978 U.S. college student: My car fucked out on me. Motor conked. You can't even jump it anymore. **1982** R. B. Wright *Teacher's Daughter* 191: I just don't want anybody to fuck out on this. We can make ourselves some nice money this morning if nobody fucks out. *Ibid.* 202: That's what the job is worth. You fucked out on us. **1985** C. Hope *Kruger's Alp* 154: "You fucked out on us, Trev," said the man called Kramer from Accounts. **1993** J. Noon *Vurt* 96: It works up to a point, and it's not much of a point. It can cure the tiny troubles; it fucks out on the big troubles.

2. to be sexually unfaithful.

*ca***1975** M. Moore *Black Trade* 62: You're a loyal boy. You've never tried fucking out on me…like sometimes I suspect the others to do. **1984** J. McCorkle *Cheer Leader* 15: "I cannot tell a lie" is important and fucking out on Martha is not.

fuck over *verb* [probably FUCK (UP) + (*work*) *over*] Especially *Black English*.

1. to treat harshly or with contempt, in any manner whatsoever; mistreat, victimize, cheat, betray, etc.; damage. [The 1961 quotation is euphemistic.]

1961 J.A. Williams *Night Song* 155: Eagle ain't even cold yet and you cats are effin' over him already. **1965** C. Brown *Manchild in the Promised Land* 98: We couldn't be fucked over but so much. **1966** in *Folk Speech* (Indiana University Folklore Archives): Used to mean that someone or something has been used to the point of abuse. *fucked over.* **1967–68** N. von Hoffman *We Are the People Our Parents Warned Us Against* 55: My head's pretty badly fucked over by life in general. **1968** W. Mares *Marine Machine* 93: You fucked over those weapons so much they probably will never fire again for other privates. **1969** D. Mitchell *Thumb Tripping* 125: He couldn't let this Brylcreamer fuck over his head. He'd have to keep it together. **1969** E. Willis in *New American Review* 6 (Apr.) 103: Fuck over the city. Do them in. **1970** D. Ponicsan *Last Detail* 17: Don't it sound like somebody's fucking over Meadows? **1970** T. Whitmore *Memphis-Nam-Sweden* 134: I was refusing to be a part of that country which was fucking over my own people. **1972–76** C. Durden *No Bugles, No Drums* 16: It was a weird scene, a noncom fuckin' over an officer in front of grunts. **1976** in S. Mack *Stan Mack's Real Life Funnies* (unpaged): Bill, it's a dog eat dog world. They gonna fuck all over you, man! **1974–77** A. Hoffman *Property Of* 221: Something gets fucked over in the store, take it out of her wages. **1977** M. Torres in R. P. Rettig et al. *Manny* ii. 63/2: Just because you can't prove me guilty of your armed robbery, now you're going to fuck over me with some phony charge. **1979** Coleman Young, Mayor of Detroit, in S. Terkel *American Dreams* 357: I was attracted to this…way of fighting back at the thing that had been fuckin' me over all my life. **1985** W.J.Boyne&S.L.Thompson *WildBlue* 453: We can't let these punks fuck over the whole goddam Air Force! **1988** S. Gray *How's that for Telling 'em, Fat Lady?* ii. 68: All that he understood was that he was being ordered not to be the actor that he is, playing the character that he's playing—his very soul as an actor was being "fucked over" in fact was how he put it. **1991** D. Simon *Homicide* (1993) 28: Is he really gonna go after a police on this Monroe Street thing? He's gonna try and fuck over another police because of some dead yo? What is he, a rat or something? **1994** *New Yorker*

(Mar. 21) 125: If Joel Silver fucked me over tomorrow, if he murdered my family, ruined me financially, I would still have to say, "But, God, when you add it all up, he was so great to me." **2001** D. Lehane *Mystic River* 370: If you give 'em half a chance, they'll fuck you over just to prove they can. **2005** N. Hornby *Long Way Down* 35: He'd been locked up for sleeping with a fifteen-year-old, and fucked over in the tabloids.

2. to beat up; work over.

1970 E. E. Landy *Underground Dictionary* 84: *Fuck over*...Beat someone up. **1971** T. Mayer *Weary Falcon* 31: The fourth mission I went on was the time they really fucked us over. **1986** College instructor, age 35: When I first heard *fuck someone over* in 1966, it meant specifically to beat them up. **2000** M. Albo *Hornito* 108: "I'm gonna fuck you up." *Just leave me alone*, I say. "No. I'm gonna fuck you over."

fuck pad *noun*

a dwelling or room used for esp. casual sexual encounters.

1975 B. Gonzales *Movin' On Down De Line* 36: When I walk into his combination office and fuck pad I see this little jive broad from Howard of Tuskegee. **1988** J. Ellroy *Big Nowhere* (1994) iii. 28: He met Howard Hughes and started bird-dogging for him, picking up star-struck farm girls, ensconcing them in the fuck pads the big guy had set up all over LA. **1997** G. Williams *Diamond Geezers* xi. 77: If it weren't for the horses this could be the fuck-pad of some Cuban cocaine king. **2002** W. Self *Dorian* iv. 57: Such was the congruity of their home with the Wotton's relationship that this was Henry's bedroom, or, more properly, his fuck pad. **2007** R. Ellis *City of Fire* 217: Burell thought he was keeping his lifestyle in the vault, but everybody in the hood knows this place is a fuck pad.

fuck-pig *noun*

British. a contemptible person. Compare PIG-FUCKER.

1922 T. E. Lawrence *The Mint* (1955) 127: "Look at me, look me in the face, you short-arsed little fuck-pig," he is yelling again. **1949** E. Partridge *Dictionary of Slang & Unconventional English* (ed. 3) 1054: *F*ck-pig*. A thoroughly unpleasant man...from ca. 1870. **1961** A. Sillitoe *Key to* *the Door* (1962) 435: They can stuff their rifles.... Next time, I turn mine against that fuckpig. **1973** K. Tynan *Diary* (Mar. 20) (2001) 126: Where most men of his age, referring to slightly unpleasant people whom they regard as inferiors, would use words like "chap," "fellow," "blighter".., L.O. [= Laurence Olivier] habitually calls them "fuck-pigs." **1981** R. Spears *Slang & Euphemism* 150: *Fuck-pig* a very low and worthless person; someone who would copulate with a pig. **1993** I. Welsh *Trainspotting* (1994) 260: I know all about the crucial role of the anaesthetist. They're the punters that keep you alive, not sadistic fuck-pigs like Howison. **1997** *Sick Puppy Comix* (Sydney, Australia) (No. 4) 13: Ahh...what's your name? Hey, ahh...fuckpig!...Where are you going? **1998** *Schizo* (#3) 5: My co-workers were all loutish...fuck-pigs. **2003** E. Docx *Calligrapher* 69: Will you stop being such a fuckpig and think of a plan?

fuckpole *noun*

the penis; FUCKSTICK, definition 2.

1965 in B. Jackson *Get Your Ass in the Water & Swim like Me* 159: A fuck-pole longer than mine. **1972** B. Rodgers *Queens' Vernacular* 49: Bone...fuckpole...meat. **1975** *Ribald* (Sydney, Australia) (May 29) 15: My fuck-pole was growing. **1985** "J. Blowdryer" *Modern English* 72: Genitalia... Male...*Fuck pole*. **1995** G. Vidal *Palimpsest* 94: The verse, what I could recall, moved him, and he would idly play with what he called his "fuck-pole" but in no provocative way. **1997** "G. Indiana" *Resentment* 35: My cunt lips grab that juicy donghead & i'm pulling your fuck pole into me. **2002** D. Porter *Rhinestone Country* 304: The deep-throating of Hank's enticingly large fuckpole.

fuckrag *noun*

a worthless, contemptible, or despicable person.

1993 *Re: From the King*, on Usenet newsgroup alt.tasteless (July 27): Yeah, sure, whatever, you dumbass Canuck fuckrag. **1996** K. Williamson *Scream* (film): It's called tact, you fuckrag. **1998** D. Gaines in *Village Voice* (N.Y.C.) (Mar. 10) 135: His gift can be used for something much more than generating chaos, using people like disposable whip- and fuck-rags, and attaining petty ego gains. **1998** *Re: Question to MonkeyMan*, on Usenet newsgroup alt.atheism (Oct. 7): Shit-for-brains...ASSWIPE! What say you now, FUCKRAG? *a2007* C. Doctorow *Overclocked* 35: ["]Whoever wins, at least we're doing SOMETHING[." "]Not if they vote for one of the fuckrags[."] Fuckrag was the epithet that some of the sysadmins were using to describe the contingent that wanted to shut down the Internet.

fuck rubber *noun*

a condom. Also **fucking rubber.**

> **1981** R. Spears *Slang & Euphemism* 150: *Fucking-rubber* a condom. **1984** K. Weaver *Texas Crude* 114: She found that fuckrubber under her pillow. **1991** M. Ruuth trans. R. Jönsson *My Father, His Son* 76: Comfortable armchairs worn to amiable perfection by a multitude of behinds, and probably more fuck-rubbers and more coins to count. **2000** L. Brown *Fay* 215: There were three knobs on the machine. She read slowly, out loud in a low voice: "Ribbed sen...shoo? Delight." Then she nodded. Oh. Fucking rubbers.

fuckshit *noun*

a despicable person.

> *a1973* S. Elkin *Condominium* in *Searches & Seizures* (1978) 239: "You ask *them*, you cheap fuckshit, you goddamn errand boy, you ass stink and cunt grease," punching him about the head and shoulders with all his might. **1998** D. Menaker *Treatment* 258: His practitioner comes to get him and he says, "Hi, fuckshit Scott." **2001** R. Joshi *Last Jet Engine Laugh* 61: "Can you tell me why Poresh babu is living in this way, here now in Calcutta, alone? Why he is not in Paris, as he was?" You slimeball little fuckshit. What business is it of yours? **2003** T. Green *Fifth Angel* 259: Listen, fuckshit.... Didn't you listen to me about who my uncle is? They can find a bag of cocaine in your cell by four o'clock, then you can eat vanilla ice cream out of your cellmate's ass for the next ten years.

fuckshit *interjection*

(used to express dismay, anger, disappointment, etc.)

> **1970** J. Bouton *Ball Four* ii. 66: "Shitfuck," he said, using one of his favorite words ("fuckshit" is the other). "Shitfuck. We've got a damned good ballclub here. We're going to win some games." **1996** *Loaded*

(Sept.) 197/1: "Oh fuck-shit," screams Tony, "it's happy bloody hardcore!"
1999 P. Quarrington *Spirit Cabinet* 203: The black creature brought its teeth together and Rodolfo muttered, "Fuckshit." **2001** C. Glazebrook *Madolescents* 74: Oh fuckshit, it's crashed! I slam the phone down so hard it bounces. **2007** S. Rao *Chambermaid* 208: "Shit. Damn. Damn it. Fuck. Fuck it." And my personal favorite. "Fuckshit."

fucksome *adjective* [perhaps punning on *buxom*]
sexually desirable.

1879 *Harlequin Prince Cherrytop* 29: Hot, wriggling, moist-lipped, fucksome Columbine. **1890–93** J. S. Farmer & W. E. Henley *Slang and Its Analogues* III. 80: *Fuckable*, adj....Desirable. Also *Fucksome*. **1962** N. Thomas *Ask at the Unicorn* (1963) 134: Fucksome but diseased. **1969** C. Logue *The Girls* in *Selected Poems* (1996) 121: Suck this—you fucksome bitch! Suck this! **1992** W. Kennedy *Very Old Bones* 171: "I think you are probably at this moment...the most fucksome woman on this planet." "What an exciting word." **1998** *Deadfuck owl*, on Usenet newsgroup alt.tasteless (July 13): She is a comely young flapper, coiffed and petite and oh, so fucksome! **2007** T. Devine *Bad As She Wants to Be* 180: Marianne was telling us you all hooked up with some real fucksome guys on your road trip this week.

fuckster *noun*
= FUCKER, definition 1.

*ca***1675** *Advice to a C—monger* in E. J. Burford *Bawdy Verse* (1983) 170: Fucksters, you that would be happy,/Have a care that C—t don't Clap yee. **1680** *School of Venus* in B. K. Mudge *When Flesh Becomes Word* (2004) 26: If all of this nature, with [what] our voluptuous fucksters know, were communicated to the world, we need not translate *French*. **1680** *Satire on the Court Ladies* in G. Williams *Dict. Sexual Language & Imagery in Shakespearean & Stuart Literature* (1994) I.564: Her house and body have a thousand wayes/To let in fucksters. **1867–92** Capt. E. Sellon *Ups and Downs of Life* 110: I'm a mere fuckster. I like women, and I have them. *ca***1890** *My Secret Life* III. xiv., I used to think her a plain woman, one of the plainest, but she was a glorious fuckster. **1890–93** J. S. Farmer & W. E. Henley *Dictionary of Slang* III. 81: *Fuckster*...A good performer...one specially addicted to the act. **1930** *Lyra Ebriosa* 20: Nearby there lived a fuckster tall. **1992** B. Unsworth *Sacred Hunger* xxx. 295: He is the only free fuckster on this ship then. **2002** S. Waters *Fingersmith* vi. 199: "You bloody swine!" I cried, twisting again, and pulling towards him. "You fuckster! Oh!"

fuckstick *noun* [perhaps modeled on British English slang *funk stick* 'a coward']

1. a worthless, contemptible, or despicable person.

1958 W. Talsman *Gaudy Image* 222: There's still the heavenly debasement of the imperturbable fuckstick. Surely that appeals to you. **1968** C. Baker et al. *College Undergraduate Slang Study* 122: *Fuck-stick.* A person who always fools around. **1967–72** T. Weesner *Car Thief* 47: Go to sleep, fuckstick. *Ibid.* 67: You dumb fuckstick. **1974** N.Y.C. man, age *ca*28: A *fuckstick* is a really foul, ugly prostitute. This was at Fort Polk and environs in 1969. It's like a *skank*. **1978** L. K. Truscott *Dress Gray* 152: Hey, fuckstick, buck up, man. **1980** P. Conroy *Lords of Discipline* 145: Get your fucking chin in....Rack it in, fuckstick. *a*1983 S. King *Christine* 362: The fuckstick had parked at the far set. **1993** R. Peters *Flames of Heaven* 190: One…spit at Samsonov's feet, saying: "Fuckstick." **1999** J. Cahill *Guy Walks into Psychiatrist's Office* in *Sopranos* (TV shooting script) (Second Series) 38: Those two fucksticks ripped off a Porsche Carrera from our own building. **2008** *New York Magazine* (July 21) 56/2: Crazybastard…drying out in Aspen, looked at all the greedheads and fucksticks, real-estate scum, resort developers.

2. the penis.

1973 E. Parnay *Stud Seeker* 63: The soldier threw his ass higher, pistoning up to the huge fuckstick as Grain went with him, in and out so fast that the soldier could hardly keep the pace. **1976** J. Vasco *Three-Hole Girl* 139: Bob had been filming the whole lewd performance she had been giving Trish's butt and Craig's fuckstick. **1977** E. Torres *Q & A* 239: My pistol is like my fuck-stick. Don't go nowhere without it. **1981** *Penthouse* (Apr.) 26: I pulled my fuck-stick out of her cunt. **1993** L. Colton *Goat Brothers* 238: I'd be happy to let Lurleen do a tongue stand on my fuck stick. **2002** S. Home *69 Things to do with Dead Princess* i. 13: Holding the base of Dudley's erection with my index finger and thumb, I took his fuck stick in my mouth. **2003** C. R. Kiernan *Low Red Moon* 44: You want to suck on my fuckstick, faggot?

fuckstrated *adjective*

sexually frustrated.

*a*1990 P. Munro *Slang U* 86: Biff broke up with his girlfriend and hasn't had sex in three weeks; he's so fuckstrated. **1995** D. E. Kaun *Ru$$ia* 136: I'm so totally fuckstrated I got cobwebs. **2007** in "Zane" *Dear G-Spot* 216: Feeling fuckstrated, my yearlong "no job-no pussy" drought felt like decades.

fuckstress *noun*

a woman who copulates.

1883 R. L. Stevenson *Letter* (May) in *Selected Letters of R. L. Stevenson* (1997) 223: To be quite frank, there is a *risqué* character. The Countess von Rosen, a jolly, elderly—how shall I say?—fuckstress. *ca*1890 *My Secret Life* VIII. x.: The red haired strumpet seemingly pleased, knelt down and licked the clitoris of my fuckstress, whilst with almost imperceptible joggings of her cunt, and heaving of my bum, we fucked. **1890–93** J. S. Farmer & W. E. Henley *Dictionary of Slang* III. 81: *Fuckster*…A good performer.…in feminine *fuckstress*. **1933** A. Crowley in L. Sutin *Do what thou Wilt* (2000) 365: The most marvellous fuckstress alive. **1990** *Footlicker* 77: Verushka and I will be waiting for your report on that little psychofuckstress. **1996** *Boarding School Adventures,* on Usenet newsgroup alt.sex.stories (Dec. 18): You are going to be an accomplished fuckstress.

fuck-struck *adjective*

obsessed with copulation; extremely lustful. Compare *cunt-struck.*

1966 E. Shepard *Doom Pussy* 160: Like a tomcat at a petting party, Alby tried to force two B-girls to sit on his knee. Tors eyed him with distaste. "He's fuck-struck," observed the Swede to no one in particular. **1990** J. Barnes *Love, Etc.* 70: I was duly fuck-struck as I waved him off on a night as foul as that which saw the return of St Mark's body to Venice. **2004** P. Reizin *Fiends Reunited* vi. 199: I was still in something of a post-coital fugue; part hungover, part sleep-deprived, part lovesick. One of those peculiar states where…it was hard to tell how much to put down to being abroad, and how much to being what Jay once…described as fuck-struck.

fucktard *noun* [from FUCK + re*tard*]

a despicably stupid person.

1994 *Re: Rush* on usenet newsgroup alt.music.alternative (June 13): You worthless fucktard. Go crawl back under whatever stinking bigoted little rock you crawled out of. **1998** *Face* (Apr.) 46/1: Beaver beer. Blow jobs. Weenies, stoners and "fucktards." Who said Kevin Smith was a borderline misogynist with limited pop-cultural imagination? **2003** *OC Weekly* (June 13) 22: So why then, aside from the fact that they're stupid and selfish fucktards, are they breaking up? **2005** M. Malkin *Unhinged* 17 The latter site allows angry leftists to leave uncensored, incoherent messages for the president, whom they refer to as a "fucktard." **2008** *New York Magazine* (June 2) 28/2: In spreading his dire message, he favors colorful curses like "asshat" and "fucktard."

fuck toy *noun*

1. a person regarded or treated as a sex object.

1988 P. Beck & P. Massman *Rich Men, Single Women* 87: This little number was for him, for his pleasure, a fuck-toy for his frequent business jaunts to L.A. **1995** D. Coupland *Microserfs* 300: I *don't* call you a piece of meat. I call you my fuck toy. **1996** I. Welsh *Ecstasy* 125: You've got it all there, access to my breasts, my cunt, my arse. Anything you like.... Just a fuck toy. **2004** J. Jameson & N. Strauss *How to Make Love Like a Porn Star* iv. ix. 368: I looked at how the other girls were being treated (basically, like Tinkertoys).... I was determined not to just be a fuck toy but also to retain as much power as possible off camera. **2006** A. Blake *Called to the Wild* 95: You're nothing but a slut. A fuck toy. Only sluts like sucking men off as much as you do.

2. a sex toy, as a dildo or vibrator.

2007 V. Crowley *Longing for Toys* 216: [She] shoved the vibrator all the way up her cunt.... Lucille felt the big fuck toy slip out of her.

fucktruck *noun*

1. a vehicle in which people engage in sexual activity; esp. a van or large car having bedding, etc., in the back.

1979 in *Australian National Dictionary*: The boys wearing blue singlets in their striped fuck trucks yelled & pressed down on the horns but fifi [*sic*] kept going. **1982** J. Breslin *Forsaking All Others* 47: An overnight stay with her husband in the trailer parked outside the prison fence—"the fuck truck," the inmates called it. **1990** T. Thorne *Dictionary of Contemporary Slang*: *Fuck truck*...another term for *passion wagon*. **1993** *Independent* (London) (June 9) ("Focus") 22: There was this Australian freak who had this van called the Fuck Truck. **1995** *Time Out New York* (Oct. 25) 25: Fucktruck...was common parlance in a certain Tennessee town in the late '70s. **1998** N.Y.C. editor: We used *fuck truck* in the '60s to mean "passion wagon." **2006** J. Iversen *High School Confidential* 221: Steve drove and old Chevy minivan with a mattress in the back that he had dubbed the "fuck truck."

2. a bus that brings prospective sexual partners together; esp. one of various shuttle buses in the Boston area running between nearby women's colleges and Harvard or M.I.T.

1990 S. Orlean *Saturday Night* 21: Many Wellesley students consider the Fuck Truck a source of personal growth. **1998** N.Y.C. woman: As a student at Wellesley, I—and most of my classmates—referred to the bus that took us from campus to M.I.T. and Harvard as the "fucktruck."... the M.I.T. and Harvard guys called it the same thing. **1998** N.Y.C. man: The fucktruck was the bus that went from M.I.T. out to Wellesley. **1998** R. Campo *Desire to Heal* 77: Frequent trips on the free shuttle bus (called the "fuck truck") to Mount Holyoke and Smith. **2002** B. Mezrich *Bringing Down the House* 118: At MIT, there was no place better to meet eager young women, bused right to the building's front steps from the nearby all-girl colleges. The bus was lovingly renamed the "fuck truck." **2005** H. Winston *Unchosen* 153: Brandeis is not actually in Boston, but nine miles west of the city, accessible to him only by commuter rail—or, he later learned, the "fuck truck" from Harvard, named for the supposed sexual libertinism of the Brandeis students.

fuck-up *noun* Especially *Military*.

1. an incompetent person; a chronic bungler; a misfit. [The 1942 quotation, collected from Australian schoolchildren, may have resulted from a misunderstanding of this term.]

[**1942** S.J. Baker *Australian Language* 206: *Fug-up.* A stodgy person, one who prefers a "fuggy" atmosphere to playing out of doors.] [**1944** *Newsweek* (Jan. 24) 68: I am not a messup any more. I like the army.] *ca*1945 J. Cheever in *Letters* (1988) 108: Last night two fuckups were discussing their disatisfactions [*sic*] with the army. **1948** N. Mailer *Naked & Dead* 224 [refers to WWII]: Bunch of fug-ups, lose a goddam gun, won't even take a drink when it's free. **1946–50** J. Jones *From Here to Eternity* ch. iv: He's such a fuckup I was afraid we'd shoot somebody on a problem. **1951** E. Hemingway in *Selected Letters* (1981) 721: To me he is an enormously skillful fuck-up and his book will do great damage to our country. **1954** F.I. Gwaltney *Heaven & Hell* 194 [refers to WWII]: You're not commanding a fuckup company. This is a regiment, and not every man in it is a fuckup. **1955** T. Anderson *Your Own Beloved Sons* 8: Whenever he screwed up they knew it. He was a fuckup. **1962** J. O. Killens *Then We Heard the Thunder* 39 [refers to WWII]: You're nothing but a first-class fuck-up. **1965** C. Brown *Manchild in the Promised Land* 145: The cats who had a little bit of sense but who were just general fuck-ups were sent to the Annex. **1967** J. Kornbluth *Notes from the New Underground* 14: What stupid fuck-ups men are! **1971** *Playboy* (May) 207: You mean we're gonna let them fuck-ups play on *our* ball diamond? **1979** in S. Terkel *American Dreams* 396: I'm not a great believer in failure as a sin. A couple of our writers are fuckups. **1980** S. Kopp *Mirror, Mask, & Shadow* 81: I become…[an] uncomfortably vulnerable fuck-up whose blunder is now exposed to my eyes and to theirs. **1985** E. Leonard *Glitz* 152: I thought maybe I was a total fuckup. *a*1990 E. Currie *Dope & Trouble* 22: I used to be a real fuck-up, you know? **1996** M. Aftel *Story of your Life* iv. 79: How do you portray yourself in this plot—as a seeker, a journeyman, a budding entrepreneur, an indentured servant, a hired hand, an expert, a fuckup, an uninspired drudge, a hotshot? **2000** R. Barger et al. *Hell's Angel* ii. 15: I was considered a fuckup. I didn't take to authority. **2000** A. Bourdain *Kitchen Confidential* 90: He, more than anyone else I encountered in my professional life, transformed me from a bright but druggie fuck-up into a serious, capable and responsible chef. **2005** K. MacNeil *Stornoway Way* 68: I wish for the ten millionth time that I enjoyed, or could even tolerate, violence. I'm a fuck-up when it comes to being anything other than peaceful.

2. a blunder; botch; FOUL-UP, definition 1. Compare 1941 quotation at FRIG-UP.

1949 E. Partridge *Dictionary of Slang & Unconventional English* (ed. 3) 1054: *F*ck-up of,* make *a.* To fail miserably at; to spoil utterly; low coll.: C.20. **1951** J. Kerouac in *Selected Letters* (1981) 321: [Interference] promises fuckups. **1958** J. O'Hara *From the Terrace* 257: Such a Goddam fuck-up. **1964** R. Allen *High White Forest* 266 [refers to WWII]: Two of our divisions got tangled up there...and the Krauts hit them from the slope. What a fuck-up! **1968–71** M. Cole & S. Black *Checking it Out* 105: Not only was that a fuck-up of LEAP's name but why the hell did I accept their stealing? **1972** *Metropolitan Review* (May) 4: No fuck-up should go unridiculed. **1977** R. Coover *Public Burning* 455: And now it scared them that somebody might catch them in a fuck-up. **1984** "W.T. Tyler" *Shadow Cabinet* 241: A royal bureaucratic fuck-up, take my word. **1986** D. Tate *Bravo Burning* 96: A small..., probably perfectly explainable fuck-up. **1994** J. Kelman *How Late it Was* 208: Whatever brains he had man he had to use them. Nay fuck-ups. **2005** Z. Smith *On Beauty* 44: He felt he couldn't tell his own family this fact; it was easier for them to believe that last year was Jerome's "romantic fuck-up" or—more pleasing to the Belsey mentality—his "flirtation with Christianity."

fuck up *verb* [compare synonyms *bugger up*, FRIG UP, *screw up*; also influenced by (if not the inspiration for) *muck up*].

 1. to ruin, spoil, or destroy; to botch; in phrase: ☞ **fuck up the detail**, *Military.* to bungle. See also earlier FUCKED UP.

 1929 F. Manning *Middle Parts of Fortune* I. v. 92: And they'll call up all the women/When they've fucked up all the men. [**1932** E. Halyburton & R. Goll *Shoot & Be Damned* 206 [refers to 1918]: That big tub of sour owl milk will jazz up the detail for all of us. You'd better dust off a court martial for him.] **1942** H. Miller *Roofs of Paris* 248: You and Sid are going to fuck up everything before you're through. **1942** in M. Morriss & R. Day *South Pacific Diary* (1996) 33: If there is any way for a thing to be fucked up, the Army will find it....Sometimes they'll even fuck it up when you'd think it's impossible. **1944** J. O'Hara in *Selected Letters* (1981) 184: I know I fucked up your afternoon schedule. **1951** in *International Journal of Psycho-Analysis* XXXV (1954) 35: When a man says: "I got my day all fucked up," he is [yet] fully aware of the primary sexual meaning of the word. **1952** in S. J. Perelman *Don't Tread on Me* 123: So many bothersome and ridiculous complications with which you'd managed to fuck up your life here. **1953** M. Harris *Southpaw* 143: Them goddam bastards would as soon f— up my ball club as not. **1956** T. T. Chamales *Never So Few* 574: They fucked something up when they moved that piece....They're missing us. **1965** S. Yurick *Warriors* 71: That fucked everything up, Hector thought. **1966–67** W. Stevens *Gunner* 119 [refers to WWII]: It's not going to do...anybody...any good if you go around fucking up the detail. **1968** W. Mares *Marine Machine* 29: Mouse, the coffee's cold! You're a Kremlin spy sent here to fuck up my stomach. **1969** R. M. Stern *Brood of Eagles* 341: Oh, I would have fucked it up for fair. I know that. **1974** P. Larkin *This Be the Verse*: They fuck you up, your mum and dad./They may not mean to, but they do./They fill you with the faults they had/And add some extra, just for you. **1984** J. Fuller *Fragments* 23: Duds, the drill sergeants would call us.... Fuck up a two-car funeral. **1991** "R. Brown" & R. Angus *A.K.A. Narc* 188: They'll fuck this up like they fucked up everything else. **1998** *Starr Report* VIII L: Ms. Lewinsky said she wanted two things from the President. The first was contrition: He needed to "acknowledge...that he helped fuck up my life." **2000** C. Bushnell *Four Blondes* 23: You really fucked it up.... You had a chance. We could have spent the summer together. You blew it. **2005** P. Jillette & M. D. Lynn *How to Cheat Your Friends at Poker* vi. 27: Don't forget that cutting the deck doesn't fuck up the order.

2.a. Of a person: to blunder badly; to make a (serious) error; (*hence*) get oneself into trouble of any kind; to fail.

1943 in M. Morriss & R. Day *South Pacific Diary* (1996) 114: They... fucked up beautifully. **1945** in T. Shibutani *Derelicts of Company K* 115: We always fuck up when we march. **1953** M. Harris *Southpaw* 201: The first man that f—s up in this respect is going to get hit in the pocketbook, and hit hard. **1944–57** L. Atwell *Private* 33: He f—ed up there too, so they sent him down to us in C Company. **1957** H. Simmons *Corner Boy* 73: People will fugg up. **1961** G. Forbes *Goodbye to Some* 53: I really fucked up. We were going way too fast. **1961** L. McMurtry *Horseman, Pass By* 48: "You fucked up," Hermy said. **1963** J. Ross *Dead Are Mine* 87: Keep your nose clean and this will all be forgotten. Fuck up and you're dead. **1964–66** R. Stone *Hall of Mirrors* 271: But in my journalistic opinion they're gonna fuck up. **1971** D. Meggyesy *Out of Their League* 189: I also watched how Ernie and Larry did and I must admit I was pleased when they made mistakes and fucked up. **1972** D. Halberstam *Best & Brightest* 281 [refers to 1963]: Americans in Vietnam...had come up with a slogan to describe the ARVN promotion system: "Fuck up and move up." **1978** Rascoe & Stone *Who'll Stop the Rain?* (film): "I've been waiting all my life to fuck up like this.""Well, you've finally made the big time." **1972–79** T. Wolfe *Right Stuff* 221: *Falling behind* put you on the threshold of *fucking up.* **1982** C. Gino *Nurse's Story* 318: Maybe somebody fucked up. **1987** M. Piercy *Gone to Soldiers* 631: I fucked up, I know it, I fucked up everything that counted, I know it, listen to me, I know it. **1987** J. D. Pistone *Donnie Brasco* 209: Tony, the responsibility I gave Donnie just now...if he fucks up, I'm a dead man. **1993** P. Roth *Operation Shylock* 259: But if he gets actively involved, he fucks up everything. Jews don't put trust in the bank, they have private trusts. **1998** E. Reid *If I Don't Six* 24: I've watched him on television kicking grass at refs, tossing his headset to the ground in fury, snapping clipboards and even smacking players in the facemask when they fuck up. **2002** D. Eggers *You Shall Know Our Velocity!* 325: "They fucked up," he said to me. "They fucked up and they're hiding something." **2006** "Iggy Pop" in L. McNeil & G. McCain *Please Kill Me* 142: Coral had had enough of me. I was no longer happening. I was fucking up, and fucking up, and losing, and losing—and she could see it.

b. Of a thing, a situation, etc.: to go awry; malfunction; break down.

1976 D. Mamet *American Buffalo* 35: There's the least *chance* something might fuck up. **1980** J. Carroll *Land of Laughs* 90: How many things are going to fuck up before we get this straightened out. **1982** D.J. Williams *Hit Hard* 175 [refers to WWII]: A-17 gun fucked up. **1985** A. Sawislak *Dwarf Rapes Nun* 193: In case you miss a transmission or the radios fuck up. **2003** *New York Magazine* (Mar. 31) 25/3: But on the other side, the global opposition, and the new, excited homegrown anti-Bush front line, are anticipating...the myriad ways this colossal and quixotic undertaking will invariably fuck up. **2004** S. Kernick *Crime Trade* 32: All I was trying to do was nail one of the bad guys. It fucked up, the whole thing fucked up, and I lost a good mate.

3.a. to confound; thwart; interfere with; to befuddle or confuse.

1945 in T. Shibutani *Derelicts of Company K* 133: I bet that fuckin' CO stays awake every night tryin' to think up some new way to fuck us up. **1950** J. Kerouac in *Selected Letters* 239: I don't see how these cocksuckers could have done a better job trying to fuck me up as a…novelist. **1968** in E. Knight *Belly Song* 15: Perhaps it was just the brother's definition that fucked me up. **1968–71** M. Cole & S. Black *Checking It Out* 223: "It will be six months before they use those rooms again.…" "That's cool…I dig fucking up white prejudiced pricks." **1971–72** L. Giovanitti *Man Who Won the Medal of Honor* 109: I said what I said because I had nothing else to go on. I ain't changing that story now. And nobody's going to fuck me up. You understand? **1972** D. Wolf *Foul!* 313: We could have won, if that dumb coach didn't fuck us up. **1976** R. E. Chinn *Dig the Nigger Up* 37: I'd sure like to do it to her!…She fucks me all up! **1978** E. Thompson *Devil to Pay* 156: It was Milt's idea to cook out. "Really fuck up the neighbors, man. They'll think it's springtime." **1983** D. Mamet *Glengarry Glen Ross* 96: What you're hired for is to *help* us—does that seem clear to you? To *help* us. *Not* to fuck us up. **1989** M. Davis *Miles* 193: But Cannonball just fucked me up the way he played the blues and nobody had ever heard of him. **1991** D. Gaines *Teenage Wasteland* 232: If you tell anybody who I am, if you fuck me up, man, I'll find you. **1995** *Journal of American Folklore* CVIII. 215: Why aren't…voices that would fuck theory up included in this collection? **1997** G. Meade *Brandenburg* 325: Don't compromise me, Gonzi. Don't fuck me up. **2004** M. Boland & M. Bodey *Aussiewood* vi. 100: Once I got into this game and saw how it fucks people up, just fucks them up, I'd grown up and knew what was bullshit.

b. to make intoxicated.

1971 in H.S. Thompson *Shark Hunt* 147: Five reds, enough to fuck *anybody* up. **1980** J. DiFusco et al. *Tracers* 46 [refers to Vietnam War]: There's enough shit here to fuck up the entire squad for at least a week. **2001** *Maximum Rocknroll* (Apr.), Man, I wanna get high!… Something to fuck us up. Drugs.

4. Especially *Black English*. to injure, especially severely; mangle; wound; (especially *Military*) to kill.

1962 in D. Wepman et al. *The Life* (1976) 23: He romped and stomped, and he fucked up his face. **1965** C. Brown *Manchild in the Promised Land* 144: Man, those bullets can really fuck you up. **1966–67** P. Thomas *Down These Mean Streets* [refers to ca1950]: I felt his fist fuck up my shoulder. *Ibid.* 209: Louie, if the motherfucker makes a move, fuck him up good. **1967** in B. Edelman *Dear America* 87: The company lost 5 KIA and about

40 wounded. We fucked up at least two times as many Charlies as far as KIA, but we have more wounded. **1970** L. Cole *Street Kids* 88: The guy who was on our kid fucked the other guy up. The guy was bleeding from his eye. **1970–71** J. Rubinstein *City Police* 358: You think it was a gun?... O.K., pal, just relax, at least he didn't fuck you up. **1972** T. O'Brien *Combat Zone* 76: You don't get mangled by a mine, you get fucked up. **1972–74** H. Hawes & D. Asher *Raise Up off Me* 84: My man from Harlem had overheard the...hassle...and asked if I wanted him to get some cats to fuck up the bass player. **1975** S.P. Smith *American Boys* 162: A few losers who'd been fucked up not quite bad enough to be sent home. **1978** W. Brown *Tragic Magic* 152: "Fuck him up!" "Waste his ass!" **1982** J. M. Del Vecchio *13th Valley* 22: Some innocent dudes always get fucked up and blown away. **1987** L. S. Whiteley *Deadly Green* 201 [refers to Vietnam War]: Fuck them up! Fuck them fuckers up!...Get some! **1996** P. Godwin *Mukiwa* xii 221: Don't wade in. Let them fuck each other up first, then arrest anything that doesn't move. **1997** *New Yorker* (July 21) 38: Or I can wait for you after work and fuck you up. **2000** G. Marinovich & J. Silva *Bang-Bang Club* xv. 221: Joao responded by telling Dave, a good friend, that if he did not leave him alone he'd fuck him up.

5. *Black English.* to fool around.

1969 U. Hannerz *Soulside* 62: I earn good money, you know, with those two jobs, and my old lady earns a lot on her job, so actually I don't have to leave too much money at home 'cause she takes care of much of that. So this means I got a lot to spend just fucking up. **1970** A. Young *Snakes* 125: We both need to get away from this old school grind for awhile. Why don't we go out and fuck up tonight? It's Friday, man....Let's go out and party!

In Phrase:

☞ **could fuck up a wet dream**, Originally *Military.* is or are exceedingly clumsy, stupid, or despicable.

1967 A. Dubus *Lieutenant* 52 [refers to 1956]: Freeman, you are nothing but a skinny turd and would fuck up a wet dream. **1971** R. Flanagan *Maggot* 242 [refers to ca1956]: They fuck-up everything. Some of them would fuck-up a wet dream. **1975** J. Wambaugh *Choirboys* 185: Roscoe Rules could fuck up a wet dream. **1966–80** J. McAleer & B. Dickson *Unit Pride* 391 [refers to ca1951]: Billy, I swear you'd fuck up a wet dream. **1984** W. J. Caunitz *One Police Plaza* 193: That guy could fuck up a wet dream.

1987 D. Sherman *Main Force* 191 [refers to 1966]: Lewis, you'd fuck up a wet dream. Go back to sleep. **1988** J. L. Burke *Heaven's Prisoners* 221: Then they see a guy that's got all the things they want and can't have because most of them are so dumb they'd fuck up a wet dream. **1990** C. Lucas *Prelude to a Kiss* 48: It's a real busman's holiday with you around, you know? You could fuck up a wet dream! **2002** M. A. Kahn *Trophy Widow* 37: Those five-hundred-dollar-an-hour yahoos could fuck up a wet dream. **2003** C. Weber *Baby Momma Drama* 76: Damn, Jasmine, you could fuck up a wet dream, you know that? Why don't you lighten the fuck up for once?

fuckwad *noun*

a stupid or contemptible person; an asshole.

1974 U.S. student slang survey: Motherfucker, fuckwad, sonofabitch, [etc.]. **1986** J. Cain *Suicide Squad* 97: I wanna see ID cards on all these fuckwads. **1987** "J. Hawkins" *Tunnel Warriors* 144: That goofy fuckwad. **1990** E. W. Rukuza *West Coast Turnaround* 8: Some fuckwad was shootin' up da scenery wit' a machine gun. **1997** S. Lopez *Sunday Macaroni Club* 209: These fuckwads decide to go swimming and now they complain about getting wet. Joey hated working with amateurs. **2002** A. Davies *Frog King* 284: Think about someone else for a change, fuckwad. **2006** J. McManus *Physical* 87: As I performed my husbandly duty sans condom, however, I was hoping, like a bona fide fuckwad, that somehow it wouldn't quite take.

fuckwind *noun*

the kestrel. Cf. WINDFUCKER *noun*.

1611 R. Cotgrave *Dictionary of the French & English Tongues* s.v. *Crecerelle*, A Rattle, or Clacke for children to play wtih; also, a Kestrell, Fleingall, or Fuck-winde. [**1847** J. O. Halliwell *Dictionary of Archaic & Provincial Words* I., *Fuckwind*, a species of hawk. North.]

fuckwit *noun*

Chiefly *Australian & British* a stupid person. Hence **fuckwittage**, *noun*, stupidity.

1968 A. Buzo in *Plays* 89: Well, ta-ta for now, fuckwit. **1970** S. Jarratt *Permissive Australia* 142: Of course they do, you fuckwit. **1979** in *Australian National Dictionary*: It sounded like a load of fuck-wit shit to me. **1986** M. Johnson *Lear* 7: It is not your turn, fuckwits! **1992** I. Banks *Crow Road* vi. 144: How can he be such a great guy, and clever and just...just a good friend, and some fuckwit forgetting to look both ways cancels out all that...probably not even a fuckwit; probably some ordinary guy thinking about something else. **1995** Will Self in *Esquire* (Feb.) 108: Dear Fuckwit. **1997** *N.Y. Press* (Aug. 27) 30: Fuckwit on a wet-bike. **1998** H. Fielding *Bridget Jones's Diary* 18: Sharon started on a long illustrative list of emotional fuckwittage in progress in our friends: one whose boyfriend of thirteen years refuses to even discuss living together [etc.]. *Ibid.* 66: I am not interested in fuckwittage. **2000** Z. Smith *White Teeth* viii. 185: I'm the sympathetic side of the service industry, I'm service with a fucking smile, I'd wear a little red tie and a little red hat like them fuckwits in Mr Burger if my fuckin' head weren't so big. **2004** *Vanity Fair* (Apr.) 222/1: I just can't believe I got mixed up with such a strange group of fuckwits. **2007** B. Eisler *Requiem for an Assassin* 98: The first time it had been in the gut, but Dox had seen it coming and even though the fuckwit knew how to punch, the damage hadn't been too bad.

fuckwitted *adjective*

Chiefly *Australian & British* stupid.

1971 in J. Hibberd *Stretch of Imagination* 40: You two-timing, fuckwitted mongrel of a slut! **1973** in *Australian National Dictionary*: That fuckwitted agent of yours is really driving me right off my brain. **1982** E. Haley & L. Rosser *Memories of an Australian Girlhood* 25: Pancho's the only guy fuck-witted enough to put up with her. **1996** *ikon* (Jan.–Feb.) 35/2: She understands business enough to know that mindlessly "political" songs about Ireland will go down a storm 7,000 miles away with fuckwitted Americans who have just decided that they are, like, rilly down with the situation in Northern Ireland. **1998** F. Brimson *Hooligan* xxxv. 98: He knew the city lads well and now had a pub full of serious drinkers rather than soppy, fuck-witted tourists. **2008** G. Canardeaux *Cuisine du Moi* iii. 66: Like, it's cost me zero to make, a few quid to serve, but—on the other side of the ledger—it's made these fuckwitted customers think their own shit doesn't stink.

fuck with *verb*

to trifle, toy, meddle, or interfere; fool; play; (*hence*) to harass, tease, or provoke; mess. [Both Chandler quotations are euphemistic; compare FUCK AROUND, definition 2 and FRIG, *verb*, definition 3.]

1938 R. Chandler *Big Sleep* ch. 26: Don't fuss with me, little man. **1940** R. Chandler *Farewell, My Lovely* 5: I'm feelin' good...I wouldn't want anybody to fuss with me. **1946** in T. Shibutani *Derelicts of Company K* 391: The Boochies won't fuck with him because they don't want to catch shit. **1948** E. Hemingway in *Selected Letters* (1981) 644 [refers to *ca*1915]: I learned early to walk very dangerous so people would leave you alone; think the phrase in our part of the country was not fuck with you. Don't fuck with me, Jack, you say in a toneless voice. **1953** M. Harris *Southpaw* 239: Do Not F— With Me. **1962** J. O. Killens *Then We Heard the Thunder* 221 [refers to WWII]: Why do you fuck with me so much, man? There are millions of other people in the Army. **1965** C. Brown *Manchild in the Promised Land* 189: It was practically a twenty-four-hour-a-day job trying to get some money to get some stuff to keep the [heroin] habit from fucking with you. *Ibid.*: If you fuck wit that rent money, I'm gon kill you. **1968** P. Tauber *Sunshine Soldiers* 169: No one fucks with chow. You eat when you're supposed to. **1968** R. Gover *JC* 100: Can't rezist fuckin with him jes one more time. **1970** T. Thackrey *Thief* 209: Took the carburetor off and soaked it in solvent and put it back on. Fiddled and fucked with it. And finally it seemed to be okay again running good. **1968–71** M. Cole & S. Black *Checking it Out* 113: I...turn around and scream, "Don't fuck with my mind!" *Ibid.* 198: Stay the fuck away.... And if you think I'm fucking with you, try me. **1971** *Playboy* (June) 216: I don't like anyone fucking with my head while I'm doing [a movie]. **1977** E. Bunker *Animal Factory* 46: "Tony tells me you're good at law." "I used to fuck with it. No more." **1977** L. Jordan *Hype* 230: Them people are fuckin' with us, man! **1981** C. Crowe *Fast Times at Ridgemont High* 92: They're just fuckin' with us! **1990** L. Bing *Do or Die* 122: 'Cause he fucked with my food...took one of my French fries. **1997** *TV Guide* (May 18) 48: "Don't f—with the Babe!" is her boldface battle cry throughout her book. **1998** *New Yorker* (Mar. 16) 34: You don't say no to the Mafia, you don't challenge the Mafia, you generally don't fuck with the Mafia. **2000** Z. Smith *White Teeth* ix. 232: But mainly their mission was to put the Invincible back in Indian, the Badaaaass back in Bengali, the P-Funk back in Pakistani. People had fucked with Rajik back in the days when he was into chess and wore V-necks.

2005 M. M. Frisby *Wifebeater* iii. 16: Do I know? You're fucking with me right? He's all you talk about. **2007** D. Johnson *Tree of Smoke* 287: Hanson's...finger's on the trigger. If it comes, the enemy will feel sincerely fucked with.

fucky *noun*

see under FUCKEE.

fucky *adjective*

sexually attractive or stimulating.

1958 J. Kerouac *Letter* (Sept. 8) in *Selected Letters 1957–69* (1999) 150: There's a girl here, J. L., rich, sexy, thin fucky who went with me to visit Latcadio last Sat nite. **1969** A. Ginsberg *Interview* in *Spontaneous Mind: Interviews* (2001) 170: I get into a deeper emotional intimacy if the chick is lissome and springy, skinny and pretty. I like little blonde furry fucky dolls. **1973** N. Mailer *Marilyn: A Biography* 102: Never again in her career will she look so sexually perfect as in 1953 making *Gentlemen Prefer Blondes*, no, never if we are to examine a verb through its adverb [*sic*]—will she appear so fucky again. **1976** in G. Legman *New Limerick* 461: I feel fucky. **1991** "Red Hot Chili Peppers" *If You Have to Ask* (pop. song): A little lust/To the fucky-ass Flea [*sc.*, the band's bass player]. **1994** *Guardian* (London) (June 29) T8: T-shirts with slogans like *Have You Wanked Over Me Yet?* and *I'm So Fucky.* **1998** *Playboy* (Dec.) 86: What was a sweet fucky marriage but the sublimation of orgies never taken? **2007** J. Sandford *Invisible Prey* 105: I know you're attracted to fucky blondes, especially the kind with small but firm breasts.

fuck-you *noun*

a statement or expression of contempt, hostility, or the like. [In 1943 and 1951 quotations, referring literally to statements of the phrase *fuck you*.]

1943 G. Biddle *Journal* (July 31) in *Artist at War* (1944) 77: Teddy's run of literary allusions is a pleasant relief after the too concentrated diet of "fuck me's" and "fuck you's" of the G.I.'s. **1951** J.D. Salinger *Catcher in the Rye* 202: I went down by a different staircase, and I saw another "Fuck you" on the wall. **1965** H.S. Thompson *Letter* (Aug. 10) in *Proud Highway*

(1997) 537: I had a bad wrangle with them on a Tom Wolfe review, and we said a mutual fuck you, with me about $500 ahead. **1976** L. Bangs in L. Bangs & J. Morthland *Mainlines, Blood Feasts, Bad Taste* (2003) 165: His entire performance, from music to personal bearing, was a giant fuck-you to everybody present. **1992** *Rolling Stone* (Dec. 10) 45: The disc was a relentlessly catchy and fuzz-filled "fuck you." **1993** *Rolling Stone* (Oct. 14) 68: Who else could insult Budweiser, Michael Jackson, Whitney Houston, Calvin Klein, the entire recording industry and MTV all in one video? "This Note's for You" is Neil Young's finest "fuck you." **1994** *Granta* 47 (Spring) 129: She never learned English, even though she had come here at sixteen: a fuck-you to the New World. **1995** *New York Magazine* (Mar. 13) 33: When it's as bad as it can be, and people still act like there's nothing wrong, then it's sort of like a fuck-you to the audience— "we don't have to be good, because we're Saturday Night Live!" **1996** *N.Y. Observer* (Apr. 1) 3: The line was a veiled fuck-you to David Letterman,... the symbolic whipping boy for how the East Coast element screwed up the Oscars. **2000** *N.Y. Press* (Mar. 29) ii. 14/1: Searching for friendly faces, I get only fuck-yous. **2007** J. Picoult *Nineteen Minutes* 114: She had pictured suicide as a final statement, a fuck you to the people who hadn't understood how hard it was for her to be the Josie they wanted her to be.

fuck-you *adjective*

that expresses or is characterized by a desire to insult or to demonstrate defiant indifference; provocative; contemptuous; hostile; confrontational.

[**1954** "Lars Lawrence" *Morning, Noon & Night* 148: The critic's immaculate mind had attracted him powerfully, though he rejected the utility of such refinement in a fuck-you-Jack, my-belly-first period of history.] **1962** J. Kerouac *Letter* (Apr. 4) in *Selected Letters 1957–69* (1999) 334: Funny how they look so old-fashioned now, they were written in '54 but not everyone writes like that (with that fuckyou freedom). **1972** *Rolling Stone* (July 20) 8: For clenched fists and gritted teeth and fuck-you rock and roll. **1973** *Rolling Stone* (Mar. 1) 42: See if you can keep your integrity without a flat out fuck-you challenge. **1981** *Times Literary Supplement* (May 15) 548: The Beatles....A pretentious gobbledygook introduction by Leonard Bernstein: "...the Fuck-You coolness of these Four Horsemen of Our Apocalypse." **1993** N. Maclean in *Harper's* (Feb.) 35: Under the influence of those dreams, some of the finest fuck-you prose in the English language has been composed but, alas, never published. **1994** *Rolling Stone* (Feb. 10) 53: We've endured so much phony Hollywood nobility about disease that Jean's fuck-you rampage against death comes off as horrifically honest. **1996** *Newsweek* (Feb. 19) 39: The bombing…is "the politics of fuck-you rage and resentment rather than political calculation."**1997** *New Yorker* (Oct. 6) 48: Youthful hubris or fuck-you candor. **1998** *New Yorker* (Dec. 1) 64: He has the real fuck-you blood. **2002** *Ministry* Jan. 91/1: I've just got to give them respect for doing something that's completely balls-to-the-wall and fuck-you. **2005** T. Brookes *Guitar* 260: He gave me his usual fuck-you stare and set his guitar…on the stage. **2008** A. Davies *Mine All Mine* 232: Pushing out of a sleeve is a chronograph the size of a biscuit. It looks like it could tell you the time, the moon phase, the weather in Tokyo, and precisely how much money you don't have in your checking account. It's a fuck-you watch, attached to the fat wrist that's attached to the kill-you hand. So this is the magus who sends agents into my life to ruin me.

fuck-you lizard *noun* [suggested by a fancied resemblance between the English phrase and the gecko's call]
Military in Southeast Asia. a tokay gecko.

[**1934** C. L. Clifford *Too Many Boats* 309: A gecko lizard in a nearby papaya tree croaked throatily. "Obscene devils, those," he went on dryly. The colonel laughed.] [**1970** *Pacific Stars & Stripes* (May 15): A 2nd Brigade chaplains's assistant is trying to put his outdoorsman's skills to work on a somewhat embarrassing problem at the 4th Inf. Div.'s Highlander Chapel. The nemesis in this case was the infamous Vietnamese "insulting lizard."] **1971** *Playboy* (Aug.) 199: From the underground comes the chant of "Fuck you, fuck you" from small lizards, not unexpectedly called fuck-you lizards. **1978** G. Hasford *Short-Timers* 151 [refers to Vietnam War]: The fuck-you lizards greet us. **1984** J. Fuller *Fragments* 78: Did you know that if you grab one of those Fuck You lizards by the tail, he just lets go and walks away? **1986** J. Thacker *Finally the Pawn* 133: That's because of the fuck-you lizard. **1987** M. L. Lanning *Only War We Had* 253: FNGs were told that the "fuck-you" lizards were NVA taunting us. **1988** M. Clodfelter *Mad Minutes* 33 [refers to 1965]: Naturally we labeled these leftovers from the prehistoric past "Fuck You Lizards." **1996** S. O'Nan *Names of the Dead* 124: They'd told him about this; it was a gecko—a fuck-you lizard. **2002** R. Hoyt *Old Soldiers Sometimes Lie* 245: American sailors at Subic Bay and airmen at Clark Air Force Base had famously called it the Fuck You lizard.

fuck-you money *noun*
Especially *Business.* sufficient money to give one personal freedom, esp. the freedom to quit one's job; (*broadly*) an (unexpected) financial windfall.

  1969 C. Blair *Board Room* 294: I don't care. I've got my fuck-you money. **1975** L. Rust Hills in *Esquire* (Dec.) 180: "But all that money...."... "Well, it's 'fuck-you' money....It gives me freedom and independence so I won't have to write something that doesn't appeal to me." **1986** *New Republic* (Dec. 8) 11: [Donald] Regan huddled in the Oval Office with the president.... "I've got something that none of those other guys have."... "What is it?" To which Regan, wealthy from his days as boss of Merrill Lynch, replied, "Fuck you money." **1988** *Granta* 23 (Spring) 246: Earning more doesn't make the problem go away unless you're saving for "fuck you" money. A month ago Brian told me about "fuck you" money. "It's the amount of money you need to be able to say 'Fuck you' to anyone." Brian reckoned the current amount to be three million pounds. **1994** N.Y.C. man, age 30: When you win the lottery, you get *fuck-you money.* Anyone you don't want to bother with, you can afford to say "Fuck you!" **1994** *Times Literary Supplement* (Nov. 18) 9: "Fuck-you-money," for having enough money set aside to tell one's boss to screw off, should the impulse to do so arise. **1995** *New York Times Magazine* (Nov. 19) 46: The Number is often used interchangeably with another term, an unprintable one that describes the sum you need to be able to tell your boss you've had enough. Its family-newspaper approximation would be Forget You Money. **1999** *Vanity Fair* (Dec.) 216/2: I came up with a figure of something like $7 million. But "fuck-you money," as the retirement number is commonly referred to out here, can be a lot less. **2004** T. L. Lee & C. M. Anthony *Gotham Diaries* 7: He had yet to make the transaction that would put him over the top, give him some fuck-you money and social respect.

fuck-your-buddy week *noun*
Especially *Military.* a hypothetical period during which betrayal and exploitation of one's friends is supposedly encouraged. *Jocular.* Also variants. Compare BUDDY-FUCK.

[**1952** Haines & Krims *One Minute to Zero* (film): John, this isn't help-your-buddy week. We might need those guys again.] **1958** T. Berger *Crazy in Berlin* 302: What is this, fuck-your-buddy week? **1960** D. MacCuish *Do Not Go Gentle* 342 [refers to WWII]: National American custom of Screw Your Buddy Week. **1962** P. Crump *Burn, Killer, Burn* 279: Don't worry about it, weed.... This is Frig Your Buddy Week. *ca*1963 in H. Schwendinger & H. Schwendinger *Adolescent Subculture* 296: It's fuck your buddy week, fifty-two weeks of the year....If you have a buddy kind and true, you fuck him before he fucks you. *a*1967 in M.W. Klein *Juvenile Gangs* 98: It's fuck your buddy week, fifty-two weeks of the year. **1971** *Playboy* (Apr.) 182: That old Army expression, "Every week is fuck-your-buddy week!" **1973** W. Crawford *Gunship Commander* 148: The whole army overreacted, filed charges against everybody in sight, good old fuck-your-brother week. **1980** W. Manchester *Goodbye Darkness* 156 [refers to WWII]: The school's shabbiest custom [was] known as "fuck-your-buddy night." Every candidate was required to fill out a form rating his fellows. **1984** E. Partridge *Dictionary of Slang & Unconventional English* (ed. 8) 1323: What *is* this?—International Fuck-Your-Buddy Week?...Prob. adopted from the US forces in Korea, 1950–53. **1997** D. DeLillo *Underworld* 690: Somebody says, "What's this, fuck-your-buddy week?" **2004** R. Arellano *Don Dimaio of La Plata* 180: You backstabbing spic! What is this, Fuck Your Buddy Week?

fuddle-duddle

Canadian. a euphemism for FUCK in various senses and parts of speech. [After an incident in the House of Commons, when Prime Minister Pierre Trudeau, being criticized by the opposition, mouthed something claimed to have been "fuck off." In an interview with CBC Television, he denied having mouthed "fuck off" but acknowledged having moved his lips; when asked what he had been thinking when he did so, he responded "What is the nature of your thoughts, gentlemen, when you say 'fuddle duddle' or something like that?" Though the exact nature of his original words remains unclear, popular perception quickly arose that he did say "fuck" and then later claimed that he had only said "fuddle-duddle."]

1971 *Globe & Mail* (Toronto) (Feb. 17) 1: Mr. Trudeau, however, said he had not mouthed any vulgar words. "I would never say anything like that." Pressed by reporters to reveal the words he had mouthed, the Prime Minister said they were "Fuddle-duddle." **1979** *Globe & Mail* (Toronto) (Nov. 22) 8/5: Pierre Trudeau is stepping down. His place in history will depend on where Quebec goes in future. I'm confident he will be ranked among the three greatest prime ministers, along with John A. Macdonald and Wilfrid Laurier. And fuddle-duddle to anyone who thinks otherwise. **1984** L. Rooke *Sing Me No Love Songs* 289: "Oh fuddle-duddle," exclaims Anne. **1986** R. Graham *One-Eyed Kings: Promise & Illusion in Canadian Politics* 112: It outraged the premiers, angered Washington, sent London into a tizzy, and fuddle-duddled the opposition. **1991** *Ottawa Citizen* (Dec. 25): When Brian Mulroney said—or did not say—fuddle-duddle in the Commons last week, he was—or was not—merely reflecting the mood of the times. There was very little Christmas cheer on Parliament Hill. **2001** *Maclean's* (June 18) 56/2: George was the first person to put the dreaded F-word into Canadian newspapers after P. Trudeau "claimed" he had just aimed "fuddle-duddle" at an opposition MP.

fug

(a written euphemism for FUCK in various senses and parts of speech; see FUCK for examples). [Associated chiefly with Norman Mailer, who was required by his publishers to use the euphemism in *The Naked and the Dead* (1948).]

fugly *noun* [blend of FUCKING + *ugly*]
Originally *Australian Military*. an extremely ugly person.

*a*1970 in R. J. Rayward *More than Mere Bravo* (1989) 122: *Fugly*—an extremely ugly woman. A blending of "fucking" and "ugly" to describe the woman. **1993** B. Moore *Lexicon of Cadet Language* 157/2: Seeing your fugly tonight, Bill? **2005** *Cosmopolitan* (U.K. edition) (Aug.) 21/1: 33% of women have dated someone "as ugly as sin" because he made them laugh. Here's to all the fuglies!

fugly *adjective*
Originally *Students*. especially of a person: very ugly.

[**1962** in H.S. Thompson *Proud Highway* 316: Get these dogs off me! These fucking ugly dogs!] **1980** E. Segal *Man, Woman, & Child* 60: "In other words she's fugly, right?" Bob smiled. "Don't you think I could pick a winner, Bern?" **1984** Mason & Rheingold *Slanguage*: *Fugly,* adj.... fucking ugly. **1988** C. Eble *Campus Slang* (Fall) 4: *Fugly*—extremely ugly. **1989** P. Munro *U.C.L.A. Slang* 41: She's so fugly she makes my mother-in-law look cute. **1993** N.Y. man, age 23: This girl asked me out yesterday, but man, she was fugly. **1998** Personal letter to editor (Aug. 25): *Fugly*—I picked up the term from my college roomie, 1974–75. **2004** J. Weiner *Little Earthquakes* 357: Do you realize I'm going to have to wear those fugly maternity clothes again? **2006** *New York Magazine* (Sept. 4) 86/1: Well, what if the show was called *Ugly Betty*—and you were playing Betty? What if the other characters routinely deride you as "fugly"?

FUJIGMO *interjection Military.*

"*fuck you, Jack, I got my* orders." *Jocular.* Compare FUIGMO under FIGMO.

1950 *Saturday Evening Post* (Aug. 5) 89: With him flew Lt. Col. "Pappy" Hatfield, in his famous bomber the "Fujigmo"—translation unprintable. **1953** in G. M. Valant *Vintage Aircraft Nose Art* 295: FUJIGMO. **1980** D. J. Cragg *Lexicon Militaris* 158: FUJIGMO. Fuck You, Jack, I Got My Orders.

futhermucker *noun* [intentional spoonerism]

= MOTHERFUCKER. *Jocular.*

1961 T. Joans *All of Ted Joans & No More.* **1965** Walnut Ridge, Ark., high school student: Every one of your Hoxie friends turns out to be a futhermucker, if you ask me. **1972** R. Wilson *Playboy's Book of Forbidden Words* 171: *Mammy-jammer,... futher-mucker.* **1972–76** C. Durden *No Bugles, No Drums* 41: Thanks, futhermucker. **1982** in G. Tate *Flyboy in the Buttermilk* 21: Well, goddamn, these furthermuckers [*sic*] must not be bullshitting. **1998** G. Tate in *Village Voice* (N.Y.C.) (Mar. 10) 124: His peers are those lofty, low-rent, high-concept, swing-baiting furthermuckers [*sic*].

futz *noun*

1. a foolish or unpleasant fellow.

1935 *Bedroom Companion* 79: Some crusty old futz who has had too much drink starts off on this tangent. **1940** W. R. Burnett *High Sierra* 35: He was an old phutz and a has-been. **1959–60** R. Bloch *Dead Beat* 84: The old futz inside the loan office gave him a cold eye. **1984** B. Haskin *Byron Haskin* 80: The screenplay was written by Sir Reginald Barclay, a puffy old futz who knew nothing about anything dramatic. **1996** M. Daheim *Auntie Mayhem* 128: "Old futz," muttered Renie. "How could you encourage him to launch his war stories?"

2. (used as a euphemism for *the fuck*, under FUCK, *noun*).

1947 B. Schulberg *Harder They Fall* 104: Nobody knows what the futz you're talkin' about. **1961** A. Maund *International* 4: He promised me three years ago he would run Nick Sarpedon the futz out of the International. **1996** L. Niven *Ringworld Throne* 318: What the futz was Bram expecting?

futz *verb*

1. [probably an alteration of Yiddish *arumfartsn*] to fool or play.—used with *around* or *with*. [Often regarded as a euphemism for FUCK, *verb*, definition 5, or FUCK AROUND.]

1929–30 J.T. Farrell *Young Lonigan* 63: Studs kept futzing around until Helen Shires came out with her soccer ball. **1932** *American Speech* VII (June) 335: *Phutz around*—to trifle; to interfere; "to horse around." **1936** M. Levin *Old Bunch* 64: There was a fellow that never wasted time. No fuzzy futzing around. *Ibid.* 249: No more futzing around being a schoolboy. **1941** C. Brackett & "B. Wilder" *Ball of Fire* (film): Why do you think we're futzin' around with these? **1941** in A. Boucher *Werewolf* 129: Futzing around with the occult. **1944** A.J. Liebling *Back to Paris* 113: Have we really started, or are we still futzing around? **1948** I. Wolfert *Act of Love* 158: What's he futzing around for? **1949** H. Robbins *Dream Merchants* 14: At least he didn't say a word about my futsing around all those years. **1959–60** R. Bloch *Dead Beat* 3: "Good crowd," said Eddie, futzing around with his mustache. **1964–66** R. Stone *Hall of Mirrors* 78: To…watch a room full of stooges futz with soap. **1968** P. Roth *Portnoy's Complaint* 263: I am nobody to futz around with. **1970** C. Harrison *No Score* 55: You futz around in the darkroom all the time. **1973** A. Schiano & A. Burton *Solo* 106: All that futzing around with bits of paper. **1984** *USA Today*

(Nov. 7) 3A: President Reagan...[suggested] it is time to "stop this futzing around." **1998** *New Yorker* (Oct. 5) [inside back cover] [advertisement]: Da Vinci didn't mess with the Mona Lisa. Beethoven didn't futz with his 5th Symphony. **1998** T. C. Wilson *Systems Librarian* 88: In its most basic definition, "futzing" is playing around with a technology to get it to work as needed or to improve its operation—tweaking so to speak. **2000** *Wired* (Jan.) 216/2: The Air Force report acknowledges the controversy inherent in futzing with Mother Nature. **2003** D. Gaines *Misfit's Manifesto* xv. 331: But I got hold of myself and started futzing with the tape recorder.

2. to treat with contempt.—used with *around*; = FUCK AROUND, *verb*, sense 3.

1966 B. Brunner *Face of Night* 165: Futz me around a little more and find out. **1989** E. Segal *Doctors* 138: "I bet you'll be back with us by spring." "Don't futz me around. I'm gonna be here forever."

futzer *noun*

= FUTZ, *noun*, definition 1.

1938 H. Miller *Tropic of Capricorn* 30. You poor old futzer, you, just wait. **2002** D. Reuter *Gaydar* 119/1: This obsessive-compulsive futzer can be one mean "queen" bee, as he endlessly buzzes around his hive, picking up pollen and depositing it in its proper place.

futz off *verb*

to loaf; FUCK OFF, *verb*, definition 2.a.

1968 C. Baker et al. *College Undergraduate Slang Study* 123: *Futz off.* Waste time, not study.

futz out *verb*

= FUTZ UP; fizzle out.

1963 G. L. Coon *Short End* 254: What happens to you, if you are Halstead...and the whole shooting match futzes out right in your face and lies there? **1992** F. Kellerman *False Prophet* 187: Peter Jedidiah Decker, don't you *dare* futz out on me! **2005** J. J. Ordover *Star Trek S.C.E.: Identity*

Crisis 14: I think they might be futzing out on us and causing feedback through the system.

futz up *verb*

to spoil, confound; mess up; FUCK UP.

1947 C. Willingham *End as a Man* 296: I've got her all futzed up. She does everything I tell her. **1948** I. Wolfert *Act of Love* 293: If you're futzing it up I want to know. **1965** R. Hardman *Chaplains Raid* 64: Not while you're futzing up the clergy I won't! **1966** A. Drury *Capable of Honor* 300: The President wants me to run...to balance the ticket, to futz up the image, and to blur the issues so that he can be elected. **1987** B. Sills *Beverly: An Autobiography* 290: Rosalinda was a pretentious lady who made Adele wear a uniform, but because Rosalinda didn't know what she was doing, Adele's uniform was all futzed up. **1992** R. W. White *Heat Islands* 125: He knew Sutter had futzed up the bilge pump of his skiff, then snuck back later and cut the boat free. **2003** G. Spence *Smoking Gun* 184: There is an ethical obligation for them not to futz up the evidence.

F-word *noun*

(used as a euphemism to refer to the word FUCK or one of its derivatives or compounds).

1956 W. E. Collinson in *Moderna Språk* (Modern Language Teachers' Association of Sweden) L. 13: Even today the British printer would draw the line at the f-word used in *Lady Chatterley's Lover*. **1964** *Labor Arbitration Reports* (Bureau of National Affairs) XLII. 494/2: Two witness stated X— used the "F-word" epithet to MM, the female jobber clerk. The gravamen of House Rule 2 lies in the use of profanity *maliciously* against others. **1970** *Evergreen Review* XIV. 72/3: Another undercover police lady said that in one defendant's speech "every other word was the 'F' word." **1973** *New York Times Book Review* (May 6) II. 10/3: I ain't got time to be outraged about these books. I dismiss them. The kids use the expression "f-word," the "f-word," when they want to talk about it without saying it. Well, I say, "f-word" them books, and "f-word" the pretentious writers who write them. **1987** F. Flagg *Fried Green Tomatoes* 41: Here she was, at her age, and she'd never said the F word. **1995** N. Hornby *High Fidelity* xvi. 194: "And don't fucking say 'Oh' like that." A couple of people look round

when I use the "f"-word, and Jo puts her hand on my arm. I shake it off.
2001 D. Lehane *Mystic River* 232: "You said the f-word, Dad."... "Sorry,
Mike. Won't happen again." **2007** L. McMurtry *When the Light Goes* 36:
These are modern times, you know.... Old ladies can say the F-word if they
want to.

F-word *verb & interjection*
(used as a euphemism for FUCK *verb* and *interjection*). Compare
EFF.

1973 *New York Times Book Review* (May 6) II. 10/3: I ain't got time to
be outraged about these books. I dismiss them. The kids use the expression
"f-word," the "f-word," when they want to talk about it without saying it.
Well, I say, "f-word" them books, and "f-word" the pretentious writers who
write them. **1989** J. Kirkwood *Diary of a Mad Playwright* 39: I thought:
Oh, F-word, I can't go around beggin on my knees anymore, it's just too
F-wording boring and demeaning. **1995** *Re: Help Me!* on Usenet newsgroup rec.bicycles.off-road (Feb. 18): I personally have witnessed "newbie"
mtb kids with the F-word off attitude. Scaring horses, walkers, and even
Me! **2003** *Detroit Free Press* 9 Oct. (Electronic ed.): That hulking groper is
not the (F-word)ing governor!

FYFI [initialism punning on standard *FYI*]
Especially *Business*. "for your fucking information." *Jocular*.

1995 N.Y.C. publisher, age 52: *FYFI* means "for your fucking information." I've seen it used on memos for at least ten years—everyone knows
what it means. **1996** *Re: 2 10,000 Maniacs Questions*, on Usenet newsgroup alt.music.alternative.female (Feb. 23): This "some guy or something"
is called Salman Rushdie, FYFI. **1998** *Re: Truth*, on Usenet newsgroup
rec.audio.tubes (July 20): FYFI, it is easy to spot an unsuccessful author.
He publishes two books and is gone.

G

---

gaggle-fuck *noun*

= CLUSTERFUCK, sense 2.

1996 *A Whole "Wack"?* on Usenet newsgroup alt.tv.x-files (Nov. 15): I wouldn't place any bets on that being an actual term. The Canadian military make up our own all the time. My personal favourite is "gaggle-fuck": a formation resembling a bunch of guys standing together. **2001** O. West *Sharkman Six* 30: He's smart enough to stay hidden; the last thing he wants is to be associated with the gaggle fuck on the beach. **2007** D. Bellavia & J. R. Bruning *House to House* 118: We've got one big gaggle fuck right in the front yard, and we're vulnerable as hell.

gang-fuck *noun*

1. a gangbang: an occasion on which a number of people copulate successively with one person; (*also*) gang rape; (*also*) a sexual orgy. Also **gang-screw**.

1941 G. Legman in G. V. Henry *Sex Variants* II 1166: *Gang-fuck*. An instance of pedication or irrumation of a single boy or homosexual by two or more men consecutively, and with or without his consent. Also used as a verb, and in both senses heterosexually. **1946–51** W. Motley *We Fished All Night* 350: The fellows had the girl back behind a stairway. She was willing. It was another gang-screw. *a***1968** in Haines & Taggart *Fort Lauderdale* 60: Gang fucks. **1972** D. Jenkins *Semi-Tough* 58: Less fun than being next-to-last on a high school gang-fuck. **1979** C. McCarthy *Suttree* (1992) 416: A female simpleton is waking naked from a gang-fuck in the backseat of an abandoned car. **2003** N. Hynd *Enemy Within* 118: The same trio wanted to share a girl for the night. The three of them with one female. They were celebrating some deal they had struck, Anna said, and their way of closing out the transaction was a gang fuck.

2. chiefly *British*. = CLUSTERFUCK *noun* sense 2.

1995 A. McNab *Immediate Action* 230: If we started losing contact, it would all go to a gang fuck. **2000** T. Carew *Jihad!* v. 121: I'd thought that Salim knew his stuff, but the move was a complete gang-fuck. We made the first ten kilometres in good time, but then they stopped to pray. We set off again half an hour later, but now we were going much slower and I could see that we certainly weren't going to get there before 10 p.m. **2006** M. J. Pass & D. Pass *Waiting for Red* 18: It's a gang-fuck. The house is far from town so the chances of shots being heard are next to nothing.

gang-fuck *verb*

to copulate with (someone) in a GANG-FUCK.

1916 H. N. Cary *Slang of Venery* I 103: *Gang Fucked*—Said of a woman who, willingly or unwillingly, submits to the embraces of the individuals in a crowd of men in succession. **1938** "Justinian" *Americana Sexualis* 24: A *gang* of boys or young men escorts a girl or young woman to its rendezvous and proceeds to *gang-fuck* her. U.S. vulgarism, C. 20. **1940** *Tale of a Twist* 77: I guess I've been gang-fucked a few times. **1959** W. Burroughs *Naked Lunch* 125: I been gang fucked. **1971** H. S. Thompson *Fear & Loathing in Las Vegas* 114: These cops will go fifty bucks a head to beat her into submission and then gang fuck her. **1975** C.W. Smith *Country Music* 84: They'd just as soon gang-fuck you as look at you! **1984** W. D. Ehrhart *Marking Time* 66: What kind of person could gang-fuck some poor starving refugee in the middle of a war? **2007** A. H. Vachss *Terminal* 33: They were gonna throw gasoline in my cell and fire me up, put glass in my food, gang-fuck me until I was dead.

genderfuck *noun*

(an instance of) reversal of normal gender roles; (*specifically*) transvestism.

1972 L. Humphreys *Out of the Closets: Sociology of Homosexual Liberation* 164: This technique (also known as "gender fuck") is a form of extended guerilla theater. **1973** *Rolling Stone* (Aug. 30): The new "macho" transvestitism, called vulgarly "gender-fuck," a curious satire of female impersonation—dresses, pumps, full make-up and beards—is represented by, among others, three men in WAC uniforms and big moustaches. **1979** Robert Christgau in Greil Marcus *Stranded: Rock and Roll for a Desert Island* 133: Ordinarily, their [*sc.* the New York Dolls'] gender-fuck was a lot subtler. **1985** *Village Voice* (N.Y.C.) (Sept. 10) 74: Part of Phranc's appeal is the genderfuck of her sweet feminine voice coming from such a masculine frame. *a*1988 *Maledicta* IX (1987–88) 173: Real transvestites and transsexuals are…embarrassed…[by] the gender-fuck Cockettes and such (in dresses and beards). **1995** E. Weisbard *Spin Alternative Record Guide* 135: Gender-fuck goddess Annie Lennox and wacky rock professor Dave Stewart were a match made in video-pop heaven. **1995** in *Village Voice* (N.Y.C.) (Jan. 2, 1996) 6: The hot-off-the-press Gender Fuck issue of Porn Free—"the Porn 'Zine Dedicated to Getting You Off for Nothin'." **1996** *N.Y. Press* (Nov. 6) 36: "The boys wanna be girls and the girls wanna be boys." He was right—the crowd was pure third-sexer gender-fuck. **2003** *Bitch* (Fall) 63/2: Representations of queer parents show them to be extremely gender-determinate gay men or lesbian women, without a hint of genderfuck anywhere in the picture…as with the super-femmy lesbian moms in *Friends*. **2005** J. Gamson *Fabulous Sylvester* 139: Sexy genderfuck was one of her signatures: she…wore her hair short and sharp; often dressed in…men's tailored suits with breasts revealed.

GFO *noun* [*general* *f*uck-*off*]
Military. a lazy individual. *Jocular.*

> **1948** *N.Y. Folklore Quarterly* 20 [refers to WWII]. **1957** A. Myrer *Big War* 213 [refers to WWII]: Snap-to, you pitiful gutless GFO!

GFU *noun* [*general* *f*uck-*u*p]
Military. an incompetent individual. *Jocular.*

> **1942** *Yank* (Nov. 25) 21: G.I. Jones…was the GFU of Bat. B 66th CA (AA). **1944** in *American Speech* XX 148: *G.F.U.* General foul up; a soldier who does not do the work he is supposed to do. **1945** *Saturday Review of Literature* (Nov. 3) 7: He had better learn. Otherwise he will be known as a GFU… and that would be just TS. **1945** *American Speech*

(Dec.) 262: *G.F.U.*, "a soldier who never does anything correctly." **1962** J. O. Killens *Then We Heard the Thunder* 208 [refers to WWII]: Sad sacks and GFUs and…goldbricks. **1991** L. Reinberg *In the Field* 93 [refers to Vietnam War]: *G F U* abbr. for General Fuck-Up, usually referring to specific persons. **2001** J. Iannuzzi *Mafia Cookbook* (ed. 2) 9: I was a GFU (General Flake-Up), so I was constantly on KP.

goat fuck *noun*

Especially *Military.* a fiasco; mess; CLUSTERFUCK. Also (*euphemistically*) **goat dance, goat screw, goat rope.**

1965 H. S. Thompson *Letter* (Jan. 29) in *Proud Highway* (1997) 481: Kentucky was a Wolfean nightmare and New York was a goatdance. **1971** T. Mayer *Weary Falcon* 15: "What a goatfuck," I said. **1981** F. Knebel *Crossing in Berlin* 89: We got a real goat fuck going here today, Mr. Simmons. **1990** E. Ruggero *38 North Yankee* 80: There seemed to be some order creeping into Barrow's "goat screw." **1991** R. Marcinko & J. Weisman *Rogue Warrior* 199: It had been one humongous goatfuck. *a***1991** W. Kross *Splash One* 34 [refers to Vietnam War]: What's a guy like you doing in a goat rope like this? **1995** *Guardian* (London) (Sept. 2) 1: Britain now has what the Americans call "goat-fucks," those swaying edifices of cameramen, snappers, sound recorders and hacks which lurch perilously round press conferences. **2004** G. Crile *Charlie Wilson's War* 384: Even in the heyday of Eisenhower and John Foster Dulles, when the Cold War was one big fucking goatfuck, no one was publicly calling for more money for the CIA to use in Guatemala or Cuba or anywhere. **2005** S. Brockmann *Hot Target* 219: What I can't figure out—and maybe you could help me with this—is the difference between a goatfuck and a clusterfuck.

goat-fucking *noun*

In phrase:

☞ **been to three county fairs and a goat-fucking** [or (*euphemistically*) **goat-roping**] *Southern.* seen many astounding sights. *Jocular.*

1974 U.S. college student: I been to three county fairs and a goat-fuckin' and I ain't never seen the like of *that.* **1981** B. Bowman *If I Tell You* 98: "I've been to three county fairs, two goat-ropings and a "'tater digging.'"

I know what's going on; I've been around. **1984** K. Weaver *Texas Crude* 30: I've seen a goat-roping, a fat stock show and a duck fart under water, but if that don't beat any damn thing I've *ever* seen, I'll put in with you!! **1988** D. Dye *Outrage* 16: Colonel, you and me been to three county fairs and a goat-fuckin' contest and I ain't seen you hit by nothin' heavier than shrapnel.

goat-fucking *adjective*

= MOTHERFUCKING.

> **1960** H. S. Thompson *Letter* (Mar. 22) in *Proud Highway* (1997) 209: I would give at least one ball for one (or three) of your sandwiches right at this goat-fucking instant. **1989** S. Hunter *Day before Midnight* 404: Drown your sorrows in vodka as better men before you have, you goat-fucking son of a bitch. **2004** D. Sosnowski *Vamped* 302: He's a dickless, ball-less, gutless, spineless, goat-fucking pederast from the bad part of hell. **2007** A. Franklin *Mistress of the Art of Death* 313: A jellybag, she called him, a snot-faced, arse-licking, goat-fucking, bum-bellied, farting, turd-breathed apology.

green motherfucker *noun*

Army & U.S. Marine Corps. the U.S. Army or U.S. Marine Corps.— usually used with *this*. Also variants. [Quotations refer to Vietnam War. The 1968 quotation is a euphemism.]

> **1968** Stuart *Typescript* (unpaged): I'll be out of this "green thing" in another year. **1973** W. Karlin et al. *Free Fire Zone* 137: Plan on getting out of this green amphibious motherfucker. **1976** C.R. Anderson *Grunts* 146: How did you ever get in this green mother anyway? **1978** J. Webb *Fields of Fire* 210: The Corps...I *love* this green motherfucker. **1982** R.A. Anderson *Cooks & Bakers* 116: They talked about how much they hated Vietnam and the Marine Corps—the "Crotch," the "Green Motherfucker." **1983** W. D.Ehrhart *Vietnam to Perkasie* 54: The Army buys... jeeps that work. But the Green Mother spend money for good equipment? **1985** D. Dye *Run Between the Raindrops* 144: Could have gotten *out* of this green motherfucker and been set, man. **1999** T. Jones *Sonny Liston was a Friend of Mine* 63: I'm in the Green Motherfucker already. I guess that makes me a citizen.

GRF *noun*

see under RATFUCK, *noun*, definition 2a.

guaranfuckingtee *verb*

to guarantee absolutely. Compare -FUCKING-, *infix*.

1948 W. Manone & P. Vandervoort *Trumpet on the Wing* 180: I guaran-(fussin')-tee you, when we got the place fixed up it was real pretty. **1961** J. Jones *Thin Red Line* 42 [refers to WWII]: I guaran-fucking-tee you! **1974** P. Roth *My Life as a Man* 19: I guaranfuckintee you gentlemen, not one swingin' dick will be leavin' this fiddlefuckin' area to so much as chew on a nanny goat's tittie. **1976** W. Goldman *Magic* 102: I'll guaranfuck-ingtee ya I'm an expert. **1986** J. C. Stinson & J. Carabatsos *Heartbreak Ridge* 141: I'll guaranfuckintee you. **1988** *New Yorker* (Dec. 5) 61: They say they never do it, but I guaranfuckintee you someone fooled with the ball this year. **1993** J. Mowry *Six out Seven* i. x. 151: Cause there gonna be a popquiz, man. I *guaran-fuckin-tee* y'all that right now, this minute, there least *one* little sucka…bleedin his little ass off in the sun! **2000** G. V. Higgins *At End of Day* 29: If that's where they're comin' from, Nova Scotia's where the crew's gonna end up—guaranfuckintee it. **2004** C Rummelkamp *Secretkeepers* 76: They are *not*, I repeat *not* Mafia. I guaran-fuckin-*tee* you they are not Mafia. **2008** A. Davies *Mine All Mine* 99: It's not a probability. It's not a fucking Miss-Cleo-says-the-future-is-cloudy-so-who-knows-what-will-happen. It's for real. It is going to happen. It's guaranfuckingteed.

H

---

ham and motherfuckers (or mothers)

see under MOTHERFUCKER.

handfuck *noun*

an act of masturbation performed (esp. on another person) with
the fingers or hands. Also **hand frig**.

1879 *Harlequin Prince Cherrytop* 4: Hand frig, stand frig,/That's the
sport for him. **1979** D. Bryan *Hard Hat Fucker* 111: Beaten into submission by the sheer, vicious force of his hand fuck. He knew the young man
could not take much of of [*sic*] this pounding. **1996** L. McK. Bienen in
Ploughshares (Sept. 1): You want hand fuck...How much you give me?
2003 V. Redel *Swoon* 8: Standing in a dark corner of our home/leaning
into your hand fuck/while in their room the children toss in sleep.

handfuck *verb*

to masturbate (another person or oneself) with the fingers or
hands. Also (as in 1989 quotation) figurative.

1975 W. B. Huie *In the Hours of Night* 189: The boy would put on a
rubber and his girl would hand-fuck him while he clutched her with one
arm, kissed her and finger-fucked her with his other hand. **1982** N. Friday
Men in Love 361: He watched as I slowly hand fucked myself and shot my
come at least five feet in the air. *a***1989** C. S. Crawford *Four Deuces* 48 [re-
fers to Korean War]: To find the break they wrap their hands around the
telephone line...and let it run between their fists. That's what they call

"hand-fucking" the line....They were out hand-fuckin' a line lookin' for a break in it. **1992** A. McGahan *Praise* 44: I set to with three fingers and finally she came...."Hand fucking is wonderful." **2006** J. Ross in *Bad Boys Southern Style* 60: The top of her dress was down around her waist, and somehow her skirt had ended up there, as well, as he'd hand-fucked her.

hate-fuck *noun*

an esp. aggressive act of intercourse motivated by animosity towards one's partner.

1968 Paul Newman in *Playboy* (July) 69: There was the hate fuck, the prestige fuck—and the medicinal fuck, which is, "Feel better now, sweetie?" *a***1976** Jack Nicholson in A. W. Read *An Obscenity Symbol After Four Decades* 3: People that I don't like are not sexually attractive to me at all. I remember in my early 20s I had a few hate-fucks and they were groovy. But not now. **1977** "Iceberg Slim" *Long White Con* 18: He was palpitating to despoil her, hurt her, violate her with a hate fuck. **1987** "Pussy Galore" *Groovy Hate Fuck* [rock album title]. **1995** R. Athey in *Village Voice* (N.Y.C.) (Feb. 14) 32: When he comes home fucked up, I'm sure to give him a good hate fuck. **1997** D. DeLillo *Underworld* 293: If you fuck me, it'll be a hate fuck. This what you want? This what you mean by aggressive? **2003** N. Kelman *Girls* 118: You had been attracted to her all those years before but had never wanted to admit it could be anything more than a "hate fuck."

hate-fuck *verb*

to engage in a HATE-FUCK with.

1966 R. Gover *Poorboy at the Party* xvi. 195: Was into it enough now to be itching for a bitch I could hatefuck, not looking for a girl who was happy and full of joy. **1975** R. Rapoport *Super-Doctors* 87: "I know if you really try, you can stop hate fucking and learn to start really loving your wife." The hate-fucker nods. **1999** R. Kean *Pledge* 208: "He's in a tough spot—us on one side, his girlfriend on the other." "*Shawn*. That girl needs to be hate-fucked." **2008** *Californication* (Showtime TV) (Oct. 26): "Something about that woman. I want to fuck her, but I kinda want to punch her in the face too, it's weird." "Ah, you want to hate-fuck her."

headfuck *noun*

1. an act of fellatio. Also: a person who performs fellatio. Cf.
MOUTH FUCK, SKULLFUCK.

1974 "T. Andrews" *Story of Harold* 208: "Marcius give me a headfuck."
"A what?" "A headfuck. A blow job." **1999** K. Cairns *Surviving Paedo-
philia* 30: Give us a head-fuck, girl. Give us your mouth. **2004** *Gay Times*
(Feb.) 237/2: A truly great storyteller and a brilliant head-fuck.

2. Chiefly *British*. a state of confusion.

1983 R. Price *Breaks* 236: I got a panicky feeling that every second that
passed in conversation was just increasing the headfuck. **1997** *Dazed &*
Confused (June) 22/1: I wrote it while I was having a bit of a head-fuck.
It's about being in an oppressive, testing situation—be it mental or physical—and at that moment when you fly out of it and feel like you're coming
alive again. **2003** D. Adebayo *Westside Storeys* 154: When you finally ex-
hale, the violent headfuck you were expecting fails to materialize. You feel
a pleasant, manageable rush.

3. something or someone that causes confusion or disorientation.

1993 "Wildhearts" (song title): My baby is a headfuck. **1996** P. Attanasio
Donnie Brasco (film script) (second Green rev. pages) 93: You sit in your little
fucking house…and you complain on the phone to your little fucking friends
and you dream up this latest hundred dollar headfuck. **2003** *Word* (May)
47/1: *Jacob's Ladder* is great because it's just a headfuck. **2004** *Vice* (Feb.)
36/2: Now we have films like Spike Jonze's *Adaptation*, a multi-levelled,
metatextual headfuck that you need to debate afterwards with your friends.

4. imaginary sexual activity; MINDFUCK *noun* sense 1.

1997 *Good Vibrations Guide to Sex* 99/1: We decided it was only unfaithful if we touched each other…so we…talked utter filth to each other while
masturbating. A true "head-fuck" that lasted for about eight hours. **2007**
A. Tyler *G is for Games* 68: I imagin[e] taking him into my mouth, feeling
his cock stiffen further….I'm lost in my headfuck when he returns.

headfuck *adjective*
Chiefly *British*. confusing; misleading.

1992 *i-D* (July) 61/3: We're trying to reflect the scene; the balearic, the techno and the late night post-club ambient headfuck music. **1999** S. Reynolds *Generation Ecstasy* 217: With its premium on headfuck weirdness and disorienting effects, darkcore opened up a vital space for experimentation. **2003** T. Neradin *Last Train* 40: Pete was now strapped firmly into his seat on the head-fuck roller-coaster and it was making its first ascent.

headfuck *verb*

1. to confuse, mislead, or the like, especially deliberately; MIND-FUCK.

1974 B. Hoddeson *Porn People* 117: Other typical *Ball* stories include…"Fucking and Headfucking." **1978** R. Price *Ladies' Man* 211: I feel like you're fucking with my head.…I feel head-fucked. **1985** R. Frede *Nurses* 287: I told you, Trina. Don't pull that headfucking with me. **1994** I. Welsh *Marriage* in *Acid House* 278: It's strong acid, real head-fucking gear, but when we get to Roxy's we start drinking like there's no tomorrow. **1999** L. Hird *Born Free* 97: Why do mentally ill people always try and bring you down to their level? I'm leaving if she's going to head-fuck me like this. **2005** B. Paloff trans. Dorota Maslowska *Snow White & Russian Red* 111: I don't know how head-fucked you have to be to ring the doorbell to a stranger's house in such an assholey way.

2. to engage in fellatio; SKULL-FUCK.

1979 F. Picano *Lure* 97: Head fucking. Cocksucking. Words from gymnasium locker rooms. **1987** T. Boyle *Post-Mortem Effects* 225: Then having head-fucked her and ejaculated in her ears, hair, eyes, nostrils, mouth, they hopped in a car and drove away, leaving the woman behind. **1988** "Ultra Violet" *Famous for 15 Minutes* 165: You know about fist fucking and head fucking? **2007** P. Frost *Deep Inside* 216: I pumped his dick, squeezed his balls, and lost myself in the sensation of being head-fucked.

headfucker *noun*

1. a person who deliberately confuses or misleads people.

1967 R. Drexler *Line of Least Existence* 23: You know something — you're a real head fucker. **1972** R. Drexler *To Smithereens* 25: If you don't stop being such a head-fucker I'm gonna walk in the other direction. **1985** R. Frede *Nurses* 314: You're a real headfucker, aren't you? **2003** *Time Out* (London) (Feb. 26) 192: While searching, people try, usually unsuccessfully, to protect themselves from wrong 'uns, of which there are many: commitmentphobics; headfuckers; manipulators; liars; and deeply damaged, addicted people who will never be able to put anyone but themselves first.

2. a powerful hallucinogenic or psychotropic drug; (also) a strong alcoholic drink.

1975 in R. Spears *Slang & Jargon of Drugs & Drink* 254: Headfucker ["a potent head drug"]. *a***1989** R. Spears *NTC Slang Dictionary* 176: This stuff is a real headfucker. Stay away from it. **2006** *Urban Dictionary* (Apr. 20) (online): *Headfucker*, A large bowl of mixed alcoholic drinks with a small amount of juice which fucks your head up and makes you do silly things and forget them.

HMFIC *noun* [probably modeled on *HNIC* 'Head Nigger In Charge'] "*H*ead *M*other *F*ucker *I*n *C*harge."

1994 T. Reed & J. Cummings *Compromised* 187: Max boasted to Terry that he had been "hand-selected by the White House" to set up and oversee this operation. He made it very clear that he would be what Terry later termed the HMFIC, "the head mother-fucker in charge." **1997** J. Crotty *How to Talk American* 200: HMFIC: Head "Military Figure" in Charge. **2001** R. Martini *Hot Straight and Normal* 114: When going below decks looking for a decision maker whether a chief or an officer a sailor would say who's the HMFIC? **2004** B. Williams *Spare Parts* 219: This is all mine, brother. I might be a private, but I'm the HMFIC of this prison camp.

honeyfuck *noun*

a sexy young woman. Also: an unusually gratifying act of copulation.

1967 F. Pollini *Crown* 259: "You're some honey," he said. "*Some honeyfuck*." **1970** E. Thompson *Garden of Sand* 295: Come on,... honeyfuck. **1979** L. Heinemann in *Tri-Quarterly* (Spring) 184: The snazziest hot-to-trot honey fuck to hit the mainland since the first French settlers. **1993** R. O'Connor *Buffalo Soldiers* 130: This is the honeyfuck of honeyfucks. She has you in her power. **2002** D. Ayres *Other Girls* 162: I got you that.... A real honey-fuck.... Instead, you fall in love with her.

honeyfuck *verb* [probably an alteration of earlier *honeyfuggle* in its sense 'to engage in kissing and hugging']
    to engage in unusually gratifying copulation.

    1954–60 H. Wentworth & S. B. Flexner *Dictionary of American Slang*: Honey-fuck...v.i., v.t. To have sexual intercourse in a romantic, idyllic way; to have intercourse with a very young girl...*honey-fucking*...extremely gratifying and slow intercourse. **1980** L. Heinemann in *Harper's* (June) 64: She's honey-fucking the everlasting daylights out of some guy. **1986** R. B. Merkin *Zombie Jamboree* 121: We were honey-fuckin', real slow and low, takin' our time. **1990** J. Fitzgerald *Belle Haven* 176: Did you know that your former husband's son has been honey-fucking your young niece, probably daily, am I right, Dabney? **2007** *Black Lace Quickies* I. 9: She remembered teenage boyfriends honey fucking her on parents' sofas in front of the television, for hours sometimes.

horsefuck *verb*
    to copulate with (someone) from behind; DOGFUCK.

    1971 R. J. Minton *Inside: Prison American Style* 60: I think you could take one of them, sit him down, and run a three-hour movie of his mother getting horse-fucked by an ape. **1972** J. Wambaugh *Blue Knight* 114: Sexy little twist....I'd like to break her open like a shotgun and horsefuck her. **1977** College student: Horsefuckin' is the best position. **2006** T. Phillips *Blacktop Cowboys* 69: You stick it in her ass or anything exciting?... Well, did she lick your balls or anything?... Did you horsefuck her?

horse-fucking *adjective*
    huge.

    *a***1968** in G. Legman *Rationale of Dirty Joke* 549: Two great horse-fucking volumes.

hot *adjective*

In phrase:

☞ **hot enough to fuck**, furiously angry.

1966 M. Braly *On the Yard* 201: The doc was hot enough to fuck. **1971** R. J. Minton *Inside: Prison American Style* 56: He's all red in the face now! He's hot enough to fuck! **1966–80** J. McAleer & B. Dickson *Unit Pride* 358: Miller's gonna be hot enough to fuck before this mess is over. **2003** N. McMahon *To the Bone* 38: I walk into my office, and first thing, I get a call from Welles D'Anton.... Hot enough to fuck twice. Yelling that we killed a patient of his.

I

IHTFP *interjection*

"*I hate this fucking place.*" [Associated with both the U.S. military (esp. the Navy) and the Massachusetts Institute of Technology.]

1962 P. Trese *Penguins Have Square Eyes* 132 [refers to 1956]: The community bulletin board, which contained...one piece of cardboard with the inscription "IHTFP!" "What's that mean?" I asked the Seabee. "Oh," he said, filling in the blank, "I hate this place." **1962** *Voo Doo Magazine* (Massachusetts Institute of Technology) (Jan.) 10: *IHTFP*—An expression of loyalty towards the Institute, meaning "Institute Has The Finest Professors." **1969** J. Crumley *One to Count Cadence* 27: All the way back to the barracks he explained why I too would soon adhere to the motto IHTFP or I Hate This Fucking Place. **1981** J. H. Webb *Sense of Honor* IV. i. 194: For those assigned to the [Naval] Academy, "IHTFP" became a slogan even before the institution formally existed. **1983** Elting, Cragg, & Deal *Dictionary of Soldier Talk* 161: *IHTFP*...gained wide currency during the Vietnam War, when it was...seen...on helmet camouflage covers or cardboard placards. **1990** J. Pournelle *Falkenberg's Legion* 124: I found a trooper painting I.H.T.F.P. on the orderly room wall. **2002** S. Williams *Free as in Freedom* 208: The cruiser's vanity license plate read IHTFP, a popular MIT acronym with many meanings.

J

JAFO *noun*

"Just Another Fucking Observer."

    1983 D. O'Bannon & D. Jakoby *Blue Thunder* (film): "I found out what JAFO is." "Just Another Fucking Observer." **1991** *Sydney Morning Herald* (Oct. 3) (Northern Herald section) 13: Among other things, he explains how he came to be a "jafo" (Antarctic slang for "just another effing observer"). **1998** *Guardian* (Aug. 20) 15: The Paras are fond of JAFO (Just Another F***ing Observer). **2002** *U.S. News & World Report* (Sept. 16) 42: From the first chaotic hours after the crash, Miller has firmly kept the media and meddling officials he calls "JAFOs" ("Just Another F - - - ing Observer") from "tromping around" in the woods and among the handful of small cabins and houses at the scene.

JANFU *noun* [*joint army-navy fuck-up*; suggested by SNAFU]

Military. a bungled military operation involving the Army and Navy. *Jocular*. [The 1943 and 1944 quotations are euphemistic.]

    1943 *Time* (Aug. 30) 36: Victory it was, but seldom has a victory been acknowledged with such wry humor. Among the echoing cliffs of Kiska a new word was born: JANFU ("Joint Army-Navy foul-up"). **1944** *Newsweek* (Feb. 7) 61: *Janfu*: Joint Army-Navy foul-up… *Jaafu*: Joint Anglo-American foul-up. **1944** in *American Speech* XX 148: *JANFU.* Joint army-navy foulup. **1945** in *Verbatim* XVI (Autumn 1989) 6: *Janfu*…"joint army-navy fxxx up." A failed amphibious military operation considered badly planned and/or executed. **1946** *American Speech* (Feb.)

72: JANFU (Joint Army-Navy FU)...became fairly common in [the Pacific] theater, especially around the time of the Saipan operation. **1993** H. J. Riker *Seals: The Warrior Breed: Silver Star* 161: "I knew the whole Navy couldn't be snafued!" "Looks to me more like a janfu."

Jesus fuck *interjection*

(used to express astonishment, fear, anger, etc.); "Jesus Christ!"

1967 M. Baldwin *Great Cham* 147: When he'd opened his mouth to say Cor Jesus Fuck, his mouth had instead said Ooomooolooo. **1974** R. Price *Wanderers* 146: She was laying in a pool of diarrhea.... "Jesus fuck! You got it onna mattress! Goddamnit! That's it! You did it an' you're gonna lay in it!" **1983** W. D. Ehrhart *Vietnam to Perkasie* 186: "We're gonna get wasted by our own people," I thought. "Jesus fuck!" **1988** W. Boyd *New Confessions* 425: Oh no, Jesus fuck no! **1993** "J. Le Carré" *Night Manager* xii. 188: "I'm going on down, Mike! I'll go start the boat, hear me? *Jesus fuck*," he complained. **1999** C. Brookmyre *One Fine Day in Middle of Night* 325: Matt heard Vale fire two rounds from his handgun. It was met by a yelp of "Jesus fuck!", then followed immediately after that by the sight of an Uzi flying through the air and skidding along the hall amidst the squillion pieces of glass. **2006** I. Welsh *Bedroom Secrets of Master Chefs* 289: Jesus fuck almighty...I get a big shock as a stunningly beautiful girl of about nineteen, twenty, appears before me.

jug-fuck *noun Military.*

1. a drinking bout.

1980 Retired U.S. Army sergeant: I first ran across this in a list of Pro Signs given to me after April, 1977. "Let's go have us a jug fuck!"

2. a confused or frustrating situation; mess; CLUSTERFUCK, *noun*, definition 2.

*a***1987** H. Coyle *Team Yankee* 116: Not until, and only if, we get this jug fuck unscrewed. **1988** D. Dye *Outrage* 10: Until we get out of this Ethiopian jug-fuck, I don't want to see you any more than six feet away from... your squad. **1992** E. Ruggero *Common Defense* 189: The FBI and the CIA, not to mention the German police, are all in on this investigation—what a jug fuck that must be.

jumble-fuck *noun*

= CLUSTERFUCK, *noun*, definition 1.

1938 "Justinian" *Americana Sexualis* 27: *Jumble-Fuck,* n. U.S., low coll., *ca*20 for *Daisy-Chain.*

L

LBFM *noun* [*l*ittle *b*rown *f*ucking *m*achine]

Military. a Southeast Asian woman who is sexually promiscuous, especially a bar girl or a prostitute. [Quotations refer to the Vietnam War.]

1971 *Playboy* (Aug.) 203: LBFM's never come. What's an LBFM? A little brown fucking machine. **1974** J. Platt *Laotian Fragments* 12: *Remember:* The Golden Palace LBFMs in their spangled padded bras saying "Melly Clistmas, GI." **1985** J. T. Heywood *Taxi Dancer* 61: The... Thais—what the airmen called Little Brown Fucking Machines, LBFMs for short. *Ibid.* 225: Where's my LBFM?...Colonel loves LBFMs. **1991** R. Marcinko & J. Weisman *Rogue Warrior* 165: No LBFM's today. *a*1992 T. Wilson *Termite Hill* 377: Swede probably thought she was just another LBFM. **1993** C. W. Henderson *Marshalling the Faithful* iii. 58: They seemed to spend every free hour searching for that fresh, young LBFM that had not yet been spoiled by too many hard nights. **2001** S. Bird *Yokota Officers' Club* 134: Bring back the LBFM with the melons!

M

mammy-dodger *noun*

Black English. (a partial euphemism for) MOTHERFUCKER. Hence **mammy-dodging** *adjective.*

1939 in A. Banks *First-Person America* 256: Hell yes, mammydodger. **1970** in *Dictionary of American Regional English* (1996) III. 493/2: Why that mammy-dodging potlicker didn't even know what shoes was till he was twenty-nine.

mammy-jammer *noun*

Especially *Black English.* (a partial euphemism for) MOTHER-FUCKER, in any sense. Also variants.

1948 J. E. Webb *Four Steps to the Wall* 100: I sure nuff show ol' white boy mammy-dugger how's feel. **1956** J. Resko *Reprieve* 48: The mammy-jammer...puts the rope aroun mah neck. **1962** J. O. Killens *Then We Heard the Thunder* 31 [refers to WWII]: I just don't like the goddamn mama-jabbing Army, that's all. *Ibid.* 32: Now ain't that a mama-jabber? *Ibid.* 195: You fat-ass mother-huncher. *Ibid.* 266: We gonna step higher than a mama-jabber. **1963** M. Braly *Shake Him Till He Rattles* 97: You know what that dirty mammy-jammer did to me? **1963** L. Cameron *Black Camp* 12: Grab your socks, mammyjammers. **1967** A. Baraka *Tales* 18: You talking about a lightweight mammy-tapper. *Ibid.* 20: Yeh, mammy-rammer. **1969** H. R. Brown *Die, Nigger, Die* 109: I'd bought a rifle, which...was a sweet mama-jammer, too. **1969** C. Gordone *No Place to be Somebody* 413: I rassle with light'nin', put a cap on thunder. Set every mammy-jammer in the graveyard on a wonder. **1971** K. W. Keith

Long Line Rider 75: Hey, Max, this mammyjammer don't like my cookin'. Y'all oughta have his butt busted. **1972** R. Wilson *Playboy's Book of Forbidden Words* 165: *Mammy-Sucker* In black slang, an insult that is felt to be even more offensive than motherfucker. **1974** U.S. college student: You mama-sticker. **1980** J. McAleer & B. Dickson *Unit Pride* 31: You...dirty Yankee mammie-jammer. **1982** B. Downey *Uncle Sam Must be Losing the War* 59 [refers to WWII]: What the fuck do we do with three of these mammy-jabbers? **1985** D. Dye *Run Between the Raindrops* 279: I'd been outa this mammy-jammer like a fuckin' shot. *Ibid.*291: We...a lucky bunch of mammy-jammers. **1987** J. Waters *Hairspray* (film) [refers to 1962]: Just to see me, the big mammy-jammer. **1991** *In Living Color* (Fox-TV): This is one bad mammy-jammer. **1992** *Jerry Springer Show* (syndicated TV series): I'm a bad mammy-jammer...I'm Wonder Woman!

mammy-jamming *adjective*

(a partial euphemism for) MOTHERFUCKING. Also variants.

1946 M. Mezzrow & B. Wolfe *Really the Blues* 105: Those Jim Crow mammyjamming whites. **1958** W. Talsman *Gaudy Image* 30: Yeah, some real mammy-lovin' goddamn cheap tinhorn place. **1969** R. Jessup *Sailor* 268: Who! The mammy-rammy *law!* That's who! **1974** R. Carter *16th Round* 55: You must be out of your mammy-jammy mind! **1974** A. Murray *Train Whistle Guitar* 117: That ain't no goddamn mammy-hunching patent leather walk. **1977** E. Bunker *Animal Factory* 59: I ain' no mammy-fuckin' *dawg!* **1977** J. Langone *Life at the Bottom* 76: Pour the stuff in the trench and it packs hard as a mammy-jammin' cement load.

maw-dicker *noun*

Southwest. = MOTHERFUCKER. Hence **maw-dicking**, *adjective.*

1984 A. R. Sample *Racehoss* 145 [refers to 1950s]: Why you Gotdam impudent shit-colored mawdicker. *Ibid.* 202 [refers to *ca*1960]: I oughta throw yore mawdickin ass in the pisser.

mercy fuck *noun*

an act of intercourse engaged in out of pity. Cf. PITY FUCK.

1975 I. Macnab *42nd Year of Mrs. Charles Prescott* 111: Having a high old time throwing mercy fucks into every cunt who thinks she needs it.

1978 T. Alibrandi *Killshot* 174: Consider your work here a mercy fuck. **1981** in *National Lampoon* (Jan. 1982) 22: But let's not consider this a mercy fuck. There's no joy in that. **1988** J. Krantz *Till We Meet Again* 506: "Please, mister, throw me a mercy fuck"—that was what a man must see when he looked at her. **1996** "Soul Coughing" *4 out of 5* (pop. song): Quantify my luck I need a mercy fuck. **2004** J. Picoult *My Sister's Keeper* 219: Who called Janet for a mercy fuck the night after she dumped you? **2005** *Vanity Fair* (Mar.) 222/3: Emily is an angel of death, falling for men….and sending them off to war with the fondest of farewells, a mercy fuck.

mercy fuck *verb*

to engage in a MERCY FUCK (with).

1968 Paul Newman in *Playboy* (July) 69: Mercy fucking…would be reserved for spinsters and librarians. **1980** M. Gordon *Company of Women* 141: "Who's this one?"…"One of Robert's rescuees. He believes in mercy fucking." **1992** M. Blonsky *American Mythologies* xv. 344: She's the beautiful American sans superego….If she has a beer too many, she'll even mercy fuck you. **2003** *Village Voice* (Feb. 9) 135/1: It seems to me that an ex who's willing to bang you on a business trip might be willing to make a special trip and mercy-fuck you right away.

m.f. or **em-eff** *noun*

(a partial euphemism for) MOTHERFUCKER.

1953 R. Ellison *Letter* (Apr. 9) in A. Murray & J. F. Callahan *Trading Twelves* (2000) 42: Doc looked at me as though to say "come on, m.f., this ain't the time to start no shit." **1959** in R.S. Gold *Jazz Lexicon* 209: You go and buy me a tenor saxophone and I'll play the m-f. **1964** C. Howe *Valley of Fire* 190: Being able to call a gook an emm-eff in pig Latin and get away with it. **1965** E. Cleaver *Soul on Ice* 58: Why'n't they kill some of the Uncle-Tomming m.f.s? **1965** in S. Sanchez *We be Word Sorcerers* 193: I'm a lucky M.F. to have found you. **1965** in W. King *Black Anthology* 304: So I stole the m—f [*sic*]. **1966–67** P. Thomas *Down These Mean Streets* 236: You poor m.f. **1968** B. Caldwell in G.M. Simmons et al. *Black Culture* 213: Let's get these m.f.'s now! **1970** S. Terkel *Hard Times* 407: Today you get a guy in court, [he] don't like what the judge says, he calls him a *m f,* you know what I mean? **1970** G. Cain *Blueschild Baby* 77: A bunch of dirty white M.F.'s. **1971** in V. Matthews & N. Amdur *My Race be Won* (1974) 246: There'd be a lot of dead "M.F.'s" around. **1971–73** G. Sheehy *Hustling* 89: Then in comes this m.f. from Midtown North, *our* precinct. **1974** R. Blount *3 Bricks Shy* 159: They say "m-f" worse than a colored person. **1976** G. Kirkham *Signal Zero* 63: *Adios,* MF! **1986** B. Clayton & N. M. Elliott *Jazz World* 101: I did provoke the fight by calling him an MF. *Ibid.* [refers to 1930s]: Billie [Holiday] called all of her close friends MF. **1987** *Newsweek* (Mar. 23) 61: He could stand out on the corner looking sharp as a MF in his Stacy-Adams wingtips and a $100 hat. **1992** *Donahue* (NBC-TV): I'm gonna take all you m.f.s with me. **1992** "Prince" *Sexy M.F.* (pop. song title). **1997** Y. Jah & Sister Shah'Keyah *Uprising*: The other day your baby was a "punk, mf, stupid, ignorant so-and-so." You've been telling him that all of his life. **2004** K. Adams *Ex-Girlfriends* 42: Life was hard core. No coddling necessary. Her mantra: bring it on, m.f.

In phrase:

☞ **MFWIC,** *motherfucker what's in* charge.

1980 D. J. Cragg *Lexicon Militaris* 285: MFWIC. Motherfucker What's In Charge. **2002** C. Bartolomeo *Side of the Angels* 52: "Can you have Nicky up there pronto?" "By this weekend. Who's the MFWIC again?" Ron asked. (MFWIC, pronounced "miffwick," was an old campaign acronym which meant "mother-fucker-what's-in-charge.") **2007** K. S. Bodman *Checkmate* 156: Anyway, after that debacle, we had a meeting, and Austin demanded to know who the MFWIC was on that project.

m.f. or **em-eff** *adjective*

(a partial euphemism for) MOTHERFUCKING. Also **emeffing**.

1958 W. Motley *Epitaph* 120: Them emeffing guards is bringing it in fountain pens. *Ibid.* 149: You emeffing right. *a***1972** in G.M. Simmons et al. *Black Culture* 219: That M-F-in' jive. **1973** A. Childress *Hero Ain't Nothin' but a Sandwich* 34: All over the emm-eff community. **1975** J. McCourt *Mawrdew Czgowchwz* (2002) iv. 83: Wait a minute, hon, I'll write it down—where's my m. f. lipstick. **1990** *New Yorker* (Apr. 2) 46: Graffiti…on the… training ship of the Maine Maritime Academy…"Only 13 more MFD's, Only 12 more MFD's, Only 11 more MFD's," and so on down a toilet stall. The "D" stood for "day."

MILF *noun* [*m*other (or *m*om) *I*'d *l*ike to *f*uck]
a sexually attractive woman who is a mother or (generally) in early middle age.

1991 (name of rock band): milf. **1995** *Re: Fabulous after Forty* in Usenet newsgroup alt.mag.playboy (Jan. 12): Those moms are babes!!... We have a term for it around here, its [*sic*] called "MILF".... "Mothers I'd Like to Fuck." **1998** A. Herz *American Pie* (film script): *Freshman guy.* Dude! That chick—is a MILF! *Freshman guy #2* What the hell is that? *Freshman guy* M-I-L-F! Mom I'd Like to Fuck! **2005** "Belle De Jour" *Intimate Adventures of London Call Girl* 45: There seems to be a leggy blonde or brunette sex goddess for every potential horny businessman on earth, with maybe a MILF or two to spare.

mindfuck *noun*

1. imaginary sexual activity. Cf. HEADFUCK *noun* sense 4. *Jocular.*

1964 I. Faust *Steagle* 265: We could lie down side by side and think. Oh, a mind fuck? That's nowhere. **1968** *Zap Comix* (No. 3) (unpaged): A mind-fuck. *a***1977** M. French *Women's Room* 574: They masturbate to it....It's a mind-fuck. *a***1991** J. Phillips *You'll Never Eat Lunch in This Town Again* 163: He rarely gets a hard-on, but the mind-fuck is really irresistible. **2008** B. Kahr *Who's Been Sleeping in Your Head?* 39: The patient from Berlin explained that he derived more pleasure from the *fantasy* than he did from the *reality*... As one of my patients admitted, "Sometimes a mind-fuck is better than the other kind."

2.a. a disturbing or overwhelming experience, esp. one caused by deliberate psychological manipulation.

1971 *It* (June 2) 19/3 The title track "The Man Who Sold the World" is possibl[y] the most spaced out cut, but each one has its own individual mind fuck inside. **1972** R. Barrett *Lovomaniacs* 385: Dolly's eyes said she was *stoned*...I...know when someone's full of the...original superfreak mindfuck. **1977** *National Lampoon* (Aug.) 33: His Pressed Wang on Stained Glass is a religious mind-fuck. **1980** M. Baker *Nam* 40: When you weren't going through that, you had your recruit regs held up in front of your face memorizing your eleven general orders. It was a real mind fuck. **1986** J. Cain *Suicide Squad* 85: Mindfuck would be terminal this time. **1988–90**

M. Hunter *Abused Boys* 279: The mind-fuck you did on me. **1993** K. Scott *Monster* 164: You simply prepared ahead of time for the mind-fuck of being a prisoner. **2001** M. Azerrad *Our Band could be your Life* viii. 289: It was…a mind-fuck of a show. **2006** *Giant Robot* No. 43 56/2: I was a film geek who was heavily mining through Euro and Asian cinema in college, and it was a total mind fuck to see all-Asian casts speaking American English when *Yellow* and *Shopping for Fangs* came out.

b. something that causes confusion or bafflement; a confusing or mentally challenging thing.

1971 L. Bangs in *Creem* (June 17) 7 : That electro-distort stuff that rocked you guys to sleep when you were first tokin' in your cradles was really unheard-of then, a real earthquake mindfuck. **1987** "J. Hawkins" *Tunnel Warriors* 37: Despite the obvious game of mindfuck. **1997** *Village Voice* (N.Y.C.) (Sept. 30) 88: Fincher's new movie…is a cynical mindfuck thriller that builds, with increasing pointlessness, to a deflating punchline. **2001** *Premiere* (Apr.) 42/2: We had a great screening early one morning.…It was packed — for a mind-fuck at 9 o'clock.… a mesmerizing meditation on memory, identity, and loss. **2007** P. Spiegelman *Wall Street Noir* 351: Time is an invidious mind fuck. You look around one day and everything's unfamiliar.

3. a counterintelligence deception; an act of psychological manipulation.

1974 C. Bernstein & B. Woodward *All the President's Men* 119: Somewhere, Bernstein had been told that the CIA did that kind of thing abroad. He had heard it called Mindfuck but the agency called it Black Operation. **2005** N. Fick *One Bullet Away* 153: A voice began to fire questions at me— name, rank, service.… I struggled to use the resistance techniques I had been taught.… I smiled in the tight confines of the cell and waited for my next mind-fuck. **2006** E. M. Katz & L. Holmes *Why You're Still Single* 57: He might be starting a bizarre mind-fuck in which he's going to cancel every fourth date in order to keep you from ever getting comfortable.

4. a crazy person; a psychotic. Also: a person who manipulates others; MIND-FUCKER, definition 2.

1977 J. Sayles *Union Dues* 312: Comes back such a mindfuck he can't remember. Fuckin space cowboy. *Ibid.* 176: He was a certifiable mindfuck and you had to keep him on a tight leash. **1992** H. Childress *Reality Bites* (film script) 25: *Lelaina stops at the door confused, kind of bummed out. Then she looks at Vickie, who has on a Cheshire cat grin. Lelaina smiles as she realizes Vickie was stringing her along.* LELAINA. You little mind-fuck. **2005** J. Trunk *Dirty Fan Male* 3: So there I was, with a job, a tiny salary, working for a shit company, working with a total mindfuck, hating it all and still seeing no way out.

mindfuck *verb*

1. to psychologically manipulate; to disturb psychologically.

1966 (quotation at *fuck (someone's) mind* under FUCK, *verb*). **1967** L. Wolf *Voices from the Love Generation* 17: Their consciousness has been permanently altered. Forever altered. They've been mind-fucked. *Ibid.* 281: Mind-fucked. Profoundly influenced by something. **1970** J. Howard *Please Touch* 235: Some [encounter] groups dismiss all abstractions as "headshit" and "mindfucking." **1971** S. Miller *Hot Springs* 66: They have nothing to teach you—they mind-fucked you. **1972** R. Gover *Mr. Big* 11: She mindfucks me again. **1976** J. W. Thomas *Heavy Number* 105: He's really mind-fucked you. **1987** R. Miller *Slob* 156: They both felt giddy, hysterical, a little confused, mindfucked, spent. **1989** E. Gilchrist *Light can be both Wave & Particle* 164: Rhoda, stop mindfucking. Love people that love you. **1991** R. Marcinko & J. Weisman *Rogue Warrior* 165: I was a veteran of mind-fucking the Vietnamese. **1997** A. Beattie *My Life, Starring Dara Falcon* 136: Suddenly she's selling his mother's ring. His mother's ring! Tell me that isn't mind-fucking him. **2006** R. Barger & K. Zimmerman *6 Chambers, 1 Bullet* 309: Was it fruitless trying to get into Vladimir's head in a last-ditch attempt to mind-fuck him?

2. to engage in imaginary intercourse (with).

1970 J. S. Grendahl *Mad Dog Press Archives* 144: And a bad stripper, really she's ashamed to be up there, isn't really into mind-fucking with everyone in the crowd. **1996** E. G. Colter et al. *Policing Public Sex* 161: Mindfucking is no longer better than the real thing if safer sex education is about sex. **2004** "Annalise" *Venus Rising* 126: You used to mind fuck me all the time. I used to come in my uniform just by listening to you whisper in my ear. **2008** K. Jaye *Good Girls Pole Riders Club* 146: I let my middle finger fall away from my clit.... It had been four days since visiting him, and my vagina was almost raw. I had mind-fucked Darius so many times, it was starting to wear on my body.

mindfucker *noun*

1. something that is extremely disturbing, amazing, or astounding.

1969 J. Sebastian in *Woodstock* (film): This thing is a real mindfucker! **1970** E. E. Landy *Underground Dictionary* 133: *Mind fucker*...Thing or situation that upsets or disturbs one. **1972** W. Pelfrey *Big V* 24: Wow man, that's a mind-fucker. **1980** A. Maupin *More Tales of City* lvii. 188: Michael rattled on about...Mrs. Madrigal's recent revelation to her "family." Jon shook his head incredulously. "That is...a mindfucker." **1985** J. P. Kelly *Solstice* in B. Sterling *Mirrorshades* (1986) 93: They would have called the Stonehenge free festival a mind-fucker. **2007** E. Schweikher & P. Diamond *Cycling's Greatest Misadventures* 30: The thought of getting lost was a complete mindfucker.

2. a person who psychologically manipulates another person; one who MIND-FUCKS.

1970 E. E. Landy *Underground Dictionary* 133: *Mind fucker n.* Individual who asserts personal pressure to persuade people to believe his way without regard for the feelings of the people he influences; person who attempts to manipulate another's thinking without regard for the other. **1980** *National Lampoon* (Aug.) 67: You're some kind of mindfucker. You're a witch. **1982** H. Gold *True Love* 140: You, mindfucker.... You've done nothing but lie to us. You think this is a liar's game? **1996** N. T. Rosenberg *Trial by Fire* 70: The woman is a mind-fucker, Stella. She'll use anything and anyone to get what she wants. **2004** K. Schwartz *Clearing the Aisle* 297: He was a mindfucker. Very charming, but a real snake.

mind-fucking *adjective*

baffling or astounding; (*also*) that psychologically manipulates.

1971 S. B. Kopp *Guru* 145: Away from intellectual "mind-fucking" words. **1977** R. A. Wilson *Cosmic Trigger* 93: "They" turned some kind of "mindfucking" machine on the two men. **1986** Atlanta, Ga., man, age *ca*30: [Hands Across America] was mindfucking, man! Such a great thing! **1990** S. Frith & A. Goodwin *On Record* 233: You think of those weird ways of ending one song and having some kind of transitional riff to get into the next one. That's really the most fun—especially when you can pull off some mind-fucking key change. **1996** E. Leonard *Out of Sight* 51: In an altogether different kind of mind-fucking incarceration. **2004** J. D. Vinge *Dreamfall* (revised edition) 399: Get off him, you mindfucking bitch!

mo dicker *noun*

(a partial euphemism for) MOTHERFUCKER.

1968–70 *Current Slang Cumulation* III & IV 84: *Mo dicker*, n. A lazy, irresponsible person.—New Mexico State. **1989** D. Sherman *There I Was* 129: It started raining like a mo-dicker....I...said "mo-dicker"... 'cause your momma don't like me saying "motherfucker," but it's really the same word.

mofo *noun*

(a partial euphemism for) MOTHERFUCKER. *Jocular.*

1965 in H.S. Thompson *Hell's Angels* 33: The "Mofo" club from San Francisco. **1966** F. Reynolds & M. McClure *Freewheelin Frank* 116: The Mofos (a motorcycle club that isn't in existence now). **1972** R. Wilson *Playboy's Book of Forbidden Words* 171: *Mother-jumper, mother-ferrier, mo'-fo', mammy-jammer,...futher-mucker.* **1973** *Oui* (Mar.) 69: And now you, too (you jive mofo) can control the minds of women! **1977** U.S. college student: I'm sincerely beginning to believe that mofo is a goddamn female impersonator. **1979** L. Blum, D. Goldberg, J. Allen & H. Ramis *Meatballs* (film): I will twist that mofo. **1982** W. L. Heat Moon *Blue Highways* 124: He's one useless black mofo. **1983** Leeson *Survivors* (film): Hey, you honky mofo, get the lead out of your ass! *Ibid.*: Your gun jammed, Mr. Honky Mofo? **1987** *National Lampoon* (June) 79: It hurt like a mofo. **1989** W.E. Merritt *Rivers Ran Backward* 20: Get your white ass in the truck, mofo. **1995** *Guardian* (May 13) (Guide) 18/1: Although Ike Turner may be a former coke-headed, woman-beating ex-con mofo, he's also one of the most important unsung figures of American music. **1999** Y. M. Murray *What it Takes to Get to Vegas* xi. 186: He'd found part-time work at a Taco Bell downtown, but his full-time job was being a radical mofo with a mission. **2005** *SL* (Cape Town, South Africa) (Feb.) 8/3: Keane better than Coldplay? You must be kidding.... I hope the Chris Martin mafia comes to take you mofos down! **2006** *Navy Times* (Aug. 28) 33: Much of the credit, of course, goes to Jackson, Mr. Mofo himself, proving anew that he's one of the baddest movie men on the planet.

mofo *adjective & adverb*

= MOTHERFUCKING. *Jocular.*

1973 O. Z. Acosta *Revolt of Cockroach People* (1989) ii. 28: What about all those books that got me through the long Mofo nights? **1989** W.E. Merritt *Rivers Ran Backward* 20: You mofo lucky they sent me along. **1996** *Observer* (Dec. 29) 31/2: Peter...has been trying to pretend he's terribly bothered about all this press attention re. personal chauffeur-driven limo from Palumbo. It's actually rather hideous— every time it draws up I expect to see Huggy Bear slink out in purple pimp-suit and mo'fo' fedora. **2007** "Zane" *Dear G-Spot* 135: She was laying there, stiff as a mofo board, while I drilled this big pipe in and out that poontang.

mofuck *noun*

= MOTHERFUCKER; MOTHERFUCKING.

1962 H. Simmons *On Eggshells* 143: Get out the way, moa-fugg. **1978** T. C. Fox *Cops* 47: If the *Killer* is played by a black actor, the following changes should be made in the dialogue... pg. 30—*Killer* I don't give a fuck, mo'fuck. **1982** J. M. Del Vecchio *13th Valley* 477: This mofuck division fucked up. **1983** R.C. Mason *Chickenhawk* 105 [refers to 1965]: [The mongoose] was young and tame, and he named it Mo'fuck. **1985** G. Bear *Dead Run* in *Collected Stories of Greg Bear* (2002) 333: "You can take us back, mister! You really can!" "Can he?" "Shit no, mofuck pig." **1990** J. Levy *Squeeze Play* 287: There were street punks in ripped-off Nikes screaming "Mo'fuck" in my ear.

Mongolian cluster fuck *noun*

see under CLUSTERFUCK *noun.*

monkey *noun*

In phrases:

☞ **a monkey fucking a football** and variants, a ridiculous or clumsy figure.

1968 P. Tauber *Sunshine Soldiers* 117: You know what you look like, Pea-zer, stupid? You look like a monkey trying to fuck a football. **1977** in S. Lyle & P. Golenbock *Bronx Zoo* 17: Jesus Christ! You looked like a monkey trying to fuck a football out there! **1981** W. T. Hathaway *World of Hurt* 47: You look like a monkey fucking a football. **1984** K. Weaver *Texas Crude* 34: That guy tryin' to change a tire looks like a monkey tryin' to fuck a football. **1988** D. Poyer *The Med* 422: You people cry like fifteen monkeys fuckin' a football. **2005** E. Puchner *Music through the Floor* 74: Watching you work is like watching a monkey fuck a football.

monkey's fuck, *British.* the least bit, a damn; FUCK *noun*, definition 2.a. Also in euphemized variants.

[**1893** R. G. Hampton *Major in Washington* 97: A poker I.O.U. that wasn't worth a monkey's snicker.] [**1942** P. Larkin *Letter* (Mar. 20) in *Selected Letters* (1992) 32: I rather liked the way the words "monkey's fuck" and "bugger" shone like sign posts in the strange country of this drunken Scotch.] **1960** G. W. Target *Teachers* 100: The Old Man's door opened and the pair of them came out, Stillwell not seeming to give a monkey's, but too casual, and poor Jimmy Taylor with his hands clenched before him. **1961** E. Partridge *Dictionary of Slang & Unconventional English* (ed. 5) Suppl. 1188/1: *Monkey's f*ck, not to care a,* not to care a rap; low (esp. Naval). **1968** M. Woodhouse *Rock Baby* xii. 116: I don't give a monkey's knee if he was with the Resistance or the Mafia. **1970** *Observer* (May 10) 33/5: Tony Martin has booked himself a vasectomy… "I was brought up a Catholic…but I don't give a monkey's; you've got to be practical." **1975** J. Wainwright *Square Dance* 26: "Not," snarled Sugden, "that I give a solitary monkey's toss what you wear." **1990** *Lancet* (June 2) 1313/2: In the words of one member of the underclass, [the government] "doesn't give a monkey's." **2006** S. Hill *Risk of Darkness* 161: "I don't give a monkey's fuck," Nathan said viciously, "about Frankie Nixon."

mother *noun*

(a partial euphemism for) MOTHERFUCKER (in any sense).

1935 in P. Oliver *Blues Tradition* 232: Dirty Mother For You. **1936** in M. Leadbitter & N. Slaven *Blues Records* 297: She's A Mellow Mother For You. **1944** in C. Himes *Black on Black* 209: That old mother, cotton, is gonna kill me yet. **1958** E. Gilbert *Vice Trap* 110: Jive and lush don't use together, you mother. **1960** in T.C. Bambara *Gorilla* 49:

Now this jive mother who is my boss thinks he can make some bread by recording some of the old-timers. **1961** J. Brosnan *Pennant Race* 74: Malone pulls that ball on a line and Willie is a dead mother. **1961** G. Forbes *Goodbye to Some* 82 [refers to WWII]: That mother Stevens dropped a crab in the beer. **1961** H. Ellison *Gentleman Junkie* 144: He just grabbed that muthuh by the neck and...beat the crap outta him. **1962** K. Kesey *One Flew Over the Cuckoo's Nest* 175: Drive, you puny mothers, *drive!*...Practice, you mothers, get that ball and let's get a little sweat rollin'! **1961–64** D. Barthelme *Come Back, Dr. Caligari* 142: You brought the darkness, you black mother. **1964** R. Newhafer *Last Tallyho* 182: If ever...I get out of this mother of a thunderstorm. *Ibid.* 302: There's nothing wrong with these mothers at all. **1965** J. L. Herlihy *Midnight Cowboy* 101: It's a powerful mothah, ain't it? **1967** G. Moorse *Duck May be Somebody's Mother* 139: Jeez, Doc,...you're about the smartest muther in the whole world. **1971** J. P. Sloan *War Games* 125: There sits a man who is going to go home and tell his wife a mother of a story. **1972** D. Jenkins *Semi-Tough* 188: Some wives is gonna read that mother you writin', you dig what I'm sayin'? **1972** C. Gaines *Stay Hungry* 34: He had worked [his calves] so hard he thought they would pop off, but the mothers wouldn't grow. **1973** W. Karlin et al. *Free Fire Zone* 164: I can take work!...I can work like a mother! **1976** C. R. Anderson *Grunts* 47 [refers to 1969]: You mean it's that hill over there, the bald mother? **1978** H. Selby *Requiem for a Dream* 247: Yeah, he be a cool mutha jim. **1984** G. Holland *Let a Soldier Die* 156: Deal those mothers! **1985** D. Killerman *Hellrider* 9: You muvva. **1986** B. Breathed *Bloom County* (syndicated comic strip) (Dec. 3): Just wing that mother. **1987** *N.Y. Daily News* (July 2) M3: Here comes that evil mother; we can't win now. **1988** *Living Dangerously* (A&E-TV): The river is one tough mother [to cross]. **1992** *New York Magazine* (Mar. 30) 61: He has never tried a case before, but he's a tough little mother. **1999** M. Foley *Have Nice Day* v. 73: I climbed into the front seat [of the car] and attempted to fire the mother up. Needless to say, the mother didn't fire. Neither did it flicker or even spark. It was one dead mother. **2007** *On Board* (Jan.) 48/2: This year's goggles come in a variety of different colours: check these gold mothers.

In phrases:

☞ **ham and mothers**, see *ham and motherfuckers* under MOTH-ERFUCKER.

1973 (quotation at *ham and motherfuckers* under MOTHERFUCKER). **1978** G. Hasford *Short-Timers* 86 [refers to Vietnam War]: Ham and mothers....I hate...ham and lima beans. **1990** G.R. Clark *Words of Vietnam War* 52: Ham and lima beans..."ham-and-mothers." **1996** D. Jauss *Black Maps* 27: You look like you've put on a couple of pounds since yesterday.... Maybe you had an extra helping of ham and mothers? **2004** R. E. Peavey *Praying for Slack* 251: Nobody eats ham and mothers up here.

☞ **your mother!** Especially *Juvenile.* (used as a derisive retort). [It is widely perceived that the phrase abbreviates *go fuck your mother* and is therefore especially provoking; it is also reminiscent of the "dozens," a game of ritually exchanging insults.]

[**1891** in J. F. Dobie *Rainbow in the Morning* (1965) 172: Talk about one thing, talk about another;/But ef you talk about me, I'm gwain to talk about your mother.] [**1929** E. Hemingway in *Selected Letters* 298: In a purely conversational way in a latin language in an argument one man says to another "Cogar su madre!"] **1937** C. Odets *Golden Boy* 243: [On telephone:] I'll bring him right over...you can take my word—the kid's a cock-eyed wonder...*your* mother too! **1939** in A. Dundes *Mother Wit from the Laughing Barrel* (1990) 288: An upper-class Negro woman [in a northern city] said...[that] in her high school group...a simple reference to "your ma" or "your mother" was a fighting challenge. The woman herself did not know why one had to fight when she heard this but did know that fight one must. **1953** "F. Paley" *Rumble on the Docks* 86: "Your mother!" Pooch murmured with thick lips. **1957** H. Simmons *Corner Boy* 79: Your mother, your mother. **1968** K. Hunter *Soul Brothers* 39: If a Southside boy wanted to start a fight, all he had to say...was, "Your mother—." He didn't even have to finish the sentence. The other boy would tear into him...in a blind fury. **1972** in W. King *Black Anthology* 145: "Your motha'!" she yelled. **1973** Lucas, Katz & Huyck *America Graffiti* 23: "What happened to you, flathead?" "Ah, your mother!" **1974** V. C. Strasburger *Rounding Third & Heading Home* 159: Carter turned around. "Your mother," he said to the guy who had just finished talking. **1977** E. Bunker *Animal Factory* 29: "I'm gonna bust you someday." "You'll bust your mother." "Your mother wears combat boots!" **1978** P. Schrader *Hardcore* 65: "You're thinking about your father."..."Keep him out of this or I'll break your balls." "Who?" "Your mother, smart-ass." **1985** *Cheers* (NBC-TV): Ya mother! **1999** F. McCourt *'Tis* xv. 118: Weber gives him the finger and says, Your mother, and Buck has to be stopped from attacking him by the duty sergeant who tells us all get out.

mother *adjective*

(a partial euphemism for) MOTHERFUCKING.

1958 Meltzer & Blees *High School Confidential* (film): You're the swingin'est chick in the whole mother kingdom. **1962** T. Reiter *Night in Sodom* 134: You a fool, Chollie. A rotten muvva fool. **1966–67** P. Thomas *Down These Mean Streets* 201: What a sick mudder scene! **1968** G. Vidal *Myra Breckinridge* 98: I am going to sell the whole mother score. *ca*1969 D. Rabe *Basic Training of Pavlo Hummel* 23: Jesus God Almighty I hate this mother army stickin' me in with weird people! **1970** La Motta, Carter, & Savage *Raging Bull* (film) 25: Everybody down on his knees, you mothers, down on your fuckin' mother knees! **1971** *Go Ask Alice* 102: The fuzz has clamped down till the town is mother dry. **1976** J.W. Thomas *Heavy Number* 44: Wait a mother-minute! *Ibid.* 115: I...can't use them...in the middle of the mother desert! **1988** D. Ing *Chernobyl Syndrome* 113: A big-motha' windmill, with 4-meter epoxy-coated high-aspect ratio blades and a capstan drive made from a wheelchair.

motherfather *noun*

(a partial euphemism for) MOTHER-FUCKER.

1991 Redd Foxx on *Royal Family* (CBS-TV): Oh, motherfather! **1993** S. Womack *Dead Folks' Blues* 231: What the motherfather you talking about? **2005** C. Coleman *Cage's Bend* 204: You son of a bitch. You don't care about me. You motherfather!

motherfouler *noun*

(a partial euphemism for) MOTHER-FUCKER.

1947–52 R. Ellison *Invisible Man* 422: Coolcrack the motherfouler! **1962** L. Hughes *Tambourines to Glory* 238: Sister Laura's going to crack-up and all over Buddy Lomax—who everybody knows is a motherfouler.

motherfuck *noun*

1. = MOTHERFUCKER, *noun*, sense 1.a., 1.b.

1964 R. Gover *Here Goes Kitten* 110: I hop back in bed beside this great big mountain of a mothahfug, an I get down t'bizness. **1967** N. Mailer *Why We Are in Vietnam* 54: Don't come near, motherfuck. **1970** E. E. Landy *Underground Dictionary* 135: *Mother fuck,* greeting to another person. It has a positive connotation... Negative connotation when used in anger to express hostility—e.g. *You mother fuck!* **1972** *N.Y.U. Cold Duck* (Apr. 17): Fuck you, motherfuck, you're trying to censor my work! **1978** P. Schrader *Hardcore* 99: You muthafuck! **1986** D. Tate *Bravo Burning* 96: Hey, motherfucks, you don't have to treat him like that. *a***1990** E. Currie *Dope & Trouble* 14: She a grown motherfuck. **2000** T. A. Kessler *D-Girl* in *Sopranos* ((TV shooting script) 2nd Ser.) 42: You miserable motherfuck, I'm the kid's [confirmation] sponsor!

2. a thing or state of affairs, esp. if hateful or infuriating; = MOTH-ERFUCKER, *noun*, sense 2.a., 2.b.

1967 N. Mailer *Why Are We in Vietnam?* 82: How'd you get this motherfuck? **1982** J. M. Del Vecchio *13th Valley* 271: How they gonna get a bird inta the middle a dis mothafuck?

3.a. a damn.

1967 "Iceberg Slim" *Pimp* 277: I wouldn't give a mother-fuck. **1970** in B. Jackson *Get Your Ass in the Water & Swim Like Me* 232: This is my friend,/this is my kin,/I don't give a motherfuck/if he don't come in. **1972** W. Pelfrey *Big V* 106: And I don't *give* a motherfuck. **1984** S. P. Smith *American Boys* 147: Tell 'em I'm like Donald Duck—got web feet and don't give a motherfuck! **1992** S. Frazier *I Married Vietnam* 94: You ever do that again motherfucker I'll kill you. I don't give a motherfuck if you got one day and a wakeup. **2006** R. Shydner & M. Schiff *I Killed* 49: We're not leaving until we get our motherfucking money. I don't give a motherfuck.

b. (used as an emphatic expletive); hell; FUCK.—used with *the*.

1975 N. De Mille *Smack Man* 70: How the motherfuck do a pimp's girl get jealous, man? **1973–76** J. Allen *Assault* 188: You better get the mother-fuck out of my place. **1982** J. M. Del Vecchio *13th Valley* 309: Where the motherfuck is the C-4? **1986** T. Philbin *Under Cover* 120: Who the motherfuck are you? **1988** J. Norst *Colors* 22: What the motherfuck was that you just did. **1994** S. Hunter *Dirty White Boys* 150: You got nothing but a staff of assholes what hates their goddamned jobs and ain't about to die for no Denny, whosoever the motherfuck he may be. **2006** J. Burke *On the Road to Kandahar* 143: I'm on fucking patrol.... Why do you think I am wearing my body armor, motherfucker? For the motherfucking fun? So shut the motherfuck up.

motherfuck *adverb*

(used for emphasis); = MOTHERFUCKING.

1970 E. Sanders in Padgett & Shapiro *New York Poets* 386: And don't you motherfuck forget it!!! **1971** S. Stevens *Way Uptown in Another World* 54: The motherfuck whites don't never look close enough at a black man to tell how old he is.

motherfuck *verb*

1. (used to express rejection, dismissal, hatred, etc.); God damn; FUCK, *verb*, definition 4a; curse; to hell with.

1942 in W. N. Hess *B-17* 32: [Inscription on U.S. bomber, with picture of Japanese Prime Minister Hideki Tojo receiving an obscene gesture:] MFU-TU [*i.e.* mother fuck you too]. **1965** in *Social Problems* XIII 351: Mother Fuck the Police! **1969** *Black Panther* (Oakland, Calif.): Well, motherfuck the police. **1972** B. Davidson *Cut Off* 29 [refers to 1944]: Mother-fuck this fuckin' war. **1968–73** M. Agar *Ripping & Running* 137: Aw man, motherfuck it. **1975** S.P. Smith *American Boys* 37: "Three tears in the bucket," he yelled. "They don't flow, mother fuck it!" **1977** E. Torres *Q & A* 16: Motha fuck you, ain't tellin' you shit. Who the hell're *you!* **1989** C. Ridenhour et al, *Fight the Power* (song, perf. "Public Enemy") in L. A. Stanley *Rap: the Lyrics* (1992) 259: Straight up racist that sucker was simple and plain/Motherfuck him [*sc.* Elvis] and John Wayne/'Cause I'm black and I'm proud. **1994** J. Berendt *Midnight in the Garden of Good and Evil* 114: If I offended anyone, two tears in a bucket, honey. Motherfuck it. **2000** J. Womack *Going, Going, Gone* 23: Half the room turned to look, and then the same half of the room turned deaf mute. "Motherfuck you," she broadcast.

2. to destroy, confuse, FUCK UP; to treat with hostility, insult.

1975 in *Urban Life* IV (1976) 489: We'll motherfuck the bastard's mind! **1990** L. Rooke *Good Baby* 136: That bitch who tried to motherfuck and hogtie me. **1991** *Vanity Fair* Aug. 169/1: I don't know if he was "motherfucking" them—if he was still being verbally aggressive. **2000** R. Barger et al. *Hell's Angel* vii. 128: We motherfucked them for a while until they finally gave up and drove away. **2007** J. R. Daniels *Mr. Pleasant* 3: I could read her lips. She was motherfucking me to her little brother.

motherfuck *interjection*

(used to express astonishment, anger, etc.).

1970 W. C. Woods *Killing Zone* 143: Mother*fuck*—what happened to you? **1976** R. Price *Bloodbrothers* 20: Mother-*fuck!* **1979** B. Gutcheon *New Girls* 249: Motherfuck, guess who that is? **1998** *GQ* (Nov.) 172: He spins around, kicks the ground, stares down the offending patch of wood. "Mother*fuck*," he mutters. **1998** J. Manos Jr. & D. Chase *College* in *Sopranos* ((television shooting script) 1st Ser.) 12: Chris's car jerks to a stop. Jacket over his head, Chris runs to a pay phone, jams his body under the shell, inserts quarters while rain pelts his back. *Christopher.* Mothefuck. **2005** "Noire" *Candy Licker* xxvi. 279: "Motherfuck!" Hurricane cursed.

motherfucker *noun*

1.a. a despicable or contemptible person. [The 1928, 1935, 1939, and 1946 quotations are euphemistic.]

1918 *Letter* in *Journal of American History* (1995) LXXXI 1585: You low-down Mother Fuckers can put a gun in our hands but who is able to take it out? [**1918** in H. De Witt *Bawdy Barrack-Room Ballads*: The little red runt he grew and grew/****ed his mother and sister too.] **1928** C. McKay *Banjo* 229: I've been made a fool of by many a skirt, but it's the first time a mother-plugger done got me like this. **1935** G.W. Henderson *Ollie Miss* 82: The man from Swanson had passed the ugly word then, and the Hannon boy had flung it back... neatly compounded, with the word "mother" preceding it. The Swanson boy... whipped out his razor. *ca*1935 in G. Logsdon *Whorehouse Bells were Ringing* 95: Motherfucker, I'll slice off your prick. **1935** in P. Oliver *Blues Tradition* 232: He's a dirty mother fuyer, he don't mean no good. [**1936** A. W. Little *From Harlem to the Rhine* 5 [refers to 1917]: And so I saiz ter him, Cap'n Suh, "Ever-ting you saiz

Ah am—yoo is double—even de part against yoo mudder....Ef yoo saiz anyt'ing mo' ter me Ah'll cut yoo heart out."] **1938** *"Justinian" Americana Sexualis* 29: *Mother-Fucker.* n. An incestuous male. The most intense term of opprobrium among the U.S. lower classes. Probable Sicilian origin. C. 20. Urban communities only. No sexual connotation; used merely as an epithet. **1939** in A. Banks *First-Person* 255: Why you poor Brooklyn motherfrigger, I'll wreck this goddamn place with you. **1946** M. Mezzrow & B. Wolfe *Really the Blues* 14: A motherferyet that would cut your throat for looking. **1946** J. Del Torto *Graffiti Transcript* (Kinsey Institute): Susie is a mother fucker. **1948** N. Mailer *Naked & Dead* 152: I was gonna shoot the mother-fugger but you were in the way. **1950** *Commentary* X 62: When asked what his chief duties were in a Negro settlement house for boys, a social worker answered, "Teaching them euphemisms for mother— (unprintable word)." **1954** R. Lindner *50-Minute Hour* 152 [refers to *ca*1938]: During my years in prison work I had observed that one expletive, that referring to intercourse between son and mother (m-f), was at once the most dangerous and the most frequent on the lips of the psychopath. I had actually seen men killed for using it. **1954** in D. Wepman et al. *The Life* (1976) 110: Cocksuckers by the dozens, motherfuckers and their cousins. **1956** in P. Oliver *Blues Tradition* 240: Your mama...she's a runnin' motherfucker, cheap cocksucker. **1957** H. Simmons *Corner Boy* 79: Kill that mother fug— . **1958** *Stack A Lee* (typescript, Kinsey Institute) 1: I'm that bad motherfucker they call Stack A Lee. **1958** E. Gilbert *Vice Trap* 44: "You mother—" she said to me, crying. **1959** W. Burroughs *Naked Lunch* 40: I'll cut your throat you white mother fucker. **1962** J. O. Killens *Then We Heard the Thunder* 284: Every time I walk up the company street I hear somebody calling somebody else a mother-fucker or a sonofabitch. **1963–64** K. Kesey *Sometimes a Great Notion* 71: My brother is a motherfucker. **1965** C. Brown *Manchild in the Promised Land* 137: Don't explain yourself to that mother-tucker. **1965** R. E. Conot *Rivers of Blood, Years of Darkness* 222: Even the word *motherfucker* takes on different connotation. For the white it is the image of incest; for the Negro it is the picture of a white man lying with a black woman who is his, the Negro's, mother. **1968** A. Montagu *Letter to P. Tamony* (June 24): Mr. Donald C. Greason has written to me that he heard the epithet [*motherfucker*] often from a friend of his at the front during late 1917. **1968** H. Van Dyke *Blood of Strawberries* 177: If you even touch it, motherfucker, you die. **1968** R. Gover *JC* 34: Sonny you nacheral sack a twenty diffrent mothalıfuggahs. **1971** O. Guffy & C. Ledner *Ossie* 46 [refers to *ca*1940]: "You're a motherfucker." "Your mama's one." **1974**

V. E. Smith *Jones Men* 18: Look at that bitch. Nasty motherfucker. **1992** T. Hosansky & P. Sparling *Working Vice* 197: People called her motherfucker...[and] bitch. **1995** *Jerry Springer Show* (syndicated TV series): Come on, motherf-cker! [vowel bleeped out].

b. Especially *Black English & Military*. (in positive contexts) a fellow; person; an admirable person; (*often*) a formidable person.

1958 *Stack A Lee* (typescript, Kinsey Institute) 1: He...said who put the hole in this motherfucker's head?/Who could the murderer of this poor man be? **1964** R. D. Abrahams *Deep down in Jungle* (Appendix II) 261: One of the best things which can be said of a man is that he is a "mean motherfucker" or a "tough motherfucker," but to call him just a "motherfucker" is to invite reprisal. **1970** E. E. Landy *Underground Dictionary* 135: *Mother fucker*...Positive, complimentary name for a friend—e.g., *Hey, mother fucker, what's happening?* **1971** in S. D. Horwitt *Let Them Call Me Rebel* 4 [refers to 1930s]: Pretty soon word of the incident spread throughout the gang. "That Alinsky, he's an all-right motherfucker," the kids would say, and... they began to trust me. **1971** J. Cheever in *Letters* (1988) 284: A puertorican drug-pusher...exclaimed: "Oh what a cool motherfucker was that Machiavelli." **1972** in W. King *Black Anthology* 101: Joe was a motherfucker. A revolutionary motherfucker. A black man made of steel iron. **1973** J.R. Coleman *Blue-Collar* 62: A word like "motherfucker" here is often just a synonym for man, no more and no less. ("Who's that new motherfucker over there?" or "I told the motherfucker we'd pick up him and his bitch at eight.") **1973** L. Bangs *Canned Heat* in *Mainlines, Blood Feasts, Bad Taste* (2003) 37: Vestine was an incredible, scorching motherfucker of a guitarist, knocking you through the wall. **1973** R. Roth *Sand in Wind* 154: Hey, motherfuckers, look at this. *Ibid.* 438: I've met some of the best motherfuckers I've ever known in the [Marine Corps]. **1972–74** H. Hawes & D. Asher *Raise Up off Me* 3 [refers to 1930s]: Anybody who *looked* good was automatically a motherfucker. *Ibid.* 98: We...talked about Debussy and Bach and what bad motherfuckers those cats were hundreds of years ago. **1974** L. A. Lacy *Native Daughter* 108: Fine...nice legs... tall...would be a motherfucker if she didn't talk so much. **1974** V.E. Smith *Jones Men* 156: I'm just as cool as the next motherfucker. **1977** L. Jordan *Hype* 44: "C'mere, you little motherfucker," he said tenderly, reaching for her. **1978** B. Johnson *What's Happenin'?* 57: Once I figured out that a "bad mother-fucker"was an all-right dude,I at least had a shot at communicating. **1978** W. Strieber *Wolfen* 127: You the scaredest motherfucker I've seen in a good long while. *a*1983 J. Baugh *Black Street Speech* 24: See, like if a brother gets on my case I can tell blood, "Hey motherfucker, you can kiss my ass," and the brother can...take it in stride—cause he know where I'm comin from. But you can't be tellin no white dude that. **1987** D. Sherman *Main Force* 96 [refers to 1966]: "That bad out there, huh?" "Worse, except we're the baddest mother-fuckers in the valley." **1984–88** D. Hackworth & J. Sherman *About Face* 510 [refers to Vietnam War]: In the Airborne, the term "motherfucker," unless spoken harshly, was among the highest terms of endearment. **1993** *Face* (Sept.) 141/1: Ice-T recorded an as yet unreleased version of Sly Stone's "Don't Call Me Nigger Whitey" with Perry Farell, who he calls "the ultimate cool motherfucker." **2003** A. Swofford *Jarhead* 25: He's an all right motherfucker.... He's all right for a reporter.

2.a. an infuriating, hateful, or oppressive thing, difficult task, etc.; (*broadly*) a thing.

1948 N. Mailer *Naked & Dead* 345: You know what the motherfugger'll be like?...We'll be lucky to get out of there with our goddam heads on. **1960** J. Peacock *Valhalla* ch. iv: "I'll get the motherfuckers [beer cans]," Dallas offered. **1962** B. Jackson *In the Life* 156: Oh, life's a motherfucker, Bruce. **1962** T. Berger *Reinhart* 386: Let me run that big motherfu—. **1967–68** N. von Hoffman *We Are the People Our Parents Warned Us Against* 98: The street is a rough motherfucker. **1969** *Playboy* (Dec.) 290: Let's burn this motherfucker down. **1973** E. Jong *Fear of Flying* 4: So I keep concentrating very hard, helping the pilot...fly the 250-passenger motherfucker. **1974** D. Goines *Daddy Cool* ix. 115: Damn, baby...whose goddamn poolroom is this anyway? To listen to him talk, you'd think he owned the motherfucker! **1975** N. De Mille *Smack Man* 108: What a motherfucker that's going to be, given the rules of evidence in this state. **1978** S. King *Stand* 84: Eight milkshakes (why...had he bought eight of the mother-fuckers?) **1981** L. Heinemann in *Harper's* (Aug.) 58: The whole company... caught some mean kind of shit and every swinging dick *but* him bought the motherfucker. **1981** *National Lampoon* (July) 16: Being 7'4" is a motherfucker. **1981** *Penthouse* (Mar.) 174: Heroin is...an insidious motherfucker. **1982** B. Downey *Uncle Sam Must be Losing the War* 23 [refers to WWII]: Some of them... cussed their native state for being a "prejudiced motherfucker." **1991** J. Lamar *Bourgeois*

Blues 32: I knew how to make those motherfuckers gleam. **1993** K. Scott *Monster* 163: The threat of being in prison for life was a muthafucka. **2005** "Noire" *Candy Licker* xxiii. 241: He tossed me a pair of sunglasses.... "Put these motherfuckers on and make sure you don't take 'em off."

b. an infuriating or surprising situation or state of affairs.

1968 in B. Edelman *Dear America* 81: Sometimes it gets pretty hairy in this motherfucker. **1970** E. E. Landy *Underground Dictionary* 135: *Mother fucker*... Hard-to-solve problem; rough situation. **1976** R. E. Chinn *Dig the Nigger Up* 61: Now ain't this a muthafucker! **1981** W. T. Hathaway *World of Hurt* 14: This is the dumbest motherfucker I ever been in. **1987** J. Ferrandino *Firefight* 98: I don't want to die in this miserable mother-fucker. **1989** Z. Chafets *Devil's Night* 44: We'll probably never solve the motherfucker. **1989** S. Robinson & D. Ritz *Smokey* 78: We're going to remember this motherfucker...'cause I don't intend to let it happen again. **1994** T. Woods *True to Game* xiii. 152: Where's Bridgette, 'cause she could get her ass kicked next up in this motherfucker.

c. an impressive or outstanding thing; humdinger.

1977 *National Lampoon* (Aug.) 33: Have I got a motherfucker of a stunt for you! **1981** C. M. Brown in *Black Scholar* (Sept./Oct.) 8/2: They got some skies in Africa that are a motherfucker, man! **2001** *Village Voice* (May 22) 124/1: The Berkeley quartet opened its set jamming and vamp-ing... From then on it was a motherfucker; nothing like the current wave of junior Black Sabbaths and Blue Cheers trudging through the low end.

3. (used as an indefinite standard of comparison).

1962 in D. Wepman et al. *The Life* (1976) 139: I just come back....Mad as a motherfucker. **1962** V. Riccio & B. Slocum *All the Way Down* 149: Something new has been added...the letters LAMF under a personal name or a gang name....It means "Like A Mother Fucker," and it's sup-posed to suggest to all who read it that the person or the gang...is rough and tough and hell-bent for war or what may come. **1966–67** P. Thomas *Down These Mean Streets* 160: He went limper'n a motherfucker. **1973** J. E. Wideman *Lynchers* 39: It be dark as a muthafucka. **1975** S.P. Smith *American Boys* 100: LaMont was [running] like fifty motherfuckers. **1976** R. Telander *Heaven is Playground* (1995) 170: Who wants to go to college?.... Where's the talent? A strong finish. I'm losing my voice. The phone never stops ringing, coaches, high schools, prep schools, colleges. I'm closing like a motherfucker!' **1990** E. W. Rukuza *West Coast Turnaround* 39: It was raining like six motherfuckers. **1991** J. Singleton *Boyz N the Hood* (film): This fool got more comics than a motherfucker.

In phrases:

☞ **beans and motherfuckers**, *Military.* a C-ration portion of lima beans and ham.

1980 M. Baker *Nam* 11: I'm not going to say he had cold beans and motherfuckers for breakfast. *Ibid.* 320: Beans and motherfuckers—C-ration delicacy composed of lima beans and ham. **1990** G.R. Clark *Words of Vietnam War* 52: Beans-and-Motherfuckers (Ham and Lima Beans). **1991** L. Reinberg *In the Field*: Beans and motherfuckers, slang for unpopular C-ration lima beans and ham. **2004** C. Burke *Camp All-American* 111: Soldiers in Vietnam complained about the food they were served: the "beans and baby dicks" (beans and franks), the "beans and motherfuckers" (lima beans and ham). **2004** L. Reardon *Mercy Killers* 86: He eats that nasty beans and motherfuckers like it's steak and eggs.

☞ **bends and motherfuckers**, *Military.* calisthenic squats and thrusts.

1980 M. Baker *Nam* 39 [refers to *ca*1970]: You look like shit, so we're going to do a little PT now. Bends and motherfuckers. Many, many, many of them. *Ibid.* 320: Bends and motherfuckers: the squat-thrust exercise. **1990** G.R. Clark *Words of Vietnam War* 55: Bends-and-Motherfuckers...squat-thrust exercises. *ca*2000 J. DiFusco et al. *Tracers* (rev. ed) 56: Bends and motherfuckers—cadence count—one hundred repetitions. Ready. Exercise. *(The five begin doing squat thrusts, counting off.)*

☞ **ham and motherfuckers**, *Military.* a C-ration portion of canned ham and lima beans.

1973 McA. Layne *How Audie Murphy Died in Vietnam* (unpaged): Packaged into the 1942 C-ration case....Ham & little muther fahckers,/Affectionately called,/Ham/&/Mutha's. **1980** J. DiFusco et al. *Tracers* 41 [refers to Vietnam War]: I haven't got anything left except some ham and motherfuckers, man. **1982** E. Leonard *Cat Chaser* 76: Ham and lima beans: ham and motherfuckers. **1987** "J. Hawkins" *Tunnel Warriors* 332 [refers to Vietnam War]: *Ham & Motherfuckers.* C-rations serving of ham and lima beans. **1988** M. Clodfelter *Mad Minutes* 258 [refers to 1966]: Cans of "ham and mother fuckers" (ham and lima beans). *a*1989 C.S. Crawford *Four Deuces* 107 [refers to Korean War]: Ham and lima beans... was considered to be one of the good rations even though we called them "ham and motherfuckers." **1990** E. M. Helms *Proud Bastards* 125: I think I've got a sudden craving for ham and motherfuckers. **2008** J. C. McManus *7th Infanry Regiment* 70: Ham and lima beans (always referred to as "ham and motherfuckers").

motherfucker *interjection*
(used to express astonishment, anger, etc.).

1968 *Nation* (Dec. 2) 595: I said how come you din' sing the National Anthem?...Motherfucker!...You a bunch of jive motherfuckers. **1974** L.D. Miller *Valiant* 21 [refers to WWII]: Mudderfucker!... I'm hit! **1985** D. Bodey *F.N.G.* 144: Muthafucker, *can this be?* **1988** J. Norst *Colors* x. 138: But the pain only incensed Hightop, rejuvenated his awesome wired strength. Motherfucker! Motherfucker! **2008** J. Picoult *Change of Heart* 56: Calloway sank down to the floor of his cell, cradling the dead bird. "Motherfucker. Mother*fucker.*"

motherfucking *interjection & infix*
(used for emphasis). [The 1962–63 quotation is euphemistic.]

1962–63 K. Kesey *Sometimes a Great Notion* 7: How do you expect *any-motherkilling-one* to know Hank Stamper's reasons? **1967** G. Ragni & J. Rado *Hair* 154: Yeah! Emanci-motherfuckin'-pator of the slave. **1977** E. Torres *Q & A* 54: Motherfuckin'-A right. **1987** J. Ferrandino *Firefight* 124: Just hats up and dismotherfuckinappears. **1999** D. Century *Street Kingdom* ii. 77: I'm gettin' ready to go up north my-muthafuckin'-self!

motherfucking *adjective & adverb*
1. goddamned; FUCKING.

1889 *Texas Court of Appeals Report* (1890) XXVIII 206: According to Sumner, he spoke of defendant as "that God damned lying, thieving son-of-a-bitch";...and according to McKinney, as "that God damned mother-f—cking, bastardly son-of-a-bitch!" **1898** *Texas Criminal Reports* XXXVII 22: You are instructed, that if prior to the shooting of deceased by defendant, the deceased called the defendant a "mother-fucking son-of-a-bitch," and the defendant...shot and killed the deceased, then you are instructed, in such a case, the defendant could not be guilty of a higher offense than manslaughter, if guilty of anything. **1933** J. O'Hara *Appointment in Samarra* 154: Why, you small-time chiseling bastard, you. You dirty mother— bastard. [**1933** J. Conroy *Disinherited* 30: Scab! Scab! O, you bloody mother-killin'bastards! O, you lowdown sons of bitches!] **1936** M. Levin *Old Bunch* 122: Listen, you mother-f— little runt, if you don't—. **1948** N. Mailer *Naked & Dead* 12: Of all the mother-fuggin luck, that sonofabitch takes it all. *Ibid*, 400: That's the mother-fuggin' truth. [**1948** W. Manone & P. Vandervoort *Trumpet on the Wing* 131: If I hurt your beat-out feelings, I beg your mother-robbin' pardon.] **1951** J. Jones *Face of War* 62: Mother fuggin' bastards. **1951** J. Kerouac *Visions of Cody* 119: I read every WORD of that motherfuckin thing. **1953–55** MacK. Kantor *Andersonville* 524: Mother-fucking old Yankee mudsills. [**1957** T.H. White *Mountain Road* 21: The next guy doesn't know a mother-frigging thing about it.] **1958** T. Berger *Crazy in Berlin* 168 [refers to WWII]: A Southerner or a Negro, passing on the sidewalk out front, described to a mute companion a succession of events that were invariably *mothafuhn*. **1961** in C. Himes *Black on Black* 69: I'll cut your motherfucking throat. **1961** G. Forbes *Goodbye to Some* 128 [refers to WWII]: You ain't home with you mother-fuckin' mother! [**1963–64** K. Kesey *Sometimes a Great Notion* 7: The whole motherkilling agreement.] **1965** S. Linakis *In Spring the War Ended* 75: He's a mother-fuckin' liar. **1962–65** R. Giallombardo *Society of Women* 49: She said..."I'm not showing you a mother—' thing." **1965** C. Brown *Manchild in the Promised Land* 140: I'm gon bust your motherfuckin' ass. **1966–67** P. Thomas *Down These Mean Streets* 129: They don't come no motherfuckin' better. **1967** W. Crawford *Gresham's War* 161: You motherhunching son of a hounddog whore. **1967** W. Stevens *Gunner* 231: It was that motherfucking *Ploesti* that reached up and tore his ass apart. **1964–69** in S. Calt *Rather Be Devil* 57 [refers to *ca*1919]: The guys...wouldn't say: "Pass me such and such a thing, if they wanted a big pan of meat or biscuits or rice....They said, "Let such-and-such a thing *walk* up that motherfuckin' table." **1970** J. Neary *Julian Bond: Black Rebel* 174: Mayor Richard J. Daley yelled "Get that motherfucking Jew out of here!" at United States Senator Abraham Ribicoff of Connecticut. **1977** T. Jones *Incredible Voyage* 284: But you tell that mother-fucking chief, Manco Quispe, I want a clan meeting right now. **1986** P. Welsh *Tales Out of School* 64: [The pupils] lapse into street dialect, saying "be" for "are," "mines" for "mine" and of course the ubiquitous adjective "mother-f—." **1989** S. Robinson & D. Ritz *Smokey* 42: This is my motherfucking house and I'm gonna live here and no one's gonna stop me. **1993** *New Yorker* (Feb. 8) 35: Motherfucking cockroach. **1993** J. Mowry *Six out Seven* ii. i. 272: It cause of what Bates say to you! That...that bullshit! That cocksuckin motherfuckin liar!

2. (used to emphasize the positive qualities of a following noun).

1954 in D. Wepman et al. *The Life* (1976) 42: I love him madly, he's my motherfucking man. **1961** R. Gover *$100 Misunderstanding* 95: Tee vee man talkin up a mothahfuggin storm! **1973** J. Flaherty *Fogarty & Co.* 157: What a motherfucking man he was, Shamus! **1978** R. Andrews *Appalachee Red* (1987) 254: From Carolina to Alabama to Mississippi back to Alabama to here, home sweet motherfucking home! *a*1990 in M. Costello & D. F. Wallace *Signifying Rappers* 79: I shoulda kicked your ass/My-motherfuckin-self. **1991** C. E. Faupel *Shooting Dope* 75: Hey man, let's go get us some good motherfucking dope. **2000** *Village Voice* (Jan. 18)107/2: Damn girl! Look at that motherfucking ass! Whatup baby! You see that ass on her? Talk about stopping traffic. **2003** "Zoe Trope" *Please Don't Kill the Freshman* 76: My beautiful fantastic motherfucking cocksucking brilliant queer.

mothergrabber *noun*

(a partial euphemism for) MOTHERFUCKER.

1963 in J. Blake *Joint* 357: You set me up, mother-grabber. **1966** I. Reed *Pall-Bearers* 34: Goofy mother-grabber! **1968** H. Sackler *Great White Hope* I. 46: Ellie. (*With Negro inflection.*) You slimy two-bit no-dick mothergrabber. **1994** A. D. Foster in *Impossible Places* (2002) 101: You lazy good-for-nuthin' orbitin' mothergrabber!

mother-grabbing *adjective*

(a partial euphemism for) MOTHERFUCKING.

1953–58 J. C. Holmes *Horn* 68: Those mother-grabbin' *slacks*…were full of *seeds!* 1961 J. Jones *Thin Red Line* 60: He's a jerkoff. A goddam mother-grabbing jerkoff. 1961 T. Williams *Night of the Iguana* in *Three by Tennessee* (1976) 95: Oh, my God, the money. They haven't paid the mother-grabbin' bill. 1962 R. Serling *New Stories* 67: Are you out of your mothergrabbing mind? 1971 *Playboy* (Mar.) 92: "Out of your mother-grabbing mind," Joanne said. 1990 M. Newton *Blood Sport* 134: "Life's hard," Flynn said. "Ain't that the mother-grabbin' truth?"

motherhumper *noun*

(a partial euphemism for) MOTHERFUCKER.

[1959 A. Anderson *Lover Man* 52: There's a *bad* mother-hubber/ Down the road a way.] 1963 T. Doulis *Path for our Valor* 81: Death, I think, you mother-humper. 1967 D. Ford *Incident at Muc Wa* 133: "C'mon, you mother-humpers!" Ski yelled at his Raiders. 1970 J. Grissim *Country Music* 281: Anybody that can follow me is a motha-humper. And they ain't many that can do it.…I'm a violent motha-humper today. Don't nobody fool with me or *I'll kill!* 1972 *National Lampoon* (Sept.) 6: There are fourteen *fuck you's*, nine *cocksucker's*, and six *motherhumper's* left over. 1986 J. C. Stinson & J. Carabatsos *Heartbreak Ridge* 77: Let's smoke this motherhumper's ass. 2000 L. Brown *Fay* 423: He was toting one motherhumper of a buzz. 2001 J. Ellroy *Cold Six Thousand* lxxiv. 395: By my lights, he's a mean motherhumper. Probably gargles with antifreeze and flosses with razor blades. 2006 *Men's Health* (July/Aug.) 118/1: "I'll mess him up so bad he'll have to eat through a straw!…I'll sue the motherhumper!" says the chairman, although maybe not with those exact words.

mother-humping *adjective*

(a partial euphemism for) MOTHERFUCKING.

1949 D. Alman *World Full of Strangers* 54: I'll fatigue you, you mother-humpin' little bastard! 1961 R. Gover *$100 Misunderstanding* 19: He kin hardly git his mothahhumpin hands roun that wad! 1963 T. Doulis *Path for our Valor* 80: Why, that no-good, sneaky, mother-humpin' rebel. 1964 H. Rhodes *Chosen Few* 99 [refers to *ca*1950]: That mother humpin' fuckoff wanted *satisfaction!* 1964 in R. Gover *Trilogy* 215: Right inta this mothahhumpin lounge. 1968 W. Crawford *Gresham's War* 197: Motherhumping cowards. **1969** C. Brown *Life & Loves of Mr. Jiveass Nigger* 20: Like, it's none of their motherhumping business, right? **1970** D. Quammen *To Walk the Line* 86: I thought we been fittin' to make it to a gray jam, not do a suicide mission with some mother-humping cage-case. **1986** J. C. Stinson & J. Carabatsos *Heartbreak Ridge* 163: Friggin' motherhumpin' Highway. **1990** J. E. Wideman *Philadelphia Fire* 122: This mother-humping play can't end no oder way. **1998** B. Bova *Moonwar* 391: We got a damned good chance of still being out here and getting fried to a crisp by the mother-humpin' nuke. **2000** P. Kerr *Mañana Mañana* (2003) 114: "Mother-humpin' faggot!" a raucous voice behind me shouted out.

mothering *adjective & adverb*

(a partial euphemism for) MOTHERFUCKING.

1951 J. Blake *Letter* (June 21) in *Joint* (1972) 21: He said if the motherin' screw ever caught up to us, he'd wish he hadn't. **1956** N. Algren *A Walk on the Wild Side* 160: His whole life he ain't worked one single mothering day! **1957** E. Brown *Locust Fire* 95 [refers to 1944]: No more mothering flying. Well, hucklety buck. I don't give a one. **1959** W. Miller *Cool World* 15: Why shitman them Colts is the same motheren piece they was usen at Cussers Last Stan. *Ibid.* 37: Them headbreakers. Motheren headbreakers. **1959** in H. Ellison *Sex Misspelled* 103: You try my mutherin' patience. **1961** R. Russell *Sound* 31: You're too motherin' much, man. **1962** V. Riccio & B. Slocum *All the Way Down* 43: We'll show these mothern bastards. **1963–64** K. Kesey *Sometimes a Great Notion* 210: I feel…pretty motherin' good. **1965** P. Matthiessen *At Play in the Fields of the Lord* 37: Them poor mothering Indians. **1966–67** W. Stevens *Gunner* 56: They got some motherin big idea. **1968** *Saturday Evening Post* (Sept. 16) 27: I hope you have four motherin' flat tires. *ca***1969** D. Rabe *Basic Training of Pavlo Hummel* 26: You ain't no motherin' exception to that whistle! **1975** *Black World* (June) 75: Not that motherin day. **1994** J. Barth *Once upon Time* 100: We are one hundred percent spent, but we seem actually to have weathered this mothering storm. **2005** J. MacGregor *Sunday Money* xii. 310: But then the misery index was high all the way around this weekend, hot and humid as gumbo…. On Sunday six cars with Hendrick engines blew up in that mothering funk.

mother-jumper *noun*

(a partial euphemism for) MOTHERFUCKER.

1949 H. Ellson *Tomboy* 5: It was that no good mother-jumper that owns the store. **1952** H. Ellson *Golden Spike* 22: What mother-jumpers you been listening to? *Ibid.* 40: Let's kill that mother-jumper! **1955** H. Ellson *Rock* 121: I hit for the candy store then, mad as a mother-jumper. **1957** L. Margulies *Young Punks* 43: But this motherjumper is a white stud. **1963–64** K. Kesey *Sometimes a Great Notion* 334: I thought…the mother-jumper wasn't even gonna. **1965** A. Borowik *Lions 3, Christians 0* 155: Yessir, you motherjumper, you'll be laughing outa the other side of your mouth when the cops come for you. **1966** R. Fariña *Been Down So Long* 120: You old benevolent motherjumper, I love you! [**1966–67** P. Thomas *Down These Mean Streets* 91: I hate all you white motherjumps.] **1970** W. C. Woods *Killing Zone* 88: He used to be a sad mother jumper. **1977** J. Wylie *Homestead Grays* 242: He was as quick as a motherjumper. **1977** M. Butler & D. Shryack *Gauntlet* 130: All right, you mother-jumpers. **1988** R. McKnight *Moustapha's Eclipse* 15: I really don't believe this motherjumper works. **2003** D. Hamill *Sins of Two Fathers* 358: I'll kill him…. I'm washing dishes for a mother jumper who knocked up my kid sister! I'll kill him!

mother-jumping *adjective*

(a partial euphemism for) MOTHERFUCKING.

   1942 K. Fearing *Clark Gifford's Body* 215: You mother-jumping cockroach, I'll cut the heart out of your breast and eat it with my bare hands. **1952** H. Ellson *Golden Spike* 19: You mother-jumping thief! **1961** R. Gover *$100 Misunderstanding* 35: He sit up like a mothah jumpin jack-in-a-box. **1962** P. Crump *Burn, Killer, Burn* 163: You're a mother-jumping coward. **1963–64** K. Kesey *Sometimes a Great Notion* 209: And good motherjumpin' riddance. **1969** in E. G. Romm *Open Conspiracy* 138: Fucking sonofabitch Fascist mother jumping cops! **1980** F. McDowell *To Keep Our Honor Clean* 156: Sanders, you seem to think you're running this mother-jumping platoon, only it's about time you learned differently. **1983** M. S. Bell *Washington Square Ensemble* 155: The dealer calls me a motherjumping guinea. **1992** B. Gifford *Night People* 96: That wife of his made him too mother-jumpin' *certain*, and that's no good. **2001** R. Green & M. Burgess *To Save Us All from Satan's Power* in *Sopranos* (HBO-TV) (Apr. 29): It's a great mother-jumping lyric, Jan.

motherlover *noun*

(a partial euphemism for) MOTHERFUCKER.

1950 L. Brown *Iron City* 69: And as for *that* mother-lover—. **1954** E. Hunter *Runaway Black* 18: You broke the mother-lover. **1955** R. Graziano & R. Barber *Somebody Up There Likes Me* 215: "Stand straight, you little mother-lover," he says. **1963** L. Cameron *Black Camp* 63 [refers to WWII]: On your *feet*, motherlover! **1996** G. Phillips *Perdition, U.S.A.* 75: All you motherlovers drop to the ground on your knees. Now. **2001** M. Azerrad *Our Band Could be Your Life* xii. 445: Mudhoney are geeky motherlovers, all matchstick arms and legs and horn-rimmed glasses and small bottoms and boyish fun.

motherloving *adjective*

(a partial euphemism for) MOTHERFUCKING.

1951 "W. Williams" *Enemy* 149: Oh, those foggers. Those mother-loving foggers. **1954** B. Schulberg *On the Waterfront* 308: You're a cheap, lousy, dirty, stinkin', mother-lovin' bastard. **1955** J. Klaas *Maybe I'm Dead* 36: The dirty mother-loving bastards. **1955** "E. Hunter" *Jungle Kids* 103: He didn't get out of that mother-lovin' cellar. **1957** Laurents & Sondheim *West Side Story* 145: On the whole! Ever—! Mother—! Lovin'—! Street! **1959** G. Morrill *Dark Sea Running* 88: Don't be so mother-lovin' nosy. **1962** J. O. Killens *Then We Heard the Thunder* 16: That's a smooth mother-loving curve you throwing. **1968** J. D. Spooner *Three Cheers for War in General* 53: We got ourselves a mother lovin' home. **1972** *N.Y. Times* (Feb. 6) 19: His one indulgence: a St. Bernard weighing 260 mother-lovin' pounds. **1975** *Atlantic* (May) 43: I'm the Paul mother-lovin Bunyan of the Interstate system. **1983** W. Prochnau *Trinity's Child* 154: He switched to the intercom and radioed downstairs: "Keep your mother-lovin' eyes peeled down there." **1991** *Creem* (Apr.–May) 108/1: Some mother-loving hi-fi crankatron that will make strong men weak with envy. **2000** *New York Magazine* (Dec. 18) 18: Has John Simon gone off the mother-loving deep end? Making theatergoing plans based on his reviews has always been akin to asking your crazy uncle Abe for hygiene tips, but Simon has outdone himself in his review of *Comic Potential*. **2003** T. Carson *Gilligan's Wake* 74: At ease, down boy, and hello sailor, which oughta cover pretty much every mother-lovin' one of you.

mother-raper *noun*

(a partial euphemism for) MOTHERFUCKER.

1959 C. Himes *Crazy Kill* v. 27: Turn me loose, you mother-rapers! He's my brother and some mother-raper's going to pay—. **1965** C. Himes *Imabelle* 92: Mother-raper, step on it! *Ibid.* 127: I bled that mother-raper like a boar hog. **1989** R. Miller *Profane Men* 62: I didn't even read that mother raper. **1991** M. Jacobson *Gojiro* 186: Gojiro turned on the Dish and saw that grinning moron of a presidential candidate stealing his best line…. How the monster longed to make that mother-raper's day—it figured that the thick electorate fell for his act. **2000** R. Skinner *Daddy's Gone a-Hunting* 278: Now, you pissant mother-raper…. You and me goin' for a li'l ride and you're gonna show me where the money is.

mother-raping *adjective*

(a partial euphemism for) MOTHERFUCKING.

1932 F. Halyburton & R. Goll *Shoot & Be Damned* 306 [refers to 1918]: When I talked to you mother-raping sewer rats at roll call I thought you were Americans. **1959** C. Himes *Crazy Kill* 57: I ain't given Dulcy any mother-raping knife. **1960** D. MacCuish *Do Not Go Gentle* 191 [refers to WWII]: An' that queer's *really* a first-class A-1 mother-rapin' gutless wonder of a horse's ass! **1962** S. Brent *Seven Stairs* (1989) 11: You mother-raping bastard, I'll cut your throat! **1965** C. Himes *Imabelle* 67: Leave me see that mother-rapin' roll. *Ibid.* 122: Let's take the mother-raping hearse, too. **1972** C. Gaines *Stay Hungry* 213: The last motharapin straw, Newton called it. **2002** R. Marcinko *Violence of Action* 16: You'd best expect the mother-raping bastards to die and die damned hard where I find them.

motorcycle *noun*

(a jocular euphemism for) MOTHERFUCKER,—usually used with *had*.

1938 in P. Oliver *Blues Tradition* 235: Ridin' Dirty Motorsickle…He's a dirty motor-cycle. **1967** H. Lit *Dictionary* 2: *Bad motorcycle* —One who is very sharp, cool, hip, and gets what he wants but, this type of cat is also a little sneaky tricky. **1973** *Oui* (Feb.) 38: She's a bad motorcycle. **1985** J. T. Heywood *Taxi Dancer* 92: We got us a bad *motor-cycle* this mornin', gents.

motor flicker *noun*

(a partial euphemism for) MOTHERFUCKER.

1967 in *Trans-action* VI (Feb. 1969) 33: This black slick head motor flicker. **1974** S. Stevens *Rat Pack* 39: Lookit what says black, you funky motorflikker nigger. **1975** B. Silverstein & R. Krate *Dark Ghetto* 107 [refers to *ca*1965]: This black slick head motor flicker got nerve 'nough to call somebody "fat head."

motor scooter *noun*

(a partial euphemism for) MOTHERFUCKER.—usually used with *bad*. Cf. earlier MOTORCYCLE.

1960 D. Frazier *Alley-Oop* (pop. song): A mean motor scooter and a bad go-getter. **1974** R. Carter *16th Round* 168: Some real bad motor-scooters!... Some bad motherfuckers! **1986** D. Tate *Bravo Burning* 44: Called "a darn great soldier" by Captain Billy Wilson, "a bad motor scooter" by others—in admiration. **2004** *Fantasy & Science Fiction* (Dec.) 123/2: Riddick is the last surviving Furyan, a race of bad motor scooters who were thoroughly Necromongered some time back, but put up one hell of a fight.

mouth fuck *noun*

an act of MOUTH-FUCKing.

*ca*1866 *Romance of Lust* 447: Finishing off with a mouth fuck from one or the other, and a double gamahuche. **1975** S. West *Blow Boy* 146: Seven mouth-fucks on a slow week wasn't my idea of salvation. **2000** R. Gordon *Sexual Service* 40: Blond eyed her pink tongue peeping between her succulent lips. "How about a mouth fuck?" **2007** "Noire" *Thong on Fire* 155: Free was really moaning now, going from some short tight humps to a straight-out mouth fuck.

mouth-fuck *verb*

to thrust the penis into (a person's) mouth; (*also*) to vigorously perform fellatio on.

1966 A. Wainhouse & R. Seaver trans. Marquis de Sade *120 Days of Sodom* in *120 Days of Sodom & Other Writings* 673: The man who mouth-fucks the little girl prostituted by her father is the same man...who fucks with a dirty prick. **1972** B. Rodgers *Queens' Vernacular* 89: [*Fuck*] *in the face*...mouth fucking...as opposed to cocksucking. **1975** M. Amis *Dead*

Babies (1991) 113: "Have Lucy last night?" "Nah—Just let her mouth-fuck me." **1976** "Studs" *Creative Head* 39: He mouthfucked her in earnest, slapping his hairy crotch against her face. **1978** L. Kramer *Faggots* 72: Holding…his hand while mouth-fucking the impaled acolyte. **1979** C. Keller *Subway Orgy* 78: She concentrated on the stiff rod in her mouth and kept on sucking and mouth-fucking the kidnapper. **1981** *Penthouse* (Apr.) 196: She popped my purple glans into her mouth.…Then she began mouth-fucking me rapidly. **1998** *Taxi!*, pornographic story on Usenet newsgroup alt.sex.stories (Oct. 26): I take his glans in my mouth.…Covering my teeth with my lips, I mouth-fuck him vindictively. Tender isn't what's required. **2005** M. Christakos *Sooner* 120: She mouthfucked and assfucked and swam in the nude. **2007** "Noire" *Hood* 234: He slid his hands up and held her head like it was an ass, then mouth-fucked her standing up.

muck *verb*

(used as a euphemism for FUCK in various figurative senses). See also MUCK UP. [Perhaps originally suggested by *mess* (*around*), but the rhyme with FUCK has ultimately given the word the euphemistic quality with which it is now used.]

*a*1890–96 J. S. Farmer & W. E. Henley *Slang & Its Analogues* VI 372: *To muck about.*…To fondle; to mess about. **1896** R. Kipling in *Oxford English Dictionary*: Our Colonel…mucks about in 'orspital. **1928** in *Oxford English Dictionary Supplement*: His art…[is] the one thing a genuine artist won't muck about with. **1929** R. Aldington *Death of a Hero* III. x. 376: Spree be mucked—one of you ** fired his rifle and muckin' near copped me. **1936** E. Partridge *Dictionary of Slang & Unconventional English: Muck!, mucker, mucking*, have from ca. 1915 represented *f **k!*, etc. **1940** F. Hemingway *For Whom the Bell Tolls* 369: You're just mucked.… Muck this whole treacherous muck-faced mucking country. **1950** E. Hemingway *Across River* 58: Now muck off. **1950** in H. Wentworth & S. B. Flexner *Dictionary of American Slang*: Too many bones mucking about. **1958** T. Capote *Breakfast at Tiffany's* 8: You got to be rich to go mucking around in Africa. **1961** *Time* (Jan. 27) 57: There is one in every outfit—the sniveling, creepy little muckup who not only fails to pull his weight but manages to add it to the load carried by others. **1982** *N.Y. Times* IV E19: Muck around with us and you'll reap the typhoon—unless you have H-bombs, rockets [etc.]. **1990** *Future Watch* (CNN-TV) (Aug. 18): I want to muck with real astrophysics.

muck up *verb*

to botch; spoil; ruin; FUCK UP. [Perhaps originally suggested by *mess up*, but now always regarded as a euphemism for FUCK UP.]

1886 (cited in E. Partridge *Dictionary of Slang & Unconventional English*). **1922** in *Oxford English Dictionary Supplement*: You seem to have pretty well mucked it up. **1949** *Saturday Evening Post* (Oct. 8) 125: That does make it bad, doesn't it? Makes a pair of us mucking things up. **1951** *N.Y. Times* (July 22) I 11: The Iranians had always done something to "muck things up." **1954–60** H. Wentworth & S. B. Flexner *Dictionary of American Slang*: *Muck up*...= fuck up, a euphem. **1967–68** N. von Hoffman *We Are the People Our Parents Warned Us Against* 91: We need the tourists even if they may have mucked up the Haight. **1968** C. Victor *Sky Burned* 44: The squad would probably muck up the mission on top of it. **1982** *N.Y. Times* (Mar. 25) D2: You mucked it all up, gang. **1987** D. Mamet *House of Games* (film): You're mucking up my timing. **1988** *Newsday* (N.Y.) (June 20) II 6: By the mid-70's, Thompson...had already mucked up nicely. **1994** *New Republic* (Nov. 28) 56: Francis Ford Coppola... has been mucking up his own career lately. **1996** *Dr. Katz* (Comedy Central TV): Dad, please. Don't muck it up with conversation!

muh fuh *noun*

(a partial euphemism for) MOTHERFUCKER.

1969 B. Beckham *Main Mother* 148: Where you muh fuhs from? **1972** B. Beckham *Runner Mack* 186: We're taking over, muhfuh. **1974** *Black World* (June) 72/2: "Okay, muhfuh, gimme whatchu got." The voice was low and even. **1975** *Black World* (Jan.) 57: Get *out* of here, you muh-fuh! **1980** H. Gould *Fort Apache* 81: Hey, muh fuh, I ain't no junkie. **1994** *Vibe* (Aug.) 108/2: If you want to hear jazz the way they probably swing to it on the rings of Saturn, you need to check in with brother Taylor. Loop this, muhfuhs!!! **2003** *Village Voice* (Oct. 1) 84/1: Verbal panache and... funk we once snootily considered the sole province of us uppity uncouth cosmopolite muhfuhs.

muscle-fuck *noun*

1. an act of rubbing the penis between a woman's breasts.

1974 (quotation at FRENCH FUCK). **1992** *Playboy* (July) 37: Sex quiz... Been involved in breast fucking (a.k.a. the Hawaiian muscle fuck)?

2. sexual intercourse in which the woman aggressively contracts her vaginal muscles as a means of stimulation. Also as *verb*.

1977 Vermont student: A muscle-fuck is one where the Jane can contract the muscles in her vagina. It can drive you up the wall. I heard about muscle-fucks in the marines. **1991** N. Friday *Women on Top* 168: In the early 1980s a man wrote to me asking if I'd ever heard of a "muscle fuck." He knew of a young woman on his college campus who had developed the talent of painfully fucking a man dry by using her vaginal muscles and thighs; the word on campus was that she was tired of macho studs and had developed her muscle fuck as revenge. **2001** in C. Taylor *Brown Sugar* 116: Just stopped, altogether, and muscle fucked me, contracting and relaxing while I grew inside her, harder, longer. **2005** W. Christie *Threat Level* 145: First time I got muscle-fucked, I almost married the girl right then and there.... She had an act. Slipped a banana right into her pussy and it came out sliced.

N

NFG *adjective*

1. [elaboration of earlier *N.G.* 'no good'; compare earlier (1903 in *OED*3) *N.B.G.* 'no bloody good'] "*no fucking good.*" Also as *interjection.*

1945 in *Verbatim* (Autumn, 1989) 6: *NFG...*Abbrev. for *no fxxxn' good....*An individual, situation or state without any redeeming features; hopeless, incompetent, utterly worthless: *I'm NFG before my coffee in the morning.* **1977** E. Torres *Q&A* 162: He's...N.F.G., with the oak leaf cluster. **1988** T. Logan *Harder They Fall* 106: N.F.G.! Start grouping your shots....Like this. **1990** G.R. Clark *Words of Vietnam War* 356: NFG...no-fuckin'-good. **1991** S. Fry *Liar* xii. 332: The other half, which the Hungoes got ahold of this afternoon, is n.f.g. without the book of words that you have so cunningly kept clasped to your sagging bosom. **2000** A. H. Vachss *Dead & Gone* 33: No matter how I played it out, it came up NFG all the way.

2. *Army.* = FNG.

1992 D. R. Rodrique *Heading Home* 152 [refers to Vietnam War]: "You're just one more N.F.G." "An N.F.G." "New Fucking Guy; a cherry."

NFW *interjection*
"*no fucking way.*"

1974 J. Mills *One Just Man* 125: Just NFW. No fuckin' *way*. **1987** *Wall St. Journal* (Oct. 26): "N.F.W." Loosely translated: "No Feasible Way." **1993** S. Manes & P. Andrews *Gates* 238: On the way up to Seattle, Hanson had been thinking "NFW. No way am I going to take this job." **2006** B. A. Masters *Spoiling for a Fight* 83: "imho" = "in my humble opinion" and "nfw" for an unprintable expletive.

O

OMFG *interjection*

"*Oh My Fucking God.*"

1997 *Re: Favorite Anime Character* on Usenet newsgroup rec.arts.anime.
misc (Apr. 7): If you don't get impressed by the harem and the OMFG
plotlines, this is a snoozer. **2002** *Thrasher* (Nov. 1) 172: The Ice Age hit
and survival of the fittest let the young'uns pass on through. Can't fight
evolution. New Found Glory! OMFG! **2005** *New York Magazine* (July
4) 79/1: But then, as the kids themselves might say: OMFG. **2008** (cap-
tion of advertising poster for *Gossip Girls* (CW TV), featuring teenagers
in sexually provocative poses): OMFG.

P

Philadelphia rat fuck *noun*

see under RAT-FUCK, *noun*, definition 4.

pigfuck *noun*

1. = PIG-FUCKER *noun*, definition 1.

    1970 in *Fire! Reports from the Underground Press* 14: You too, you racist pig-fuck with your star badge and your crippled trigger mind. **1990** P. Monette in G. Stambolian *Men on Men 3: Best New Gay Fiction* 25: Nevertheless, the last thing I will do is acknowledge Jerry Curran, the pigfuck who rode shotgun through my brother's arrogant youth. **2003** A. Swofford *Jarhead* 200: I turn against my brother, and I insult the U.S. Army and any pigfuck who would join such a shitpoor organization. **2003** T. Carson *Gilligan's Wake* 219: No I did not you pigfuck bastard shitass fucker.

2. a genre of music, associated with the late 1980s and typically regarded as an outgrowth of punk and a precursor to grunge, characterized by a gritty, noisy sound.

    1989 *Sound Choice* (Autumn) 87/1: This LP packs a wallop...and keeps the noise/pigfuck crown firmly entrenched on Trench 'N' Go's mantle. **2001** *Terrorizer* (Sept.) 68/4: Good ol' American pigfuck—politely known as noise rock—nearly fell of the map in the late 90's, as the once-mighty Amphetamine Reptile label fizzled out and took its influence with it. **2001** M. Azerrad *Our Band could be your Life* xi. 402: They didn't socialize with the SST bands or the so-called "pigfuck" bands on Homestead and

Touch & Go. **2005** *New Yorker* (Apr. 11) 80/1: Slint and Slaughterhouse had roots in a subgenre of nineteen-eighties independent rock which was sometimes called "pig-fuck" by the music press.

3. a confused or disappointing situation or state of affairs.

1998 B. J. Nelson *Keepers* 200: The car ahead finally careened from the road… Acne and Toothy were looking back, throwing the finger. What a pigfuck. **2001** M. Wynne *No Other Option* 247: It's a pigfuck. FUBAR from start to finish. **2007** R. Leleux *Memoirs of a Beautiful Boy* 5: "Pig Fuck" was Mother's phrase for the absolute nadir of something…. So when Daddy left, taking Nana and Papa's money with him, Mother and I quickly realized we were nouveau poor. Which was the pig fuck of all time. **2009** J. Stewart on *Daily Show* (Comedy Central TV) (Jan. 13): Abu Ghraib and the weapons of mass destruction are international pig-fucks.

pig-fucker *noun*

a worthless, disgusting, or despicable person.

1938 "Justinian" *Americana Sexualis* 31: *Pig-Fucker,* n. A concupiscent man whose sensibilities are so atrophied that he would even "fuck a pig."… Obsolete Br., U.S., C. 19–20. Obsolescent. **1965** H.S. Thompson *Letter* (Apr. 18) in *Proud Highway* (1997) 509: Ah, this fucking rotten machine. One more strike against those pigfuckers. **1970** in H.S. Thompson *Shark Hunt* 40: Bug off, you worthless faggot! You twisted pigfucker! **1972–76** C. Durden *No Bugles, No Drums* 263: Five fuckin' people against five thousand pissed-off pig fuckers. **1976** C. Rosen *Mile Above the Rim* 82: Wayne Smalley was a racist white pigfucker and Jeremy hated him. **1982** D.A. Harper *Good Company* 70: Why I'd be a lyin' pigfucker if I told you that! **1983** R. Thomas *Missionary* 145: Just call him a pig fucker and let him deny it. **1987** Robbins *Ravens* 69: "Pig Fucker."… The name hails from the early days of Vietnam when fighter pilots called each other by it as a form of affectionate…abuse. *a*1989 R. Herman, Jr. *Warbirds* 97: All *right,* you pig-fuckers. I do *not* like surprises. **1990** "My Life with the Thrill Kill Kult" *Days of Swine & Roses* (pop. song): Fuck you, pig fucker! **1992** D. Allison *Bastard out of Carolina* vii. 100: "Your daddy's a son of a bitch himself, a purely crazy pigfucker," Grey was always telling me with a little awe in his voice, a hunger to be half again as dangerous. **2007**

Believer (Nov.–Dec.) 56/2: He refers to John Wayne as an "evil white racist honky pigfucker."

pig-fucking *adjective*

worthless; disgusting; despicable.

1948 I. Wolfert *Act of Love* 503: Frig you, you pig-frigging turd. **1968** H. S. Thompson *Letter* (Jan. 3) in *Fear & Loathing in America* (2000) 14: That evil pigfucking skunk. For the past year he's been hounding me like some sort of cop out of Dostoyevsky. **1972** B. Bertolucci *Last Tango in Paris* (film): You goddam pig-fucking liar! **1972–76** C. Durden *No Bugles, No Drums* 175: I knew the pig-fuckin' cocksucker was settin' me up. **1977** T. Jones *Incredible Voyage* 371: The fair-haired bastard of a pig-fucking detective... kicked out the boy's eye! **1978** E. Thompson *Devil to Pay* 103: They'll hung your ass in this pigfucking country and look for justification later. **1999** T. Parker et al. *South Park* (film script) 138: Dripping vagina eating son of a pigfucking crack whore!!! Hairy cock slurping maggot fuuuuuck!!!! **2005** L. Purdue *Perfect Killer* xxxvi. 146: You pig-fucking shit-bird.

pity-fuck *noun*

→ MERCY FUCK.

1969 J. Nuttall *Pig* 33: He'd reached two hands to her, face to her belly, willing tears to his eyes to lure her to a pity-fuck. **1993** O. Goldsmith *Flavor of the Month* 27: It might have started as a pity fuck, but she blew him away. **1994** B. Maher *True Story* 107: "Need some loving," she had said—what was this, a pity fuck? **1996** *Frontiers* (Sept. 1): We have a horror of the pity fuck. We cannot face the charity of the mercy orgasm. **1997** *Re: Daniel Mocsny's writing style*, on Usenet newsgroup soc.singles: Why are you banging a woman so repulsive she wouldn't rate a pity-fuck from me on my worst day? **2006** "L. Burana" *Try* xii. 137: A stark contrast to Alex who, despite his best efforts, made going down on me feel like a pity fuck delivered by mouth.

R

rat-fuck *noun*

1. (used as a term of abuse), "asshole," etc.

1922 in E. Wilson *Twenties* (1975) 116 [undefined list of terms]: Dumbbell upstage lousy highhat rat-fuck to crab someone or someone's act. **1955** in D. Wepman et al. *The Life* (1976) 171: That dirty rat fuck—/ He thought he was slick. **1970** T. Southern *Blue Movie* 173: *Yes,* you rat fuck! What heinous deception! **1970** G. Sorrentino *Steelwork* 16: He stood in front of them and kicked their balls off! The rat fucks. **1973** J. Breslin *World Without End, Amen* 109: Is that where the rat-fuck… is going? **1976** L. Bangs in *Psychotic Reactions* (1987) 199: Those rat-fucks in Chicago can suck my asshole. **1990** E. W. Rukuza *West Coast Turnaround* 230: He was watching…, the ratfuck! **1991** *Southern Atlantic Quarterly* XC 836: The ratfuck FCC….The…fuckwad station manager. **1996** D. McCumber *Playing off the Rail* 95: That's right, you ratfuck bastard. **1999** T. Parker et al. *South Park* (film script) 138: Fuck a hunk a shit, you rat fuck!!! **2006** G. Lawson & W. Oldham *Brotherhoods* 132: There were no references to "motherfuckers" or "cocksuckers" or "rat fucks"—the streams of expletives that were standard on the street.

2.a. Originally *Army.* a confused or bungled situation, especially an assault. [The 1930 examples are euphemistic.]

1930 L. H. Nason *Corporal Once* 139 [refers to WWI]: This here gigantic rat-copulation they call a war. *Ibid.* 171: This isn't going to be the same kind of a damned disgusting…rat-copulation such as we've been going through on the Border. *Ibid.* 260: This will be just the same old rat dinging all over again. **a1964** A. J. Liebling in *Mollie & Other War*

Pieces 151: "Whoever checked them out in a bomber ought to have his head examined! What a ratfuck!" He explained that a ratfuck was "a rat race, but all bollixed up." **1968** H. S. Thompson *Letter* (May 31) in *Fear & Loathing in America* (2000) 85: You are one of the few people who read my book on the Hell's Angels closely enough to realize that the whole thing was a wonderful rat-fuck and—as you put it—"a perpetual ball." **1971** R. Vaughan & M. Lynch *Brandywine's War* 57: A GRF...means Giant Rat Fuck....It's a nickname the men have for an aerial assault mission. **1983** J. Groen & D. Groen *Huey* 217: Every insertion was a Romeo Foxtrot (RF), translated rat fuck, the name given by flyers to doomed missions. *Ibid.* 272: He was mad as hell about that rat fuck already. **1984** G. Holland *Let a Soldier Die* 184 [refers to 1967]: I was on this rat fuck down south...and on short final the whole world went up. **1987** P. D. Chinnery *Life on the Line* 35 [refers to 1965]: The next day was my first combat assault or GRF (Grand Rat F***) as they were called. **1991** *Vanity Fair* (Sept.) 244/1: It's been a real rat fuck at Columbia and I'll bet the Japanese don't have the vaguest idea what's happening in their own company. **2004** J. F. Mullins *Into the Treeline* 237: Damn good thing I was there.... What a ratfuck operation that was!

b. an unimportant task or mission.

1987 P. D. Chinnery *Life on the Line* 227 [refers to 1970]. As a new scout pilot they send you out on...rat-f*** missions, in areas where you don't expect to see much....They generally sent him on the rat-f***s so that no one would have to depend on him in a bad situation. **1990** M. Brennan *Hunter-Killer Squadron* 237: Nobody wanted to fly real combat missions with him, so they usually sent him on the rat fucks.

3. a damn; FUCK *noun* definition 2.a.

1971 H. Dahlskog *Dictionary of Contemporary & Colloquial Usage* 48: *Ratfuck, R.F.*...a damn, as: I don't give a *rat-fuck* what you do! **1980** D. Hamill *Stomping Ground* 245: Me, I couldn't give a hairy rat fuck. **1996** J. Diaz *Drown* in *Drown* 102: With our bus drivers you didn't have to hide. Two of them didn't give a rat fuck and the third one, the Brazilian preacher, was too busy talking Bible to notice anything but the traffic in front of him. **2000** T. Clancy *Bear & Dragon* xlvi. 696: Wars are not rational acts. They are not begun by rational men. They're begun by people who don't care a rat-fuck about the people they rule.

4. a crowded or frenetic social event.—sometimes in phrase: ☞ **Philadelphia rat fuck.**

[**1965** R. Gehman *The Had* 135: I would go if you invited me to a ratfuck.] **1979** J. Houseman *Front & Center* The flashiest, richest, swiftest, best conducted theatrical rat-fuck ever staged in this city. **1986** P. Klein *Growing up Spoiled in Beverly Hills* 185: He has described certain parties to me as "rat fucks." **1987** W. McPherson *Sargasso Sea* ii. 87: "I much prefer a quiet supper to one of these"—he was about to say "rat fucks," but restrained himself—"one of these after-the-opening feeding frenzies in some designer shark tent." **1987** S. Quinn *Regrets Only* 162: "You could tell from a glance that it was going to be"—she lowered her voice—"what the late Mrs. John T. used to call a Philadelphia rat fuck." **1995** in *Vanity Fair* (Jan. 1996) 118: The only thing I went to was that Michael Fuchs HBO thing in Sag Harbor arranged by Peggy Siegal, and I'd never go again. It was a real rat fuck. **1997** *Guardian* (London) (June 3) ("Feature") 18: The luxe preview of the Harriman goods...was "the ratfuck to end all ratfucks," attracting about as repellent a collection of people as can be imagined. **1997** *N.Y. Observer* (Oct. 6) 42: Glenn Bernbaum...throws a Philadelphia rat-f*#k for Joan Collins and her new autobiography. **1997** S. Quinn *The Party* 42: A huge cocktail party where you've invited everyone you've ever known and everyone you've ever owed....This sort of event has a name, coined by the late Marie Harriman, the dazzling second wife of statesman Averell Harriman. It is called a "Philadelphia rat fuck"—"P.R.F." or "rat fuck" for short. **2003** M. Atwood *Oryx & Crake* x. 292: Every week there was a Compound social barbecue, a comprehensive ratfuck that all employees were expected to attend. **2008** J. J. Salem *Tan Lines* 296: Everything had been beautifully decorated and lavishly appointed with food and liquor, but the overall affair was a total ratfuck—shoulder to shoulder with the likes of Tommy Lee, Bruce Willis, Pamela Anderson, [etc.].

rat-fuck *verb*

1. to botch; FUCK UP.

1966 *Folk Speech* (Indiana University Folklore Archives): Used as a verb meaning to botch in the worst possible way. *Rat-fuck.* **2006** T. Phillips *Blacktop Cowboys* 119: Jensen was always getting rat fucked, which is his way of describing a plan that goes terribly awry.

2. to outwit; trick.

1964 in *American Speech* (Oct. 1965) 195: *Rat fuck, n. v....* This was a widely used slang term at Stanford... It is seldom used except in abbreviatory coinage (*R. F.*)... An *R. F.* is a practical joke...but this...has been broadened in its use. To some undergraduates, it connotes anything unacceptable to the Establishment.... *To R. F.*, however, may mean also simply having a good time, or perhaps doing something that has no practical purpose. **1989** S. Chapple & D. Talbot *Burning Desires* 290: Gotta rat-fuck those guys, Missy! It's the only way. **1989** W. Brashler *Traders* 299: Here I was in the middle of the most irresponsible, self-centered, selfish, rat-fucking business in the world and doing well at it. **1989** F. A. Leib *Fire Dream* 400: Poor rat-fucked back-stabbed...bastard. **2000** P. Baker *Breach* 188: Somebody in this room rat-fucked the president last night. **2002** D. Brock *Blinded by the Right* 81: David Sullivan was...a master of bureaucratic intrigue and strategic leaking to the press—"rat fucking" the enemy, in Sullivan's words.

3. to harm irreparably, victimize; FUCK *verb* definition 2.a.

1989 M. Kittredge *Dead & Gone* 94: Unless I could get a goddamned thesis written in three weeks, I was, you should excuse the expression, ratfucked. **1993** J. L. Burke *In the Electric Mist* 282: You got wax in your ears, you talk shit, you rat-fuck your friends. **2006** T. Phillips *Blacktop Cowboys* 119: If a steer walks all over him, Jensen got rat fucked. If a horse bucks him off, again rat fucked. **2008** T. Bell *Tsar* 437: That no-man's-land between safe and totally rat-fucked.

4. *Military.* to rummage through with the intent to steal; to rifle.

1997 M. C. Hodgins *Reluctant Warrior* 28: Curry had rat-fucked (rifled) a case of C rations on the deck under his rack. **2000** G. P. Pellecanos *Shame the Devil* 15: Go ahead, Maroulis.... Just keep ratfucking through that closet. **2006** P. K. O'Donnell *We Were One* 113: In the rubble-strewn rooms, the men "rat fucked" several boxes of MREs (Meals Ready-to-Eat), picking out the cookies, candy, and other goodies. **2007** M. Eriksen *My River Home* 91: "Who ratfucked my pack?" one might say in response to a pair of goggles missing from an unbuttoned pouch. **2007** A. Bay *Embrace the Suck* 39: *Rat-fuck*, slang meaning "to ransack something and take what you want." ("Private Baggadonuts rat-fucked that whole case of MREs just to get all the Pop-Tarts.")

rat fuck *interjection*

(used as an interjection); = FUCK *verb* definition 1.d.

> **1996** S. King *Desperation* 449: "Dear me," he said. "I've lost the respect of a man once in charge of throwing out Steven Tyler's barf-bags. Ratfuck." **1997** D. Hunt *Magician's Tale* 264: Ratfuck! Kids don't give a damn. **2006** S. King *Lisey's Story* 89: "Oh, ratfuck," Darla said dismally, and began to cry again. **2007** M. Davidson *Undead & Uneasy* 60: "Rat fuck," Tina muttered, and I nearly toppled off the counter. Tina, ancient bloodsucking thing that she was…had the manners of an Elizabethan lady and almost never swore. She was perfectly proper at all times. "Mother fuck," she continued.

rat fucker *noun*

a hated or offensive person.—used as a term of abuse. Also: one who engages in RAT-FUCKING; a dirty trickster, a saboteur. [The 1914 quotation may be a chance coincidence.]

> [**1914** J. London *Jacket* 19: It is so absurd, my dear Warden, to think that your rat-throttlers of guards can shake out of my brain the things that are clear and definite in my brain.] **1967** P. Welles *Babyhip* 61: "Scum," John mumbled. "Ratfucker, prick," George said. **1974** C. Bernstein & B. Woodward *All the President's Men* 135: For the first time, he considered the possibility that the President of the United States was the head ratfucker. *ca*1978 P. Schrader & L. Schrader *Blue Collar* (film script) 62: We'll get the fifty grand those ratfuckers are getting from the insurance company. **1987** H. Zeybel *Gunship* 138: Them dirty… Commie ratfuckers. **2000** G. Blunt *Forty Words for Sorrow* lvii. 370: Rick Bouchard…is a subliterate ratfucker. They'll have to add a special extension onto hell just to house that creep. **2007** A. Theroux *Laura Warholic* 242: I could not possibly list all the mendacious shitwads and unconscionable scum and thieving ratfuckers who, taking complete advantage of the woman, stuck to her like remoras.

rat-fucking *noun*

destructive activity, as pranks; (specifically) dirty trickery or sabotage; (*also*) a confusing situation. [The early examples are probably euphemisms; the 1930 euphemistic quotation at RAT-FUCK, definition 2a, may belong here instead.]

1928 L. H. Nason *Sgt. Eadie* 110 [refers to 1918]: This time to-morrow, Jake, I'll be with my own outfit and that's the only ray of sun in my black sky at present. All other troubles fade when I think of that. No more of this rat-kissing. **1928–29** L. H. Nason *White Slicker* 88: You know, I had a sergeancy clinched if we hadn't run into all this rat-kissing! **1944** in P. Smith *Letters from Father* 391: *Rat fucking*…at Hanover [New Hampshire] means the raiding of the students rooms on one floor by the students from another floor—the boys go in groups of eight or ten—turn everything upside down…even fire buckets of water are employed to make the wreck complete. **1972** in C. Bernstein & B. Woodward *All the President's Men* 132: Yes, political sabotage is associated with Segretti. I've heard a term for it, "ratfucking." *Ibid.* 138: Ratfucking? He had heard the term. It meant double-cross and, as used by the Nixon forces, it referred to infiltration of the Democrats. **1992** *Vanity Fair* (June) 111: Donald Segretti… was an alumnus of the U.S.C. Republican Mafia and a practitioner of the dirty tricks campaign tactics known as "rat fucking." **1993** J. Hubner *Bottom Feeders* 335: Known as "rat fucking," the tricks could be Jim slipping a huge cockroach in an enchilada Hunter Thompson was about to eat. **1996** G. Gordon Liddy *Will* 282: By this time I knew that *rat-fucking* was a University of California fraternity term for glorified Halloween pranks. **2007** M. Eriksen *My River Home* 91: "Ratfucking" is a brute phrase that collectively describes looting, pillaging, trophy hunting, stealing, souvenir collecting, scavenging, and borrowing with no intention to return.

rat-fucking *adjective*

despicable; MOTHERFUCKING *adjective*.

1977 J. Cheever *Falconer* 36: You rat-fucking, cock-sucking, ass-tonguing, sneaky, stinking fleabag. **1992** N. DeMille *General's Daughter* 429: You fucking well better, you rat-fucking, mother-fucking —. **1993** *Dangerous Game* (film): Some rat-fucking bastard who's leading a little girl…to a concentration camp, that rat-fucking cocksucker isn't feeling anything. If he was, he couldn't take her to the gas chamber. **2006** J. Karp *Futile and Stupid Gesture* 307: If a stranger objected, he would scream that the hapless interrupter was "a rat fucking, mother fucking son of a bitch."

REMF *noun* [from *r*ear *e*chelon *motherf*ucker]
a soldier in a support or administrative role; any non-combatant soldier.

1971 *Newsweek* (Jan. 11) 31/3: "Those REMF's don't even know what Vietnam is all about," sneered one grunt. **1982** J. M. Del Vecchio *13th Valley* 2: Hey, REMF,...you seen Murphy? **1993** *Soldier of Fortune* (Feb.) 54/1: One of my favorites is KGB General Vadim Kirpichenko. No REMF here. Vadim has been out in the streets doing things to the bad guys. **1998** T. Clancy *Rainbow Six* Prologue p. 2: He was respectable now as Director of the new agency. Director. A polite term for a REMF. **2007** A. Bay *Embrace the Suck* 1: But God—or the first sergeant—help the fake macho and especially the "REMF," "fobbit," or "suit" who talks the talk but hasn't walked the walk.

RTFM *interjection*
Computers. "*r*ead *t*he *f*ucking *m*anual."

1983 *Wanted VMS BACKUP for UNIX* on Usenet newsgroup net.unix-wizards (Sept. 30): The VMS people have a cute little piece of advice for people who are too slug-headed to read the manuals: RTFM. **1988** *MacUser* (Mar.) 73: RTFM [heading of question-and-answer column]. **1991** E. Raymond *New Hacker's Dictionary*: *RTFM*...Used by gurus to brush off questions they consider trivial or annoying. **1993** S. Lambert & W. Howe *Internet Basics* 472: *RTFM* (Read The Fine Manual) This acronym is often used when someone asks a simple question for the 100th time. The word "fine" is only one way to translate the acronym. **2003** C. Crawford *Art of Interactive Design* x. 122: Does this line of argument boil down to RTFM? **2008** G. A. Landis in *Analog Science Fiction & Fact* (Jan./Feb.) 109/2: When in doubt RTFM, he thought.

S

---

shitfuck *noun*

a despicable person; FUCK *noun* definition 4.

1985 A. Lamott *Joe Jones* 26: You're a rotten shitfuck slut, and I hope you rot in hell. *Ibid.* 58: Joe's shitfuck soul cringes. **1991** M. Weller *Lake No Bottom* 71: You fuck. You lunatic bastard king hell crazy shitfuck, this isn't funny any more. **2004** B. Land *Goat* 137: Fuck him. He's a shitfuck.

shitfuck *interjection*

(used to express dismay, anger, disappointment, etc.); FUCK, *interjection.*

1970 J. Bouton *Ball Four* ii. 66: "Shitfuck," he said, using one of his favorite words ("fuckshit" is the other). "Shitfuck. We've got a damned good ballclub here. We're going to win some games." **1975** J. Wambaugh *Choirboys* v. 45: "Shit fuck!" said Roscoe Rules, an expression he seldom used anymore…"Shit fuck! Give her the handcuffs, partner." **1989** *Blind Fury* (film): "Shit!" "Fuck!" "Shitfuck!" **1995** D. Hays & D. Hays *My Old Man & the Sea* 112: Last night I woke up to "*Shitfuck!*" which is how Dad gets himself really angry. **2007** R. Curtis *Twenty Grand* 11: Shitfuck! he screamed.

shitfuck *verb*

(used as an intensified elaboration of FUCK, *verb,* in various senses).

1988 M. Montecino *Crosskiller* 233: I didn't ask for this shitfucking job, and I don't want it now. I never wanted it. **1994** T. O'Brien *In the Lake of* *the Woods* 54: "Well, sure," he was saying. "Shitfuck Jesus." **2001** S. Lipsyte *Subject Steve* 109: How many times have I used my gift of language to explicate myself out of this or that shit-fucked situation?

skull fuck *verb*

1. = MOUTH FUCK. Also as *noun,* an act of skull fucking.

[**1972** B. Rodgers *Queens' Vernacular* 34: BJ...knob job...skull job.] **1985** R. Daniell *Sleeping with Soldiers* 62: The macho man never asks whether he can indulge in "skull-fucking" (semi-forced oral sex). **1993** B. Moore *Lexicon of Cadet Language* 345: *Skull fuck*...the act of fucking a woman in the mouth. **1996** *Skull-fuck Me,* title of advertisement on Usenet newsgroup alt.sex.telephone (Aug. 23). **1997** *L.A. Weekly* (Oct. 24) 27: A woman advertising over the CB that she would "skullfuck" anyone listening for $50. **1998** *Review: "Sex Lies,"* review of pornographic movie on Usenet newsgroup rec.arts.movies.erotica (Apr. 27): Both ladies take turns sucking him off when he says he wants to skull-fuck them. **1998** N.Y. man: You ever hear the term *skull fuck* for a blowjob? **2004** *Vice* (Feb.) 63/1: Stop skull-fucking me like that, you're hitting my gag reflex. **2005** B. Mullen *Whores* 281: He just dropped jaw right there in front of me and gave Perry a blowjob on my couch. I was only mildly interested in watching my boyfriend getting skullfucked.

2. to thrust the penis into the eye socket of (a person).—chiefly as an exaggeratedly violent threat.

1986 P. Nobile & E. Nadler *United States of America vs. Sex* 149: She unveiled the new paraphilia of "skull-fucking."... These are films in which a woman is killed and the orifices in her head are penetrated with a man's penis—her eyes, her mouth, and so on. **1987** *Full Metal Jacket* (film): I'm going to give you three seconds, exactly three fucking seconds, to wipe that stupid-looking grin off your face, or I will gouge out your eyes and skull-fuck you. **1996** C. Logan *Hunter's Moon* 153: Call off the tribe or I swear to God I'll pop out your left eyeball and skull-fuck you to death. **2000** A. Bourdain *Kitchen Confidential* 144: I made the mistake of telling a garde-manger man that if he didn't hurry up with an order I'd tear his eyes out and skull-fuck him. **2002** J. Goad *Shit Magnet* vii. 93: This from someone who had slaughtered at least thirteen people and skull-fucked an elderly woman after murdering her and plucking out her eyeball. **2002**

J. Dee *Palladio* 225: I want to rip his head off and shit into it, I want to pop his lying eyes out with a spoon and skullfuck him. **2009** J. Stewart on *Daily Show* (Comedy Central TV) (Feb. 9): This bill will fuck our economy in the eye. And after skull-fucking our economy this bill—this bill and Hitler will laugh and laugh.

snafu *noun* [*s*ituation *n*ormal: *all f*ucked *u*p; often interpreted in euphemistic variants, especially with *f*ouled].

1. *Army.* Especially in early use: used as an expression indicating the botched or confused nature of the military.

1941 *San Francisco Chronicle* (June 15) 5/4: "Snafu" means "situation normal, all fuddled up." **1941** *American Notes & Queries* I (Sept. 4) 94: *Snafu*—situation normal [*sic*]. **1942** *Time* (June 15): The Army has a laconic term for chronic befuddlement: *snafu,* situation normal; all fouled up. **2002** T. Lott *Rumours of Hurricane* i. 22: The local binmen are in the midst of a dispute. This does not seem extraordinary to Charlie, merely an irritatingly private blip in an otherwise consistent pattern of public life. "Snafu," thinks Charlie, his mind skipping back to army language. Situation normal, all fucked up.

2. Originally *Army.* a botched or confused situation, especially a military operation botched by incompetent planning or execution of orders. Also in mass use: confusion, disorder.

1943 *Best from Yank* (Sept. 10) 9: They worked hard and steadily, with a minimum of snafu. **1946** W. W. Haines *Command Decision* 11: But yesterday they [*sic*] was a SNAFU at the Quartermaster's and he run clean out of Spam. **1948** J. G. Cozzens *Guard of Honor* 184: It's a stupid damn snafu. **1953** M. Dibner *Deep Six* 23: He's chasing down another of your snafus. **1958** A. Hailey & J. Castle *Runway Zero Eight* 9: It would have to be a big show in Vancouver to justify this snafu. **1962** E. Shepard *Forgive us Our Press Passes* 60: On the housing snafu, he displayed the statement of a leading Soviet lawyer [etc.]. **1963** T. Doulis *Path for our Valor* 223: There's gonna be a big snafu....It means situation normal, all...fucked up. **1982** J. M. Del Vecchio *13th Valley* 1: It was one more snafu in a series of snafus. **1983** J. Groen & D. Groen *Huey* 105: John, your orders won't be coming in for two or three weeks. Some kind of a snafu. **1984** *N.Y. Post*

(Aug. 2) 60: Bettors furious over Big A snafus. **1992** H. N. Schwarzkopf *It Doesn't Take a Hero* xvii. 311: All were competing for space in the same airplanes and cargo ships, and an enormous amount of my time was devoted to untangling snafus. **1999** *Scientific American* (Nov.) 35/3: Two years ago corporate and individual domain name registrants were united in their hatred of Network Solutions, complaining of billing snafus, unwarranted suspensions and technical ineptitude.

snafu *adjective Army.*

1. Of a situation, etc.: hopelessly botched or confused. [Most early quotations refer to WWII.]

1941 *Kansas City Star* (July 27) 5A: That time you wrote you'd been talking to your captain for half an hour and everything was snafu, you got us terribly worked up.... Everything is strictly snafu. **1942** in C.R. Bond & T. Anderson *Flying T. Diary* 183: What a SNAFU operation. **1943** J. Twist *Bombardier* (film): You'll be plenty snafu if Captain Oliver hears about this. **1943** R. L. Scott *God Is My Co-Pilot* 22: And so we began our airmail flying—slightly SNAFU, as we have learned to say from the gremlins in World War II. **1944** *Collier's* (Apr. 1) 21: This all sounds snafu. **1945** Chase *This Man's Navy* (film): This place is all mixed up, snafu. **1945** Scowley & Friel *513th Retrospect* (unpaged): Once on shore things began to go SNAFU. **1947** *Startling Stories* (May) 112/2: Poor printing and snafu artwork keeps this Detroit zine down in the doldrums despite a high-powered lineup that includes Brazier, Elsner, Tigrina and Joe Kennedy. **1948** A. Murphy *To Hell and Back* 1: If the landing schedule had not gone snafu, we would have come ashore with the assault waves. **1953** K. Dodson *Away All Boats* 285: This is the most snafu beach I ever did see. **1959** B. Cochrell *Barren Beaches of Hell* 84: "Jesus," Willy said. "Sounds sort of snafu." **1970** J. W. Corrington *Bombardier* 53: The coffee splashed out, and the sugar fell into the eggs, and it was snafu. **1995** T. Clancy *Op-Center* xxxv. 157: They were all part of the same SNAFU scheme of things.

2. Or a person: worthless, useless; mentally confused; crazy.

1946 I. Gershwin *My Son-in-Law* in R. Kimball *Complete Lyrics of Ira Gershwin* (1993) 346/2: He may look good to you,/Your son-in-law:/To me he's just snafu,/Your son-in-law. **1975** J. Stanley *WWIII* 87: He's snafu, Sarge, snafu. I'm on your side. I swear it.

snafu *verb* Originally *Army.*

1. to bring into a state of great confusion; ruin through incompetence; botch; confuse; FUCK UP. Usually **snafued**, *adjective.*

1943 L. Cane *Letter* (July 6) in *Fighting Facism in Europe* (2003) 56: Gosh everything seems to be snafued for me the past few days. **1943** F. Wakeman *Shore Leave* 66: "There you go," the P-Boat pilot said. "Letting a lot of big sloppy words get you all snafued." **1944** B. Stiles *Serenade to the Big Bird* 74: It can snafu the works. **1948** B. Lay & S. Bartlett *Twelve O'Clock High!* 45: The warning order just came down....Snafu'd as usual. It says we're low group at *nine* thousand feet. **1970** J. R. Lincke *Jenny Was No Lady* 20: St. Jude, the patron saint of snafued ventures. **1979** in J. Raban *Old Glory* 348: He ain't going to allow some dumbhead bargeman to snafu the whole rest of his life for a can of Bud. **2002** J. J. Gobbell *When Duty Whispers Low* 74: Whoever snafued that plane's engine saved my life.

2. to blunder elaborately; FUCK UP.

1946 J. H. Burns *Gallery* 317: I snafu'd just like the rest of them. **1948** *Military Engineer* (Vol. XL) 64: Too often men seemed not to care if they "snafued." **1951** R. Leveridge *Walk on Water* 179 [refers to WWII]: Maybe the Army Post Office snafued again! **1992** A. Codevilla *Informing Statecraft* 327: Soviet factories have been known to snafu in grand style all by themselves.

3. Originally *Military.* to go wrong, especially to become botched or confused.

1957 W. P. McGivern *Odds Against Tomorrow* 175: But when things snafu they start acting like a bunch of crazy women. **1991** L. Niven et al. *Fallen Angels* 122: If the targeting system snafued... No, you're probably right. **1992** *Car* (Feb.) 86/1: Munich's weekend bound traffic snafus and we travel four miles in 40 minutes. **2001** E. H. Rosen *Think Like a Shrink* 157: Every move, every encounter has the potential to snafu.

snefu *adjective* [*s*ituation *n*ormal: *e*verything *f*ucked *u*p; variant of SNAFU]

Military. = SNAFU *adjective.*

1942 in P. Jordan *Tunis Diary* 38: SNEFU, as an American officer said at dinner....Snefu means Situation Normal: Everything F—d Up. **1943**

Hartford Courant (Mar. 6) 6/4: The same man reports that a common expression now at the Capitol when one is asked about the state of affairs is that it is "Snefu." After considerable probing this turns out to be "situation normal, everything fogged up."

sportfuck *noun*

an act of casual sex. Also: a person regarded as a casual sexual partner.

1990 L. Hutchins *Bi Any Other Name* 328: Lesbians who end up doing what some call a "sport fuck" with a man have been in a situation, such as travel, in which a good time with a kindred spirit just happened along. **1991** D. Jenkins *Gotta Play Hurt* 43: Even enjoying a sport-fuck occasionally. **1994** J. L. Burke *Dixie City Jam* 275: "Wouldn't you like a little sport fuck on the side?" I opened her car door and fitted my hand tightly around her upper arm. **1996** C. Logan *Hunter's Moon* 55: I gave up *a lot* for him. And not just to be his sport fuck. So yeah, I got him to make it legal. **2005** P. Levine *Solomon Vs. Lord* 292: Chet, you're adorable in your own way, but you're just a sport fuck and we both know it.

sportfuck *verb*

to engage in casual, indiscriminate copulation [with].

1968 Paul Newman in *Playboy* (July) 69: There was sport fucking. There was mercy fucking. **1976** J. Bode *View from Another Closet* 91: After we separated and eventually divorced, I went through the typical reactions of sport-fucking, long-term affairs, brief interludes, but always with men. **1987** C. Hiaasen *Double Whammy* xxiv. 235: Lanie gave a shallow laugh. "The sportfucking, he didn't mind. A different fella each night and he'd never say a word to me." **1989** S. Chapple & D. Talbot *Burning Desires* 124: I still sportfish. I no longer sportfuck. **1991** University professor, age 60: You'd think he'd have some better form of recreation than sportfucking some groupie on the lawn.... *Sportfuck* is a word I remember from Chicago, about 1959. **2003** J. McManus *Positively Fifth Street* 143: As far as she was concerned, getting sport-fucked by Tabish before they burked [*sc.* suffocated] Ted made perfect sense. **2005** R. Hoban *Come Dance with Me* xv. 91: I've had my share of one-night stands and sport fucking and I don't know if any of those men who didn't mean anything to me ran into the Curse of Christabel. **2006** L. Kipnis *Female Thing* 4: Feminism Plan A: Strive for empowerment, smash those glass ceilings, sport-fuck like the guys.

starfucker *noun*

= CELEBRITY-FUCKER. Hence **starfucking.**

1970 J. Barnes *Deceivers* 72: Those star-fuckers at the other agen
cies were probably sucking up to Curtis and Lang till hell wouldn't have
it. **1970** J. Grissim *Country Music* 259: In the rock and roll fifties they
were called star-fuckers. In the acid rock world of the Sixties (and now
Seventies) they were called groupies. **1972** *Playboy* (Aug.) 70: Groupies and star-fuckers abound and you certainly don't have to marry them,
though a lot of poor fools do. **1973** M. Jagger & K. Richards *Star Star*
(song, perf. "Rolling Stones"): Lead guitars and movie stars get their
tongue beneath your hood.Yeah! You're a star fucker, star fucker, star
fucker, star fucker. **1978** C. Crawford *Mommie Dearest* 277: They were
the "starfuckers," people who...would go to any lengths to have their
own names associated with anyone famous. These people were not just
fans, they had professions and services to sell. **1981** C. Nelson *Picked
Bullets Up* 181: Because of his notoriety as a bisexual star-fucker. **1990**
Nation (June 4) 796: Wenner,...inveterate starfucker (he once claimed
to have started the magazine [*Rolling Stone*] in order to meet John Len-
non). **1992** *Vanity Fair* (Nov.) 283: Some people might say he's starfucking. **1993** *New Republic* (Nov. 15) 34: The '60s turned even serious
people into starfuckers. **1998** "M. Manson" & N. Strauss *Marilyn Manson* xvi. 253: Another starfucker and sycophant sucking the life out of
me and distracting me from the conversation that I want to have. **2003**
L. Block *Small Town* 286: That didn't mean he could abandon her and trot
off after some tail-wagging cupcake.... This wasn't the night for a romp
with a starfucker.

STFU *interjection*

"Shut The Fuck Up."

1991 *Re: ALL: How to Save alt.evil!!!* on Usenet newsgroup alt
.evil (Dec. 29): When you find your brain, let us know. Until then,
STFU. **1997** C. Parker *Joy of Cybersex* 183: *STFU* Shut the fuck up.
1998 *Independent* (Apr. 2) 6: Unfortunately the "STFU-During
Performances" sign was too subtle a warning. **2002** E. Jansen *NetLingo*
458: STFU "Shut The F*#k Up." **2006** *Bucks County Courier Times*
(Jan. 26) 2G: I bet they doodle on their paper and write things like,
stfu kerry.

sympathy fuck *noun*

= PITY FUCK.

1973 J. Harrison *Good Day to Die* 68: Nobody wants a sympathy fuck. I would never fuck a girl again if it was a sympathy fuck. **1978** W. Brown *Tragic Magic* 97: You'd be surprised how many sympathy fucks I got cause I didn't have no hand. **1987** C. J. Hribal *American Beauty* 38: "So he wants a sympathy fuck." Mia exhales at the ceiling. "Exactly." **2001** J. Weiner *Good in Bed* 203: "You're not back together?" "No. It was…"…"Not to worry," she said, effectively ending my attempts to think of an appropriate euphemism for sympathy fuck. **2007** J. McPhee *Man of no Moon* 208: You should know by now that every time I fuck it's a sympathy fuck.

T

tarfu *noun & adjective* [*t*hings *a*re *r*eally *f*ucked *u*p; suggested by SNAFU]

Especially *U.S. Army.* = SNAFU.

1942 *Time* (Nov. 30) 70: "Snafu," pronounced "snaffoo"—a good, grumbling Army word, now has a superlative… The new superlative, discovered by correspondents in Britain: "tarfu" ("things are really fouled up"). **1944** E. Pyle *Brave Men* 212: The colonel had a coal-black Labrador retriever named Tarfu. That's one of those mytic military names which you'll have to get somebody else to explain to you. *ca*1944 in G. M. Valant *Vintage Aircraft Nose Art* 295: Tarfu. **1945** in *California Folklore Quarterly* V (1946) 387: *TARFU.* fouled up. **1948** J. G. Cozzens *Guard of Honor* 409: On the side of the plane's black nose, spiritedly sketched in dark red paint, was a cavorting skeleton who danced with a nude woman. Under it, in fancy letters, were the words: *Tarfu Tessie.* **1972** B. Davidson *Cut Off* 30: Tarfu, a word coined around the time of the Battle of the Bulge, was…the acronym for Things Are *Really* Fucked Up. *Ibid.*: In a Tarfu like this, nothing surprises me. **2007** R. Atkinson *Day of Battle* 78: The action, in Gavin's assessment was "self-adjusting," a SAFU, as well as a TARFU and a JAAFU.

throat-fuck *verb*

= MOUTH-FUCK, *verb.*

1975 N. Jennings *Bondage & Boyflesh* 96: The others gathered around to watch their thick-cocked leader throat-fucking the handsome young queen. **1980** S. McCarthy in *Humanist* (Sept./Oct.) 15: The

February *Penthouse* contains an ugly letter from someone who claims to be a sophomore at a large midwestern university and is "into throat-fucking." He writes of Kathy and how he was "ramming his huge eleven-inch tool down her throat." **1990** G. Fisher *Journal* (Apr. 14) in *Gary in your Pocket* (1996) 234: Jan sucks Ham near climax (he throat-fucks her)... Description of the face-fuck. **2007** J. Norton *Happy Endings* 126: Twenty minutes later you're back in your hotel room throat-fucking her bareback while praying she's HIV negative.

tit-fuck *noun*

an act of rubbing the penis between a woman's breasts; FRENCH FUCK. Also as *verb*. Also **titty-fuck.**

[**1879** *Harlequin Prince Cherrytop* 4: Breast fuck, best fuck, Cherry's prick shall ne'er be in it.] **1972** R.A. Wilson *Playboy's Book of Forbidden Words* 285: *Tit fuck* Insertion of the penis between a lady's breasts. **1975** *Ribald* (Sydney, Australia) (Sept. 18) 2: "Down in the valley something stirred." English-speaking people called it a tit-fuck. **1976** J. Vasco *Three-Hole Girl* 20: Lisa's jugs looked like they'd feel great if she pressed them down around his dick and let him tit-fuck her. **1984** R. Coover in *Playboy* (Jan. 1985) 122: Safely closeted off in his rooms over the town saloon, tit-fucking the hero's wife. **1986** *Penthouse Letters* (Mar.) 89: In the soft version of Annie's flick, we lose a great tit-fucking scene. **1987** *Penthouse Letters* (Oct.) 27: Her scene...ends quite rightly with a tit-fuck. **1991** B. E. Ellis *American Psycho* viii. 79: I tell her I would like to tit-fuck her and then maybe cut her arms off. **1998** *Schizo* (#3) [back cover]: I heard Gary Coleman titty-fucked your DAD! **1999** F. Renzulli *Toodle-fucking-oo* (television shooting script) in *Sopranos* (2nd Series) 35: Shaen: (*Ed Sullivan*) And now for you youngsters, with visions of tit-fucking in your heads, the Bing girls! Come on out here. *Pole-dancing resumes.* **2007** S. Seligson *Stacked* 72: Have you seen this month's issue of *Hard Nipple Hotties*? They ran a feature about tit fucking.

tongue fuck *verb*

to perform oral sex on (a person, or a body part). Also as *noun*.

1870 *Cythera's Hymnal* in G. Legman *Limerick* (1954) 91: He shyly confessed,/"I like tongue-fucking best." **1870** *Cythera's Hymnal* in

G. Legman *Limerick* (1954) 91: His whores said he always was poking 'em,/But all he could do/Was to tongue-fuck a few. **1968** L. Harrington *In Drag* 98: He felt for sure, Jeff had managed to tongue-fuck him. **1974** R. Price *Wanderers* 203: Tokyo had whorehouses where they did Japanese tongue fucks that drove a man crazy. **1979** P. J. Farmer *Image of Beast* 89: He...tongue-fucked her while his fingers increased the speed of their in-and-outs into her cunt and anus. **1982** S. Hite *Hite Report on Male Sexuality* 728: I also "tongue-fuck" her by shoving my tongue in and out of her hole. **1982** N. Friday *Forbidden Flowers* 184: After a while, she takes it out and tongue fucks me and after a while would place her finger in my juicy wet cunt up and down till I had an orgasm. **1991** R. Meltzer *Of Peep Shows & Piano Bars* in *Whore Just Like Rest* (2000) 429: A little overboard on anilingus..., lines like "'Ooooh,' she wailed, 'you're tongue-fucking my shitter!'" **2005** "Noire" *Candy Licker* ii. 27: I got my first tongue fuck when I was fourteen.... Not one person had prepared me for what it would be like when a man actually opened me up and touched me with his tongue. **2007** H. Hunter *Insatiable* 149: I licked the juices off the side of her thighs...before I began to tongue-fuck her.

U

---

unfuck *verb*

1. (used as an imprecation or oath); God damn; to hell with; curse. [Used as a substitution for FUCK *verb* definition 4.a., on the grounds that *fuck* denotes a pleasurable act that one would not want to wish on the person being cursed.]

1963 A. Ellis *If This be Sexual Heresy* 95: By the same token you should say "I had an *un*fucking *bad* time." Q. I can see this, you know?—In the subways, two or three centuries from now: "Unfuck you!" *a***1966** L. Bruce in S. Pinker *Stuff of Thought* (2007) 346: If I really wanted to hurt you I should say "Unfuck you, Mister." Because "Fuck you" is really *nice*! **1966** B. Deming *Prison Notes*: A former prisoner has scratched in wide letters: FUCK THE COPS! It should really be UNFUCK THE COPS, one peacewalker has suggested; unlove them is what is meant.

2. to correct (a fault); fix (a problem); etc. Sometimes used with *up*.

1971 S. Stevens *Way Uptown in Another World* 148: She was just a nice little fox who was all fucked up and didn't know how to unfuck herself. **1973** *Psychiatry* XXXVI. 145/2: These residents don't know nothing. These poor patients. The staff has to unfuck what the doctors fuck up. **1975** O. Hall *Adelita* 164: "I'll keep them plenty busy if I can just get this fucker unfucked," Birdwell said. Nicanor sat slumped with the sack on his shoulder until this was accomplished. **1976** B. A. Floyd *Lance Corporal Purdue Grace, USMC* in *Long War Dead* 21: Know this about this fucked-up war/that will never unfuck itself—/Life in Vietnam is a sea of shit. **1978** W. B. McCloskey Jr. *Highliners* xix. 242: Go on, now, un-fuck those room assignments before something else happens. **1988** W. Gibson *Mona Lisa Overdrive* 11: Little Bird fumbled the Mech-5 microsoft from the socket behind his ear—instantly forgetting the eight-point servo-calibration procedure needed to unfuck the Judge's buzzsaw. **1995** S. Rushdie *Moor's Last Sigh* 49: If you fuck up what I unfucked for you once, you better hope on I'm around to unfuck it for you twice. **1997** 2nd Lieutenant, USMC: "Unfuck it, Corporal!"...That means "fix it," "make it not fucked up." Almost any kind of screw-up. **2003** K. Friedman *Kill Two Birds & Get Stoned* 43: It's a fucked-up world...and sometimes you gotta just try to unfuck it. **2004** in M. Eversmann & D. Schilling *Battle of Mogadishu* 161: I did some last-minute coordination with the commo guys trying to unfuck the confusion surrounding communication.

unfuckable *adjective*

sexually unavailable; (*also*) sexually undesirable. Hence **unfuckably** *adverb*.

*a***1968** P. Levine *By Animals, By Men, and By Machines* in *Not This Pig* (1968) 73: The doctor, he tells me, is a "nice nigger,"/the nurses are all unfuckable,/even the tight-assed one who calls him Sugar. **1970** L. Gould *Such Good Friends* 8: I was the failure. Hopelessly unfuckable. **1981** T. McGuane *Nobody's Angel* 85: In the Castilian walk-up an unfuckable crone has the say of things and brings vegetables. **1984** B. Woodward *Wired* 293: She was sophisticated, sensual and hard, but they wanted even more of the stonelike, unreachable side: she was the elusive, truly unfuckable woman. **1991** Z. Z. Gabor *One Lifetime is not Enough* 262: If a woman wants to be attractive to a man, she should have a little flesh on her body and not just be skin and bones. All the men I ever met in my life, when they look at these models' pictures exclaimed, "My God, how could I ever make love to that?" Rubi used to describe them as "unfuckable." **2001** A. Dangor *Bitter Fruit* xxiii. 247: Dull afternoon shadows on her face. Prissy Priscilla, unshockable, and unfuckable. **2003** R. Liddle *Too Beautiful for You* 168: Duvalier is thin and sharp with a *recherché* quiff and keeps trying to paw Sophie who is acting all cool and above it all and unfuckable. **2006** *Esquire* (Jan.) 65: When you are a male entering the 10th grade, there are only four kinds of people on the entire planet: girls you want to fuck, girls who are unfuckable, guys you want to kill, and guys who generally seem OK. **2006** *Time Out N.Y.* (Mar. 30)147/2: She is fat. Unfuckably fat.

unfucked *adjective*

1. not having engaged in sexual intercourse.

*ca*1890 *My Secret Life* X. iv.: The lass kneeling over me, sucked my prick as if she loved it, and had practised the art of gamahuching from her infancy,—yet this girl was unfucked and but fourteen years of age.—I pushed up her bum, and I pulled open her little cunt lips—yes she was still intact, unbroken. **1952** J. Kerouac *Visions of Cody* 115: I'm hot and unfucked. **1973** E. Jong *Fear of Flying* 213: I began to hate myself, to feel ugly, unloved, bodily odoriferous—all the classic symptoms of the unfucked wife. **1975** C. Willingham *Big Nickel* 260: Your poor little unfucked pussy. **1979** J. Friedman *Queen of Gang-Bang* in *Tales of Time Square* (1993) 95: Mobs of unfucked men were milling about in the lounges and getting restless. **1983** A. Codrescu *In America's Shoes* 136: Needless to say, the ad didn't net [him] any lovers. He went unfucked and grew more menacing by the day. **1997** C. Shields *Larry's Party* 127: He thinks of Sally as a random force, a zephyr, who by chance crossed his path and—with purpose, pity, giggling a little as she unzipped his pants—rescued him from shame. There he was, a mere boy at eighteen, unkissed, untouched, unfucked, numbly average, bashfully unexamined. **2000** *GQ* (Nov.) 372/1: The plan was Hemingway simple. Experience. Women. Novel. Instead, I wrote one slim poem, then came home broke, unfucked and even more confused. **2003** K. Saunders *Marrying Game* 210: He had been trained to fall asleep in tanks and trenches, and other places even more uncomfortable than a double bed with an unfucked wife in it.

2. not fucked (in other senses).

1967 N. Mailer *Why Are We in Vietnam?* 184: They got the unfucked heaven of seeing twelve Dall ram on an outcropping of snow two miles away across two ridges. **1968** P. Roth *Portnoy's Complaint* 259: Yes, this was my kind of girl, all right— innocent, good-hearted, zaftig, unsophisticated and unfucked-up. **1972** *Black World* (May) 80/1: Fuck over no one so you will not have to worry about whose [*sic*] going to fuck over you. The "unfucked-over" are both unfuckable and have no need to fuck over

266

anybody else. **1988** L. McMurtry *Texasville* 239: I doubt my life will ever be unfucked again. **1993** *Guardian* (Sept. 25) (Weekend Suppl.) 66/1: Their other children, especially the delightful Catherine Zeta Jones, are paragons of unfuckedupness. **1999** K. Sampson *Powder* 281: They were like a breath of fresh air—cool, young, motivated team players, unfucked by drugs or baggage, mad on music, ready to go in to bat for you. **2000** E. Reid *Midnight Sun* 138: This is one of the last unfucked-up places you're going to find. It's too remote for the timber and oil companies to get their grubby paws on it and no way the National Park Service is going to be bussing tourists in here. **2005** J. MacGregor *Sunday Money* i. 30: For white folks about the only thing left unscorched or unsullied or unstolen or unfucked with in the South after the Civil War were stories and ideas.

un-fucking-believable *adjective*
see under -FUCKING-, *infix*.

W

windfucker *noun*

a type of kestrel; (*hence*) (used as a vague term of opprobrium). Cf. FUCKWIND *noun*.

1599 T. Nashe in *Oxford English Dictionary*: The Kistrilles or windfuckers that filling themselues with winde, fly against the winde euermore. **1602** in *Oxford English Dictionary*: I tell you, my little windfuckers, had not a certaine melancholye ingendred with a nippinge dolour overshadowed the sunne shine of my mirthe, I had been I pre, sequor, one of your consorte. **1609** B. Jonson *Epicene, or the Silent Woman* I.iv: Did you euer heare such a Windfucker, as this? *ca*1611 G. Chapman *Iliad* (preface): There is a certaine enuious Windfucker, that houers vp and downe, laboriously ingrossing al the air with his luxurious ambition. **1614** F. Beaumont & J. Fletcher *Wit Without Money* IV.i: Husbands for Whores and Bawdes, away you wind-suckers [*sic*].

WTF *interjection*

"*what* (or *where* or *who*) the fuck?"

1985 *Ramblings 5/85*, on Usenet newsgroup net.micro.mac (May 18): I asked myself, "W.T.F.?" **1985** *Proline C preliminary review*, on Usenet newsgroup net.micro.cbm (May 26): WTF do I need a C primer if I am buying the compiler for the language? **1988** *sgipie.ps (file 2 of 5)*, on Usenet newsgroup comp.windows.news (Aug. 28): wtf did all that junk on the stack come from? **2006** *New York Magazine* (July 24) 28/2: So I told her it must be nice to afford designer clothes & go on luxurious vacations 2x a yr. Now she is mad at me! WTF? **2007** *Wired* (Oct.) 80/2: If the voice in your head doesn't scream "WTF?!" it's not strange enough.

X

XXXX *noun*

British. = FUCK *noun* definition 2.a. [After an advertising campaign for Castlemaine XXXX beer, having the tagline "Australians couldn't give a XXXX for any other lager."]

[**1944** M. Elevitch *Letter* (Jan. 15) in *Dog Tags Yapping* (2003) 35: We sat around talking softly—not knowing what had been accomplished and not giving a xxxx.] **1985** *Times* (London) (Sept. 6) 19/1: Allied does not give a XXXX for Elders. **1988** *Guardian* (June 10) 6/7: Quite a few of the party's MPs don't give a XXXX for the whole affair, since they don't fancy either of the candidates. **1991** *South* (Aug.) 6/2: Algerians like their rams to be rams, and it was foolish to expect them to give a XXXX for anything else. **1995–6** *Arena* (Dec.–Jan.) 59/1: Most of the world couldn't give a XXXX about it, something that has long rankled with the marketing men who run the game in the States. **2001** *Adrenalin* (No. 9) 133/3: He said it was corrupted by the West, and, because the presence of so many ugly yobbo Australians who couldn't give a XXXX for anything remotely connected to Indonesian culture, it made him feel ashamed of his nationality. **2006** *Independent* (Nov. 25) 39/1: Labour did it before the last election when they circulated, via text message, the loutish slogan: "Don't give a xxxx for last orders? Vote Labour."

Z

zipless fuck *noun*

an act of intercourse without an emotional connection; (*hence*)
a person with whom one has such an act of intercourse.

    1973 E. Jong *Fear of Flying* 11: My fantasy of the Zipless Fuck....Zip-
less because when you came together zippers fell away like petals. **1978**
G. Vidal *Kalki* 79: Girls who feared flying tended to race blindly through
zipless fucks. **1984** T. C. Boyle *Budding Prospects* 158: Talk about the zipless fuck, this was real anonymity, cold and soulless as an execution. **1992**
in *Esquire* (Jan. 1993) 109: I stumbled through the early '80s and an address book filled with zipless fucks. **1994** *Village Voice* (N.Y.C.) (Aug. 2)
38: Ever dedicated to the zipless fuck, Patsy, the predator, exhibits the
kind of natural cleavage that renders the Wonderbra irrelevant. **2001** F.
North *Fen* 22: You can't go on the rebound with your ex-girlfriend. It de-
feats the objects of the exercise. You need a good old zipless fuck.